The Basics

Also by Shirley King
Saucing the Fish
Dining with Marcel Proust

THE BASICS

An Illustrated Guide
to Selecting and Cooking Fresh Seafood

REVISED AND UPDATED

Shirley King

Illustrations by Glenn Wolff

CHAPTERS PUBLISHING LTD., SHELBURNE, VERMONT 05482

Copyright © 1996, 1990 by Shirley King
Illustrations copyright © 1996, 1990 by Glenn Wolff
Cover illustration copyright © 1999 by Ann Field

For information about permission to reproduce selections from this book, write to
Permissions, Houghton Mifflin Company, 215 Park Avenue South,
New York, New York 10003.

Library of Congress Cataloging-in-Publication Data

King, Shirley.
    Fish, the basics: an illustrated guide to selecting and cooking fresh seafood/
Shirley King; illustrations by Glenn Wolff. —Rev. and updated.
    p.   cm.
Includes bibliographical references and index.
ISBN 0-618-00203-0 (pbk.)
1. Cookery (Fish). 2. Cookery (Seafood). I. Title.
TX747.K52 1996
641.6'92—dc20   95-52720

Printed and bound in Canada by Webcom Limited, Scarborough, Ontario

Cover design by Susan McClellan
Cover illustration by Ann Field
Interior design by Eugenie Seidenberg Delaney and Susan McClellan

QWT 10 9 8 7 6 5 4

I dedicate this book to my family, friends and students and to all those who find seafood cookery somewhat of a mystery. I hope I have explained it well and that by reading and using this book, all becomes clear.

Acknowledgments

MANY PEOPLE helped me to garner information for this book. Richard Lord, a walking reference on seafood who was the head of Fulton Fish Market Information Services and whose joy in life comes from collecting new species of seafood to write about and photograph, gave me invaluable help with the fish profiles and lots of other information.

Ken Gall of the New York Sea Grant Extension Program at Stony Brook, Long Island, collected and gave me information, especially on the fat, cholesterol and omega-3 content of the fish and shellfish in this book.

Susan Herrmann Loomis sent me exquisite fish and shellfish from Seattle when she lived there. Jon Rowley and Peter Redmayne, also of Seattle, have made invaluable contributions to this book, for which I thank them.

Lawrence Skrivanek of Mister Wright, a liquor store in New York City, and my dear friend Stephen R. Lawrence, both wine connoisseurs, have kept me up to date on many fine wines that I enjoy with fish.

I am also most grateful to those friends who shared in the creation of many of the recipes and to my students, who (without knowing it) gave me much invaluable input during my seafood workshops.

Very many thanks to Nach Waxman, owner of the Kitchen Arts and Letters bookstore in New York City, for his continuing support and for brilliantly suggesting the title for this book.

Glenn Wolff did the drawings for the original book and painstakingly recreated them for this edition; my admiration of this work is boundless.

My thanks to Kerri Conan, editor at Simon and Schuster, for her meticulous follow-ups on the editorial details in the 1990 version. And to Rux Martin, editor at Chapters Publishing, for her foresight and confidence in republishing this book, my sincere thanks.

Contents

Preface

THERE IS NO GREAT TRICK to cooking seafood. What you need is a good piece of fresh fish and a good recipe. The same holds true for shellfish.

First a comment about the use of the word "seafood." It is a general term that I use for all kinds of fish and shellfish which come from the oceans of the world and from fresh water, such as streams, rivers and lakes.

If you go to the fish store with a preconceived notion of the seafood you want to cook, you may end up going home with something less than fresh; it is better to be flexible in your choice, once you've learned how to judge freshness. And once you've become familiar with the textures and tastes of different kinds of fish and shellfish, it will be easy to choose a recipe or make up one of your own. Even if you do not recognize some of the "new" fish which are appearing in the markets, you need not avoid them, for undoubtedly they are similar to other fish that you know.

This book will show you how easy it is to master the simple techniques necessary to produce perfectly delicious seafood dishes. You will learn how to select that choice piece of fish at the store.

This book is designed to present basic information and then send you on your way to prepare seafood confidently and to learn to create dishes on your own. With the help of this book, seafood cookery will become as fascinating as you choose to make it.

In Part I, you will become familiar with seafood nomenclature and learn to distinguish among the varieties of seafood you encounter at the market. You will learn how to buy fresh seafood and what to do with it once you get it home. Learning how to fillet a fish and alternative ways of cutting fish and their fillets will help you either to direct the fish-store personnel to do it for you or to do it yourself. You will also learn how to be sure you are enjoying the many health benefits of seafood.

Part II consists of some 57 basic recipes and methods for preparing the seafood you buy. Most of the methods and recipes can be used with many different kinds of seafood, and you will find that once you know them, your own inventiveness will lead you to create new and exciting taste experiences. In this part of the book, you will also find recipes for sauces and salads, as well as advice on which vegetables, herbs and spices are best for different kinds of seafood and which wines are the most suitable to drink with them.

Finally, Part III is an alphabetical listing of the profiles of virtually every kind of seafood you may find in your fish market or supermarket, with references to the basic recipes useful for each. You will learn about the forms in which these fish and shellfish are available and the seasons when they are at their best.

HOW TO USE THIS BOOK

Fish: The Basics is meant to become one of the cookbooks you use constantly, a great resource and aid in preparing dishes based on the wonderful fruits of the sea.

All the information that you need to identify, choose, store, prepare and cook fish and shellfish is contained in the three parts of this book. These sections work both independently and together.

You may begin by selecting a particular fish or a specific cooking method. Let's say, for instance, that you want to serve salmon. If you don't often go to the fish store, you might first want to read through Part I to get an idea about how to select the freshest fish. Next, look up the salmon profile in Part III. While scanning the entry, you will see that salmon is usually available whole, in steaks or in fillets, and you will learn how much of each form is needed per person. A list of recommended salmon preparations follows.

Suppose you choose to broil a salmon fillet. Turn to Part II and read first about broiling, then go to the broiling recipe that catches your eye. In reading the instructions, you note a couple of other fish that are suitable for this same preparation. Now you are ready to go to the fishmonger, certain to leave with the right amount of the freshest fish possible.

Or suppose you fancy a particular fish preparation—say, poaching, for example, because you crave a plainly cooked fish accompanied by a healthful sauce. Begin by looking up poaching in Part II. Reading through the text, you decide to poach a whole fish rather than a fillet, and you note several fish you can poach. Perhaps you leaf through a couple of profiles in Part III to become acquainted with the fish mentioned. Again, it's off to the fish store, and you're ready to select the freshest fish possible to bring home and poach. You can even clean it yourself if you wish—easy instructions are in Part I.

Don't forget to plan the rest of the meal. There's information on sauces and condiments, as well as discussions of side dishes and wines. Have fun, because it's easier than you think— and so satisfying—to cook seafood well.

Basic

Information

About Fish and Shellfish Cookery

IN THE FISH STORE, you can find fish in a wide variety of forms—whole as well as cut into steaks, fillets and chunks, which are also known as roasts. Whole fish is delicious cooked on the bone. The scales, guts and gills have to be removed before the fish is cooked. Fish fillets cut from whole fish are practically boneless, and for that reason, they appeal to many. Steaks are convenient for individual portions, and chunks (weighing 1½ to 5 pounds, cut from a whole fish) can easily be stuffed and served to several people. Once you learn to recognize the advantages of the different forms, you can make better choices when planning your meals.

Although frying, broiling, grilling and baking are popular ways of preparing fish, there are as many cooking methods for fish as there are for meat. In fact, cooking is not always necessary to enhance the flavor of fish. Some fish, like tuna and yellowtail, taste great raw, as attested by the popularity of sushi and sashimi—raw fish as served by the Japanese.

Cooking fish is simple, since it is naturally tender and needs only to be heated through to attain its fullest flavor and texture. It is important to cook fish for a short enough time so that it does not become overdone or fall apart in the cooking utensil, but for long enough that it is still juicy and practically melts in your mouth. Elaborate sauces are not necessary, as you will see. Nowadays, it isn't considered essential to "sauce" a fish; the natural juices from both fish and vegetables are enough to flavor and moisten the fish. If you do want to add a sauce, see the recipes in Part II.

The taste of cooked fish ranges from delicate/mild/bland (flounder, sole) to flavorful (mackerel). Adjectives such as nutty and sweet can be applied to the taste of many fish. Most lean white-fleshed fish not only need to be enhanced but are perfect vehicles for subtle seasonings. They are cooked with little added fat, mild herbs, spices, seasonings, vegetables and, if necessary, some liquid, such as wine or stock. Fish with higher fat content, like salmon, mackerel, herring, whitefish, tuna, eel, sturgeon, sablefish and trout, can be cooked with stronger-flavored accompaniments, such as the more emphatic herbs and spices. These fish are also excellent for smoking.

For shellfish, freshness and proper cooking methods are of the utmost importance. In addition, you will need to learn several simple techniques—for opening oysters and clams, cleaning mussels, and so on. These techniques are described in the profiles in Part III.

Some shellfish are expensive, while some cost less than most finfish. If you live near the coast, of course, you may garner some shellfish on your own for free. Always be sure to check your sources with the local fisheries department to avoid bad effects from contaminated waters and to make sure it is the legal season to gather shellfish. Also be sure to store them properly. Under those circumstances, picking your own is the best way to ensure absolute freshness.

Shrimp are the most popular shellfish—practically every restaurant across the country serves shrimp in some form or another. Though relatively expensive, small shrimp cost less per pound than flounder fillets. Blue crabs, mussels, squid, conch, octopus and periwinkles are just some of the shellfish that are cheap. To my mind, the best shellfish in the world are the lobsters from the East Coast, stone crabs from Florida, blue crabs from the Chesapeake Bay area, Dungeness crabs from the Pacific Northwest and crawfish from Louisiana, California and Oregon. But each to his or her own taste.

Shellfish had better be cooked properly. There is nothing as awful as rubbery shrimp or tough, dried-out lobster. Nowadays, perhaps as a reaction against dreadful cooking habits, many seem to like their shellfish nearly raw. This is not to my taste, but I do want my morsels moist, tender and sweet. Fortunately, the endless variety of seafood and recipes means that every palate is sure to be satisfied.

Seafood and Health

SEAFOOD IS GREAT FOOD for old and young, since it is so easily digested and so healthful. Fish and shellfish are variously rich in vitamins, high-quality protein, major minerals, such as calcium, phosphorus, magnesium and potassium, and trace minerals, such as iron, copper, zinc, iodine, vitamin B_{12}, folic acid, fluoride and selenium. Calcium is found in those fish having bones that we eat, bones that are soft and harmless when cooked—I refer especially to canned sardines, salmon, anchovies and pickled shad and herring. The unsaturated omega-3 fatty acids that are found in seafood are useful in combating high blood-cholesterol levels and therefore heart disease and in preventing immune and inflammatory ailments. Generally speaking, fattier fish such as salmon, whitefish and mackerel have higher levels of omega-3s—the exception is eel, which has low omega-3s.

Fish and shellfish are low in calories (most have fewer than 150 calories in 3½ ounces of cooked flesh), low in sodium (except canned seafood preparations and smoked and cured seafood) and low in saturated fats and cholesterol (most have less than 100 milligrams of cholesterol in 3½ ounces of raw flesh). Since the American Heart Association and the National Heart, Lung and Blood Institute recommend that we limit our intake of cholesterol to 300 milligrams or less per day, it is best to eat only a little red or organ meat, fewer dairy products and saturated oils and a variety of seafood often.

Recently, mussels, oysters, scallops and clams have been discovered to have far less cholesterol than previously thought because the plant sterols in them (which work against cholesterol) had been erroneously counted as cholesterol. Crab and lobster have about the same cholesterol count as chicken with its skin removed (75 to 90 milligrams per 3½ ounces). As a point of reference for all fish and shellfish, two large egg yolks have 550 milligrams of cholesterol.

Nearly all fish have less than 20 percent fat when raw—most have less than 5 percent, others less than 2.5 percent, which is far less than a beefsteak, which has 37 percent fat, or a pork chop, which has 21 percent fat, or even chicken. The percentage will change depending on the cooking method and vary according to the season and other factors. All raw shellfish have less than 2.5 percent fat. The fat in seafood is high in polyunsaturated fatty acids and tends to lower the blood lipids, thereby helping to prevent blood clots from forming. It also helps combat arthritis, asthma, multiple sclerosis, diabetes, lupus, psoriasis, migraines, prostate tumors and cancer of the breast, colon and pancreas.

In recent years, studies have revealed the crucial role of omega-3 fatty acids in seafood-rich diets. Until recently, the Japanese have had very little incidence of heart disease, because they ate fish on most days. Now that they are beginning to eat like Westerners, heart disease is on the rise. In Greenland, heart disease was nearly unknown, because the Eskimo diet relied heavily on fish, in addition to seal and whale. The Dutch, too, were found to benefit from eating a fair amount of fish—even though the fish was mostly lean. It seems that even the smallest amount of omega-3s, when taken regularly, combats heart disease.

In general, except for the oil necessary to keep fish from sticking to a pan or grill, little added fat is needed when cooking seafood, for it tastes best simply prepared—broiled, grilled, roasted or baked in the oven, cooked in a microwave oven, poached or steamed. And, of course, any oil that is used is choles-terol-free. What varies among the oils is their saturated fat. The more saturated a fat, the more cholesterol your body will produce. Olive oil, which is monounsaturated, and saf-flower, corn, sunflower, soybean, walnut and cotton seed oils, which are polyunsaturated, are considered better for health than the coconut and palm oils, which are saturated.

Don't deep-fry or sauté high-fat fish (in fat), for those methods do nothing for their taste or your health.

When considering the effect of fish and shellfish on your health, keep in mind the following:

♦ Shellfish and fish are low in fat. A low-fat diet in turn lowers cholesterol production in our bodies. You can safely eat a variety of seafood, which is what most people do naturally, without raising your cholesterol level. Even though some seafood is high in choles-terol, many of these are high in omega-3s, which combat it. Consider cutting down your fat in other foods so that you can benefit from the fattier fish and their omega-3 fatty acids.

♦ It is all right to eat moderate amounts of shellfish when on a low-cholesterol diet, because shellfish is low in saturated fat. But if you are on a strict low-cholesterol diet, eat small portions infrequently.

I have found that various sources may give slightly different figures for fat, satu-rated fat, omega-3 and cholesterol content for individual fish and shellfish. There are three main reasons for this: There are natural variables that occur between individual fish; there are differences within each fish tested (some sections are more fatty than others, for instance); and modes of testing vary some-what. However, the following tables give rel-atively accurate and valuable guides.

Fat, Omega-3 and Cholesterol of Raw Fish

All values are for raw 100-gram (3.5-ounce) portions.

LEAN FISH (LESS THAN 5 PERCENT FAT)

NAME	PERCENTAGE TOTAL FAT	SATURATED FAT G	OMEGA-3 G	CHOLESTEROL MG
Anchovy, fresh	4.1	1.1	1.4	N/A
Bass, freshwater	3.7	0.8	0.6	68
Bass, sea	2.0	0.5	0.6	41
Bass, striped	2.3	0.5	0.8	80
Blackfish	0.2	N/A	N/A	N/A
Blowfish	0.7	N/A	N/A	N/A
Bluefish	4.2	0.9	0.8	59
Catfish, freshwater	4.3	1.0	0.4	58
Catfish, ocean	2.9	0.36	N/A	50
Cod or Scrod, Atlantic	0.7	0.1	0.2	43
(Cod) Cusk	0.7	N/A	N/A	41
Cod, Pacific	0.6	0.1	0.2	37
(Cod) Pollock, Atlantic	1.0	0.1	0.4	71
Croaker	3.2	1.1	0.2	61
(Croaker) Spot	4.9	1.5	0.6	N/A
Dolphinfish (mahi-mahi)	0.7	0.2	0.1	73
Drum, Black	1.5	N/A	0.2	N/A
(Drum) Freshwater sheepshead	4.9	1.1	0.5	64
(Drum) Redfish	0.8	0.2	0.1	64
(Flatfish) Flounder	1.2	0.3	0.2	48
Eel (conger)	N/A	N/A	N/A	49
Grouper	1.0	0.2	0.2	37
Haddock	0.7	0.1	0.2	57
Hake, red (ling)	0.6	0.1	N/A	35
Hake, white	0.5	N/A	0.2	39
Halibut	2.3	0.3	0.4	32
(Jack) Amberjack	1.8	N/A	N/A	43
(Jack) Pacific crevalle	3.9	1.2	0.7	N/A
Lingcod	1.1	0.2	0.2	52
Mackerel, king	2.0	0.4	0.3	53
Monkfish	1.5	N/A	N/A	25
Mullet	3.8	1.1	0.3	49
Ocean Perch	1.6	0.2	0.3	42
Ocean Pout	0.9	0.3	N/A	52
Orange Roughy	0.7	0.1	N/A	23

Name	Percentage Total Fat	Saturated Fat G	Omega-3 G	Cholesterol MG
Perch, freshwater	0.9	0.2	0.3	90
(Perch) Walleye	1.2	0.2	0.3	86
Pike, northern	0.7	0.1	0.1	39
Porgy, northern (scup)	2.7	N/A	N/A	N/A
Rockfish, Pacific	1.6	0.4	0.3	35
Salmon, chum	3.8	0.8	0.6	74
Salmon, pink	3.5	0.6	1.0	52
Sea Robin	1.9	N/A	N/A	32
Sea Trout	3.6	1.0	0.4	83
Shark	4.5	0.9	0.8	51
Sheepshead	2.4	0.6	0.3	N/A
Sheepshead, Freshwater—see Drum				
Skate and Ray	0.7	0.1	0.3	56
Smelt	2.4	0.5	0.7	70
Snapper	1.3	0.3	0.3	37
Sole—see Flatfish				
Spot	4.9	1.5	0.6	N/A
Sturgeon (ocean species)	4.0	0.9	0.3	N/A
Sunfish	0.7	0.1	0.1	67
Swordfish	4.0	1.1	0.6	39
Tilapia	0.9	N/A	0.1	19
Tilefish	2.3	0.4	0.4	N/A
Trout, brook	3.2	0.7	0.4	68
Trout, rainbow	3.4	0.6	0.6	57
Tuna, bigeye	1.6	N/A	N/A	66
Tuna, bluefin	4.9	1.3	1.2	32
Tuna, skipjack	1.0	0.3	0.3	47
Tuna, yellowfin	1.0	0.2	0.2	45
Weakfish—see Sea trout				
Whiting (mixed species)	1.3	0.2	0.2	67
Whiting, Pacific	1.6	0.3	0.5	N/A
Wolffish	2.5	0.4	0.6	46

Fat, Omega-3 and Cholesterol of Raw Fish

All values are for raw 100-gram (3.5-ounce) portions.

MODERATELY FATTY TO FATTY FISH (MORE THAN 5 PERCENT FAT)
(Fish with high fat content are also high in omega-3 fatty acids.)

NAME	PERCENTAGE TOTAL FAT	SATURATED FAT G	OMEGA-3 G	CHOLESTEROL MG
Anchovy, canned in oil	9.7	2.2	2.0	N/A
Buffalofish	16.6	N/A	N/A	N/A
Butterfish	8.0	N/A	N/A	65
Carp	5.6	1.1	0.4	66
Char, Arctic	7.9	1.7	N/A	27
(Drum) Kingfish, southern	5.1	1.6	0.4	N/A
Eel (other than conger eel)	11.66	2.4	0.1	126
(Flatfish) Turbot	13.8	2.4	0.9	46
Herring, Atlantic	18.0	2.0	1.6	60
Herring, Pacific	16.4	3.3	1.7	77
Mackerel, Atlantic	13.9	3.3	2.3	70
Mackerel, Pacific and chub	7.9	2.2	1.4	47
Mackerel, Spanish	6.3	1.8	1.3	76
Pompano, Atlantic	9.5	3.5	0.6	50
Sablefish, black cod	15.3	3.2	1.4	49
Salmon, Atlantic	6.3	1.0	1.4	55
Salmon, chinook	10.4	2.5	1.4	66
Salmon, coho	6.0	1.1	0.8	39
Salmon, sockeye	8.6	1.5	1.2	62
Sardine, Atlantic, canned in oil	11.5	1.5	1.0	142
Sardines (mixed species)	6.8	N/A	1.5	52
Shad	13.6	2.0	1.4	N/A
(Shark) Dogfish, spiny	12.2	3.2	1.8	60
Trout, lake	9.4	1.2	1.4	36
Tuna, albacore	7.2	1.9	2.1	38
Tuna, bonito	5.5	N/A	N/A	N/A
Whitefish	5.9	0.9	1.3	60
Yellowtail	5.2	N/A	N/A	N/A

SHELLFISH

NAME	PERCENTAGE TOTAL FAT	SATURATED FAT G	OMEGA-3 G	CHOLESTEROL MG
Abalone	0.8	0.2	N/A	85
Clam, Manila	0.8	N/A	N/A	N/A
Clam (mixed species)	1.0	0.1	0.1	34
Clam, quahog (hard)	1.0	0.2	0.2	40
Clam, razor	1.5	0.3	0.3	107
Clam, soft-shell	1.2	0.2	0.2	25
(Clam) Cockles	N/A	N/A	N/A	N/A
Crab, blue	1.1	0.2	0.3	78
Crab, Dungeness	1.0	0.1	0.3	59
Crab, Jonah, red and rock	1.3	0.1	0.3	74
Crab, king	0.6	N/A	N/A	42
Crab, snow	1.2	0.1	0.4	55
Crab, stone	N/A	N/A	N/A	N/A
Crawfish (crayfish)	1.1	0.2	0.2	139
Cuttlefish	0.7	0.1	0.1	112
Lobster, northern	0.9	N/A	N/A	95
Lobster, spiny	1.5	0.2	0.4	70
Mussel, blue	2.2	0.4	0.4	28
Octopus	1.0	0.2	0.2	48
Oyster, Belon	1.7	N/A	0.2	N/A
Oyster, eastern	2.5	0.6	0.4	55
Oyster, Olympia	2.5	N/A	0.4	N/A
Oyster, Pacific	2.3	0.5	0.7	N/A
Periwinkle, common	3.0	0.5	0.4	N/A
Scallop (mixed species)	0.8	0.1	0.2	33
Scallop, sea	0.8	N/A	0.19	37
Sea Urchin	3.2	N/A	3	498
Shrimp	1.7	0.3	0.5	152
Squid (mixed species)	1.4	0.4	0.5	233
Whelk	0.4	0.1	0.1	65

Sources

Composition of Foods: Finfish & Shellfish Products. U.S. Department of Agriculture Handbook 8-15, Washington, D.C., U.S. Government Printing Office, 1987.

Faria, Sue. *Northeast Seafood Book.* Boston, MA: Division of Marine Fisheries, 1984.

Nettleton, Joyce A. *Seafood Nutrition.* Huntington, NY: Osprey Books, 1985.

NOAA Technical Reports: NMFS 55, 1987 and *NMFS F/Sec-11, 1981.*

Seafood Leader Buyer's Guide. Seattle, WA, 1995.

Handling Seafood Safely

IT ALMOST GOES WITHOUT SAYING that the first criterion when cooking and eating seafood is that it be fresh. Simply put, bad seafood smells bad and should not be eaten.

We know that bacterial growth hastens contamination, and we have to learn how to combat it.

TIPS FOR CAREFUL SEAFOOD COOKERY

♦ Handle seafood properly, making sure that utensils and boards are clean, to prevent cross-contamination that can provide a breeding ground for salmonella.

♦ Always buy from a reputable source. If you catch fish, treat it scrupulously from the moment you catch it.

♦ If you collect your own shellfish, check with the department of fish and game or local health authorities to be sure that the water is safe.

♦ Be extra careful when eating raw fish and shellfish, particularly raw bivalves. When buying bivalves, you may ask to see the tag held at the fish store which verifies that the shellfish came from clean, tested waters. The waters are identified on the tag. Fish suppliers, supermarkets and restaurants are obliged to keep the tag for 90 days, in case a bad bivalve needs to be traced. Many oysters and clams are farmed in controlled waters nowadays and therefore are less prone to contamination.

♦ Eat a variety of seafood rather than one kind exclusively.

♦ People who are already suffering from disease or are otherwise debilitated should limit their raw seafood intake to once a week.

♦ Cook seafood to 140 degrees F or freeze it for two days to kill parasites.

♦ Contaminants can collect in the viscera of a fish, in some of its fatty areas (such as the belly flaps), in the dark fat muscle that runs along its lateral line and, to some extent, in its skin. Avoid eating these parts if there is any possibility that the fish may be contaminated.

Environmental Pollutants

BESIDES THE NATURAL SPOILING PROCESS, the environment can compromise the safety of even otherwise fresh fish. Bivalves such as clams, mussels and oysters, which are sedentary creatures, filter their food from the water, so they may be infected by pollutants in the water. Among the polluting effects is red tide, a natural phenomenon that occurs worldwide. Though called "red tide," it is neither red nor a tide but an algae bloom caused by a combination of nutrients, carbon dioxide, cool waters flowing into warm, and sunlight. Red tide is of much concern in Maine and around San Francisco, especially during the summer months. Not all red or brown tides are toxic for fish and shellfish, but the affected creatures are poisonous to humans and can cause paralytic shellfish poisoning (PSP), which is usually lethal. The various potential dangers are greatest when bivalves are eaten raw. But I must emphasize that waters are tested regularly and advisories are put out when there is any danger.

Pollution may also occur in the form of harmful chemicals or pesticides that drain into water. Such chemicals include PCB—polychlorinated biphenyl—deposits, which are found in rivers where fish spawn. PCBs concentrate in the guts of a fish, especially in the liver, the strip of dark fat found along the lateral line and the fatty flesh of the belly. There are advisories and restrictions on the catch of bluefish and striped bass, partly because they have been overfished and also because they spawn in rivers and thus have been affected by PCBs. As these regulations change from time to time, it is a good idea to refer to your local Environmental Conservation Bureau of Finfish and Crustaceans for an update.

Very occasionally, one encounters small, slender worms in the bodies of fish, such as mackerel, herring, rockfish, cod and haddock. As a precaution, a fair amount of cod and haddock is candled—fillets are laid on top of light boxes so the parasites can be seen and removed. Other parasites of the *Diphyllobothrium* genus can be present in freshwater fish, such as pike, perch and salmon. Wild salmon, although most often caught in the sea, do spend time in streams, rivers and lakes. Lightly smoked or cured fish may also be affected. The tiny worms can be killed by cooking fish to 140 degrees F or by freezing it for two days. If ingested, these tiny worms may promote nausea but seldom cause more lasting complications.

Most poisons are resistant to heat, so cooking will not guarantee safety. Scombroid or saurine poisoning can occur in jack, mackerel, tuna, swordfish and dolphinfish (mahimahi), fish that are usually perfectly safe to eat. This poisoning develops when the fish are left in warm temperatures and not chilled when caught. A bad smell is a clue to scombroid poisoning. Symptoms are headache, skin rash and upset stomach. Saurine poisoning may be combated with antihistamine drugs.

Ciguatera poisoning is due to a toxin that concentrates in large fish, which probably get it by consuming smaller fish that eat affected phytoplankton. Jacks, snappers, groupers and parrot fish are some of the fish that are affected. The toxin can't be discerned, for it concentrates in the liver and viscera. Ciguatera is a much greater problem in the Caribbean than in North American waters.

Botulism occurs in canned or vacuum-packed seafood. In normal processing, these fish are heated to specific temperatures for specific times in order to kill the organism that produces the botulism toxin. If botulism does occur, it is most certainly because the can or box has the smallest of holes in it, which allows the organism to enter and grow.

It should be remembered, however, that relatively few people get sick from eating fish and shellfish, and most cases probably are due to poor food handling, since waters are monitored often and fish and shellfish are tested.

Buying and Storing Fish and Shellfish

Some Names Fish Go By

IDENTIFYING FISH may, at first glance, seem to be difficult. There are many species within each family, and a species known by one name may be given other, perhaps confusing, names in the fish store. Sometimes these are colloquial names used in particular localities, which may differ from the names you are used to. Sometimes a fish with a homely name—such as pollock—will bear a grander label, such as "Boston bluefish," although a pollock in no way resembles a bluefish. Fish stores may give a species a more becoming name or the name of a similar, possibly more popular fish. Or a fishmonger may aim to pass off a cheaper fish as a more expensive one. This is illegal, of course; the Food and Drug Administration has a list of approved market names.* In the fish-by-fish profiles in Part III of this book, you will find the vernacular and local names given to the different species as well as the approved market names.

Many fish with even the slightest tinge of red on the skin are passed off as "red snapper." I've seen ocean perch fillets called "snapper" fillets and skinned tilefish fillets called "red snapper." I have also seen tilefish labeled "white snapper," and although there is a species of snapper that has whitish skin, it does not in any way resemble a tilefish in looks, flavor or texture. All this may confuse you, but usually a good look at the fish (if you have some prior knowledge of how it should appear) or a question to the fishmonger will help you figure out the correct name.

By correct, I mean the common or usual

*The Food and Drug Administration's Guide to Acceptable Market Names for Food Fish Sold in Interstate Commerce, 1993. Superintendent of Documents, U.S. Government Printing Office, Washington, D.C.

name established by law. Each species and its family have scientific Latin names, and fish stores and suppliers may use their own market names for different species. Monkfish, for example, is called "belly fish" by fish purveyors. Monkfish is often referred to by its French name, *lotte*, especially in restaurants.

The word squid is subject to translation as well, and squid are often known as *calamari*, the Italian name; as *calmar*, the French; or as *calamar*, the Spanish.

Peter Redmayne, editor and publisher of *The Seafood Leader*, a seafood magazine published in Seattle, Washington, writing in an editorial for that magazine (Spring 1987), noted some name changes he had seen in restaurants. The New Zealand fish called permit had been served as "New Zealand pompano," but there are no true pompano in New Zealand waters. Another restaurant offered "Chesapeake Bay pollock" because the manager said it was trying to give the "poor pollock some pizzazz." (Pollock is not available as far south as Chesapeake Bay.) Redmayne also heard about some Alaska pollock that was being passed off as "Georges Bank cod" by a distributor. Another distributor took arrowtooth flounder—a fish with little going for it because it cooks up soft and thus is usually used as mink food or fertilizer—repacked it in boxes marked "petrale sole" and marked it up two dollars a pound.

Very likely, you will see labels that say "fresh fish." Well, it had better be fresh; or if it was frozen, it should have been frozen properly and, if defrosted, defrosted properly. (More about frozen fish later.) I have seen the word "fancy" on some labels in Seattle markets. This, in fact, means previously frozen, now defrosted. Other markets are more honest and use labels that read "previously frozen."

On the positive side, more and more markets are identifying the source of seafood—the name of the lake, river, bay, ocean or state it was fished from. This is a good practice and tends to increase our interest in all seafood. And the FDA is now insisting that fish stores and suppliers use correct nomenclature.

When you are at the fish store, you see a great variety of fish and shellfish in many different forms on display. It's often easiest to look for a familiar fish in a familiar form, but there are more adventurous ways to buy fish. It is possible to group fish according to their different forms (fillets, steaks, etc.) and their textures and tastes.

Once you've become familiar with the cooking methods and the fish and which is most appropriate for which, shopping for seafood and cooking it will become very simple. For instance, you may decide on a mild-tasting fish that is easy to sauté or a more emphatically flavored fish to broil. Or you will soon learn that when you see a fresh-looking, firm and flavorful fish, you can grill or blacken it.

Useful Terms You Will Need to Know

Drawn fish: Fish that have been gutted.

Dressed fish: Whole fish that have been gutted and scaled and from which the gills have been removed. They are ready to cook.

Often, fish-store people are in the habit of cutting off the fins and trimming the tails. If cooking a whole fish, I want the fins, for they are part and parcel of the look of the fish.

Pan-dressed fish: Gutted and scaled fish with the head and fins cut off and the tail trimmed. Pan-dressing is usually done to small fish that will fit in a medium-sized frying pan.

Fillets: Boneless sections or pieces of fish flesh, cut from both sides of the fish. Fillets are just the ticket for those who want the pleasure of eating boneless fish.

Filleted fish abound at the fish store. The fillets may be skinned or not. They come in various sizes. You can, for example, buy a whole large salmon fillet or part of one.

Fillets are conducive to all sorts of cooking methods.

Butterflied or *split fish*: Fish that have been split open, producing two sides of the fish joined by the belly skin or the back (see page 47). They may or may not be boned.

Steaks, *loins*, *wheels* and *center cuts*: Steaks come near to solving the bone problem too. They make fine individual portions.

The flesh of a steak is cut against the grain, sliced straight through the backbone, and only a small cross section of the backbone and sometimes a rib bone or two are left attached to the flesh.

Most large roundfish—salmon, cod and tilefish, for example—can be cut into steaks, as can halibut, a large flatfish. Steaks from these fish should be cut 1 inch thick. Other smaller flatfish may also be cut into steaks to good effect, though these should be smaller—¼ to ½ inch thick.

Tuna are cut off the central bone into round fillets, called "loins," and then into boneless, skinless steaks. Sharks and swordfish are cut into "wheels" and "center cuts" from which steaks are then cut; this practice is unique to these large varieties. To stay moist, tender and attractive when cooked, these steaks should be cut 1 to 1¼ inches thick.

Chunks (roasts): Chunks, also known as roasts, may not be visible to you when you visit the fish store. Chunks are cut from the heaviest part of a large fish, which typically weighs between 5 and 10 pounds. These are fish from which the fishmonger cuts steaks, such as salmon, striped bass, lingcod, cod, pollock and tilefish.

You can ask the fishmonger to cut you a chunk weighing 1½ to 4 pounds or more. You can also ask him to bone it, or you can do this yourself by following the instructions on page 48. The chunk can be stuffed with vegetables, herbs and a fillet of another fish (for contrast) and then baked, roasted, poached or cooked on an outdoor grill.

How Shellfish Are Graded and Sold

CLAMS

Hard-shell clams from the bays and seas along the East and West Coasts are graded and named by their size. They are sold by the dozen or half-dozen.

Littlenecks are about 1½ inches in diameter and are the smallest and the most expensive; next come *cherrystones*, which are about 2½ inches in diameter.

Chowder or *quahog clams* are about 4 to 5 inches in diameter and are sold whole or minced for chowders, soups, pies and fritters.

The large (6 to 7 inches in diameter) *Atlantic surf*, *bar* or *sea clams* are processed and cut into strips to be battered and deep-fried for clam rolls. They are also minced and sold canned.

Manila clams come from the West Coast and Canada. They are gorgeous little thin-shelled clams that are best sautéed. They are sold by the pound.

Cockles from New Zealand are similar to Manila clams, but usually smaller. They are best sautéed or added to soups, stews or rice dishes such as paella or risotto. These clams are sold by the pound.

Soft-shell clams (called steamers, softs, gapers, squirts or even "pissers") are sold by the pound.

Razor clams are also sold by the pound.

Geoduck clams (pronounced "gooeyduck") from the Pacific Northwest are very large, weighing 2 pounds or more each. They are sold by the pound, and their neck and strip flesh is also sold by the pound.

CONCH

Conch are sold by the piece when alive in their shells. Conch meat, cooked or raw, is often frozen. Conch meat is sold by the pound.

CRABS

Crabs are sold alive or cooked. Crabmeat picked from cooked crabs is sold in different grades as follows:

Lumpmeat or *backfin crabmeat* consists of large whole lumps from the body and the backfin.

Special crabmeat consists of lumpmeat and flakes from the rest of the body.

Flake or *regular crabmeat* consists of all the meat from the whole body, except the choice lumpmeat.

Claw crabmeat consists of only the meat from the claws.

All of the above are sold by the pound; most are pasteurized and canned.

Cocktail claws are cooked crab claws with shells partially removed. They are usually available frozen and are sold by the pound.

Soft-shell crabs from Maryland are graded according to size and sold by the piece. They are sold both live and frozen, but I think soft-shell crabs should still be alive when you buy them. Often the fish stores clean them in advance, thereby killing them. I prefer to view the live crabs and have the fishmonger clean them in front of me, or do it myself.

Crabs may not be graded by the following names at your fish store, but these are the names most commonly used by processors. Generally speaking, the larger they are, the more expensive.

Whales: over 5 inches

Jumbos: 4½ to 5 inches

Primes: 4 to 4½ inches

Hotels or *primes*: 3½ to 4 inches

Mediums: 3 to 3½ inches

Hard blue crabs from Maryland are graded by size. The males are known as *jimmys*. The females are called *sooks*. Jimmys are popular in the Chesapeake Bay area. The red-tipped clawed sooks are more attractive to New Yorkers, who also enjoy the extra fat in the female blue crab. Jimmys and sooks are sold by the dozen or half-dozen. The largest are #1 jimmys, then come mediums.

Stone crabs are found in waters from the North Carolina coast to the Gulf of Mexico. Claws are all that is sold of the stone crab. The claws are always previously cooked, and some are frozen. Stone crabs are graded by the number of claws that make up a pound. The largest claws are the most expensive.

Dungeness crabs are sold by the pound, either live, cooked or cooked and then frozen. Picked crabmeat is also available from these crabs, as are crab claws and legs, either attached to the body or not.

King crabs have two claws and six long walking legs. These and the shoulder meat are what is sold. Seldom sold fresh, most king crabmeat is frozen or canned. The legs—some of which have the shell split open for easy eating—and the claws are sold by the pound, with the larger pieces fetching higher prices. Claws, legs and shoulders are also sold in clusters. The most expensive picked king crabmeat is from the upper part of the legs (called the *merus meat*), followed by the meat from the claws and the lower part of the legs, which are edged in red; the least choice part is the white meat from the shoulder and other body meat. *Fancy meat* refers to a mixture of these three. *Salad meat* consists of chunks of red-edged and white meat and the smaller pieces from the body.

Snow crabs, also called *tanner* and *queen crabs*, have 10 legs, two of which end in claws. The shells are much smoother than those of the king crab. The claws, legs and shoulders are sold in clusters, as is king crab meat. Meat picked from cooked snow crabs is canned or frozen. Leg meat is the most expensive.

Jonah, *rock* and *red crabs*, all from the northern Atlantic Ocean, are not often sold in fish stores at the moment, because they yield less meat than other crabs. The claws are processed and usually sold frozen or in cans as picked meat. Rock crabs are sometimes seen live in tanks along with lobsters and Dungeness crabs.

OTHER SHELLFISH

Crawfish (crayfish), which are bought alive, are graded by size—the larger they are, the higher their price. Whole live crawfish are sold by the pound. The tail meat is sold fresh or frozen by the pound. Whole crawfish are quite often available cooked and chilled, sold by the pound.

Gooseneck barnacles, mostly found off the coast of the Pacific Northwest, are sold by the pound, live.

North Atlantic lobsters are sold by the pound, live or cooked. Cooked meat from these lobsters, sold by the pound, is expensive, as is canned meat. Live, these lobsters are graded by size: *Chicks*, or *chicken lobsters*, weigh around a pound; *culls* have one claw and are less expensive. Lobsters weighing 1 to 2½ pounds usually cost the same per pound, although prices vary according to the season or at holiday times. Very large North Atlantic lobsters may cost less per pound.

Spiny or *rock lobsters*, from cold and warm waters, have no claws, so mainly the tails are sold. The tails are mostly frozen and are graded by their weight, which ranges from 2 ounces to 2 pounds. Many are imported from South Africa, Australia, the Gulf of Oman, Iran and New Zealand. They are also available from Florida and farther south.

Northern Atlantic mussels are sold by the pound. The number per pound ranges from 8 to 18, approximately. They are not graded by size.

New Zealand green-tipped mussels are also sold by the pound, usually cooked and frozen.

Octopuses are usually cleaned and frozen; they weigh 1 to 4 pounds. They are sold by the pound.

Oysters are sold in the shell or shucked. They are also shucked, breaded and frozen or shucked and canned. Live in-shell oysters are sold by the dozen, sometimes by the pound. Suppliers grade them by size, but you may not see them graded in the store. Different species and different-sized oysters command different prices.

Periwinkles are sold by the pound. There may be as many as 60 to the pound.

Scallops are sold by the pound in the United States. The adductor muscle is all we eat of the scallop here. The shell and the rest of the animal are thrown away at sea when the scallop is shucked. In Europe, scallops are sold by the piece, most often with each scallop still lying on its bottom flat shell with its coral (roe). *Sea scallops* are the largest: there are 6 to 25 per pound. Sea scallops are found way out at sea. *Bay scallops* are found in bays. There are 50 to 80 bay scallops per pound. *Calico scallops* are smaller: there can be 100 to the pound. (Beware—these are sometimes called bay scallops.)

Sea urchins are sold live by the piece or by the pound. Japanese sources sell the edible part—the ovaries (called *gonads* or *roe*) of these animals already shucked, lying on little wooden boards. Each board holds about 20 pieces, equal to half a pound.

Shrimp are sold by the pound, except, of course, when canned. They are graded by size. Most shrimp are previously frozen; they come headless with the shell on or off. They are defrosted before being sold and are sometimes cooked, peeled and deveined for your convenience.

The largest, 8 to 15 to the pound, are the most expensive, and they may be called anything from *extra-colossal* to *colossal* to *jumbo*. There is no hard-and-fast rule about how fishmongers name the sizes—the names are given quite arbitrarily. Other grades available in stores are *large* (16 to 35 per pound), *medium* (36 to 50 per pound) and *small* (51 to 60 per pound). There can be as many as 400 to the pound. Fresh head-on *prawns* (*freshwater shrimp*) are sold by the pound: there are about 12 to the pound.

Squid are available both fresh and frozen, although most are cleaned and frozen at sea.

Fresh squid may have been cleaned at the fish store. Squid are sold by the pound. Heads, tentacles and bodies are sold.

Freshness

FIRST OF ALL, it is best to go to the fish store with no set idea of the fish or shellfish you want to prepare. I hardly ever plan a seafood meal ahead; the freshest is what I buy and serve. The whole experience of eating fresh fish is quite different from eating something that was taken from the water a few too many days ago and then was not carefully gutted or, most important, thoroughly chilled. Ideally, fish should be enjoyed within 48 hours after capture.

In order to realize a large enough catch for their huge markets, fishing boats in the United States and Canada must stay at sea a day or more at a time. What fishmongers then call "fresh" may already have been out of the water for a week or more. However, there are many day fishing boats that go out from all the coasts and lakes of the United States, Canada and Alaska.

The fact is that most of our fish reach us after many days out of water, but if the fish are properly handled, they can still be excellent. Many companies are making the right sort of effort to get fish to the consumer in less time nowadays, and consumer tastes are forcing the suppliers to ensure better quality. An example of this is the recent innovation of bleeding, gutting, icing down and boxing fish on board fishing vessels, initiated some time ago in Europe and Japan and now in New England. This method results in delivery of superior cod and haddock.

Optimum handling begins the moment the fish is caught. Fish guru Jon Rowley, who helps restaurants and fish stores buy the best seafood, describes the process: "The fish must be stunned and bled immediately after it is caught. Then it must be drawn—gutted, washed and chilled—before rigor [stiffness] sets in. The fish must go into rigor slowly and come out of rigor slowly. A fish kept in rigor for six days is the same as if it came right out of the water." If you catch your own fish and dress it before rigor sets in, you will be amazed at how wonderful it tastes.

All fish have some bacteria on their skin, in their gills and in their guts. The flesh of a fish is slightly acidic during rigor, so bacteria growth is inhibited, but bacteria spread into fish quickly after rigor passes. The growth of bacteria is greatly reduced when fish are gutted and properly iced or refrigerated by the supplier at 32 degrees F (0 degrees C). Unfortunately, our home refrigerators are set at around 39 degrees F (4 degrees C), so once home, fish should not be stored uncooked longer than a day. Some markets sell ungutted fish, which is not a good idea if they are to be kept for any length of time, even if properly chilled. (Exceptions include farmed fish such as striped bass, which have a good shelf life. Also note that freshwater fish have a longer shelf life than marine fish.) Ask the fishmonger to gut the fish for you, or follow the simple directions on page 41 and page 51.

Buy from reliable stores where the fish are displayed on a lot of ice or in a good refrigerated state. The place should smell fresh and be well patronized by the local community so that there is an abundant turnover.

Some live shellfish, such as lobsters and Dungeness crabs, should be kept in tanks of running salt water. Live clams, oysters, mussels, crawfish, sea urchins, periwinkles, conch and abalone should be refrigerated, preferably in airy sacks, so that they stay alive. They are displayed on ice. Soft-shell crabs are kept on a bed of seaweed in flat boxes. Hard-shell blue crabs are kept in bushel baskets.

The store display should look bright and lively, with sparkling ice, glistening skins, brilliant fish eyes and translucent fish fillets and steaks.

Ideally, you would use smell, sight and touch to tell the freshness of a fish. Even if you cannot use all your senses in a store—for sanitary reasons, your server should not let you touch fish or bring it up to your nose to smell it—your eyes can tell you a lot.

The questions that follow are clues to freshness—if the answers to most of the questions are yes, then we can assume that you have chosen well.

WHOLE FISH

Smell: Does the fish have an aroma of the sea?

An ammonia smell might be found in the cartilaginous species, such as sharks, rays and skates, but this can usually be gotten rid of by soaking. See the methods described in the fish profiles on pages 335 and 343 in Part III of this book.

The iodine smell and flavor sometimes found in flounder and brown shrimp can be attributed to their diet.

Sight: Does the fish look fresh?

Are its eyes clear and bright and flush with the surface of the head?

Are the scales (if any) shiny and intact, coated with a clear, glossy, thin mucous layer?

Are all the fins in good shape so you know that the fish has not been mishandled?

Are the gills of a strong red color and not gray, discolored or misshapen? A thick, gray, viscous coating is a bad sign. *Note:* Some fish are bled through the gills, and this process will turn the gills pale; this is acceptable.

Touch: Is the flesh firm?

Does the flesh bounce back if you make an indentation with your finger?

Does the fish feel rigid when you pick it up? The flesh (muscles) around the backbone should still be in rigor. When the fish is first out of the water, it is supple, but when rigor sets in, the muscles stiffen. Later, when the fish loses this stiffness, bacteria start to invade the flesh, and the peak of freshness has passed. *Note:* Rigor can last from a few hours up to one week; if a fish struggles during capture, rigor will last a very short time.

FILLETS, STEAKS AND OTHER CUTS OF FISH

Smell: Does the fish have an aroma of the sea?

Sight: Is the flesh unblemished, with no traces of bruises or blood spots?

Does it have a translucent look?

Does the flesh look firm, not flaking or falling apart due to a condition called "gaping?"

Touch: Is the flesh firm?

Does the flesh bounce back if you make an indentation with your finger?

PACKAGED FISH

If buying packaged fish, use the above criteria as much as you can. You can smell bad fish and shellfish right through the packaging.

SMOKED FISH

Smoked fish, whether packaged or not, should look moist and be firm to the touch, with no telltale excretions of oil or salt. They should not be dry—dryness denotes an old article. Keep them well refrigerated.

FROZEN FISH AND SHELLFISH

Frozen fish and shellfish, whether labeled "frozen" or "thawed," should look much like any packaged fresh fish. You must use the same criteria as for fresh fish when choosing it. The package must be intact, with no sign of freezer burn—drying out caused by dehydration. Freezer burn turns the flesh white and opaque, and it becomes soft and spongy. Solidly frozen fillets should look glossy, and whole fish should be carefully packaged and unblemished. *Note*: Frozen fish will turn rancid in long-term frozen storage; it has a characteristic smell and taste that is not appetizing.

Preparing and Storing Seafood

IF YOU CATCH FISH YOURSELF or others bring you fresh fish, be sure that the fish are gutted as soon as possible and stored properly. Follow the simple instructions on page 41 and page 51 if your friends did not gut the fish. If the fish have been well handled—that is, if they have not been allowed to bruise themselves on the deck of the boat or on the dock, their skin has not been broken and they have been bled, gutted and iced down promptly—they will stay fresh longer. As a rule of thumb, you can keep well-handled fish in the refrigerator for up to three days before you eat them.

For a whole, drawn, dressed or pan-dressed fish, put crushed ice into its belly cavity and use more ice to cover the outside skin. Place the fish, in an upright position as if it were still swimming, in a draining pan with holes, in a colander or on a rack, and put this container on top of another pan so the ice moistens the skin and removes bacteria as it melts and drains away. Restaurants use this method, and I recommend it, especially if you have a big fish or a big catch. You can also store a whole dressed fish, fillet or steak in a plastic bag (or cover it with plastic wrap) and place it in the refrigerator.

Remember that seafood should be eaten as soon as possible. It is not like beef, which can improve with age, although fish probably does improve for up to 48 hours after capture—the sweetness of the flesh intensifies in that time and then fades.

LIVE SHELLFISH

If you buy live shellfish, be sure they are still alive when you cook them.

Lobsters, *crawfish* and *crabs* should be lively. Lobsters picked out of marine tanks should splay their legs, claws and tails or curl their tails in. At any rate, they should react. Blue crabs from the East Coast are not kept in marine tanks, but Dungeness crabs from the West Coast are. Both hard- and soft-shell blue crabs are kept chilled in baskets or boxes of seaweed, while crawfish are kept in sacks or boxes in a moist but cool place. All should definitely show signs of life before they are cooked.

Bivalve mollusks—that is, those sea creatures with two shells, such as *clams*, *mussels* and *oysters*—must not have broken shells, gaping shells, empty shells or heavy shells that might be filled with mud or sand. If they do, they should be discarded. Bivalve mollusks must have tightly closed shells. The exceptions are geoduck clams, razor clams and soft-shell steamer clams whose siphons protrude, so they can never totally close their shells. Touch these siphons, or necks, and if they retract or move a little, the creatures are alive. With clams, mussels and oysters, if the shells are slightly open but close after a hard knock, you may be sure they are alive. When oysters, clams and mussels are sold shucked, the plump creatures should lie in plenty of their own clear, natural liquid.

Sea scallops are mostly shucked at sea and are therefore dead when we buy them. They must glisten, be firm and smell sweet. This applies also to the smaller *bay* and *calico* scallops. If they are packaged, put the package to your nose.

Univalves, such as periwinkles, conch and abalone, each have only one shell. They are considered sea snails because each has a single foot that rests on rocks. A periwinkle or conch has an *operculum*, a hard protective shield that covers the opening to the shell when its foot is withdrawn. When you touch the operculum, it should move slightly, showing that the creature is alive.

Sea urchins have spherical shells, called *tests*, covered with spines. If the prickly spines move when touched, the urchins are alive. You can buy sea urchin *roe* or *gonads* (*uni*) packaged on little wooden trays from Japanese markets. There are five little tongues of bright orange-yellow roe within each sea urchin. They should look and smell fresh.

Most *shrimp* are sold frozen; 65 to 70 percent are imported. Most are sold as raw frozen tails (with shells), and in fish markets, they are called green (raw) headless shrimp. Some farmed freshwater prawns—colorful blue shrimp from the South, the Caribbean, Hawaii (the largest domestic producer) and Brazil—are beginning to appear in New York markets with lingering signs of life. In California and Hawaii, some are kept alive in tanks. Some live white shrimp are now available in New York City's Chinatown. It is essential that fresh shrimp and prawns be eaten as soon as possible, because their flesh disintegrates quickly and becomes soft and mushy.

Whole raw shrimp with heads on come from Maine and the Gulf of Mexico at different seasons of the year and should look fresh, colorful and in pristine condition. The deterioration of a head-on shrimp is quick—pull off the head, and it will last longer. However, when it is cooked, you will miss sucking out the "fat" (liver, roe and pancreas) in the head, which tastes so good.

Most of the shrimp we eat have come from the warm-water oceans of the world, and nearly all are frozen headless, but with shells on. Whether in their shells or not, they must look shiny, moist, translucent, all of a piece, uncrushed and bright. Some raw shrimp have such pink shells that they may be mistaken for cooked shrimp. Cooked shrimp must look firm to the touch, no longer translucent but not dried out—a dry appearance denotes overcooking and toughness. This also applies to cooked lobster and crabmeat.

Squid, *cuttlefish* and *octopus* are sold fresh, frozen or defrosted. Look for good color—that is, creamy white flesh under the outer membrane, which is light brown on the summer *Illex* (short-finned) squid and white on the winter *Loligo* (long-finned) squid but turns purple with age; look for the same creamy white flesh when the squid are cleaned. Cuttlefish have varicolored membranes, ranging from a brownish beige to sepia to a dark bluish tinge. Under the membrane should be the same creamy white flesh as on the squid. On the octopus, look for gray skin (which turns white when cooked) and white flesh.

All packaged *crabmeat* is cooked before it is sold, and the shells are picked clean. Fresh crabmeat should be kept very cold and used as soon as possible. Canned *pasteurized* crabmeat lasts several months in the refrigerator.

Dungeness crabs from the West Coast are sold live from tanks, but they are mostly sold whole—cooked, in sections or as picked meat. Some Dungeness crabmeat is frozen, as are whole crabs.

Snow crab (also called *tanner* and marketed as *queen crab* in Atlantic Canada) and *king crab* are cooked and sold mostly frozen in the shell or as picked crabmeat. It is hard to tell when shell-on crab legs are of good quality for obvious reasons—you can't see the flesh inside. However, when they are sold split open, you can see whether the flesh is moist and shows no signs of freezer burn.

Red, *rock* and *Jonah* crabs from the Atlantic are mostly used for picked crabmeat, although they are sometimes available live. Red rock crabs from the West Coast are very similar to Jonah and rock crabs.

Claws are all that is sold of the *stone crab*. Either the left or right claw is picked off a live crab, which is then thrown back into the water to grow another claw. These claws are immediately cooked, cooled and chilled. A good deal of them are also frozen. Buy only claws that look freshly caught and cooked. Barring breaking open the shell, the only way to tell freshness is by smell. You want no odor or, at best, one of the sea.

STORING LIVE SHELLFISH

Live shellfish need air and moisture. Store them in the refrigerator in open plastic or paper bags, preferably with seaweed or wet paper towels to keep them moist. Cook lobsters the day you buy them. You can pretty safely keep mussels, oysters and clams refrigerated for one or two days before eating.

FREEZING TIPS

It is hard for me to be enthusiastic about freezing seafood unless it is flash-frozen in supercold commercial freezers at -40 degrees F (-40 degrees C); the home freezer proves inadequate. The Japanese freeze tuna at -76 degrees F (-60 degrees C) and may keep it frozen for a year before thawing it for sashimi. The home freezer that reaches only 0 degrees F (-18 degrees C) can be used to store previously frozen seafood or to store fresh seafood for a short time—a week for fatty fish, a month for lean fish and shellfish.

If you plan to eat raw fish, freeze it for two days to kill any parasites it may have. Few fish have parasites—for further information see page 21.

Defrost seafood overnight in the refrigerator. Don't hurry the process, except by defrosting in the microwave oven. Don't defrost the seafood all the way through in the microwave, however, otherwise it will start to cook on the outside edges. Complete the defrosting at room temperature.

Before freezing fish, all you need to do is clean it (gut it and remove the gills). Then wrap it well with freezer wrap or put it in a heavy plastic self-sealing bag, making sure it is airtight to prevent freezer burn. Push or suck the air out before sealing the bag. Put shellfish, such as scallops and squid, in self-sealing bags also. Don't freeze previously frozen shrimp.

How Much to Buy

THE AMOUNT OF FISH you buy does, of course, depend much on appetite. When buying whole fish with head and tail, you need 10 ounces to 1¼ pounds per portion. Portions of filleted fish can vary from 3 ounces to ½ pound per person. Some fish lose more water than others in cooking, particularly skinned filleted fish; to compensate for this loss, buy more than usual.

The fishmonger should be able to help you with the amount to buy for a certain number of people, but when buying whole fish, you need to be aware of those fish which lose water in cooking, those which are heavy with bones and those with large, heavy heads. In general, you do not need to buy as much of rich and flavorful fish as you do of milder and leaner fish. Smoked seafood, such as trout, salmon, tuna, mackerel, mussels, bluefish, chub, haddock, eel, scallops, sable and sturgeon, is usually used for an appetizer or salad, and only a few ounces need be bought for each person—I suggest 2 to 4 ounces per person. The amount you buy is your choice; however, you can refer to the guide that follows and, of course, to the different recipes.

Fish	Pan-Dressed or Whole	Fillet	Steak	Chunk
		Amount Per Person		

Fish	Pan-Dressed or Whole	Fillet	Steak	Chunk
Anchovy	¾-1 lb.			
Bass:				
black sea, white sea, white (freshwater)	1 lb.	5-8 oz.		
smallmouth, largemouth	1 lb.	6-8 oz.		
striped (wild and freshwater)	1 lb.	6-8 oz.	6-8 oz. (wild)	¾ lb. (wild)
Blackfish (tautog, hardhead, black trout, steelhead)	1 lb.	6-8 oz.		
Blowfish (sea squab, chicken of the sea)		6-8 oz. (tail ends)		
Bluefish (snapper, tailor, chopper)	¾-1 lb.	6-8 oz.		¾ lb.
Buffalofish		6-7 oz.		
Butterfish, Atlantic	8-10 oz.			
Carp		6-7 oz.	6-7 oz.	
Catfish: channel, white, brown bullhead, flathead	¾ lb.	6-10 oz.		
Char, Arctic	¾ lb.	5-8 oz.		
Cod or Scrod:				
Atlantic cod and scrod	¾ lb.	6-8 oz.	6-8 oz.	
Pacific (gray cod)	¾ lb.	6-8 oz.	6-8 oz.	
salt cod in dry state	¾ lb.	3-4 oz.		
Croaker	¾ lb.			
Cusk	¾-1 lb.	6-10 oz.		
Dolphinfish (mahi-mahi)		4-8 oz.		
Drum	¾ lb.	6-10 oz.		
Eel	2-3 oz.	7 oz.	7 oz.	
Flounder: summer, Southern, black-back, fluke, yellowtail	1-1¼ lb.	6-8 oz.		
Grouper	¾-1 lb.	6-8 oz.		¾ lb.
Haddock	¾ lb.	6-8 oz.	6-8 oz.	
Hake:				
white	¾ lb.	6-8 oz.	6-8 oz.	
red (ling)	¾ lb.	4-8 oz.		
Halibut	¾-1 lb.	6-8 oz.	6-8 oz.	
Herring: Atlantic, Pacific	½-¾ lb.	8 oz.		
Kingfish: Atlantic, Southern	¾ lb.	6-8 oz.	6-8 oz.	
Lingcod	¾ lb.	6-8 oz.	6-8 oz.	

FISH	AMOUNT PER PERSON			
	PAN-DRESSED OR WHOLE	FILLET	STEAK	CHUNK
Mackerel:				
Atlantic, Pacific	¾–1 lb.	6–8 oz.		
king (kingfish)	¾ lb.		6–8 oz.	
Spanish, jack, chub, Japanese	¾ lb.	6–8 oz.	6–8 oz.	
Mahi-mahi (dolphinfish)		4–8 oz.		
Marlin		4–8 oz.		
Monkfish (anglerfish, bellyfish)	¾ lb.	8 oz.		
Mullet, striped	¾–1 lb.	6–8 oz.		
Ocean Perch (Atlantic redfish)		6–8 oz.		
Ocean Pout				6–8 oz.
Orange Roughy		6–8 oz.		
Perch, yellow	½–1 lb.	6–8 oz.		
Pike	¾–1 lb.	6–8 oz.		
Pollock: Atlantic, Pacific, Alaskan	¾–1 lb.	6–8 oz.		
Pompano	¾–1 lb.	6–8 oz.		
Porgy (scup)	¾–1 lb.	6–8 oz.		
Redfish		6–10 oz.		
Rockfish:				
Pacific (black, canary, orange, yellow, widow, blue, yelloweye, bocaccio, rock cod)	¾–1 lb.	6–8 oz.		
Sablefish (black cod; butterfish when filleted)	¾ lb.	6 oz.	7 oz.	⅔ lb.
Salmon:				
Atlantic, chinook (king), chum (keta), coho (silver), pink (humpback), sockeye, baby coho	½–¾ lb. 8–10 oz.	6–8 oz.	6–8 oz.	½–¾ lb.
Sardine	¾–1 lb.	6–8 oz.		
Sea Robin	½–1 lb.	6–8 oz.	6–8 oz.	
Sea Trout, spotted—see Weakfish				
Shad and Roe		4–7 oz.		
Shark:				
Atlantic, Pacific, mako, thresher, silky, dusky, shovelnose, nurse, blacktip (spinner)			6–10 oz.	
sand shark (dogfish)		4–8 oz.	6–8 oz.	
Sheepshead	¾–1 lb.	6–10 oz.		
Skate	½–¾ lb.	6–8 oz.		
Smelt	½–¾ lb.	5–8 oz.		

Fish	Amount Per Person			
	Pan-Dressed or Whole	Fillet	Steak	Chunk
Snapper: red, American red, gray (mangrove), lane, silk (yelloweye, day, red day, longfin, pargo de la alto), yellowtail, vermilion (beeliner)	¾-1 lb.	6-10 oz.		1 lb.
Sole:				
Pacific (West Coast Dover, English, petrale, rex, rock, sand, yellowfin)	¾-1 lb.	4-8 oz.		
Atlantic (gray, lemon)	¾-1 lb.	4-8 oz.		
European Dover	¾-1 lb.	4-8 oz.		
Spot (Norfolk)	¾ lb.			
Sturgeon: Atlantic, lake		6-8 oz.		
Sunfish, various	¾-1 lb.			
Swordfish (broadbill, billfish)			7-10 oz.; cubes: 4-8 oz.	
Tilapia (St. Peter's fish)	¾ lb.	6 oz.		
Tilefish (blueline, gray, golden, rainbow)	¾-1 lb.	6-8 oz.	10-12 oz.	
Trout:				
freshwater (rainbow, lake, brook, brown, steelhead) (bone in or out)	8-10 oz.	6-8 oz.		
Tuna:				
bigeye, bluefin, skipjack, yellowfin, blackfin			6-10 oz.	
albacore, bonito, little tunny	¾-1 lb.		6-10 oz.	
Wahoo		4-8 oz.		
Weakfish	¾-1 lb.	6-8 oz.		
Whitebait (silversides)	6-8 oz.			
Whitefish, freshwater	¾ lb.	6-8 oz.		
Whiting, American (silver hake, New England hake)	¾ lb.	4-8 oz.		
Wolffish (ocean catfish)		6-8 oz.		
Yellowtail:				
raw		3-4 oz.		
cooked		6-8 oz.		
Yellowtail Flounder—see Flounder				
Yellowtail Snapper—see Snapper				

FISH	AMOUNT PER PERSON
Fish Roe, various	4-6 oz.

NUMBER CRUSTACEAN, MOLLUSK OR CEPHALOPOD	AMOUNT PER PERSON	PER PERSON
Abalone		½-1 4 oz. (flesh)
Clams:		
littleneck, cherrystone	6-9	
soft-shell (steamers)		¾-1 lb.
Manila		6-8 oz.
cockles		6-8 oz.
geoduck		4 oz. (flesh)
Conch		6-8 oz.
Crab:		
hard-shell blue (depending on size)	2-6	
soft-shell blue (depending on size)	2-4	
red, rock, Jonah		1-2
king, snow (tanner, queen)		½-1 lb. (legs) or 4-8 oz. (flesh)
Dungeness	1	1 lb.
stone crab claws		¾-1 lb.
crabmeat (various kinds)		4-8 oz.
Crawfish (crayfish):		
whole	6-12	½-1 lb.
tail meat		6-8 oz.
Gooseneck Barnacle		½-¾ lb.
Langostino (Dublin Bay prawn)		½ lb.
Lobster:		
Atlantic	1	1-2 lb.
spiny (tails)	1-2	6-8 oz.
cooked meat		4-6 oz.
Mussels, northern Atlantic		¼-1 lb.
Octopus		6-8 oz.
Oysters:		
in shell	6-9	
shucked		½ pint
Periwinkle, common		4-8 oz.
Scallops: sea, bay, calico		4-8 oz.
Sea Urchin	1	1-4 oz.

Crustacean, Mollusk or Cephalopod	Number Per Person	Amount Per Person
Shrimp:		
in shell		6-8 oz.
cooked meat		5-6 oz.
Squid:		
uncleaned		6-8 oz.
cleaned		4-6 oz.

Methods of Preparation

A N UNDERSTANDING of anatomy is necessary for complete mastery of fish cooking.
Once you know the anatomy of a fish, you
can cut it in various ways, such as into steaks,
chunks or fillets, and make different cuts
from fillets, such as medallions (thick slices),
escalopes (thin slices) or slivers. With this
knowledge, you can create a variety of dishes
and also ensure even cooking, which is so
important with fish. Becoming familiar with
the bone structure also allows you to separate
the flesh from the bones easily, once the fish
is cooked.

Roundfish

ANATOMY

When we refer to a roundfish, we mean
any fish, whether with a rounded or a compressed body, that has eyes on both sides of
its head, such as cod, tuna, salmon, whiting
and rockfish. By contrast, a flatfish has a
compressed body (hence the name) and has
both eyes on the top of its head. Examples
include flounder, fluke, dabs, turbot and rex,
Dover sole, lemon sole and halibut. On the
West Coast, roundfish is the term given to
any fish that is whole, not filleted.

The skeleton of a roundfish consists of a
central backbone with a row of straight bones
reaching upward to the dorsal fins and two
rows of curved rib bones that enclose the visceral cavity—that is, the stomach cavity.

Most roundfish have another row of
bones, called pin bones, sticking outward at a
right angle from the backbone. In general,
pin bones of small fish are few, feathery, thin
and short and extend only along the backbone above the rib cage. When a roundfish is
filleted, these bones remain in the center of
the fillets but are easily removed.

Not all roundfish are round. Their shapes
vary from round to oval to compressed. If we
look at cross sections of different parts of a
roundfish, we learn that although the fish is

PIN
BONES

DORSAL FINS

GILL COVER

PECTORAL FIN

PELVIC FIN

VISCERAL
CAVITY

VENT

ANAL FIN

roundish in shape, the cross sections will not always produce a solid disk of flesh. A cross section of the flesh behind the head shows

the hollow of the visceral cavity; it is shaped somewhat like a horseshoe. Cross sections taken beyond the visceral cavity, nearer to the tail, will be solid disks of flesh.

The rib bones of roundfish jut out from the backbone either at a curve or—as in the case of cod, whiting and eel—at a sharp, nearly right angle. It is said that the Mercedes-Benz symbol derives from the cross section of an eel's backbone. The angle at which the rib bones stick out in a particular fish, of course, alters the shape of the fillet. The flesh over the rib bones is always thinner than the flesh from the back of the fish.

UTENSILS NEEDED

♦ A hard plastic or wooden chopping board, perhaps used only for fish.

♦ For any size fish: a boning or filleting knife. I prefer to use a boning knife with a nonflexible 5½-inch blade. For a smaller fish, you can use a sharp paring knife with a 4-inch blade. Some people (including fish-mongers) use a flexible filleting knife with an 8-to-10-inch blade.

♦ A chef's knife with an 8- or 10-inch blade.

♦ For fish with sturdy pin bones: a pair of pin-nose or needle-nose pliers. For fish with thin, feathery pin bones: a pair of tweezers.

GUTTING

It is important that a fish be gutted as early as possible to prolong its shelf life. The gills must also be removed before cooking. Usually, a fish has been gutted by the time you see it, either at sea or by the fishmonger. However, if you catch a fish or a friend gives you a whole undressed fish, you must gut it, scale it and remove the gills yourself.

To gut a fish, take a sharp-pointed knife and insert it in the anal vent. Make a slit up the belly to the head, cutting around or between the pelvic fins. Empty out the visceral cavity. You may find the roe (fish eggs) enclosed in a thin-skinned elongated sac.

Save it to cook and eat (it can be delicious), or discard. The dark secretion of blood (the kidney) on the backbone can give a bitter taste to the fish; this blood is often hidden, covered by a skinlike lining along the backbone. Cut through the lining if necessary, scrape the blood away, and rinse out the inside of the fish. The blood is often present in a cleaned fish too—if so, remove it.

You can also gut a fish through the head. In this case, you don't have to make a slit in the belly cavity at all. The appearance is neat, and head gutting is suitable for such small fish as anchovies, sardines, smelts, mackerel, freshwater trout, small sea trout (weakfish) and red mullet (rouget).

To gut a small fish through the head, first take hold of the gills with your fingers. If you pull carefully, the gills and guts will come out more or less all together. Retrieve any guts left inside with a small knife or your fingers. If there is roe in the fish, leave it in or squeeze the fish carefully (like a toothpaste tube) to extrude the roe. Rinse the inside of the fish.

It is more difficult, but not impossible, to gut a large fish through the head, for the gills are large and strong.

SCALING

Not all fish need to be scaled. Some, such as catfish, monkfish, wolffish, shark and swordfish, are scaleless. On others, such as mackerel, trout and pompano, the scales are very small, fine and negligible.

Before scaling, you can remove all the fins with shears or scissors, if you like, but if you intend to cook the fish whole, I believe you should leave the fins and tail on, so you can see the complete fish in all its glory. Be careful of the dorsal fins, for the spiny ones can puncture your skin easily.

Scale a fish with a fish scaler, a dull kitchen or table knife or a spoon. You want to avoid splitting the skin, so don't use too sharp a knife. Holding the fish by the tail, put it headfirst in a large see-through plastic bag, such as a self-sealing bag, or directly into a garbage pail or a sink full of water, so that the scales do not fly all over. If it is a large fish, handle it without bending it too much so that you do not break the backbone.

Remove the scales from the tail end by inserting the knife under the scales and pushing them off in short strokes, working up to the head.

REMOVING THE GILLS

Gills, the breathing and, in some fish, the filtering mechanism, are J-shaped pieces of cartilage or bone with filaments (which are bright red and feathery when the fish is very fresh) attached to the outside and, frequently, gill rakers—a row of little "bones"—protruding from the inside. (In herbivorous fish, the gill rakers behind each gill arch prevent food from escaping out of the gill opening and direct it down the gullet; large carnivorous fish often lack gill rakers.) The gills must be removed, for they contain bacteria and blood and can spoil the taste of the fish.

remove the gills, as they might impart a bitter taste to the stock. Also, rinse any traces of blood from the bones before using them.

FILLETING

Now let's learn about filleting and what can be done with fillets once they are free of the bones. The aim in filleting a whole fish is to take as much flesh from the bones as possible, while producing a beautiful fillet. A roundfish produces two fillets, one from each side of the body.

Take the time to examine the fish *before* filleting. Look inside the visceral cavity, and acquaint yourself with the angle of the rib bones and the shape and size of the cavity. You shouldn't see any pin bones sticking out of the backbone at this point. At any rate, the knife will cut through them without much difficulty, unless they are very large and strong. They can be removed afterward.

Your knife must always be in contact with the bones, and you need to make long, smooth strokes as you cut.

Place the fish on a cutting board at an angle, with the head to your right pointing away and the top dorsal fin (the back of the fish) nearest to you. (Reverse this if you are left-handed.)

They lie under the gill covers behind the eyes. There are four gills on each side of a fish's head.

The gill nearest to the head is attached by a membrane and must be freed by cutting alongside it. Lift up the gill cover, and with a sharp knife or kitchen shears, cut along the innermost gill to free it from the head. Cut the gills free at each end also. Use a cloth to pull them out so that the gill rakers don't stab you. Discard. Rinse the inside of the fish, and pat the outside dry with a paper towel. (Even fish supposedly cleaned at the store may retain some of the gills; if so, remove them.)

When making stock with fish "frames" (skeletons, heads, tails and skin), be sure to

Cut downward with your boning knife, following the line of the head behind the pectoral fin and the armored gill cover, until you hit the backbone. Also cut down through the flesh just above the tail.

Now, take your knife and insert it just behind the head, and with one hand on the fish (but of course out of cutting reach), make a cut through the skin along the back, close to but avoiding the dorsal fins, all the way down to the tail. Cut in a long, continuous stroke, not with a jaggedy motion. Then, following the same cut, cut deeper into the fish until you reach the backbone. You will feel a slight or substantial bump, depending on the size and kind of fish.

Now, fold back the flesh so you can see what you are doing.

Again, take your knife to the head end to complete the cutting of the fillet. Your next cut must curve slightly upward and then down over the rib bones to release the flesh. You will be cutting through the pin bones that extend from the backbone as you do this. Even if you can't see the pin bones, you will hear your knife going clickety-click as it severs them. Look inside the cavity to check the angle of the rib bones so you can tell how sharply your knife must curve upward. (The rib bones of some fish that have large visceral cavities, such as cod, protrude greatly, and so the knife must curve upward, nearly at a right angle to the backbone. I find that nobody ever explains this, and unless you are aware of the undulations of the bones, you can miss a lot of the flesh.) I repeat, your knife must always be in contact with bones. The flesh that covers the rib bones is thin and one can easily cut through it by mistake.

After you have made the upward curve with the knife, angle your knife downward so that you can clean the flesh from the rest of the bones along the length of the fish. Try for a clean cut, so the fillet is neat and not jagged. Do not cut the fillet completely off, because you need its bulk in place as you fillet the other side.

Now, turn the fish over. You will cut the second fillet starting at the tail end.

Cut down through the flesh just above the tail. Cut closely, as before, along the back skin, but avoiding the dorsal fins, until you reach the head.

Now, make another deeper cut, following the previous cut, until you reach the backbone.

Make a diagonal cut behind the pectoral fin and gill cover. Gently pull back the flesh, and angle the knife slightly downward, slicing to free the flesh above the straight bones near the tail.

As you reach the rib bones, curve the knife upward and over them, until you reach the head.

Free this fillet entirely from the bones. Turn the fish over, and free the other side as well.

Check to see whether any rib bones are still attached to the fillets. Insert your knife under them to release them.

SKINNING A FILLET

You can skin a fillet if you wish. To do so, take the fillet and place it on the board, skin side down, so the tail end is nearest you. Pin the tail end to the board with the fingertips of one hand. Take a chef's knife with an 8- or 10-inch blade (no other knife works as well) and slip the blade at an angle between the fillet and the skin just in front of your fingertips. Saw gently back and forth, separating the flesh from the skin all the way up. Lift the fillet as you work to make sure that it is coming smoothly off the skin. You can pull on the skin as you are cutting. Discard the skin, or save it to make a stock. Trim any raggedy edges off the fillet.

REMOVING PIN BONES

Check to see whether there are any small pin bones at the head end of each fillet, or find them by running your fingers over the center of the fillet. If a fillet is thin, take pin-nose pliers or tweezers and pluck out the bones by pulling toward the wide (head) end of the fillet. When the pin bones fillet off the bone, then slide the other one off, taking care to lift it free of the rib bones, which sometimes want to stick on. If the rib bones come away with the flesh, slide your knife under them to remove them. When the skeletal bones are exposed (with the other fillet underneath), pull the tail up all the way to the head, lifting the backbone away from the flesh. The whole bone structure, including the head, should come away in one piece if the fish has been cooked through properly.

are big and strong, take your knife and cut down into the fillet on both sides of the bones (without cutting through the skin). Angle your knife and slide it across the skin, removing the thin strip of flesh with the pin bones embedded in it.

When removing the pin bones this way on a skinless fillet, you will have a V-shaped fillet.

FILLETING A COOKED WHOLE ROUNDFISH

It is not as easy to lift a *whole* fillet from the top side of a whole cooked fish as it is to remove one from a raw fish. The easiest way to fillet a cooked fish is to cut the top fillet down the middle, above the backbone, and lift it off the fillets in two sections.

Make a cut down the middle of the flesh on top of the backbone and lift off the skin, if desired. Gently lift one-half of the upper

Discard the skeleton, or put it to the side of the plate. The entire bottom fillet is now free too. Eat and enjoy.

When serving a large cooked fish, you may find it convenient to bone the fish completely and then reassemble it. Do this in the manner described above, taking large *pieces* of the fish fillets off with a long spatula. Put the pieces aside, neatly and in order, and remove the backbone. Put back the pieces of fillet to reassemble the fish. This method works beautifully with a celebratory salmon. Or, if more convenient, bone the fish before cooking (see page 48).

BUTTERFLYING OR SPLITTING

To *butterfly* a fish is to make two fillets from it that are connected by either the belly skin or the back. Incidentally, it is not possible to butterfly a flatfish, because the fillets are not joined together anywhere. They are separated by bones.

One method of butterflying a roundfish is to split it open from its back and bone it at the same time, producing two fillets joined by the belly skin. Be sure there is no belly slit. This can only be done to an ungutted fish or a fish that has been gutted through the head. It makes a pleasant variation in presentation and is used mainly for smaller fish which are served as individual portions, such as herring, sardines, mackerel, trout, whiting, black sea bass, flying fish and other fish that weigh 1½ pounds or less.

To butterfly using this method, first scale the fish and cut off its head and fins. Then cut into the back of the fish, first on one side

of the dorsal fins, then on the other, down and over the rib bones until you reach the visceral cavity. *Do not cut through the skin at the bottom of the fish*. Lift out the viscera. Spread the joined fillets open and remove any remaining bones.

Another method produces two fillets connected by the back. Follow the directions for boning on page 48. You can leave the head and tail on if you like. Spread the fish open. This method is good for small fish such as trout, herring, mackerel and sardines; baby coho salmon is usually prepared this way by processors.

You can also butterfly filleted fish. For this method, see page 59.

In cooking, butterflied fish are treated as fillets.

BONING

Boning is useful when you are stuffing a chunk, or roast, or when you just want to make a nice presentation of a whole fish such as a bake-poached or roast salmon for a party so that you do not need to deal with the bones when serving.

For a whole fish, once it is scaled and gutted, continue the cavity cut all the way to the tail. Spread the fish open a little, and cut through the rib bones and up toward the back on either side of the backbone (first one side, then the other), without actually cutting through the skin along the back of the fish. Do not cut off the dorsal fins if you are going to close up the fish again for the final presentation. Find the tops of the rib bones at the point where they were attached to the backbone, and strip them clear of the flesh with your fingers, or insert a knife under them to loosen them, then discard them. Try to keep the flesh intact. Then cut or detach the central backbone (kitchen shears are good for this) at both the head and the tail, and pull it free. Most likely, you will not be able to remove the row of smaller bones near the dorsal fins unless you have a large fish. Don't worry about them—they are easily removed after the fish is cooked.

Trout and baby coho salmon are usually prepared this way by processors. Whole fish, such as large salmon, bluefish, tilefish, groupers and red snappers, can certainly be prepared this way before they are roasted, bake-poached or stuffed and then roasted.

Bone a chunk, or roast, in the same way.

The chunk will most likely come already scaled and cleaned and won't have the head or the tail.

ANOTHER WAY TO DRESS A ROUNDFISH THAT WEIGHS TWO POUNDS OR LESS

A whole fish is cut in half lengthwise to separate the two halves, producing two fillets with half the head attached to each.

Take, for instance, a whole pompano, whose beautiful skin should be shown to advantage. (Incidentally, pompano, though technically a roundfish, has a compressed flat body.) Gut it, and then slice it in half lengthwise. Here's how: Starting at the head, place the knife at a right angle across the mouth, cut into the mouth, then cut through the head and body, following the backbone from head to tail. One side of the fish will still contain the backbone, so loosen it with a sharp knife and also remove the rib bones from each fillet. Trim the edges of each fillet. This method works best for fish with fairly compressed bodies, such as pompano, John Dories, porgies, butterfish and small black sea bass or farmed striped bass.

A fish prepared this way can be bake-poached in the oven, broiled or grilled on a barbecue. The skin should show for the presentation, so either bake-poach the fish in the oven skin side up or broil it skin side down in a pan filled with ⅛ inch of white wine and present it skin side up. Grill the halves flesh side down to preserve the skin. This way, you do not waste any flesh—it is all

available to you, particularly the small amount of delectable flesh in the head (the cheek), which is lost when filleting.

It is also a good way for two to share a fish.

Flatfish

ANATOMY

The flatfish group includes all flounder, sole, dab, fluke, plaice, Greenland turbot and halibut, as well as Dover sole, turbot and brill from Europe.

Flatfish have flat, compressed bodies. They swim in a horizontal position and look like oval plates as they swim. The skin on the top side of a flatfish is dark, acting as camouflage so the fish will not be easily seen from

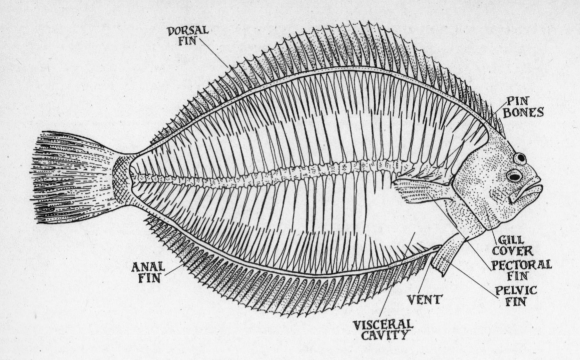

DORSAL
FIN

PIN
BONES

ANAL
FIN

GILL
COVER

PECTORAL
FIN

PELVIC
FIN

VENT

VISCERAL
CAVITY

above and will blend in with the sandy bottom of the ocean, where flatfish like to live. The underside is usually white or nearly white. (The underside of the gray sole is gray and that of the Greenland turbot is black.) The scales on a flatfish are not large; on small fish, they are negligible and only a gentle scrape is necessary to remove them.

The dorsal and anal fins of a flatfish run the length of its body. Its relatively small visceral cavity and anal vent lie near the head, just behind the gill cover, like a little pocket.

If there are any male or female roe sacs, they lie along both sides of the fish and next to the straight bones behind the visceral cavity.

A flatfish starts life with an eye on either side of its head and the same coloring all over. When it is but half an inch long, it begins to flatten out, and one eye joins the other on the top of its head. The eyes can be on the right or left side of the head, depending on the species, but most flatfish from U.S. waters are right-eyed, although most flukes, Southern flounder and sand dabs from Florida waters and the Gulf of Mexico are left-eyed.

How do you tell whether a flatfish is right-eyed or left-eyed? With the dark skin facing upward, place the fish horizontally in front of you with the visceral cavity, pelvic fin and mouth nearest you. A right-eyed flatfish has its eyes to the right of the visceral cavity; a left-eyed flatfish, to the left. Recognizing right- and left-eyed flatfish will help you to identify different fish and also make it easier to follow instructions on filleting those fish.

The skeleton of a flatfish is very simple. It consists of a central backbone with straight bones extending out to the little bones supporting the dorsal and anal fins. The basic skeletal structure is so simple and strong that if you remove the fillets and let the skeleton dry, you can use it to comb your hair. But we won't do that. Instead, we will learn how to gut a flatfish and how to cut fillets and steaks from it.

UTENSILS NEEDED

♦ A hard plastic chopping board, perhaps used only for fish. This board can easily be scrubbed with bleach.

♦ A boning or filleting knife. (I prefer a boning knife with a nonflexible 5½-inch blade.)

♦ A chef's knife with an 8-to-10-inch blade.

GUTTING

Note: It's not necessary to gut a flatfish before filleting it, but it is necessary before cooking it whole.

Insert the tip of the boning knife in the anal vent. Cut a slit toward the head, between the two pelvic fins. Empty the cavity with your fingers, loosening the guts with the knife and pulling the remainder away. Rinse.

VISCERAL CAVITY

FILLETING

Roundfish fillets (see page 43) taper at the tail end and are usually very thin over the rib bones. Flatfish fillets are of a more even

thickness, therefore they cook more evenly, although the top fillet of a flatfish is a little thicker than the bottom one. Flatfish fillets are boneless, save for a few pin bones at the head end, which can easily be removed. These bones are all that remain of the rib cage when the fish is filleted. (They can also be left in if they are very fine, for they will be harmless once cooked.) Flatfish fillets are simplicity itself to eat, for they are easily lifted off the flat bone structure.

At the fish store, we see double fillets of flatfish that have been deftly cut by processors or, preferably, have been cut by the fishmonger that day. When filleting flatfish ourselves, we can take either two or four fillets from each fish.

To Produce Two Fillets: Place a right- or left-eyed fish, dark skin uppermost, diagonally on the cutting board, with the head to your left and the tail pointing away to the right.

Take your knife and first make a slit across the flesh next to the tail, then cut into the skin along the fins, starting at the tail and

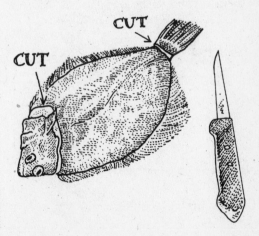

CUT

CUT

finishing just before the head. You should feel the little bones that support the fins all the way along. Make a cut behind the head, the pectoral fin and the visceral cavity.

Now, cut in deeper with long strokes until you reach the slight bump of the backbone. Again, you should feel the bones at all times with your knife.

Gently fold back the fillet, ease your knife over the backbone, and continue to cut, slightly downward at first, then flatten out the knife to free the rest of the fillet from the bones. Do not free it completely, for you need its bulk in place as you fillet the other side.

Turn the fish over, and place it with the head to your right.

Repeat the above operation, starting at the head end. Free this fillet completely from the bones, and turn the fish over to free the other fillet.

Trim the edges of each fillet. Trim any pin bones from the head end.

You now have two nice fillets.

To Produce Four Fillets: Place the fish on the cutting board, underside up, with the head away from you and the tail toward you.

Take your knife and make a cut down the middle of the fish, above or just to one side of the backbone (you can feel the backbone with your fingertips), from the head to the tail.

Cut the left-hand fillet away starting at the head end, using long strokes to obtain a smooth fillet, with the knife at an angle to free it from the bones. Do not cut the fillet completely off, because you need its bulk in place as you fillet the other side of the fish.

Turn the fish around with the head toward you, and cut the other fillet away, but again not completely off.

Turn the fish over, and repeat the procedure, cutting the two fillets from this side completely free from the skeleton. Release the fillets on the other side of the fish.

Trim the edges of the fillets. Trim any pin bones from the head end.

You now have four nice fillets.

Note: If you should find roe sacs in these fish during filleting, lift them up and put them aside. They can be cooked with the fillets or served separately but can also be used to make a sauce, a custard or a mousse.

SKINNING A FILLET

This method is the same as for roundfish fillets: Take the fillet and place it on the board, skin side down, so the tail end is nearest to you. Pin the tail end to the board with the fingertips of one hand. Take a chef's knife and slip the blade at an angle between the fillet and the skin just in front of your fingertips. Saw gently back and forth, separating the flesh from the skin all the way up. Lift the fillet as you work to make sure that it is coming smoothly off the skin. Discard the skin, or save it to make a stock.

In Europe, the white underskin is often left on, because its color does not offend and because it tastes good (as does the dark skin).

FILLETING A COOKED WHOLE FLATFISH

Make a cut down the middle of the flesh to the central backbone, and gently lift one side—that is, one-half—of the fillet off the bone, then slide the other side off. When the skeletal bone is exposed (with the other fillet underneath), lift it up from the tail end all the way to the head. The whole bone structure, including the head, should come away

in one piece if the fish has been cooked properly. Now, you are free to eat the rest of the fish.

FLATFISH STEAKS

The halibut, a large flounder, is most often cut into steaks by processors or fishmongers. Halibut steaks should be cut 1 inch thick for best cooking results. As halibut are usually very large fish, weighing up to 750 pounds, they have strong backbones that are best cut with a cleaver or a saw. Leave this job to an expert if the fish is very large.

Smaller flatfish, such as sole, flounder, brill and turbot, can be cut into steaks for variety also. To do this, cut down against the grain of the fish as you would for roundfish, in slices about ⅜ to ½ inch thick. You will need a heavy chef's knife or a cleaver and a mallet to get through the backbone. A few little steaks arranged in a star pattern on a plate look marvelous.

Other Anatomies
BLOWFISH AND MONKFISH

Blowfish and monkfish have very simple anatomies: Both have sturdy backbones with no other bones protruding from them. Both of these fish are a bother to skin, but one hardly ever sees the skin or heads of either of these fish, as these parts are unpleasant to look at and touch and thus are either discarded at sea or removed by the processor. We eat the tail end of the blowfish, but not the tail itself. In the case of the monkfish, we eat the tail end or fillets cut from each side of the backbone. These pieces are very simple to prepare for cooking and eating.

Blowfish: The blowfish, which is also known as the pufferfish, sea squab or chicken of the sea, inflates its prickly skin when chased by a predator in order to make itself into an unpleasant mouthful too large to swallow. Apart from its head bones, the blowfish has a simple backbone with no other bones. When the head, tail, skin and guts of a blowfish have been removed, what

remains is a firm, glistening piece of tail flesh surrounding the backbone.

In Japan, where there are 15 varieties of blowfish (*fugu*), it is important that a professional do the skinning and gutting because tetrodotoxin, which is highly toxic, can be present in the liver, ovaries and viscera and can contaminate the flesh. Sushi chefs with 10 years' experience are the only ones entrusted with this task. By contrast, the U.S. species of blowfish is harmless. If you catch your own blowfish, cut off the head and tail with a boning or filleting knife, and then pull

off the skin, using a cloth or pliers so you don't get scratched. The skin comes off easily, the guts spill out, and you are left with a tender morsel of blowfish meat, ready to cook.

Blowfish tails are sold already prepared for cooking; they are usually small, weighing 2 to 6 ounces each, so that several pieces are required for a helping. They are delicious quickly sautéed, barbecued or broiled, and they can be picked up and eaten much like chicken drumsticks.

Monkfish: The monkfish tail has wonderful sweet flesh surrounding a simple backbone resembling a rod. Under the silky skin is a layer of pinkish-purplish tissue covering the white flesh. The dark layer must be removed because, although tasty enough, it shrinks around the flesh as it cooks and distorts the shape, and it turns even darker when cooked. You have to be ruthless when cutting it off, and some of the white flesh may come away with it as you cut.

If you buy an unskinned monkfish, cut the skin loose with a boning or filleting knife and throw it away (most of it can be pulled off). Cut the fins off the top and bottom of the fish. Insert your boning or filleting knife under the dark tissue, starting at the head end. Following the rounded shape, curve the knife around and under the dark flesh to free it from the white flesh. Do the same on the other side of the fish.

You can cook the whole tail end very successfully. Cutting the tail end into steaks is useless, because in cooking, the flesh tightens up and the bone tends to pop out, making it impossible to cook on the other side, but you can easily cut fillets from each side of the backbone. You will find some tough white flesh on the side of the fillet that was next to the backbone. Trim this away. Cook the fillets whole, or cut them, on a diagonal, into escalopes, medallions or cubes (see pages 57 through 59).

TUNA

Although tuna weighing up to 500 pounds are commonly caught, we never see a whole tuna in a fish store, apart from small bonitos and little tunnies. Skilled cutters carve large tuna into "loins" from which we cut steaks (preferably 1 to 1¼ inches thick) or cubes (1 to 1¼ inches square). The skin is easily removed and must be, as it is as tough as leather. The dark, nearly black part of the flesh is muscle rich in myoglobin, a blood pigment. It has a stronger taste than the rest of the tuna and can be cut off or not, as you prefer. I find it perfectly delicious, as do the Japanese.

SWORDFISH

Swordfish weighing up to 1,000 pounds are caught commercially. The head, fins and guts are usually removed at sea, and at the fish store, we see center cuts and wheels, which are cross sections of the fish. All cuts can be made into steaks (1 to 1¼ inches thick) or cubes (1 to 1¼ inches square). The skin is thick and can be removed before cooking if desired. The flesh color ranges from gray to white to pink-orange. The dark part is the red muscle. Apart from the red muscle, the flesh turns white when cooked.

SHARK

There are 350 species of shark, but those we see the most of are mako, thresher and blacktip. Sharks weigh up to several thousand pounds. They never cease to grow as long as they have food to eat. Sharks have cartilaginous skeletons that are easily broken by handling. Because their skeletons are so fragile, it is difficult to catch sharks in a way that allows them to be kept alive. Sharks are marketed, much like swordfish and tuna, in loins, center cuts and wheels and then cut into steaks. When available, the smaller sand sharks (also known as dogfish) are sold filleted or cut into steaks.

Different Cuts Possible From Fillets

NOW THAT YOU HAVE LEARNED to fillet fish—or even if you haven't learned but are used to buying fillets—you can choose to leave the fillets as they are (with pin bones removed before cooking) or cut them into a variety of shapes.

The decision whether to cut a fillet or cook it whole depends to a large extent on the size of the fillet. If fillets are left whole, a small one (6 to 8 ounces) will be enough for an individual helping, while a whole fillet from the side of a 6-to-9-pound fish obviously can serve several people. (The amount you want for each portion is usually 6 to 8 ounces, depending on appetite and choice of fish—perhaps you will opt for a lesser amount if you choose a rich or expensive fish. See page 34 for suggested amounts to buy.)

Whole fillets can be broiled, baked, fried, deep-fried (if small), poached, steamed or grilled. The cooking method will depend on the size of the utensils you have at hand. For instance, you can easily fry a small fillet in a small frying pan, but if you want to cook more than one, you may have to fry them in batches, placing the fillets in a large frying pan with sufficient space around them. If you want to bake a whole large fillet, you must have a large enough baking or roasting pan.

Thin or thick slices, either on the diagonal or straight across the grain, can produce escalopes, medallions or slivers, while other cuts can produce butterfly shapes or cubes. You have undoubtedly noticed that fillets, especially from roundfish, are usually of uneven thickness. Some of the cuts I describe here ensure even cooking, and all of them will help you to attain a neat and attractive presentation.

Before cutting a fillet, skin it if desired (see pages 45 and 53), then remove the pin bones, if any, with pin-nose pliers, your fingers or tweezers, or cut them out.

ROUNDFISH

Slices: Take your boning, filleting or chef's knife and cut even-sized portions right down against the grain of the fillet, 2 to 3 inches apart, or make diagonal cuts for a sleeker, more generous look. To make diagonal cuts, place the fillet with the head end to your right. Hold your knife at an angle so the sharp edge is closer to the tail end and the top of the knife is closer to the head end. Cut toward the tail end.

Repeat for the other portions. Remember to cut the tail portion wider than the other portions, because it is thinner. Of course, it is possible to cut more than one slice for each portion, making the slices 1½ inches wide. If the slices are narrower than that, they may fall apart in cooking.

To even out thick fillets, take your knife and cut through the thickest part of the fillet, crosswise, nearly all the way through. Fold back the top piece to level the fillet out.

Escalopes and Rosettes: Escalopes are slices cut against the grain, ¼ or ½ inch wide. When they are laid flat on a broiler pan, they will cook perfectly evenly. When you serve them, you can lay them out concentrically like rosettes, in rows or in a star shape.

designs—three in the center of the plate, in a row, whatever you fancy.

Slivers: Fillets of fish with brightly colored skin, such as red snapper, pompano, John Dory, salmon and black sea bass, can be cut into slivers on a diagonal and bake-poached, skin side up, to show off their perfectly beautiful skins.

Medallions: A medallion is thicker than an escalope. Cut the slices 1 inch thick straight down against the grain of the fillet. Each medallion will have a thin "tail," rather like a lamb chop. Lay each slice out, then curl the thin part of the slice around the thick part until you have a nice, neat, round medallion. Insert toothpicks to keep them together if necessary. When cooked, these medallions can be placed on the plate in different

Place a fillet in front of you with the head end, where you will start your cuts, to your right. Hold your knife at a diagonal angle, with the sharp edge of the blade facing you.

Make slivers about 1 to 1½ inches wide. These slivers show both flesh and skin. Then use a wide spatula to transfer the slivers onto a baking dish or baking pan.

Butterflies: To make butterfly-shaped portions of fish another way, take a skinless fillet or loin and cut a slice 2 inches thick straight down against the grain, then cut down the middle of it (against the grain again), but not all the way through. Spread the two halves out to create a butterfly shape 1 inch thick. This is best done with fish like salmon, swordfish or tuna.

Cubes: Cubes taken from filleted fish are used for brochettes, kebabs, soups and salads. They are obtained from thick fillets of firm-fleshed fish such as swordfish, monkfish, tuna and shark.

Cut your fillets into slices 1 to 1¼ inches thick, then tailor the cubes.

FLATFISH

The flesh of flatfish is more evenly distributed than that of roundfish—that is, no one part of a flatfish fillet is very much thicker than the rest, except in large fish such as halibut. Flatfish fillets are therefore much easier to cook evenly than roundfish fillets.

If flatfish fillets are very thin, fold them in thirds or roll them up and fasten them with toothpicks.

Strips: If you want variety, you can cut flatfish fillets into diagonal strips, which are then deep-fried (these are called *goujonettes* in French) or prepared as seviche.

You will need the complete fillet from each side of the fish for this preparation. Feel for any small pin bones at the head end of each fillet, and cut them out. Slice each fillet every ¼ or ½ inch straight down against the grain on a diagonal.

Cubes: Halibut and large turbot can be cubed. Follow the instructions for cubing roundfish.

The Attraction of Cooking Whole Fish

IT IS MY STRONG BELIEF that fish tastes and cooks better on the bone. The backbone is an excellent heat conductor, and the skin keeps the moisture in.

Cooked whole fish, whether large or small, look marvelous. You can cook small fish as individual portions and display large fish on a big platter for a more formal and dramatic presentation.

Many fish have beautifully colored skin. The skin of red snappers, striped bass, black sea bass, trout, pompano, porgies and salmon should be displayed to advantage. If you don't like to eat the skin, which can be delicious, show it anyway, since it can be easily lifted off with a knife at the table. In any case, to keep in moisture, do not remove the skin before cooking, but by all means scale it.

By cooking whole fish, we are sure of eating all the flesh without wasting any, and there is the delight of eating the cheek muscles of the fish—delicious morsels that are fought over by some. The eyes can be removed easily when the fish is cooked and the head made a little more glamorous with sprigs of parsley or small pieces of cut vegetables inserted in the hollows where the eyes were.

Fear of getting a bone in the mouth does discourage some from eating a cooked whole fish. I encourage people by saying, "Any bone that gets in your mouth can always be taken out." However, once you know a little fish anatomy and can choose a fish with a simple bone structure (one whose flesh lifts easily off the bone after cooking), you will have greater confidence.

This is not to say that all fish should be cooked whole, for this would be impractical. Swordfish, tuna and most sharks are too large by far.

Of the fish featured in this book, I recommend cooking the following ones whole (gutted, gilled and scaled) for individual servings when they weigh 1½ pounds or less: black sea bass, striped bass, bluefish, catfish, flounder, sole, whiting, trout, sardines, mackerel, monkfish tails, pompano, porgy, rockfish, entire ray, or skate, wings, smelt, red snapper, whitefish and weakfish (also known as sea trout). All these fish have very simple bone structures, and their flesh can be easily lifted off as fillets with your knife and fork.

Large fish of these species can also be served whole. You can poach, bake-poach, roast, broil, steam or grill them.

PART II

Basic

Cooking Methods,

Techniques

and Recipes

Cooking with Confidence

IN THE FOLLOWING PAGES, I have provided easy-to-understand descriptions of the different methods of cooking seafood, as well as basic recipes for each method. From the descriptions, you will learn which kinds of seafood are suitable for different methods of preparation and which herbs, spices and seasonings are best for different kinds of fish and shellfish. You will also learn about cooking times, temperatures, ways of recognizing when seafood is cooked and health benefits. All the recipes given are for main courses, unless otherwise noted, and since all are suitable for several different kinds of seafood, I have noted the best choices for each. Also provided are lists of vegetables, herbs, spices and seasonings that can be used in place of those in the recipes. Feel free to mix and match as you like or as the market dictates.

The recipes include approximate preparation times; I know that everyone works at his or her own speed, and I cannot correctly gauge yours. You will also find approximate cooking times and whether all or some of the preparation can be done beforehand. A large number of fish and shellfish have been listed in alphabetical order with each recipe. When you see generic names such as salmon, rockfish, flounder, sole or bass listed, feel free to use any one of the species.

Broiling, grilling, frying, deep-frying and baking are the most common ways of cooking seafood, but there are many more methods. To benefit from the health-giving properties of fish and shellfish, we are now devising ways of cooking them so that added fats (such as oil, butter and margarine) and coatings (such as bread crumbs and batter) do not significantly decrease the health benefits. Of course, sauces play a good part in enhancing the flavor of seafood, but they need not be fattening. Using vegetables, herbs, spices and seasonings to flavor seafood can produce delicious results, as you will see. Healthful and, happily, nonfattening ways of preparing seafood are poaching, steaming, broiling, grilling, baking and roasting.

There are many quick ways to cook fish and shellfish. Since most seafood is naturally tender and needs only to be cooked through— that is, until the flesh turns opaque all the way through—just large whole fish, octopus and large squid require long cooking. The rest take minutes—individual portions of seafood take 3 to 15 minutes to cook, depending on thickness. Don't forget that seafood continues to cook as it makes its way to the table.

Since the purpose of this book is to teach you *how* to cook seafood, precise cooking times are rarely given. Some kinds of seafood cook faster than others because of the density of the flesh or its thickness, but rather than relying on hard-and-fast rules about how long seafood should cook per inch of thickness, you will find that it is better to learn how to recognize when it is cooked and then check for yourself to see whether it is done. With a little practice, you will learn the approximate times and temperatures for cooking different kinds of seafood. Then you can apply this knowledge to a seafood recipe from any cookbook.

In the recipes, you will notice that you are required to distinguish the *skin side* of a fillet when the fillet has been skinned. Often, the instruction reads, "Lay the fish skin side down in the pan."

You can tell the skin side because it is not as translucent as the side carved from the skeleton. It is usually not a clear white, as with most fish fillets, and you can see the darker fatty flesh that lies along the central lateral line of the fillet. There may even be shiny thin remains of the skin left on.

CHECKING FOR DONENESS

♦ Use your finger to feel whether the flesh is firm but bouncy. Feel the tip of your nose with your finger—that's it, firm but bouncy.

♦ Insert a fork or knife into the thickest part of the flesh, and pull it apart to see if it is opaque all the way through.

♦ Insert a small, thin instant-read thermometer (Taylor makes a good one) into the thickest part of the flesh; if it reads 140 degrees F, the fish is cooked.

♦ If you can easily pull out a spine from one of the fins when roasting or poaching a whole fish, the fish is cooked.

♦ For shellfish, cut a piece in half to see whether it is opaque all the way through.

♦ Mussels and clams should be cooked only until they open, or they will toughen.

Note that overcooked fish produces white fat globules on the opaque flesh. If you over-salt the fish, the fat will rise to the surface faster.

So, let's take the cooking methods one by one and see the advantages of each.

Before you start to cook, take the fish or shellfish out of the refrigerator for a little while. This will take the chill off, so it will cook more evenly.

AVOIDING FISHY SMELLS

People often ask me how to avoid getting a fishy smell in the kitchen when cooking fish. Well, fish is not naturally smelly when fresh, and belief in this "smell" is probably not based on fact. I cook fish nearly every day, and I would say that the only smell which knocks me for a loop is that of the guts of some fish. The guts and any bits of fish garbage should be enclosed in separate garbage bags or plastic bags and thrown out immediately.

Accompaniments to Seafood

SOME VEGETABLES, fruits and herbs enhance the character of fish and shellfish more than others. Here's what I contemplate when deciding what goes alongside the seafood:

First, there are the traditional companions. A squeeze from a wedge, slice or curl of a lemon or lime is nearly always essential to a fish dish—the acidity balances the sweet flavors of fish. Chopped parsley, or even whole sprigs, may enhance the visual appeal of the dish, although other herbs often add more interesting flavors. I use garlic in many seafood recipes because I consider its flavor important in practically any cooking. Peeled, steamed and turned potatoes are time-honored and always appealing—in fact, potatoes cooked by any method are delicious with seafood, as are simple rice and pasta dishes. Legumes are good companions because of their mild taste; white navy beans especially suit a tuna salad.

When planning the rest of the meal, think of vegetables whose taste will not overwhelm the seafood. Because fish is often sweet-tasting, serve vegetables that sweeten as they cook, and remember that roasting is one of the best cooking methods to bring out the sweetness.

I suppose onions and tomatoes—both raw and cooked—are my favorite vegetables to serve with fish. They are easily prepared and can be cooked on top of, underneath or on the side of fish. The pale purple color and mild, sweet flavor of red onions, for example, make them wonderful with practically any seafood. Yellow tomatoes—the delicious acid-free variety available in the summer months—are also favorites. I have cooked them along with broiled cod and then strewn them with a few anchovies and purple basil leaves with dramatic results. Tomatillos—those little green tomatolike vegetables with papery husks—make a great salsa to go with fish (see page 197). Cook some wedges with shallots or chopped onion for a slightly acidic accompaniment to any oily or grilled fish.

I find that corn goes very well with steamed or grilled lobster and other shellfish dishes. Asparagus, by the same token, particularly suits lobster as well as other firm, sweet-fleshed fish and shellfish and is pretty too. And don't overlook grilled or sautéed eggplant—its slight bitterness does not overpower most fish.

Sliced cool cucumbers, crisp jicama and daikon work as foils to the soft texture of fish. These may be raw or lightly sautéed. Snow peas, green beans, lima beans and sugar snap peas are all appropriate and pleasant for the same reason.

Red, green and yellow bell peppers may be sautéed or roasted and served with practically any fish. See page 203 for a delightful sweet red pepper sauce. The various hot chili peppers—both fresh and dried—are indispensable for bringing heat to a sauce, soup or stew, but they should be used sparingly, or you will cancel out the flavor of the seafood itself.

Sliced or whole baby carrots work well sautéed, steamed or roasted with any seafood. A combination of leeks and celery cut into julienne slices and then blanched is a perfect bed for a fish fillet or steak. Chopped celery definitely belongs in shellfish salads, particularly those featuring lobster or tuna.

Fennel bulb, or anise (again, either cooked or raw), is a delicious choice. The licorice taste is an elixir with fish. If you can find dried fennel stalks, buy them, because they make a fantastic bed for a roast fish and will flavor whatever is cooking on an open grill. A drop or two of Pernod or Ricard added at the last to a fish soup is delicious.

Lemongrass works well in the same dishes as celery, although its lemon-lime taste is not at all similar. The tender inside can be thinly sliced, and the dry grassy top is superb in soups and stews.

Then there's an elusive, thin, asparagus-like grass that grows in saline marshes both here and in Europe, known in France as *pousse-pierre*, in England and the United States as samphire or glasswort and in Latin by the genus name *Salicornia*. It is a spectacular vegetable to serve with seafood—slightly salty, with a taste of fennel—and it looks extremely pretty. Just steam it for a few minutes. Glasswort is usually available in the spring and summer in specialty produce stores.

Scallions can be added to fish salads and salsas or grilled along with seafood. Leeks have a pronounced sweetness that complements especially sweet-tasting seafood, such as crab and scallops as well as flounder and sole.

Sorrel, sometimes seen in produce markets but often found in vegetable gardens, is enjoyable with salmon in particular. The taste of sorrel is sharp and acidic, so it should be either used sparingly or mixed with spinach, which blunts its sharpness. Spinach, similarly, has a certain sharp flavor that counteracts the blandness of some fish. Steamed endive is featured with sole in the recipe on page 174. It is a good counterpoint to this potentially bland fish.

Some of the common leafy vegetables go better with fish than others. Cabbages such as savoy cabbage may be very thinly sliced into a chiffonade and steamed. Savoy cabbage is a great accompaniment to a sweet-tasting fish such as monkfish. Lightly sautéing bok choy and Chinese cabbage brings out their sweet flavors; these cabbages are a delight with any fish dish. However, I find kale, mustard greens, collards and turnip greens a little too strong to place alongside most seafood.

Broccoli and broccoli rabe—either sautéed or steamed—are colorful, crisp additions to any plate. Because broccoli rabe is rather bitter, it goes well with strong-tasting oily fish. Cauliflower is also fine with seafood, especially if prepared with something acidic, like lemon or tomato.

Squashes of all kinds are sweet and attractive. They are best with baked or roasted fish. On the other hand, parsnips and yams are so sweet that I don't recommend them with fish.

Because cooked mushrooms have a texture very similar to that of fish, I avoid using them as a sole accompaniment to fish. However, some dried wild mushrooms work well in sauces.

A few fruits go well with seafood. I like the tropical flavors of orange, mango and papaya. Serve them raw or lightly sautéed.

For additional garnishes on the plate, try fennel fronds or assorted greens, such as radicchio, arugula or mâche.

Remember to choose the accompaniments to seafood dishes with the same care you use in selecting the seafood itself. Look for the freshest, most attractive vegetables, fruits and herbs.

Baking, Bake-Poaching,
Oven Steaming and Casserole Baking

Baking*

BAKING IS A HEALTHFUL and easy way to cook fish. You can bake fillets, steaks and butterflied fillets of many fat and lean fish. Shellfish, such as clams, can be baked in foil, and oysters can be warmed through (on the half shell) in the oven.

Oils and butter are not used in great quantities, if at all. You need these fats only to add flavor, to help nonfatty fish brown nicely or to provide a glaze. Sometimes the broiler should be used briefly to brown the fish, either before or after baking. You may also sear the fish in some fat in a skillet or frying pan before baking to produce a light brown glaze.

Herbs, spices and seasonings play an important part in baking. Generally, you will want to use stronger-tasting herbs like thyme, rosemary, marjoram, oregano and savory in recipes for oily, strong-tasting fish, along with zestier spices and seasonings such as allspice, ginger, chili peppers, paprika, cumin, coriander, garlic and mustard. Add such flavorings as dill, tarragon, basil, parsley, chervil and lemon juice to light, lean-fleshed fish. (See page 218 for a more detailed discussion of herbs.)

Use a baking pan, a casserole or a gratin dish for fillets. Lay them on a bed of chopped or sliced vegetables—the vegetables make a rack for the fish and provide added flavor. Finely slice or chop the vegetables so that they cook in the little time needed to bake a fillet. Vegetables that take longer, such as carrots and potatoes, must be cooked until just tender before being baked with the fish—you

---

* *Note*: For clarity, I use the term *baking* for fillets or steaks of fish and *roasting* for whole fish and large chunks. (See page 87 for information on roasting.)

can bake, sauté or blanch them beforehand. In general, you do not cover baked fish.

Pouring dry white wine or water to a depth of ⅛ inch keeps the fish from sticking to the baking pan and gives tasty results.

Baked fish dishes rarely need to be sauced, as the moisture from the fish and vegetables is usually adequate; all that's needed is a squeeze of lemon juice. If you want a sauce, by all means look at the recipes beginning on page 195. Some casserole and gratin-dish recipes do require sauces.

Bake-Poaching and Oven Steaming

BAKE-POACHING is an easy way to poach a piece of fish without submerging it in a liquid. No added fat is used in this method, and the fish will not brown. All that is needed is some dry white wine or water in the bottom of a shallow baking pan and a covering of some sort to keep the moisture in. The fish can be covered with wilted lettuce leaves that you discard before serving or covered loosely with a piece of parchment paper or even aluminum foil.

This is a very plain way of cooking fish— it will taste quite bland and you will certainly get the true unadulterated taste. You can enhance it with a sauce or with accompanying vegetables, herbs, spices, seasonings or even liquor.

This method is a good way to show off fillets of fish with beautiful, edible skin. Such fish include black sea bass, bluefish, mackerel, pompano, rockfish, smelt (butterflied), red snapper, salmon, tilefish, tilapia, trout, weakfish and whiting. Of course, not only fish with good-looking skin can be bake-poached—use any fish you like.

You can take advantage of this method to cook a whole large fish for a special occasion.

The fish is tightly wrapped in foil and baked on a baking sheet. All the juices will be retained inside the foil, and they can be clarified and made into a flavorful aspic when you are decorating the fish. Large fish can also be poached in a fish poacher, but the bake-poaching method obviates the need for a poacher and, to my mind, is much more satisfactory, for there is no chance of the fish juices and their flavors seeping away into the poaching liquid. Of course, a flavorful poaching liquid does enhance the flavor of a dull-tasting fish.

In the oven-steaming method, the seafood is cooked in a tightly closed paper package. This is called cooking *en papillote*. This method is a good one, for all the moisture is retained in the package and a wonderful aromatic steam escapes as the package is opened. Serve this as a romantic meal for two. You can mix vegetables and seafood together and, if you like, bake a potato to go with them; you will have a potless meal and very little washing up.

Casserole Baking

SEAFOOD CAN BE COMBINED with vegetables or a sauce in a shallow earthenware, Pyrex or ovenproof china casserole dish, then simply baked uncovered in the oven until done. Vegetables may have to be sautéed or blanched in advance, because the seafood takes little time to cook, and a coating sauce must be prepared beforehand as well.

You can assemble a casserole several hours before cooking. Cover it with plastic wrap, and refrigerate it until you are ready to cook. Remove it from the refrigerator 10 to 15 minutes before baking to take the chill off, or if you want to cook it straight from the refrigerator, lengthen the cooking time specified in the recipe. Most casseroles can be prepared and cooked in about 45 minutes.

For variety, cut fish fillets on a diagonal into ¼-to-½-inch-thick slices or slice large sea scallops across into wafers. Intersperse them with sliced cooked vegetables, such as potatoes. Add a few herbs or a basil leaf or Coriander Pesto (page 208), as well as some seasonings and chopped tomatoes, to finish the dish. Or put a layer of toasted bread, fresh bread crumbs, mashed potatoes or sliced cooked potatoes on the bottom of the dish. Lay the fish or shellfish on top of the bread or vegetables, and pour an appropriate sauce on top. This way, the bread or vegetables absorb the delicious seafood juices.

I recommend using a hot oven (400 to 475 degrees F), as I prefer to sear the fish rather than letting it "sweat" in the oven and lose moisture. This temperature assures quick cooking.

Health

THE METHODS described here require that very little fat be added to the fish or shellfish. As we have noted, little or no oil, butter or margarine is needed to give oily fish a nice glaze. The same is true of sprinkling on bread crumbs to give a fine crust: few are needed.

Baked Fatty Fish Fillets

Serves 4

THIS SIMPLE BAKED FISH is enhanced by the addition of a hearty herb such as rosemary and a garnish of red, yellow or green bell pepper.

	Dry white wine or water
1	medium onion, thinly sliced
2	tablespoons chopped fresh rosemary or 1 tablespoon dried
2	tablespoons olive oil or unsalted butter or margarine, melted
	Salt to taste
	Freshly ground black pepper to taste
1½-2	pounds fish fillets, skin on, pin bones removed
¼	cup lemon or lime juice
1	tablespoon diced red, yellow or green bell pepper (optional)
4	rosemary sprigs for garnish

1. Preheat the oven to 475 degrees F.

2. Pour wine or water to a depth of ⅛ inch into a shallow baking pan or baking sheet with ½-inch-high edges.

3. In a bowl, mix the onion with 1 tablespoon of the fresh or 1½ teaspoons of the dried rosemary, 1 tablespoon of the oil, melted butter or melted margarine and salt and pepper.

4. Spread the onion mixture in the middle of the baking pan.

5. Place the fillets on top of the onion mixture, skin side down.

6. Brush the fish with the lemon or lime juice and the remaining 1 tablespoon oil or melted butter or margarine.

7. Sprinkle with the remaining 1 tablespoon fresh or 1½ teaspoons dried rosemary and diced bell pepper, if desired.

Fish choices
Choose fillets of fish such as
bluefish
buffalofish
lake trout
mackerel
salmon
shad
sturgeon
whitefish
or see the list of fatty fish on page 18

Make-ahead tip
The preparation can be done ahead of time, and the fish can be refrigerated until you are ready to bake it. Remember to bring it to room temperature before putting it in the oven.

Special equipment
Baking pan or sheet with ½-inch-high edges

Preparation time
15 minutes

Baking time
10 to 20 minutes

8. Bake for 10 to 20 minutes, depending on the thickness of the fillets. Check for doneness after 7 minutes (see page 66).

9. If the fish has not taken on enough color to suit you, quickly heat the broiler and brown it a little. This should take less than 1 minute. Keep in mind that you don't want to overcook the fish.

10. Sprinkle with salt and pepper.

11. Use one or two wide spatulas to lift the onion mixture and fish onto a serving platter or individual plates. Pour any juices that are left in the baking pan over the fish.

12. Garnish with the rosemary sprigs.

Baked Lean Fish Fillets

Serves 4

SWEET LEAN FISH benefits from the addition of a little lemon juice and parsley.

	Dry white wine or water
1½-2	pounds fish fillets, skin on or off, pin bones removed
4	tablespoons (½ stick) unsalted butter or margarine, melted
¼	cup lemon juice
	Salt to taste
	Freshly ground white pepper to taste
2	tablespoons finely chopped fresh parsley
4	lemon wedges

1. Preheat the oven to 450 degrees F.

2. Pour wine or water to a depth of ⅛ inch into a shallow baking pan or baking sheet with ½-inch-high edges.

3. Place the fish skin side down in the pan.

4. Brush the fish with the melted butter or margarine.

5. Bake for 7 to 20 minutes, depending on the thickness of the fillets. If the fillets are very thin, check for doneness after 3 minutes (see page 66).

6. If the fish has not taken on enough color to suit you, quickly heat the broiler and brown it a little. This should take less than 1 minute. Keep in mind that you don't want to overcook the fish.

7. Use one or two wide spatulas to lift the fish onto a serving platter or individual plates. Pour some or all of the juices from the pan over the fish, and sprinkle it with the lemon juice, salt, white pepper and chopped parsley.

8. Garnish with the lemon wedges.

Fish choices
Choose fillets of fish such as
bass
catfish
dolphinfish (mahi-mahi)
gray sole
grouper
haddock
lingcod
mullet
petrale sole
pike
red snapper
rockfish
scrod, cod
spotted sea trout
tilefish
weakfish (sea trout)
or see the list of lean fish on page 16

Special equipment
Baking pan or sheet with ½-inch-high edges

Preparation time
10 minutes

Baking time
7 to 20 minutes

Variations
Use ground cumin or paprika in place of the white pepper. Use fresh chervil, tarragon or dill in place of the parsley.

Bake-Poached Whole Fish

Fish choices

*Choose a fish weighing
6 to 9 pounds, such as*
bluefish
grouper
red snapper
salmon
tilefish
weakfish (sea trout)

Special equipment

*Heavy-duty aluminum
   foil*
*Baking pan or sheet with
   ½-inch-high edges*

Preparation time

10 minutes

Bake-poaching
time

35 minutes to 1¼ hours

Variation

*The fish can also be
cooked on an open fire
(see page 104). Follow
the instructions, except
steps 1, 7 and 8.*

THIS METHOD OF PREPARING FISH is a good one when, for instance, you want to make a showy piece for a buffet. For such an occasion, it is best to buy a large fish (more than 6 pounds), but for other occasions, you can use any size whole fish. You will skin the fish after it is cooked and display the flesh in all its glory or partially cover it with razor-thin slices of cucumber to resemble fish scales. Have fun with the decoration.

Note: Adjust the number served, as listed in the table below, according to the weight of the fish's head (buy a heavier fish if the head is large, a lighter fish if the head is small). Also note that salmon has the greatest yield of the fish listed below.

NUMBER SERVED	AMOUNT OF FISH NEEDED	APPROXIMATE BAKE-POACHING TIME AT 425°F
6 to 8	1 fish weighing 6 pounds	40 minutes
8 to 10	1 fish weighing 7 pounds	50 minutes
10 to 12	1 fish weighing 8 pounds	1 hour 5 minutes
12 to 14	1 fish weighing 9 pounds	1¼ hours

4 tablespoons olive oil or unsalted butter or margarine, melted
1 whole fish weighing at least 6 pounds, gutted and scaled, gills removed, head, tail and fins left on
¼ cup lemon juice
  Salt to taste
  Freshly ground white pepper to taste
1 large or 2 small bunches dill or parsley

FOR DECORATION

1 seedless (European hothouse) cucumber
1 bunch chives or tarragon or 1 scallion
  Sprigs of dill
1 red, yellow or green bell pepper cut into rings and/or fennel cut into quarters and/or tomato wedges
2 lemons, quartered
1 cup Basic Mayonnaise (page 198) or store-bought

1. Preheat the oven to 425 degrees F.

2. Measure out a length of heavy-duty aluminum foil 8 inches longer than the fish (double this if the foil is lightweight). You will use the foil to enclose the fish completely.

3. Pour 2 tablespoons of the oil or melted butter or margarine down the middle of the foil lengthwise, and lay the fish on it.

4. Pour the remaining 2 tablespoons oil, melted butter or margarine inside and on top of the fish.

5. Pour the lemon juice all over the fish, and sprinkle the inside and outside with salt and white pepper. Lay 12 dill or parsley sprigs inside the cavity.

6. Bring the two sides of the foil up over the fish, and make a double fold down the middle and at both ends of the fish, so the juices cannot escape.

7. Pour water to a depth of ⅛ inch into a baking pan or baking sheet with ½-inch-high edges, and place the wrapped fish in it.

8. If the fish overlaps the pan and is too long to fit in the oven straight on, place it diagonally in the baking pan so that its head is in a corner of the oven and, if necessary, curve the tail up against the oven door.

9. Bake-poach the fish for as long as necessary, depending on its size. Halfway through cooking, turn the fish over, so it cooks evenly. Remove the fish from the oven, open up the foil, and check to see that it is cooked all the way through (see page 66). If it is not cooked, wrap it up and cook it a little longer.

10. When the fish is cooked, lift it from the pan, open the foil and let the fish rest for 15 minutes.

11. Put a bowl in the kitchen sink, and tip the fish so the juices go into the bowl. Don't let the fish fall into the sink.

12. Strain the juices through a fine sieve into a bowl. Set aside.

13. Now, carefully lift off the skin, using your fingers or a blunt

knife. Turn the fish over on the foil to skin the other side. Keep the head and tail intact.

14. If you like, remove the dark flesh that appears along the lateral line of the fish. It is fatty and distasteful to some, although this is where many of the healthful omega-3 fatty acids come from.

15. Lift the fish by the aluminum foil onto a platter, then rip one side of the foil away from under the fish; hold the fish in place, and pull the other side of the foil away neatly.

16. If you would like to bone the fish and return it to its original shape, follow the instructions on page 48.

17. If you wish to decorate the fish, use a sharp knife to cut very fine, nearly transparent slices of cucumber. Dip them in the fish juices, and overlap them so that they look like scales. Cut the chives into 2-to-3-inch lengths, and stretch them from the middle of the fish outward so they resemble the bone structure. If using tarragon, pull the leaves from the stalks. If using a scallion, cut the green part lengthwise into very thin strips to resemble chives and then cut into 2-to-3-inch lengths. Put little sprigs of dill down the natural lateral division.

18. Clean the platter with a paper towel and surround the fish with more dill sprigs, cucumber slices, bell pepper rings and/or fennel and/or tomato wedges, quartered lemons and mayonnaise piped into rosettes. Finally, remove the fish eye, and insert some dill or a piece of lemon in the cavity. Serve warm or cold.

Bake-Poached Fish Fillets

Serves 2

COLORFUL FISH combined with fennel creates an attractive, delicious presentation.

2 6-to-8-ounce fish fillets, skin on, pin bones removed
Dry white wine or water
½ small fennel bulb, very thinly sliced (¾ cup); save some pieces of the green fennel frond for garnish (fennel is called anise in some stores)
Salt to taste
4 lettuce leaves (outer leaves of romaine) or parchment paper or aluminum foil
¼ teaspoon paprika or freshly ground white pepper

1. Preheat the oven to 425 degrees F.

2. Cut each fillet through the skin on a diagonal, to make 8 slivers in all (see page 58).

3. Pour wine or water to a depth of ⅛ inch into a shallow baking pan or baking sheet with ½-inch-high edges.

4. Put the sliced fennel in the pan. Sprinkle the fennel with salt. Bake the fennel for 10 minutes, or until nearly tender.

5. Remove the pan from the oven and place the fish slivers, skin side up, on top of the fennel.

6. Cover the fish with the lettuce leaves, parchment paper or aluminum foil.

7. Bake for 8 to 10 minutes, until the fish is just cooked through (see page 66).

8. Discard the lettuce leaves, paper or foil. Using a wide spatula, serve the fennel, fish and juices on individual plates, sprinkle with the paprika or white pepper, and garnish with fennel fronds.

Fish choices
Choose fish fillets, preferably with attractive, edible skin, such as
black sea bass
bluefish
freshwater striped bass
haddock
mackerel
mullet
pompano
red snapper
rockfish
salmon
tilapia
tilefish
weakfish (sea trout)
whiting
wild striped bass

Special equipment
Baking pan or sheet with ½-inch-high edges

Optional
Parchment paper or aluminum foil (see ingredients)

Preparation time
15 minutes

Bake-poaching time
8 to 10 minutes

Variation
You can use celery, red onion or bell pepper (red, green or yellow) in place of the fennel.

Oven-Steamed Seafood en Papillote

Serves 1

Fish choices

Choose butterflied fish such as

baby coho salmon

brook trout

rainbow trout

or fillets of fish such as

black sea bass

blackfish

bluefish

mackerel

ocean perch

pompano

red snapper

scrod, cod

shad

sheepshead

sole

tilapia

tilefish

weakfish (sea trout)

whitefish

or shellfish such as

large butterflied shrimp

or

sea scallops

STRAIGHT FROM THE OVEN, a puffed-up heart-shaped package of fish and vegetables bursts with delightful aromas when opened.

1	tablespoon unsalted butter or margarine, melted
2	tablespoons coarsely grated carrot
1	small leek, trimmed, halved lengthwise, rinsed and cut into julienne strips 3 inches long
½	celery stalk, cut into julienne strips 3 inches long
	Salt to taste
	Freshly ground white pepper to taste
8-10	ounces butterflied fish *or* 6-8 ounces fish fillet, skin on or off, pin bones removed, *or* 4-6 ounces butterflied shrimp (16-20 per pound) *or* 4-6 ounces sea scallops, small tough muscles removed, cut into ½-inch-thick wafers
1	tablespoon chopped fresh dill or 1½ teaspoons dried
2	tablespoons lemon juice
1	large egg white

1. Preheat the oven to 400 degrees F.

2. Fold the parchment paper in half. Draw half a heart shape, beginning at the fold and going out to the edge. If you are using a microwave oven, cut the heart shape small enough that it will fit inside the oven. Use scissors to cut it out. Unfold the paper.

3. Rub 1 teaspoon of the melted butter or margarine over one-half of the paper heart.

4. Mix the carrot, leek and celery together, and place three-quarters of the mixture on the buttered side of the heart.

5. Pour 1 teaspoon of the melted butter or margarine over the mixture on the heart, and add salt and white pepper.

6. If you are using a butterflied fish, spread it open, cut off the head and tail and then cut across it in three places, making four slices. If you are using a fish fillet, do the same: cut across it in three places, making four slices.

7. Place the fish slices, skin side down, or the shrimp or scallops on top of the mixed vegetables on the heart.

8. Place the rest of the vegetable mixture on the fish, then sprinkle the fish with the remaining 1 teaspoon melted butter or margarine, the dill and the lemon juice.

9. Brush the empty half of the paper heart with the egg white and also all around the edges. Fold the paper over and crimp the edges together well. Fold the edges over twice, ending with a twist at the bottom of the heart.

10. If you are using a conventional oven, place the package on a baking sheet and bake for 20 minutes. If you are using a microwave oven, put the package on a plate and microwave for 10 to 12 minutes on High. (Here you have to be precise about the time, for there is no way to tell whether all is cooked until you open the package.)

11. When the paper is nicely puffed up and starting to brown, remove the package from the oven and transfer it to a warm serving plate.

12. You will need sharp pointed scissors to pierce the package and then cut around the edge. Slide the contents of the package onto the plate, and discard the paper.

Make-ahead tip

The preparation can be done up to 6 hours ahead of time, and the package can be refrigerated. Take the package out of the refrigerator 10 minutes before baking, to take off the chill.

Special equipment

Aluminum foil or parchment paper 12 to 15 inches square
Baking sheet, 24 x 16 inches

Preparation time

25 minutes

Cooking time

20 minutes, or 10 to 12 minutes in a microwave on High

Variations

You can use red, yellow or green bell pepper or tiny green beans in place of the carrots. You can use scallions (cut into thin strips) or chives (cut into 3-inch lengths) in place of the leek. You can use fresh basil, coriander, thyme or parsley in place of the dill.

Baked Fish Fillet Casserole

Serves 6 to 8

Fish choices

Choose thick fillets of fish such as

blackfish
catfish
cod
dolphinfish (mahi-mahi)
grouper
haddock
halibut
lingcod
red snapper
rockfish
sand shark (dogfish)
shad
tilefish
weakfish (sea trout)
wolffish

or see the list of lean fish on page 16

Make-ahead tip

The preparation can be done up to 6 hours ahead of time, and the casserole can be refrigerated until you are ready to bake it.

Special equipment

Oval earthenware, Pyrex or ovenproof china casserole dish (about 12 inches long)

Preparation time

25 minutes

Baking time

20 to 30 minutes

ADDING TOMATO AND YELLOW SQUASH to a plain-tasting fish is a colorful and flavorful way to brighten it up. The vegetables create a sauce for the fish.

3 tablespoons olive oil or unsalted butter or margarine, melted
3 pounds thick fish fillets (two 1½-pound fillets), skin on or off, pin bones removed
1 small onion, thinly sliced lengthwise (from top to bottom)
3 medium tomatoes, sliced lengthwise (from top to bottom)
1 small yellow squash or zucchini, sliced on the diagonal into five ¼-inch-thick slices
3 tablespoons fresh basil or coriander or parsley, chopped at the last moment
Salt to taste
Freshly ground black pepper to taste

1. Preheat the oven to 425 degrees F.

2. Brush the casserole dish with 1 tablespoon of the oil or melted butter or margarine.

3. Lay the fillets skin side down in the casserole dish with the thick parts of the fillets toward the outside of the dish (where they will get the most heat).

4. Sprinkle the sliced onion over the fish.

5. Lay the tomato slices, alternating with the yellow squash or zucchini slices, down the middle of the fish.

6. Place more tomato slices around the side of the casserole dish.

7. Brush the fish and vegetables with the remaining 2 tablespoons oil, melted butter or margarine.

8. Bake for about 20 minutes or longer, depending on the thickness of the fillets. Check for doneness (see page 66).

9. Sprinkle with the chopped basil, coriander or parsley, salt and pepper.

Baked Fish Fillet Casserole with Light Tomato Sauce

Serves 4

FISH IS COVERED WITH A SIMPLE TOMATO SAUCE, enhanced with basil—a great combination for many fish.

4	tablespoons olive oil
1½-2	pounds fish fillets, skin on or off, pin bones removed
1	medium onion, finely chopped (1 cup)
3	garlic cloves, minced
4	medium fresh tomatoes, peeled, seeded and chopped, or 2 cups drained, seeded and chopped canned tomatoes
	Salt to taste
	Freshly ground black or white pepper to taste
	Freshly grated nutmeg
¼	cup dry white wine
12	fresh basil leaves, finely chopped at the last moment

1. Preheat the oven to 425 degrees F.

2. Brush the casserole dish with 1 tablespoon of the oil.

3. Lay the fillets skin side down in the casserole dish with the thick parts of the fillets toward the outside of the dish (where they will get the most heat). Set aside.

4. Heat the remaining 3 tablespoons oil in a frying pan over medium heat.

5. Add the onion, and sauté until it begins to brown, stirring occasionally.

6. Add the garlic, stir, and cook until softened, about 20 seconds.

Fish choices
Choose fillets of fish such as
bluefish
buffalofish
cod, scrod
mackerel
ocean perch
perch
red snapper
rockfish
salmon
sand shark (dogfish)
tilapia
weakfish (sea trout)
whitefish
or see the lists of lean and fatty fish on pages 16 and 18

Make-ahead tip
This casserole can be prepared up to 6 hours ahead of time and refrigerated until you are ready to bake it.

Special equipment
Oval earthenware Pyrex or ovenproof china casserole dish (about 12 inches long) Frying pan

Preparation time
20 minutes

Baking time
10 to 20 minutes

7. Add the tomatoes, salt, pepper and 10 rasps of nutmeg.

8. Add the wine, and cook, stirring occasionally, for 5 minutes. You want a fairly dry sauce, for the fish will exude some juice as it cooks.

9. Chop the basil, and add all but 1 tablespoon to the sauce.

10. Pour this sauce over the fish, and bake it for 10 to 20 minutes, depending on the thickness of the fillets. Check for doneness (see page 66).

11. Sprinkle with the remaining 1 tablespoon basil, and serve.

Baked Cajun Fish Casserole

Serves 4

FISH FILLETS are sprinkled with a hot, spicy mixture and baked with red bell pepper strips.

 3 tablespoons olive or vegetable oil
 1½-2 pounds fish fillets, skin off, pin bones removed
 1 tablespoon chili powder
 1 tablespoon paprika
 1 teaspoon dried thyme
 1 teaspoon dried oregano
 ¾ teaspoon salt
 ½ teaspoon freshly ground white pepper
 ½ teaspoon freshly ground black pepper
 ⅛ teaspoon cayenne pepper
 Pinch ground cloves
 1 small onion, thinly sliced
 ½ red bell pepper, cored, seeded, veins removed and thinly
 sliced lengthwise from top to bottom

1. Preheat the oven to 425 degrees F.

2. Brush the casserole dish with 1 tablespoon of the oil.

3. Lay the fillets in the casserole, skin side down, overlapping each other, and brush them with 1 tablespoon of the oil.

4. Mix the spices and seasonings together in a small bowl.

5. Sprinkle 3 to 4 tablespoons of the spice mixture over the fish.

6. Toss the onion and red bell pepper strips with the remaining 1 tablespoon oil in a bowl, and scatter them over the fish. Place the casserole in the oven to bake.

7. Bake for about 20 minutes or longer, depending on the thickness of the fillets. Check for doneness (see page 66).

Fish choices

Choose thick fillets of fish such as
blackfish
bluefish
catfish
dolphinfish (mahi-mahi)
gray sole
grouper
halibut
lingcod
orange roughy
redfish
rockfish
sand shark (dogfish)
sheepshead
spotted sea trout
tilefish
wolffish

Special equipment

Round or oval earthen-ware, Pyrex or ovenproof china casserole dish (about 10 inches in diameter or 12 inches long)

Preparation time

10 minutes

Baking time

20 to 30 minutes

Casserole of Fish Fillets or Large Sea Scallops with Potatoes and Coriander Pesto

Serves 4 to 6

Fish choices

*Choose fillets of fish
such as*

blackfish

catfish

dolphinfish (mahi-mahi)

fluke

lingcod

petrale sole

spotted sea trout

trout

weakfish (sea trout)

*or shellfish, such as large
sea scallops*

Special equipment

*Round or oval earthen-
ware, Pyrex or ovenproof
china casserole dish
(about 10 inches in
diameter or 12 inches
long)*

Preparation time

30 minutes

Baking time

20 to 25 minutes

THE COMBINATION of sliced potatoes and fish or scallops makes a homey dish. Coriander Pesto brightens the combination.

1½	pounds red-skin potatoes, scrubbed
1	tablespoon olive oil
1½-2	pounds fish fillets, skinned, pin bones removed, *or* large sea scallops (9-12 per pound, similar in diameter to the potatoes if possible)
1	recipe Coriander Pesto (page 208)
1	medium-large tomato, peeled, seeded and chopped (½ cup; see page 216)
	Freshly ground white pepper to taste

1. Boil the potatoes for about 15 minutes, until they are just tender. Cool them under cold running water.

2. Preheat the oven to 425 degrees F. Brush the casserole dish with 1½ teaspoons of the olive oil.

3. Cut the potatoes into ¼-inch-thick slices.

4. If using the fish, cut the fillets into ⅜-inch-thick slices on a diagonal, starting at the tail end. If using sea scallops, remove the tough part on the side of each one and cut them crosswise into ⅜-inch-thick wafers.

5. Place alternate pieces of sliced seafood and potatoes all around the casserole dish. They should fit snugly.

6. Spread Coriander Pesto all over, and sprinkle with the chopped tomato, white pepper and the remaining 1½ teaspoons oil.

7. Bake for 25 minutes. Check for doneness after 20 minutes (see page 66).

Roasting*

Fish

THE LATE CHEF FELIPE ROJAS-LOMBARDI, my friend and colleague, helped me to appreciate roasted fish. I find roasted fish to be hugely popular with everyone.

Roasting a large whole fish or several small whole fish takes little effort. The fish does not need constant attention, and cooking time does not need to be as exact as with some other cooking methods. The skin encasing the flesh keeps it moist and flavorful, and the central backbone acts as a heat conductor. Large roasted fish are wonderful for buffets and dinners for eight or more. They may be served hot from the oven or at room temperature. Any number of small fish can be roasted for individual servings.

The best fish to roast are those with richly colored skins, such as salmon, red snapper, grouper, porgy, spot, pompano, all bass, tilefish, bluefish, mackerel and sardines.

There are a number of ways to flavor roasted fish. You may fill the cavity with herbs and spices to permeate the flesh as it cooks. I like a combination of fresh thyme, finely chopped ginger and garlic, perhaps with some ground cumin and salt, or a combination of fresh dill, grated lemon rind, black pepper and salt. You may also sprinkle the fish with a drop or two of dry white wine, dry vermouth or Pernod. And you may use sliced vegetables as a bed for the fish to lie on. A roasted fish, surrounded by the vegetables it was cooked on, with its colored skin lightly browned and a little crisp, is irresistible.

Large fish or chunks (roasts) can be

---

* *Note:* Whole fish and large chunks are *roasted*. Fillets and steaks are *baked*. You can also roast some shellfish.

boned and stuffed; a particularly dramatic presentation is a fish stuffed with a fillet of another fish that has flesh of a contrasting color—for example, a pollock stuffed with salmon or a salmon stuffed with flounder. When a roasted stuffed fish is sliced, it looks like a terrine or sandwich, with contrasting colorful layers.

Shellfish

YOU CAN TREAT SCALLOPS the same way as fish—that is, place them on a bed of vegetables and flavor them with herbs, spices and seasonings. Coat them with a little oil or butter to produce a nice glaze.

Small unpeeled shrimp roasted in the oven are delicious. The roasted shells impart a wonderful flavor. The shells of small shrimp are certainly edible; if the shrimp are large, equip your guests with napkins and finger bowls and let them take off the shells themselves. No doubt some of you will be kind enough to shell each shrimp for your guests, but leave on the tail and the section of the shell nearest to it. Peeled shrimp can also be roasted to good effect.

Health

THERE IS NO NEED to use a lot of oil or fat to roast seafood. Some stuffings require a little butter or oil for flavor, but otherwise, the fish should be free of added fat. Roasting is a simple and clean way to cook seafood.

Times and Temperatures

TO ROAST A FISH, you will want a relatively high temperature. Preheat the oven to 425 degrees F. A small fish—one that weighs a few ounces to a pound—will take 10 to 20 minutes. A 3-pound fish, serving four people, will take about 35 minutes. A large fish weighing 9 pounds will take 1 hour or more.

Obviously, the thicker the fish, the longer it will take to cook. But remember that the central spine will conduct heat and speed the cooking.

Shellfish need a higher oven temperature, 450 to 470 degrees F, and take 10 to 20 minutes to cook, depending on size and thickness.

Roasted fish really needs no sauce to accompany it, since its skin ensures that it will retain all its moisture if it is not overcooked.

Serve the fish with its stuffing and some of the vegetables on which the fish has been cooked. If you do want a sauce, however, there are many suggestions beginning on page 195.

Roast Whole Fish

Serves 4 to 5

THIS DISH IS EASILY ACCOMPLISHED, good-looking and delicious to eat. The basic method is the same no matter what size fish you use; only the cooking time will differ. (Domestic ovens will only be able to handle a fish weighing up to 9 pounds.) Large roast fish can be served at a dinner or as part of a buffet. Choose fish with colorful skins, and decorate the plate with fresh vegetables and herbs.

If the baking pan or the oven does not quite take the length of the fish, have no fear—you can curl the tail (covered with foil) up to fit behind the door or even against the wall of the oven. Put the fish in headfirst, because the back of the oven is usually hotter than the front, and the head end will need more cooking than the tail.

NUMBER SERVED	AMOUNT OF FISH NEEDED	APPROXIMATE ROASTING TIME AT 425°F
1	2 or 3 fish weighing a few ounces each	15 minutes
	or	
	1 fish weighing ½ pound	20 minutes
2 or 3	1 fish weighing 1½ to 2 pounds	30 minutes
4 or 5	1 fish weighing 3 pounds	35 to 40 minutes
6 to 8	1 fish weighing 6 pounds	45 minutes
12 to 14	1 fish weighing 9 pounds	1 to 1¼ hours

1 large onion, thinly sliced
2 carrots, peeled and very thinly sliced
2 tablespoons olive oil, plus more for coating
2 bunches parsley (2 tablespoons chopped; reserve the rest for decoration)
2 tablespoons finely chopped ginger
1 tablespoon minced garlic
1 teaspoon finely grated lemon rind
½ teaspoon salt
1 3-pound fish, gutted and scaled, gills removed, *or* 3 pounds small fish weighing a few ounces each— leave the tail and fins on (even if spiny)
   Dry white wine
2 lemons, sliced
2 tomatoes, cut into wedges

Fish choices
Choose whole fish such as
black sea bass
bluefish
croaker
freshwater striped bass
grouper
herring
ling
lingcod
mackerel
mullet
pike
pollock
pompano
porgy
red snapper
rockfish
salmon
sardines
scrod, cod
sheepshead
smelt
sunfish
tilapia
tilefish
trout
walleye
weakfish (sea trout)
whitefish
whiting

Special equipment
Aluminum foil
Baking pan or sheet with ½-inch-high edges

Preparation time
20 minutes

Roasting time
35 to 40 minutes

1. Preheat the oven to 425 degrees F.

2. Lay the onion and carrots on a baking pan or baking sheet with ½-inch-high edges, and sprinkle with the oil.

3. Roast for 10 minutes while you get the fish ready. *Note*: There is no need to precook the vegetables if you are roasting a fish weighing 6 pounds or more, for they will take the same time to cook.

4. Combine the chopped parsley, ginger, garlic, lemon rind and salt in a small bowl.

5. Place this mixture in the cavity of the fish.

6. When the vegetables have cooked for 10 minutes, take them out of the oven and place the fish on top.

7. Rub olive oil all over the fish, head to tail, to protect the skin and keep it moist.

8. Wrap the head and tail of the fish with aluminum foil so they don't burn: Take an 8-by-12-inch piece of foil, lift up the head, and slide the foil under it. Bring the edges of the foil together, and pinch or fold them over, leaving a space of 2 to 3 inches above the head. (This space is necessary so the heat will circulate but not burn the head.) Don't let the foil touch the top of the head, for it will stick to the head and ruin its looks. Fold another piece of foil over the tail. (*Note*: Small fish such as smelt, sardines, herring and small mackerel do not need the foil; they will take less time to cook and thus won't have time to burn.)

9. Sprinkle the fish with white wine, and roast it in the oven for as long as necessary, depending on the size of the fish. In the case of a 3-pound fish, check to see if it is cooked after 35 minutes.

10. Using one or two wide spatulas, lift the fish onto a platter and decorate it with the onions and carrots if they are not burned and look good enough to eat. Decorate with the reserved parsley sprigs, lemon slices (curled into twists) and tomato wedges.

11. If the skin is thick, cut across it behind the pectoral fin and along both the top and bottom of the fish. Then put the tines of a fork in the skin, and roll the skin back off the fish as if you were rolling up a window shade.

Variations

You can use shallots, scallions, fennel, celery, bok choy or leeks in place of the onion and carrots. You can use chopped scallions, fresh basil, fresh thyme and ground coriander in place of the parsley, garlic, ginger and lemon rind. For the decoration and final presentation, you can buy whatever takes your fancy at the market. You can use bunches of scallions, chives, dill, carrot tops, beet tops, fennel tops, spinach leaves, kale, turnips, yellow squash, zucchini (sliced on the diagonal) and sliced limes.

Roast Stuffed Fish Chunk

Serves 5 to 6

Fish choices

Choose a 1½-to-4-pound
chunk (roast) of a large
fish such as
bluefish
cod
halibut
lingcod
pollock
sablefish
tilefish
wild striped bass
and stuff with a skinned
fillet of
baby coho salmon
salmon
or choose a 1½-to-
4-pound chunk of
salmon
and stuff with a skinned
fillet of
cod
flounder
lingcod
sole
tilefish

SERVING A LARGE PIECE OF FISH like a boned roast is unusual. Stuffed with onions, garlic, tomato, basil and a slice of another fish, this dish is good cold at a picnic or other summertime occasion.

You want to stuff the fish with a skinned fillet of contrasting color. This dish is best eaten at room temperature or chilled; start the preparation either the day before or at least 5 hours before needed.

> 3-pound fish chunk, boned from the belly, but with the back intact (ask the fishmonger to do it, or follow the instructions on page 48)
> Salt to taste
> Freshly ground black pepper to taste
> ¼ cup lemon or lime juice
> 1 large tomato, sliced from top to bottom into ¼-inch-thick slices
> 10 basil leaves, rinsed if necessary, dried and thinly sliced, plus a few for decorating the plate
> 2 garlic cloves, thinly sliced lengthwise
> 1 medium onion, very thinly sliced
> 1 8-ounce thin-skinned fish fillet, pin bones removed
> 3 tablespoons olive oil
> Dry white wine

1. Preheat the oven to 400 degrees F.

2. Open up the chunk of fish, and lay it flat on a board.

3. Sprinkle the inside of the fish with a little salt and pepper and 2 tablespoons of the lemon juice.

4. Place the tomato, basil, garlic and half of the onion on one-half of the chunk. Season with salt and pepper and then place the fish fillet on top.

5. Fold the other half of the chunk over the fillet. Take string and tie the chunk like a roast, once around every inch or so.

6. Arrange one-quarter of the remaining onion in a baking pan, sprinkle it with oil, and pour white wine to a depth of ¼ inch

Special equipment

Baking pan or sheet with
½-inch-high edges or
other ovenproof pan
String

Preparation time

20 minutes

Roasting time

50 minutes to 1¼ hours

in the pan. Place the chunk on top of the onions, and brush with the oil. Place the remaining one-quarter onion on top of the chunk, and sprinkle with the remaining 2 tablespoons lemon juice.

7. Roast for 50 minutes, basting occasionally with the juices in the pan. Add more wine or water if necessary. Be generous with the basting, for the fish tends to dry out around the edges before the inside is cooked. Check for doneness (see page 66). If using an instant-read thermometer, the fish should be removed from the oven when the inside reaches 120 degrees F; it will continue to cook as it cools.

8. Remove the fish from the oven. With wide spatulas, lift the fish and vegetables out of the baking pan and onto a platter. Pour over the juices. After 15 minutes, cut the string off the fish and remove it carefully. Let the fish cool to room temperature—this will take at least 3 hours. (If you want to eat it chilled, wrap it in aluminum foil and put it in the refrigerator after it has cooled. Make sure to take it out of the refrigerator 30 minutes before serving, so it is not icy cold.)

9. Decorate the plate with the basil leaves.

10. Cut the fish into ½-inch slices with a very sharp knife.

Variations

You can use coarsely grated zucchini or carrot in place of the tomato; fresh parsley, coriander, dill or mint in place of the basil; and scallions or shallots in place of the onion.

Broiling

BROILING IS ONE of the most popular methods for cooking fish, and it produces the most satisfactory results. The fish is seared by the heat from above so that a nice crust is formed, with moist flesh underneath. I can't think of a single fish or shellfish that cannot be broiled, except for tiny fish like whitebait (silversides). Even mollusks, such as oysters, clams and mussels, can be broiled if stuffed and cooked on the half shell.

Turn the broiler to its fullest heat to do the job well, and always preheat the broiler for 5 to 10 minutes before cooking. Place the seafood on a metal pan about 3 to 6 inches away from the heat (closer if the heat is not sufficient), for it is important to sear the flesh. The heat will reach the metal pan, and the flesh will cook from the bottom upward as well as from above, so there is no need to turn the seafood over, except in the case of large whole fish.

It is important to place thin pieces of fish as close as possible to the broiler to get a nice crusty top without drying out the inside flesh. To get them close, lay another pan upside down underneath the pan you are using, or use some other object to elevate the seafood.

Pour wine or water in the pan to a depth of ⅛ inch to ensure that the seafood does not stick to the pan and will easily lift out and also to keep the seafood moist. Lightly coat the seafood with oil or melted butter, and flavor it with your choice of herbs and seasonings, adding them toward the end of the cooking time so that they do not burn. Serve the seafood with a sauce or a simple squeeze of lemon juice and/or the juices in the pan. (See the sauce recipes starting on page 195.)

If you broil a thick fish or fillet, its surface may burn before it cooks through, so you will need to finish cooking it in the oven or the microwave oven after broiling it. Check doneness at 5-minute intervals.

You can broil brochettes (shellfish or skewered cubes of fish and vegetables) rather than grilling them on an open fire. To broil them, lay the brochette sticks inside or on the edges of a baking pan. Cook them for 10 minutes, basting and turning them every 2 minutes. (For the grilling recipes, see Open-Fire and Indoor Grilling, beginning on page 104.)

Before you broil a lobster, you must split it down the middle lengthwise. The fish-monger can do this for you if you are too tenderhearted, or you can kill it by putting it into boiling water for 2 minutes, then split it down the middle. (See the method on page 290.) Lay the lobster on the broiler pan, split side up, and gently broil it about 5 inches below the heat. You may add fresh herbs and some butter or oil. Watch carefully, and be sure to remove the lobster as soon as the flesh is cooked through.

Restaurant broilers can often act like grills. Although their heat comes from above, they have grilling rods below which retain heat so well that they make grill marks on the food being cooked. If you have such a broiler and you want the marks, be sure to preheat the broiler for about 15 minutes so the rods get very hot. Oil the rods lightly before putting the seafood on to cook.

Times and Temperatures

BROILING A SMALL WHOLE FISH, fillet, butterflied fish, medallion, steak or most shellfish is fast, as long as the broiler is capable of giving off efficient heat. Depending on the thickness of the seafood, it should take 2 to 10 minutes. A ¼-inch-thick escalope will take as little as 1 minute to cook. Large whole fish and lobsters will take quite a bit longer.

Broiled Whole Flatfish

Serves 1

Fish choices

*Choose whole flatfish
such as*
flounder
sand dabs
sole
*or see the flatfish profiles
starting on page 273*

Special equipment

*Broiler pan or baking pan
or sheet with ½-inch-
high edges*

Preparation time

10 minutes

Broiling time

5 to 15 minutes

Variation

*Read the instructions on
page 53 to see how easy it
is to fillet a cooked whole
flatfish.*

T HE THIN BODIES of flatfish are ideal for broiling, since the flesh is easily carved off the simple bone structure.

For large broiled flatfish (those weighing more than 1½ pounds), it may be necessary to finish the cooking after the fish is well browned, in either a conventional oven or a microwave oven. If you have separate units, preheat the broiler and the oven at the same time. If the broiler is located under the oven or inside the oven at the top, the broiler will heat the oven somewhat, so when you turn the oven on, it will be only a few moments before it reaches the required temperature of 425 degrees F. A microwave oven can be used on High. Check doneness at 5-minute intervals.

NUMBER SERVED	AMOUNT OF FLATFISH NEEDED	APPROXIMATE BROILING TIME
1	2 or 3 flatfish weighing approximately 4 ounces each	5 to 10 minutes
	or	
	1 flatfish weighing 1 pound	10 to 15 minutes
2 or 3	1 flatfish weighing 2 pounds	20 to 25 minutes
4	1 flatfish weighing 3 pounds	30 to 35 minutes

1 1-pound flatfish
or
2 or 3 flatfish weighing approximately 4 ounces each,
    gutted and scaled, skin on or off
Dry white wine or water
2 tablespoons unsalted butter or margarine, melted
Freshly ground white pepper to taste
2 tablespoons lemon or lime juice
1 teaspoon chopped fresh parsley or thyme or dill or
    tarragon or basil

1. Preheat the broiler to its highest setting.

2. Place the fish, dark skin side up, on a board. Make a slit down the middle of the fish, above the backbone, from head to tail.

3. Cut under the fillets close to the bones to loosen them. Do not cut all the way to the edge of the fish.

4. Pour white wine or water to a depth of ⅛ inch in the broiler pan.

5. Place the fish in the wine or water. Spread the fillets open, pour 1 tablespoon of the melted butter or margarine on them, and sprinkle with white pepper.

6. Broil the fish 5 to 6 inches away from the broiler until the edges brown, about 10 minutes.

7. Check after 7 minutes to see whether the fish is cooked (see page 66).

8. If the fish is browned but undercooked, finish it in a conventional oven preheated to 425 degrees F or a microwave oven on High. Check doneness at 5-minute intervals.

9. With the aid of one or two spatulas, place the fish on a serving plate.

10. Pour the remaining 1 tablespoon melted butter or margarine and the lemon or lime juice into the juice in the pan. Give it a swirl, or stir it with a spoon, then pour it over the fish.

11. Sprinkle the fish with the chopped herb.

Broiled Whole Roundfish

Serves 4

Fish choices

Choose whole fish
such as
anchovy
black sea bass
bluefish
croaker
freshwater striped bass
freshwater white bass
grouper
lingcod
pompano
porgy
red snapper
sardines
weakfish (sea trout)
whitefish

Special equipment

Broiler pan or baking pan
or sheet with ½-inch-
high edges

Preparation time

10 minutes

Broiling time

5 to 35 minutes, including
the time needed to finish
cooking in the oven

WHOLE ROUNDFISH, both large and small, are broiled with garlic, scallions, ginger and soy sauce to heighten their taste.

Number Served	Amount of Fish Needed	Approximate Broiling Time*
1	2 or 3 fish weighing 3 to 4 ounces each	5 to 10 minutes
	or	
	1 fish weighing 1 pound	7 to 15 minutes
2 or 3	1 fish weighing 2 pounds	20 to 25 minutes
4	1 fish weighing 3 pounds	30 to 35 minutes
6 to 8	1 fish weighing 6 pounds	45 to 55 minutes

* Includes the time needed to finish cooking the fish in the oven after it has browned under the broiler.

1   3-pound whole fish *or* several small fish with a total weight of 3 pounds, gutted and scaled, gills removed, with head, tail and fins left on

3   scallions, trimmed of roots and some of the green part, cut into quarters lengthwise, then into 3-inch-long pieces

2   garlic cloves, minced

1   tablespoon finely grated ginger

2   tablespoons soy sauce

2   tablespoons light or dark molasses

2   tablespoons vegetable oil

1   tablespoon dry white wine, plus enough to fill the broiler pan to a depth of ⅛ inch

1   bunch parsley

1   lemon, sliced

1. Preheat the broiler to its highest setting. If you have a separate oven unit, preheat it to 425 degrees F when you are cooking a fish weighing more than 1½ pounds.

2. Make three diagonal slashes in the skin on both sides of the fish.

3. Insert scallion strips, garlic and ginger inside the fish and then in the slits. (If you are cooking small fish, put some of these ingredients inside the fish and scatter the rest on top.)

4. Whisk the soy sauce, molasses, oil and 1 tablespoon of the white wine together in a small bowl.

5. Pour wine to a depth of ⅛ inch into the broiler pan, and lay the fish in the wine. Brush the fish with some of the soy-sauce mixture.

6. Broil for 10 minutes, brushing more of the mixture on the fish after 5 minutes. Check to see whether the fish is browned.

7. When the fish is browned on one side, carefully turn it over using two wide spatulas and brush the exposed side with more of the soy-sauce mixture. Add more wine to the pan if necessary, and return to the broiler.

8. When the fish is nicely browned, check to see whether it is cooked all the way through (see page 66).

9. If the fish needs further cooking, finish it in a conventional oven or microwave oven.

10. Using wide spatulas, place the fish on a serving plate, and garnish it with the parsley and lemon curls. (To make curls, make a cut from the center of each slice outward, then twist each slice into a curl.)

Variations

You can use a julienne of carrots, leeks or chives in place of the scallions. You can use finely chopped celery or fennel in place of the ginger. You can use Lea & Perrins original or white-wine Worcestershire sauce in place of the soy sauce.

Broiled Fillets, Butterflied or Split Fish, Steaks, Escalopes, Medallions or Shellfish

Serves 2

Fish choices

Choose any filleted fish, butterflied or split fish, steaks, escalopes or medallions (for instructions on escalopes and medallions, see pages 57 and 58), or see lists of lean and fatty fish on pages 16 and 18, or choose shellfish such as

octopus *(previously cooked; see page 305)*

scallops

shrimp

soft-shell crabs

Special equipment

Broiler pan or baking pan or sheet with ½-inch-high edges

Preparation time

5 minutes

Broiling time

2 to 10 minutes

B ROILING GIVES AN ESPECIALLY FINE FLAVOR to fish. After cooking, it need only be sprinkled with salt, pepper and lemon juice.

> Dry white wine or water
> 2 6-to-8-ounce fillets *or* one ¾-pound fillet, skin on or off, pin bones removed
> *or*
> 2 butterflied or split fish weighing 8-10 ounces each
> *or*
> 2 6-to-8 ounce steaks
> *or*
>   escalopes or medallions weighing ¾ pound
> *or*
> ¾ pound shrimp, shelled and deveined, *or* octopus (cooked) *or* scallops, small tough muscles removed
> *or*
> 4 soft-shell crabs, cleaned
> 2 tablespoons unsalted butter or margarine, melted, or olive oil
> 1 tablespoon finely chopped fresh thyme or parsley
>   Salt to taste
>   Freshly ground black or white pepper to taste
> 1 lemon, cut into 6 wedges
>   Sauce of your choice (optional; see recipes beginning on page 195)

1. Preheat the broiler to its highest setting.

2. Pour wine or water to a depth of ⅛ inch into the broiler pan.

3. Lay the fish or shellfish in the wine, and brush with the melted butter, margarine or oil.

4. Broil 1 minute for escalopes, 2 minutes for very thin fillets or up to 10 minutes for thicker fillets, 4 to 5 minutes for octopus, 5 minutes for steaks or medallions, 5 minutes for shrimp, 7 min-

utes for scallops, 7 minutes for soft-shell crab (turn shrimp, octopus, scallops and crab halfway through cooking) and 7 minutes for butterflied or split fish. Sprinkle the fish with the chopped herb just before the end of the cooking time. Check for doneness (see page 66).

5. Sprinkle with salt and pepper.

6. Using wide spatulas, place the fish or shellfish on a plate, and pour over any juices left in the pan.

7. Garnish with the lemon wedges, and serve with the optional sauce or with none at all. It will be delicious as is.

Broiled Lobster

Serves 2

SPECIAL CARE IS NEEDED in the cooking, but it is worth it, for the lobster takes on an especially delectable flavor when broiled in its shell. The lobster must be killed before broiling. The preparation is not for the squeamish. See page 290 for instructions on how to kill lobsters humanely, or ask the fishmonger to do this for you (in this case, you will have to cook the lobster almost immediately—within 4 hours). Otherwise, always buy live shellfish and cook them promptly. It may be necessary to finish the cooking, after the lobster is well browned, in either a conventional oven or a microwave oven. If you have separate units, preheat the broiler and the oven at the same time. If the broiler is located under the oven or inside the oven at the top, the broiler will heat the oven somewhat, so when you turn the oven on, it will be only a few moments before it reaches the required temperature of 425 degrees F. A microwave oven can be used, set on High. (Crack the lobster claws first.) Check doneness at 5-minute intervals.

Special equipment
Broiler pan or baking pan or sheet with ½-inch-high edges

Preparation time
8 minutes

Broiling time
15 to 20 minutes

NUMBER SERVED	SIZE OF LOBSTER	APPROXIMATE BROILING TIME
1	1 pound	10 to 15 minutes
1	1¼ pounds	15 to 20 minutes
1	1½ pounds	20 to 30 minutes
1 or 2	2 pounds	30 to 35 minutes
2 or 3	3 pounds	35 to 45 minutes

2 1¼-pound lobsters
4 tablespoons (½ stick) unsalted butter or margarine,
   melted, or 2 tablespoons mayonnaise
3 tablespoons chopped scallions or shallots or fresh
   tarragon or chives
  Salt to taste
  Freshly ground black pepper to taste
1 lemon, halved

1. Ask the fishmonger to kill the lobsters, or do it yourself. Let them rest for 10 to 15 minutes until their muscles relax.

2. Put each lobster on its back, and cut through the middle of its body lengthwise. *Do not cut all the way through the back shell.* Use kitchen scissors to cut through the middle of the shell on the underside of the tail. Spread the two halves apart with your hands, leaving each lobster partly joined together at the back.

3. Remove the little sac from behind the eyes of each lobster. Leave the dark green coral (roe), if there is any, inside each body. It is advisable to discard the pale green tomalley (liver), because it may be contaminated. Try to remove the vein that runs along the back of the tail meat by the methods described on page 291. If you don't succeed, don't worry—it can be easily discarded as you are eating.

4. Preheat the broiler to its highest setting.

5. Put the lobsters in a broiler pan. Inside the bodies and tails of the lobsters, spread the melted butter, margarine or mayonnaise. Sprinkle with the scallions, shallots or herb and salt and pepper. Detach the lobster claws, and tilt them against the edge of the broiler pan.

6. Place the lobsters 5 to 6 inches below the broiler element, and broil until they begin to brown. Turn the claws over after 10 minutes, and turn the pan around. The tails usually curl up, so crack each shell across (using oven gloves or pot holders) halfway through cooking to straighten it out. Be conscientious! You must look often so you will know when to remove the lobsters from under the broiler. You don't want them to burn.

7. The lobsters may not fully cook under the broiler, so when their flesh is brown, check to see if they are cooked all the way through: Insert a fork or knife into the thickest part of the tail meat, and pull it apart to see if the meat is opaque all the way through. The claws will be cooked in the same length of time.

8. If the lobsters are not cooked through, crack the claws and then put the lobsters in a conventional oven preheated to 425 degrees F or a microwave oven set on High to finish cooking. (The total cooking time in the broiler and the oven should be approximately 20 minutes.) Serve with the lemon halves.

Broiled Mussels with Garlic, Basil and Tomato Butter

Serves 6 as an appetizer

PREVIOUSLY STEAMED MUSSELS combined with a flavored butter are heady with aromas and taste.

1 recipe Steamed Mussels Marinière (page 148)
1 recipe Garlic, Basil and Tomato Butter (page 212)

Preparation time
10 minutes, plus 20 minutes to make the butter

Broiling time
2 to 3 minutes

1. When the steamed mussels are cool enough to handle, pick them out of their shells, saving one-half shell for each mussel. Pick out any remaining bits of beard that you see, and place each mussel on a half shell.

2. Spread each mussel with a little flavored butter, and put them on a broiler tray. They can be covered with plastic wrap and refrigerated until you are ready to broil them.

3. Preheat the broiler to its highest setting.

4. Broil the mussels just until the butter melts and the mussels brown very lightly.

Open-Fire and Indoor Grilling

GRILLING IS QUITE SIMPLY one of the easiest and most delicious ways to cook almost any fish or shellfish. Grilling on an open fire is very similar to broiling except that the fish is cooked by direct heat from below. The combination of direct heat and smoke gives a particularly good taste to fish and shellfish.

Both the grill and the seafood should be lightly oiled to prevent sticking. Most of the oil will disappear as the seafood cooks.

The heat source for grilling and barbecuing can be wood, charcoal (preferably hardwood charcoal) or gas. I dislike charcoal briquettes, for the flavor they give off seems chemical. I also recommend that you avoid using charcoal lighter fluid; though it is convenient, it contaminates the taste of delicate fish. For the same reason, avoid buying charcoal with lighter fluid already in it. Hardwood charcoal is undoubtedly the best heat source to use.

The fire must be very hot, with ash-covered coals or embers if it is of charcoal or wood. Leave enough time before the meal to get the heat source ready. I find that a charcoal fire takes anywhere from 20 to 45 minutes to reach the desired state. However, if you use a small chimney with newspaper at the bottom and charcoal on top, it will take only 10 to 20 minutes. These chimneys are available from hardware stores and from Williams-Sonoma, which sells one called the Easy Embers Charcoal Starter for about $16. Gas-fired coals are quicker to heat. The time it takes to heat wood depends on its density and size. If the wood is not very dense, remember that it will not give out prolonged heat.

When the fire is ready, you can mix the charcoal (if that's the heat source you're using) with a small amount of cherry, hickory, sugar maple or mesquite wood chips; grapevines; corncobs; or dried wild fennel stalks that have been soaked in water for an hour or so. Let them smoke and char and begin to turn to ashes before laying the seafood over the heat. Throw strong herbs, such as rosemary, thyme, sage or savory, onto the fire for flavor, and also sprinkle them on the seafood just before grilling. If the seafood has been in a marinade, it should be drained before cooking to prevent flare-ups.

If the seafood begins to burn, take it off the fire immediately. (It may be that you have overoiled the seafood or placed it too close to the fire or that the fire is still too hot.) Wait until the heat has subsided, or finish cooking the seafood in a conventional oven that you have prudently preheated to 425 degrees F or a microwave oven set on High. Check doneness at 5-minute intervals. Another reason to heat an oven for backup is that the fire may fade on you before the seafood finishes cooking. There is not much use trying to revive the fire by adding more charcoal or wood, because of the time it would take for the fire to burn down and the flare-ups that are likely to occur.

A little salt and pepper and a large wedge of lemon are all you need to accompany grilled seafood.

You can also grill seafood using a grill pan, which is a cast-iron pan with raised ridges on the bottom. This is a fast, easy, nonfattening method of cooking seafood indoors. In the city, I find that I use my grill pan more often than any other utensil. The ridges should be lightly brushed with oil, and the pan should be preheated before cooking. You can easily make grill marks on seafood: Let the hot ridges sear the flesh, then after a few moments, move the seafood 90 degrees for the second set of marks.

Oily fish such as tuna, mackerel, sardines, bluefish and salmon are perfectly suited to grilling—the fish oils baste the flesh from within. White, lean-fleshed fish, such as weakfish, monkfish, porgy, snapper and bass, are enhanced by grilling too. Wrap soft-fleshed fish, such as mature bluefish, in aluminum foil (with a few holes poked in it), and cook them over the fire—you will still get a good taste of smoke in the fish.

It is best to put small fish, such as baby bluefish (snappers), in an oiled, two-sided hinged grill with a handle, which is simple to turn. Whole fish can be cooked in a fish basket, which can also be turned.

You can turn a whole fish to cook on both sides, but a fillet, especially one of a flaky fish, cannot be turned with much success, so be especially careful. If possible, use firm-fleshed skin-on fillets. Place them skin side up on the grill, then turn them skin side down. A fine-mesh stainless-steel grill makes it very easy to grill thin, flaky fillets, such as flatfish fillets, and any other seafood; a whole flounder can be grilled beautifully. You can also place fillets on foil with holes in it or wrap them in foil before putting them on the grill.

Fish steaks are excellent cooked on the grill or in the grill pan.

Firm-fleshed fish cut into 1¼-inch cubes and shellfish can be skewered on wood or steel brochette sticks, oiled or marinated, and then grilled.

Shellfish, such as shell-on shrimp and lobster, is delicious cooked on the grill. The cooked shell heightens the taste of the meat.

You can grill lobster successfully if care is taken to prevent it from drying out. It should be killed as for broiling (see page 290) and split down the middle before being put on the grill. Cook it shell side down first, then turn it, and cook it for a few seconds flesh side down.

Hard-shell crabs and crawfish, which also have to be killed before cooking, are wonderful on the grill.

Octopus (previously cooked) and squid can be skewered on steel brochette sticks and grilled.

You can open mollusks, such as clams, mussels and oysters, on a grill. Steamed in foil over an open fire, they are fabulous. When you open the package, the steam will delight you.

Times and Temperatures

APART FROM THE TIME it takes to get the fire going and in a perfect state to grill seafood, grilling is swift. The time depends on the thickness of the seafood and the temperature of the fire. Additional time may be needed to finish cooking the seafood in a conventional oven or microwave oven.

Health

VERY LITTLE OIL is used in grilling seafood. Although the seafood and grill have to be oiled, the oil tends to disappear into the fire.

Special Equipment

YOU'LL NEED an outdoor grill, hardwood charcoal, a newspaper chimney, a two-sided hinged grill for small fish, a fish basket for large whole fish, a fine-mesh grill, aluminum foil, wood chips, grapevine cuttings, a pastry brush, spatulas, pronged forks, skewers (wood or steel), a baby bottle with water to put out flare-ups or a cast-iron grill pan.

Grilled Whole Fish or Shellfish

Serves 4

FISH AND SHELLFISH are marinated in lime or lemon juice and olive oil. When grilled over a fire strewn with thyme leaves, the seafood takes on great flavor.

If you use a whole dressed fish, leave the fins on, even if they are spiny, for they are part and parcel of the final presentation.

NUMBER SERVED	AMOUNT OF FISH NEEDED	APPROXIMATE GRILLING TIME
1	2 or 3 fish weighing a few ounces each	15 minutes
	or	
	1 fish weighing ½ pound	20 minutes
2	1 fish weighing 1½ to 2 pounds	30 minutes
4	1 fish weighing 3 pounds	35 to 40 minutes
8	1 fish weighing 6 pounds	45 minutes, plus time to finish cooking in the oven

12	sprigs fresh thyme or 1 tablespoon dried thyme
2	tablespoons minced garlic
3	pounds whole small or large dressed fish
	or
8	soft-shell crabs, cleaned
	or
1½-2	pounds sea scallops, small tough muscles removed
	or
1½-2	pounds large shrimp (16-35 per pound), shelled and deveined
½	cup lime or lemon juice
½	cup olive oil
	Salt to taste
	Freshly ground black pepper to taste
2	limes or lemons, cut in half for garnish

1. Prepare an open fire.

2. Pull the leaves off 6 of the thyme sprigs. Mix the fresh or 1½ teaspoons of the dried leaves with the garlic, and stuff the fish cavities, or if grilling shellfish, sprinkle them with the mixture.

Fish choices

Choose whole dressed fish such as

anchovy

baby coho salmon

black sea bass

blackfish

blowfish

bluefish or baby bluefish (snapper)

butterfish

croaker

freshwater striped bass

gray sole

grouper

herring

largemouth bass

mackerel

petrale sole

porgy

rockfish

sea robin (skinned)

sheepshead

smallmouth bass

spot

sunfish

trout

weakfish (sea trout)

white bass

whiting

or shellfish such as

scallops

shrimp

soft-shell crabs

*Two-sided hinged grill for
small fish or shellfish
Fish basket for a whole
fish weighing 3 pounds
or more
Outdoor grill and heat
source*

Preparation time

*10 minutes, plus 20
minutes marinating time*

**Open-fire
preparation time**

20 to 45 minutes

Grilling time

10 to 40 minutes

Variations

*You can use rosemary,
oregano, tarragon or mint
in place of the thyme. You
can use chopped scallion,
shallot or onion in place of
the garlic.*

3. Mix together the lime or lemon juice and the oil in a shallow pan, and marinate the seafood in it for 20 minutes. Turn a couple of times.

4. Oil the hinged grill or fish basket, if using.

5. Lift the seafood out of the marinade, and drain it a little before putting it in the oiled grill or fish basket or directly on the grill. Reserve the marinade.

6. Sprinkle the seafood with salt and pepper, and close the grill or fish basket.

7. Throw 4 sprigs or the remaining 1½ teaspoons dried thyme on the fire before grilling.

8. Put the seafood on the grill, and cook it until done, turning it halfway through. See the table on the previous page for approximate grilling times for fish; scallops, shrimp and soft-shell crabs will take 7 to 10 minutes. Check for doneness (see page 66). *Note*: If the seafood needs further cooking but is browning too quickly on the grill and will burn if left on or if the fire dies out, finish the cooking in a conventional oven preheated to 425 degrees F or a microwave oven set on High. Check for doneness at 5-minute intervals.

9. Carefully take the seafood off the grill or out of the hinged grill or fish basket—you want to avoid tearing the skin. Put the seafood on a platter. Pour some or all of the reserved marinade over it.

10. Decorate the platter with some thyme sprigs, if desired, and lemon or lime halves.

Grilled Fish Fillets, Butterflied or Split Fish, Steaks, Medallions or Shellfish

Serves 1

THIS RECIPE can be used for any fish and for some shellfish. Grilling shellfish in their shells imparts an especially delightful taste.

GLAZE FOR SHELL-ON SHRIMP
- ¼ cup oil
- 1 tablespoon fresh thyme
- Pinch cayenne

- 2 tablespoons olive oil
- 6-8 ounces fish fillet, skin on, pin bones removed
  or
- 8 ounces butterflied or split fish
  or
- 6 ounces medallions
  or
- 1 1-inch-thick fish steak
  or
- 6-8 ounces previously cooked conch or octopus; scallops (small tough muscles removed); or shell-on shrimp
  or
- 2-4 soft-shell crabs, cleaned
- Salt to taste
- Freshly ground black pepper to taste
- ½ lemon
- Flavored butter such as Anchovy Butter (page 211) or Tomato Salsa (page 196); optional
- 1 parsley sprig for garnish

1. Prepare an open fire, or preheat the grill pan over medium-high heat for 2 minutes. If you are grilling shrimp, mix glaze ingredients in a small bowl. Add shrimp and mix. Otherwise, pour 1 tablespoon of the oil on a plate, and coat both sides of the fish or shellfish with it.

2. Brush the grill or grill pan with the remaining 1 tablespoon oil. The oil should smoke a bit when you brush it on the grill pan, indicating that the pan is now hot enough to use.

Fish choices
Choose any filleted fish, butterflied or split fish, steaks or medallions. Avoid very flaky fish (such as flounder or sole) unless you have a fine-mesh grill. Or choose shellfish, such as
conch *or* **octopus** *(previously cooked; see pages 255 and 305)*
scallops
shell-on shrimp
soft-shell crabs

Special equipment
Outdoor grill and heat source or cast-iron grill pan
Two-sided hinged grill (optional)
Fine-mesh grill (optional)

Preparation time
5 minutes

Open-fire preparation time
20 to 45 minutes
or
Time needed to preheat the cast-iron grill pan
2 minutes

Grilling time
5 to 30 minutes

Variations

You can use a vegetable oil, such as canola, safflower, peanut, corn or Oriental-style sesame oil, in place of the olive oil. You can use a pinch of cayenne, white pepper, cumin, ground coriander or paprika in place of the black pepper. You can use lime juice in place of the lemon juice. You can cook a few vegetables on the grill or in the grill pan at the same time you are cooking the fish. Use trimmed and sliced scallions; thin slices of red, green or yellow bell pepper; sliced tomato, zucchini or yellow squash; or previously parboiled and sliced potatoes.

Fish choices

Choose firm-fleshed fish such as
dolphinfish (mahi-mahi)
halibut
monkfish
salmon
shark
swordfish
tuna
or shellfish such as
sea scallops
shrimp

3. When the grill or grill pan is hot, lay the fish (skin side up) or shellfish (drain shrimp of any glaze) on it and cook.

4. Using a wide spatula, move the fish or shellfish 90 degrees to make attractive crisscross grill marks on the seafood.

5. Cook the fish or shellfish until it is nearly cooked through, then turn it over and repeat the procedure on the other side until it is just cooked through. The cooking time depends on the thickness of the fish or shellfish. Previously cooked octopus needs only to brown. Check for doneness (see page 66). *Note*: If the open fire dies out before the fish or shellfish is cooked, finish the cooking in a conventional oven preheated to 425 degrees F or a microwave oven set on High. Check for doneness at 5-minute intervals.

6. Place the fish or shellfish on a plate. Sprinkle it with salt and pepper. Squeeze lemon juice over it, and serve it with the flavored butter or salsa, if desired. Garnish it with a parsley sprig.

Grilled or Broiled Seafood Brochettes

Serves 4

FIRM FISH IS CUT into large cubes and marinated for a short time. Skewered on brochette sticks, the cubes are alternated with short lengths of scallion, and when nearly cooked through, they are sprinkled with chives and sesame seeds.

½ cup sesame oil (Oriental style)
¼ cup lime juice
½ teaspoon salt
　 Freshly ground black pepper to taste
1½-2 pounds fish fillets or steaks, skinned, cut 1¼ inches thick
　　 or
1½-2 pounds large shrimp (16-20 per pound), shelled and deveined
　　 or
1½-2 pounds sea scallops, small tough muscles removed

½ cup sesame seeds

2 teaspoons finely chopped fresh chives

2 bunches scallions, green part cut into 1½-inch lengths (reserve white parts for another use)

1. Prepare an open fire, if you are grilling.

2. To make the marinade, whisk together the sesame oil, lime juice, salt and pepper in a medium bowl.

3. Cut the fish into 1¼-inch cubes. *Note*: Be sure not to cut the fish any smaller—you will have trouble keeping it moist as it cooks.

4. Place the seafood in the marinade for 20 minutes only. *Note*: Do not marinate for longer than 20 minutes, because the seafood will begin to "cook" in the acid of the lime juice and will become mushy.

5. Preheat the broiler, if you will be using it.

6. Mix the sesame seeds and chives in a shallow pan.

7. Skewer the fish or shellfish, alternating 5 pieces of scallion with each piece. Reserve the marinade.

8. Grill or broil the brochettes for about 10 minutes, 5 to 6 inches away from the heat, turning and basting them with the marinade every 2 minutes. After 6 minutes, baste again and coat the brochettes completely in the sesame-seed mixture.

9. Finish the cooking. Check for doneness (see page 66). *Note*: Firm-fleshed fish tends to lose moisture quickly, so be very careful not to overcook it.

Special equipment

Four 12-to-13-inch-long metal or wooden skewers (if wooden, they should be soaked in water for ½ hour)

Outdoor grill and heat source or broiler pan or baking sheet with ½-inch-high edges

Preparation time

5 minutes, plus 20 minutes marinating time

Open-fire preparation time

20 to 45 minutes

or

Broiler preheating time

5 minutes

Grilling or broiling time

Approximately 10 minutes

Soaking time

½ hour

Variations

You can use vegetable oil, such as peanut, safflower or corn oil, in place of the sesame oil. You can use lemon juice or dry white wine in place of the lime juice.

Grilled or Broiled Seafood and Vegetable Brochettes

Serves 2

Fish choices

Choose firm-fleshed steaks or fillets of fish such as **dolphinfish (mahi-mahi)** **halibut** **monkfish** **salmon** **shark** **swordfish** **tuna** *or shellfish such as* **sea scallops** **shrimp**

Special equipment

Two 12-to-13-inch-long metal or wooden skewers (if wooden, they should be soaked in water for ½ hour)

Outdoor grill and charcoal or broiler pan or baking sheet with ½-inch-high edges

Preparation time

30 minutes

Open-fire preparation time

20 to 45 minutes
or

Broiler preheating time

5 minutes

CUBES OF FISH, shrimp or scallops are combined with tomatoes, onion and bay leaves to make a basic brochette for a summer cookout.

- ¼ cup dry white wine
- 2 tablespoons light or dark molasses
- 2 tablespoons soy sauce
  Freshly ground black pepper to taste
- ½ pound fish steaks or fillets, skinned, cut 1¼ inches thick
  or
- ½ pound large shrimp (16 to 20 per pound), shelled and deveined
  or
- ½ pound sea scallops, small tough muscles removed
- 6 cherry tomatoes (or 1 tomato cut into six 1-inch pieces)
- 1 medium onion, cut into 1¼-inch pieces
- 1 tablespoon olive oil
- 6 bay leaves
- ½ lemon

1. Prepare a charcoal fire, or preheat the broiler.

2. To make the marinade, mix together the wine, molasses, soy sauce and pepper in a small bowl with a wire whisk.

3. If you are using fish steaks or fillets, cut them into eight 1¼-inch cubes. *Note*: Be sure not to cut the fish any smaller—you will have trouble keeping it moist as it cooks.

4. Put the cubed fish or shellfish in the marinade, and stir to cover all the surfaces. Let sit for 5 minutes. *Note*: The marinade is used to glaze the seafood.

5. Put the tomatoes, onion and oil in a small bowl, and stir until the vegetables are covered with the oil.

6. When the fish or shellfish has marinated for 5 minutes, skewer it with the vegetables and bay leaves like this: onion, seafood, onion, tomato, bay leaf—three times in all per skewer, then end each with onion, seafood, onion (4 pieces of seafood per skewer).

7. Put the skewers on the grill (or, if broiling, on a broiler pan), and cook for 10 minutes, 5 to 6 inches away from the heat. Turn the skewers every 2 minutes or so, until the seafood is cooked through. Check for doneness (see page 66). *Note*: Firm-fleshed fish tends to lose moisture quickly, so be very careful not to overcook it.

8. Place the skewers on plates, and squeeze lemon juice on them.

Grilling or broiling time
10 minutes

Soaking time
½ hour

Variations
In place of the tomato, you can use sliced red, yellow or green bell pepper; 1-inch pieces of zucchini, yellow squash or corn on the cob; or small mushrooms. You can use mint, rosemary, savory, tarragon or thyme in place of the bay leaves.

Grilled Lobster

Serves 2

Special equipment
Outdoor grill and heat source or cast-iron grill pan

Preparation time
8 minutes

Open-fire preparation time
20 to 45 minutes
or
Time needed to preheat the cast-iron grill pan
2 minutes

Grilling time
15 to 20 minutes

Grilled lobster is a treat, especially as the shell gives such a smoky flavor to the lobster. For extra flavor, apply the optional spicy coating.

The lobster must be killed before grilling. The preparation is not for the squeamish. See page 290 for instructions on how to kill lobsters humanely, or ask the fishmonger to do this for you (but, in this case, you will have to cook the lobster almost immediately—within 4 hours). Otherwise, always buy live shellfish and cook them promptly.

Number Served	Size of Lobster	Approximate Grilling Time
1	1 pound	10 to 15 minutes
1	1¼ pounds	15 to 20 minutes
1	1½ pounds	20 to 30 minutes
1 or 2	2 pounds	30 to 35 minutes
2 or 3	3 pounds	35 to 45 minutes

2 1¼-pound lobsters

OPTIONAL COATING
   2 tablespoons vegetable oil
   1 tablespoon paprika
   ½ teaspoon salt
   ½ teaspoon freshly ground white pepper
   ⅛ teaspoon cayenne

   4 tablespoons (½ stick) unsalted butter or margarine, melted, or 2 tablespoons mayonnaise
   ¼ cup chopped scallions or shallots or fresh tarragon or fresh chives
   Salt to taste
   Freshly ground black pepper to taste

   1 lemon, halved

1. Prepare an open fire, if you are using one.

2. Follow the instructions on how to kill a lobster. Let them rest for 10 to 15 minutes, until their muscles relax.

3. Put the lobsters on their backs, and cut through the middle of their bodies lengthwise. *Do not cut all the way through the back shells.* Use kitchen scissors to cut through the middle of each shell on the underside of the tail. Spread the two halves apart with your hands, leaving each lobster partly joined together at the back. Remove the little sac from behind the eyes. Leave the dark green coral (roe), if there is any, inside the body. It is advisable to discard the tomalley because it might be contaminated. Try to remove the vein that runs along the back of the tail meat, by the methods described on page 291. If you don't succeed, don't worry—it can be easily discarded as you are eating.

4. If you want to use the coating to give added flavor to the grilled lobster, put the oil, paprika, salt, white pepper and cayenne into a bowl, and mix with a spoon. Coat the outside shells, claws and legs of the lobsters with this mixture.

5. If you are using a grill pan, preheat it over medium-high heat for 2 minutes.

6. Spread the melted butter or margarine or mayonnaise inside the body and tail meat of each lobster. Sprinkle in the scallions, shallots or herb, salt and pepper. Detach the lobster claws.

7. Put the lobsters on the grill or grill pan, shell side down, with the claws beside them. (You may be able to fit only one lobster at a time on the grill pan. In this case, cook them one at a time.) Turn the claws on the grill as they cook.

8. When the lobsters have cooked for three-quarters of the required time (in this case, 12 to 15 minutes), see whether their tail meat is becoming opaque all the way through (see page 66). If a lobster is nearly cooked, turn it over, flesh side down, for 5 minutes, and press down on the tail so that it can take some color and flavor from the fire or grill pan.

9. Serve with the lemon halves. Have nutcrackers, little picks (or lobster forks) and napkins ready for the feast.

Whole Fish Steamed in Foil on the Grill

GRILLING GIVES THESE FISH a slightly smoky taste. To cook whole soft flaky-fleshed fish such as bluefish or weakfish (sea trout) in foil on the grill, follow the instructions for bake-poaching whole fish on page 76, except put the packaged fish (with a few holes poked in it) on the grill instead of in the oven to cook. Turn the packaged fish every so often, for 40 minutes to 1¼ hours, depending on the size of the fish and the heat of the fire.

Note: The open fire must be substantial enough to last for 40 minutes to 1¼ hours. If the fire dies out, use a conventional oven or microwave oven to finish the cooking.

Fish Fillets Steamed in Foil on the Grill

Serves 4

A SPICY TOPPING will enhance the flavor of the sweet lean fish. Fillets of sole and flounder cannot be grilled directly on an open fire because all but the most sturdy, such as petrale sole and gray sole, will fall apart. However, fillets can benefit marvelously from the flavors of fire and smoke if they are wrapped in foil or laid on foil that has a few holes in it or if you use a fine-mesh stainless-steel grill.

Fish choices

Choose fillets with soft flaky flesh such as
cod, scrod
flounder
gray sole
lemon sole
petrale sole
sole

Special equipment

Outdoor grill and heat source
Aluminum foil or fine-mesh stainless-steel grill

2	tablespoons olive oil or soft unsalted butter or margarine
1½-2	pounds fish fillets, skinned, pin bones removed
1	recipe Spicy Basic Topping or Lemon, Parsley and Garlic Topping (page 205)
2	tablespoons lemon juice
	Salt to taste
	Freshly ground white pepper to taste

1. Prepare an open fire.

2. Cut 4 pieces of aluminum foil, if using, into 12-inch squares, and poke a few holes in them with the point of a knife or a skewer.

3. Lightly oil or butter the foil, or fine-mesh stainless-steel grill.

4. Place the fillets on the foil, and put equal amounts of the topping down the middle of each fillet.

5. Brush the fillets with the remaining oil, butter or margarine.

6. Sprinkle the fillets with the lemon juice, salt and white pepper.

7. Fold the foil over the fish, and put the packages on the grill; *or* place the foil, with a few small holes in it, on the grill and cook the fillets, uncovered, on the foil; *or* put the fillets directly on the oiled fine-mesh grill.

8. Check for doneness after 5 minutes (see page 66). *Note*: Some fillets are so thin that they will cook in a very short time, so be careful not to overcook them.

Preparation time
10 minutes

Open-fire preparation time
20 to 45 minutes

Grilling time
5 to 10 minutes

Clams or Mussels
Steamed in Foil on
the Grill or in the Oven

Serves 3 as an appetizer or 2 as a main course

Special equipment
*Aluminum foil 18 inches
  wide
Outdoor grill and heat
source (optional)*

Preparation time
20 minutes

**Open-fire
preparation time**
*20 to 45 minutes
or*

**Oven preheating
time**
10 minutes

Steaming time
15 to 25 minutes

I T IS MOST ENJOYABLE to open packages of clams or mussels with aromatic vegetables and herbs that have been steamed on the grill.

The preparation can be done ahead of time. The packages of clams can be made up to 6 hours ahead and the mussels up to ½ hour ahead and refrigerated until you are ready to cook.

18 littleneck or small cherrystone clams, scrubbed
    or
 2 pounds Manila or butter clams or cockles or mussels,
       scrubbed
 2 celery stalks, finely chopped
 1 small onion, finely chopped
 ½ red or green bell pepper, finely diced
 2 garlic cloves, minced
 2 tablespoons finely chopped fresh parsley
 1 tablespoon fresh thyme leaves or ¼ teaspoon dried
 ¼ cup lemon juice or dry white wine
 2 slices bacon, fried until crisp, crumbled (optional)

1. Prepare the open fire or preheat the oven to 450 degrees F.

2. Cut 4 pieces of aluminum foil into 18-inch squares. Use double foil for each package.

3. Place cleaned clams, cockles or mussels on each double thickness of foil, then sprinkle with equal amounts of celery, onion, bell pepper, garlic, parsley, thyme, lemon juice or wine and bacon, if desired.

4. Fold the foil over the clams, cockles or mussels loosely to give the shells room to open.

5. Fold the edges of the foil together several times to seal the packages properly.

6. When the fire is ready or the oven is hot, place the packages on the grill or on the middle oven rack, and cook them for 15 to 25 minutes, until the clams, cockles or mussels open. *Note*: Cook them a little longer if the packages have been taken straight from the refrigerator. Mussels will take less time than clams to open. Cook only until the shells open. You can unfold the foil to see whether the mollusks are open.

7. Eat the clams or mussels out of the foil, or empty the contents of the packages onto plates.

Frying and Sautéing, Including the Blackening Method

Fried or Sautéed Seafood

THE WORDS *frying* and *sautéing* are used more or less interchangeably here. Both methods are similar, in that the food is cooked with fat, be it butter and oil, butter or clarified butter alone or simply oil in a shallow frying pan or skillet over medium to high heat. Margarine is fine too. I recommend that you use butter and oil together, so that the butter will have less chance to burn, or clarified butter (see page 217), which will not burn. The hot fat should just cover the bottom of the pan so it sears the outside of the food quickly. Frying should not be confused with deep-frying, where the food is totally immersed in very hot fat.

When frying and sautéing, be sure the fat is hot enough, otherwise it will be absorbed and produce a soggy, oil-filled piece of seafood. If the fat is too hot, it will burn the outside of the fish or shellfish before the inside has cooked through. You should heat the fat over medium to high heat to sear the flesh, then lower the heat to finish the cooking. Don't crowd the fish or fillets in the pan, because the temperature of the fat will cool. The flesh must become crisp on the outside and remain moist inside.

Make sure you have a wide spatula to turn fillets over and to lift them out in one piece. Use tongs or a slotted spoon to lift out smaller pieces of seafood.

You can fry small whole fish such as trout, whether or not they have been previously boned. They can be stuffed with herbs such as tarragon, dill, basil, mint and garlic. The fish need only be garnished with a lemon wedge and, like many fried fish dishes, can be served with Tomato Salsa (page 196).

Pan-dressed fish are easy to fry indoors or outdoors on a campfire.

Small skinless fillets of flounder or sole, lightly coated with flour, are also simple to fry. Sole à la Meunière, floured and sautéed fillets that are sauced with melted butter, lemon juice and chopped parsley, continues to be a very popular dish (see page 122 for the recipe). Fillets of oily fish such as herring and mackerel are better baked or broiled. Although fried or sautéed fillets of salmon are acceptable, there are better ways to cook this fish, such as broiling, roasting and bake-poaching. A quick sauté of shrimp, scallops, soft-shell crabs or squid is delicious. Croquettes of all kinds of fish are easily fried.

I recommend using heavy aluminum frying pans for good frying and sautéing results. Nonstick Teflon-coated frying pans are useful, for they require less fat. They are relatively inexpensive. When they lose their coating, throw them away.

To sauté successfully, use medium to high heat to begin with and always add the food when the fat is hot, nearly smoking. After the initial searing, turn the heat down slightly to cook the item through. To become a good sauté person, you need a lot of practice.

Frying and sautéing are quick: Depending on the size and thickness of the seafood, cooking can take from 2 to 20 minutes.

Blackened Fish

BLACKENING IS, and will continue to be, a favorite way to prepare fish, although the hot and spicy flavorings that are used tend to obliterate a fish's character. I do enjoy the zesty taste now and again, and the method is a good one. Because the fish is seared in a very hot skillet, it gets a good crust but remains moist inside.

Take any firm-fleshed fish cut into fillets or steaks—for example, tuna, blackfish, grouper or redfish, if you can find it. (The famous Cajun blackened redfish became so popular that redfish was just about fished out, and a preservation order had to be imposed.) Fillets and steaks should be at least ¾ inch thick to withstand this aggressive method of cooking. Coat the fish with a fairly thick mixture of herbs, spices and seasonings. Then heat a heavy cast-iron skillet over high heat for 5 minutes or so until it is very hot. Coat the fish lightly with oil, melted unsalted butter or margarine, and place it in the hot pan. It will char on the outside, and a crust will form. Turn it over. When there is a crust on both sides, turn the heat down a little so the fish cooks through.

The herbs, spices and seasonings used on blackened fish include thyme, oregano, marjoram, paprika, chili powder, cayenne, salt and pepper. The coating has to be dry, so real garlic and onion cannot be used, since they will burn. Some people add garlic and onion powders or salts or granulated garlic and onion, but I do not do this: they contain preservatives and, often, monosodium glutamate and leave an unpleasant taste.

Health

DEPENDING ON THE COATING and the amount of butter and/or oil you use, fried or sautéed fish might end up with more calories than you want in your meal. However, if the fat is at the correct temperature, the fish will not absorb a great deal of it.

A heavy nonstick frying pan can be used to good advantage. Less fat is needed, and the fish browns easily, as long as the pan is no larger than 8 to 12 inches in diameter. A pan larger than this can't get hot enough on a domestic burner; the heat is dispersed across the pan, and the fish cannot sear.

In blackening, a negligible amount of fat is absorbed, so this is relatively healthful.

Fish choices

Choose fillets or 1-inch-thick steaks of fish such as

blackfish *(fillets)*

cod *(steaks)*

flounder or **sole** *(fillets)*

freshwater striped bass
  (fillets)

grouper *(fillets)*

largemouth bass *(fillets)*

monkfish fillets *(cut into*
  medallions)

mullet *(fillets)*

ocean perch *(fillets)*

ocean pout *(fillets)*

perch *(fillets)*

pike *(fillets)*

red snapper *(fillets)*

rockfish *(fillets)*

sand shark (dogfish)
  (steaks)

shad *(fillets)*

skate wings

smallmouth bass *(fillets)*

smelt *(fillets)*

sturgeon *(fillets or steaks)*

tilefish *(fillets or steaks)*

turbot (Greenland
  halibut) *fillets*

weakfish (sea trout)
  (fillets)

whiting *(fillets)*

wolffish *(fillets)*

or shellfish such as

abalone *(slices)*

geoduck clam *(slices)*

Fried Fish Fillets, Fish Steaks, Skate Wings or Abalone or Geoduck Clam Slices à la Meunière

Serves 2

À LA MEUNIÈRE always refers to cooking methods in which flour is involved. In this recipe, fillets are coated with seasoned flour, then fried and finished off with a little more butter, lemon juice and parsley.

Note: Tuna, swordfish, mako shark, salmon and halibut steaks are best broiled or grilled, but if you choose to fry these fish, there is no need to coat them with the seasoned flour called for in this recipe.

½ cup all-purpose flour

1 teaspoon salt

Freshly ground white pepper to taste

1 teaspoon fresh thyme or oregano or marjoram or dill or
  ½ teaspoon dried (optional)

1 teaspoon paprika or chili powder or ground cumin
  (optional)

⅛ teaspoon cayenne (optional)

1 tablespoon unsalted butter or margarine, plus
  2 tablespoons more (optional)

2 tablespoons olive or vegetable oil or 3 tablespoons
  clarified butter (page 217)

¾-1 pound fish fillets, skin on or off, pin bones removed,
  or steaks or skate wings
  or

½ pound abalone or geoduck clam slices

1 teaspoon lemon juice (optional)

2 lemon quarters

2 sprigs parsley

Sauce of your choice (optional; see recipes beginning on
  page 195)

1. In a bowl, mix the flour with the salt, white pepper and any of the herbs and seasonings you like, then spread the mixture out on a plate.

2. Put a medium-sized frying pan over medium to high heat.

3. Add 1 tablespoon of the butter or margarine and the oil or clarified butter.

4. Coat the fish or shellfish in the seasoned flour, and shake off the excess.

5. When the fat is hot, but before the butter or margarine has browned, put the fish in to fry.

6. When you see the fish or shellfish getting opaque and crisp on the edges, take a wide spatula and turn it over. Cook only until it is opaque all the way through. This will take from 2 to 10 minutes, depending on the thickness of the fish. Abalone and geoduck clam slices will take barely 60 seconds to cook. *Note*: When a thick piece of fish is browned on both sides and is still not cooked through, turn the heat down to finish cooking. Check for doneness (see page 66).

7. Lift the fish or shellfish out of the pan using a wide spatula, and drain it briefly on a double layer of paper towels.

8. Optional: For an extra special effect, throw away the remaining butter or margarine or oil in the pan. Clean the pan with paper towels (without burning yourself), and put it back on the heat. Melt the remaining 2 tablespoons cold butter or margarine in the pan. When it bubbles and gets frothy, add the lemon juice. Swirl the sauce around the pan, and pour some over each piece of fish.

9. Serve with the lemon wedges, and garnish with parsley sprigs.

Special equipment
Frying pan

Preparation time
5 minutes

Frying time
2 to 10 minutes

Variations
You can use lime in place of the lemon. You can use watercress in place of the parsley.

Fried Whole Fish
or Pan-Dressed Fish

Serves 2

Fish choices

Choose small whole dressed or pan-dressed fish that have somewhat compressed bodies (not too thick or rotund), each weighing from a few ounces to 1 pound, such as

butterfish

croaker

perch

porgy

sheepshead

small freshwater or saltwater bass

spot

sunfish

tilapia

or boned, butterflied or split fish, gutted and scaled, such as

black sea bass

brook trout

rainbow trout

red snapper

rockfish

weakfish (sea trout)

Special equipment

Frying pan

Preparation time

5 minutes

Frying time

5 to 20 minutes

THE FISH IS COATED with a mixture of flour and cornmeal, then fried. Proceed exactly as in the previous recipe for Fried Fish Fillets, but buy about twice as much fish (1½ to 2 pounds). These whole fish will take longer to cook than fillets.

Try this coating:

½   cup all-purpose flour

¼   cup fine cornmeal

1   teaspoon paprika

¾   teaspoon salt

¼   teaspoon freshly ground black pepper

⅛   teaspoon cayenne

Fish Croquettes or Crab Cakes

Makes 12 croquettes

THESE FISH CROQUETTES or cakes are made with cooked fish or shellfish. The fish is extended with a small amount of bread crumbs, and the seasonings are fresh and lively.

- 4 cups coarsely flaked cooked fish, skin and bones removed

  or

- 2 pounds steamed or baked fish fillets, skin and pin bones removed

  or

- 4 pounds steamed or bake-poached whole fish, skin and bones removed

  or

- 2 pounds crabmeat, picked over for any cartilage
- 2 cups fresh bread crumbs, made from 6 slices white bread (cut off the crusts and pull apart, then process in the food processor until fine crumbs form)
- ½ cup Basic Mayonnaise (page 198) or store-bought
- 2 tablespoons lemon juice
- 2 large eggs, beaten
- 1 jalapeño pepper, seeded and finely chopped
- 2 scallions, finely chopped
- 2 tablespoons chopped fresh parsley
- 1 garlic clove, minced

  Salt to taste

  Freshly ground white pepper to taste

- 1 cup all-purpose flour
- 6 tablespoons vegetable oil
- 1 recipe Tomato Salsa (page 196) or Aioli (page 200) *or* 2 lemons, cut into wedges

1. Flake the fish or crabmeat into a bowl, and add the bread crumbs, mayonnaise, lemon juice, eggs, jalapeño, scallions, parsley, garlic, salt and white pepper. Mix well but lightly.

2. Put the flour on a board or counter. Flour your hands, and form croquettes about 3 inches in diameter and ¾ inch thick. Add a little flour to the mixture as you work if it is very sticky. The stickiness depends on the moisture of the fish.

Fish choices

Choose cooked fish (leftovers are handy) such as

blackfish
catfish
cod
halibut
lingcod
mullet
orange roughy
perch
porgy
rockfish
salmon
salt cod *(rehydrated and cooked; see page 250)*
sea robin
tilefish
various bass
walleye
weakfish (sea trout)
whitefish
or
crabmeat

Special equipment
Frying pan

Preparation time
20 minutes

Frying time
Approximately 25 minutes, plus 15 to 30 minutes to cook the fish, if cooked fish is not available

3. Heat the oil in a large frying pan over medium heat.

4. When the oil is hot, cook a few fish croquettes at a time, being sure not to crowd the pan.

5. After they start to brown at the edges, turn the croquettes over with a wide spatula. Fry each side for about 3 minutes.

6. Drain on paper towels, and serve with Tomato Salsa, Aioli or lemon wedges.

Sautéed Shrimp, Scallops, Soft-Shell Crabs, Squid or Blowfish

Serves 2

Special equipment
Frying pan

Preparation time
5 to 20 minutes

Sauté time
4 to 12 minutes

SAUTÉING TAKES PRACTICE, but this combination of fish or shellfish with basic flavorings, such as garlic, scallion, lemon juice and parsley, is easy and delicious.

2	tablespoons unsalted butter or margarine
2	tablespoons olive oil
¾	pound large shrimp (16-35 per pound), shelled and deveined
	or
¾	pound sea or bay scallops, small tough muscles removed
	or
4-6	soft-shell crabs, cleaned (see the cleaning instructions on page 262, or ask the fishmonger to do it for you)
	or
¾	pound squid, cleaned by you or the fishmonger and cut into ¼-inch-thick rings
	or
1	pound blowfish tails, cleaned
	Salt to taste
	Freshly ground white pepper to taste
1	scallion, thinly sliced
2	garlic cloves, minced
3	tablespoons lemon juice
2	tablespoons finely chopped fresh parsley

1. Heat 1 tablespoon of the butter or margarine and the oil in a 12-inch frying pan over high heat.

2. When the fat is hot, but before the butter or margarine has browned, add the seafood in one layer. *Note*: Both sea and bay scallops and squid must have lots of space around them as they are sautéed, otherwise they will lose moisture. Cook them in batches if necessary.

3. When you see that the seafood pieces (all except the soft-shell crabs) are becoming opaque on one side, turn them over with tongs or a wide spatula so they will cook on the other side. Check for doneness (see page 66). Soft-shell crabs should be turned when they start to crisp and turn golden. (Incidentally, they pop and crack as they cook, so stand back.) You can tell soft-shell crabs are cooked when they feel a little more solid in the body and have turned dark brownish red. A medium crab takes about 8 minutes to cook.

4. Quickly throw on some salt and white pepper, add the remaining 1 tablespoon butter or margarine, the scallion and the garlic, and toss the seafood in this mixture.

5. Finally, add the lemon juice and parsley, stir, and turn out onto a serving platter.

Blackened Fish Fillets

Serves 2

Fish choices

Choose fillets at least ¾ inch thick from any large, fairly firm-fleshed fish such as

blackfish

bluefish

catfish

dolphinfish (mahi-mahi)

grouper

lingcod

red snapper

redfish

rockfish

sablefish

sheepshead

swordfish

tuna

Special equipment

Cast-iron frying pan or heavy skillet that you don't mind discoloring (reserve one of your skillets just for cooking blackened fish)

Time needed to preheat the frying pan

5 to 10 minutes

Preparation time

5 minutes

Frying time

4 to 7 minutes

THIS COOKING METHOD was popularized by the famous chef Paul Prudhomme of New Orleans. He found that searing fish with a highly seasoned coating in a "white-hot" pan gives it a delicious moist interior and a crusty exterior. But this method can hardly be called his anymore, because practically every seafood chef in the country has cooked fish this way since Chef Paul first put the method on the map. This is my version.

A word of caution: Cooking fish in a very hot cast-iron frying pan may not be for the novice, unless you are very careful.

1	tablespoon paprika
1	teaspoon chili powder
1	teaspoon salt
½	teaspoon freshly ground black pepper
½	teaspoon freshly ground white pepper
½	teaspoon dried thyme
½	teaspoon dried oregano or marjoram
¼	teaspoon cayenne
3	tablespoons vegetable oil or unsalted butter or margarine, melted
2	8-to-10-ounce fish fillets, skinned, pin bones removed

1. Put a large cast-iron frying pan over high heat.

2. Mix the herbs and seasonings together, and place them on a plate.

3. Pour the oil, butter or margarine on another plate.

4. When the pan is extremely hot—that is, smoking and looking gray with heat—coat the fish thoroughly on both sides with the herbs and seasonings. Then moisten the fillets with the oil, butter or margarine.

5. Lay the fillets in the pan. They will splatter and pop and smoke, so it is best to stand back. The fish will char and get a fine crust in 2 minutes or so. Be prepared to turn the fish over when it is charred on one side, and remove it after you have checked that it is cooked all the way through (see page 66).

Deep-Frying

DEEP-FRIED SEAFOOD can be most delicious, and it is not necessarily very fattening. If it is made correctly—that is, if you use a light coating and a good-quality oil which is hot enough—the oil will not penetrate the fish or shellfish, so it will be perfectly cooked, not soggy or oily, but crisp on the outside and moist on the inside.

You will need an electric deep-fryer with temperature control, a deep saucepan or a wok. You should also have a deep-fry thermometer and a frying basket or a large slotted spoon to retrieve the fish from the hot oil.

Use 1 or more quarts of oil, depending on the amount of seafood you want to fry and the size of the cooking receptacle. As a rule, the oil should be at least 2 inches deep in the pant. To guard against splashing, never fill a pan more than halfway with oil.

The quality of the oil and its temperature are the important factors in deep-frying. The oil must be vegetable oil—use canola, corn, sunflower, peanut or safflower oil. The temperature of the oil must be 375 degrees F. The best way to test it is with a deep-fry thermometer, which is cheap and easy to come by. If you don't have one, test the oil by dropping in a 1-inch cube of bread. If it turns golden brown in 20 seconds, the oil is ready.

The coating of deep-fried seafood is the first thing to hit the hot oil, and it seals the flesh. It can simply be seasoned flour (a mixture of flour, salt, pepper, paprika and a pinch of cayenne), or you can make a heavier coating by dipping the fish in seasoned flour, then in beaten egg or milk and, lastly, in bread crumbs or cornmeal. You can coat the fish with a plain batter made by mixing seasoned flour, egg and milk, or you can use a tempura batter made with flour, egg, water or beer plus, if you like, a beaten egg white folded in to lighten the batter. Fresh or dried herbs and spices such as paprika, chili powder, cayenne, salt and pepper can be added to the coating.

The color of the coating will alert you to when the seafood is cooked. You will want an appetizing golden color, not a burnt dark brown.

You may have to fry the seafood in batches to avoid a steep drop in temperature; be sure the oil has time to regain the correct temperature after frying each batch. If you have to do this, preheat the oven (200 degrees F) to receive the seafood. But try to eat the seafood as soon as possible, before it loses its crispness.

Have a rack or paper towels ready on which to lay the seafood so that the excess oil will drip off.

Also have plenty of lemon wedges on hand to squeeze over the seafood and maybe a fresh salsa (see page 196) or the ever popular tartar sauce if you wish.

The oil can be used two or three times, until it becomes dark or odorous. When it is cool, strain it through cheesecloth or a fine sieve, pour it back into the original container through a funnel and store it covered.

Lean fish, shrimp, scallops, squid rings and clams can be deep-fried. Whole fish, from the smallest (whitebait) to black sea bass and skinned catfish, are also fine for deep-frying.

Fish such as sole and flounder can be deep-fried, but they need to be filleted first. Cut these fillets on the diagonal ½ inch to 1 inch wide or cut squid rings ¼ inch wide, and dip them in seasoned flour a few at a time. Then put them in a sieve to shake off the excess flour. When coating fish with batter, let some of the excess batter drip off before deep-frying.

Fritters made with finely chopped or flaked fish or shellfish can be deep-fried. They are likely to absorb a little oil between the flakes.

Times and Temperatures

BE SURE TO LEAVE ENOUGH TIME for the oil to get to the right temperature, 375 degrees F, before starting to fry. Deep-frying times vary: Squid rings take no more than 30 seconds to cook, while a whole catfish, depending on its size, will take from 10 to 30 minutes.

Health

THE HEAVIER THE COATING or batter, the more fattening the dish. If you are on a diet, forget about deep-frying—you don't need the oil or the coating at all.

Deep-Fried Seafood with Seasoned Flour

*See Fritters (page 134) for suggestions
on type of oil and control of heat.*
Serves 1

MOST PEOPLE LOVE DEEP-FRIED FISH if it is properly done. The crisp exterior along with the moist flesh are addictive. Lemon wedges, parsley sprigs and a flavored mayonnaise or tomato salsa are fine accompaniments.

SEASONED FLOUR (ENOUGH FOR 4 SERVINGS)
- ½ cup all-purpose flour
- 1 teaspoon salt
- ½ teaspoon freshly ground black pepper
  Herbs and seasonings (optional; page 218)

- 1 quart or more vegetable oil
- 6-8 ounces seafood
- 2 lemon wedges
- 2 parsley sprigs
  Flavored mayonnaise (optional; pages 198-200) or
  Tomato Salsa (optional; page 196)

1. Mix the seasoned-flour ingredients together in a medium bowl.

2. Pour the oil into an electric deep-fryer, deep sauté pan or wok to a depth of at least 2 inches. Heat to 375 degrees F.

3. Place some seafood in the seasoned flour, and coat well.

4. Then put it in a sieve above the bowl, and shake off the excess flour. Be sure all the pieces are separate from one another.

5. When the oil reaches 375 degrees F, fry the seafood (in batches if necessary, because overcrowding will lower the heat considerably) for just over 1 minute (taste a squid ring after 10 seconds). Check the other seafood for doneness (see page 66).

Fish choices
Choose 6 to 8 ounces of one or an assortment of the following:
anchovy *(very small, gutted through the head)*
cod *or* **tilefish fillet** *(cut into 1-inch slices or cubes)*
crawfish tails *(shelled and deveined; available frozen)*
shrimp *(shelled and deveined)*
smelt *(gutted through the head)*
sole fillet *(cut into diagonal ½-inch-wide strips)*
squid *(cleaned and cut into ¼-inch-wide rings)*
whitebait *(rinsed and drained)*

Special equipment
*Electric deep-fryer with a temperature control or deep saucepan or wok
Frying basket or large slotted spoon
Deep-fry thermometer*

Preparation time
5 to 10 minutes

Deep-frying time
10 seconds to 3 minutes

Time to heat the oil
7 to 10 minutes

6. Drain the seafood on paper towels. Keep in a warm oven if you are making several batches. Always let the oil reach 375 degrees F before adding another batch.

7. Serve with the lemon wedges, parsley sprigs and a flavored mayonnaise (like tartar sauce) or Tomato Salsa if desired.

Deep-Fried Seafood with Cornmeal Coating

*See Fritters (page 134) for suggestions
on type of oil and control of heat.*

Serves 1

See Fritters (page 134) for suggestions

Fish choices
*Choose lean whole fish
such as*
black sea bass
ling
whiting
or choose shellfish such as
soft-shell crabs

Special equipment
*Electric deep-fryer with a
    temperature control or
    deep saucepan or wok
Frying basket or large
    slotted spoon
Deep-fry thermometer*

Preparation time
5 to 10 minutes

Deep-frying time
10 to 20 minutes

**Time to heat
the oil**
7 to 10 minutes

Large whole fish and soft-shell crabs are coated with a cornmeal-flour mixture for added texture.

FLOUR-AND-CORNMEAL COATING (ENOUGH FOR 4 SERVINGS)
- ½ cup all-purpose flour
- ¼ cup fine cornmeal
- 1 teaspoon salt
- 1 teaspoon paprika
- ¼ teaspoon freshly ground black pepper
- ⅛ teaspoon cayenne

- 1 ¾-to-1-pound whole fish, gutted and scaled, fins removed
    or
- 2-3 soft-shell crabs, cleaned
- 1 quart or more vegetable oil
- 2 lemon wedges
- 2 parsley sprigs

Proceed just as in Deep-Fried Seafood with Seasoned Flour (page 131), except that frying the whole fish may take 20 minutes and frying the soft-shell crabs, 10 minutes. Check for doneness (see page 66). *Note*: Soft-shell crabs will feel more solid and should be a lovely golden red color.

Deep-Fried Seafood with Beer Batter

*See Fritters (page 134) for suggestions
on type of oil and control of heat.*
Serves 2

This BEER BATTER is light and tasty, although it is heavier than a flour or cornmeal-flour coating.

BEER BATTER

¾   cup all-purpose flour
½   cup fine cornmeal
2   teaspoons paprika
1   teaspoon salt
½   teaspoon freshly ground white pepper
2   large eggs, separated
1   cup light beer at room temperature
1   tablespoon olive oil

2   12-ounce catfish on the bone, skinned, with head, tail
    and fins removed
    or
24   oysters, shucked and drained
    or
24   soft-shell (steamer) clams, shucked and drained
2   lemon wedges
1   recipe Tomato Salsa (page 196)

1. *Beer Batter*: Put the flour, cornmeal, paprika, salt and white pepper in a medium bowl, and stir well.

2. Make a well in the mixture, and add the egg yolks, beer and oil. With a wire whisk, gradually mix. Let stand for 1 hour.

3. Before coating the seafood, beat the egg whites until stiff and fold into the batter.

4. Proceed as for Deep-Fried Seafood with Seasoned Flour (page 131). The catfish will take about 20 minutes to cook (see page 66), the oysters and clams, 1 minute per side, or until crisp on the outside and juicy in the middle.

5. Serve with the lemon wedges and Tomato Salsa.

Fish choices
*Choose seafood
such as
catfish
oysters
soft-shell clams*

Special equipment
*Electric deep-fryer with a
   temperature control or
   deep saucepan or wok
Frying basket or large
   slotted spoon
Deep-fry thermometer*

Preparation time
1¼ hours

Deep-frying time
2 to 20 minutes

**Time to heat
the oil**
7 to 10 minutes

Variation
*You can add 1 teaspoon
fresh (or ½ teaspoon dried)
thyme, oregano, marjoram
or dill, ¼ teaspoon cayenne
and/or 1 tablespoon
paprika, chili powder or
cumin to any of the
coatings.*

Fritters

Makes about 40 teaspoon-sized fritters

Fish choices

*Choose seafood
such as*

conch

crabmeat

salt cod

Special equipment

*Electric deep-fryer with a
    temperature control or
    deep saucepan or wok
Frying basket or large
    slotted spoon
Deep-fry thermometer*

Preparation time

20 minutes

Cooking time

20 to 30 minutes

**Time to heat
the oil**

7 to 10 minutes

FRITTERS ARE ALWAYS POPULAR, especially at cocktail parties or buffets. No matter what they are made with—here with crabmeat, conch or salt cod—they are sure to be consumed with gusto.

You can use canola, corn, peanut, safflower or sunflower oil to fry with. It can be used two or three times. When it is cool, strain it back into the original container and keep it in the refrigerator. If you are using a deep saucepan or wok, you will be able to control the heat more easily if you have a deep-fry thermometer.

¾   cup all-purpose flour

1   teaspoon baking powder

1   large egg

½   cup milk

1   pound crabmeat, picked over for any cartilage
    or

1   pound conch, precooked and chopped by hand or
    ground through the fine cutting blade of a meat
    grinder
    or

1   pound salt cod, previously soaked (see page 250) and
    shredded (cod weighs more when it is rehydrated,
    so put ½ cup aside for another use)

3   tablespoons finely chopped fresh parsley

1   jalapeño pepper, seeded and finely chopped
    (1 tablespoon)

2   garlic cloves, minced

1   teaspoon salt (or less, depending on how salty the
    seafood is)

¼   teaspoon freshly ground black pepper
    Pinch cayenne

¼   cup lemon juice

2   tablespoons white-wine Worcestershire or plain
    Worcestershire sauce

8   drops Tabasco sauce

1   quart or more vegetable oil (preferably corn or
    safflower oil)

1   lemon or lime, cut into 6 wedges

1   recipe Tomato Salsa or Tomatillo Salsa (optional; pages
    196 or 197) or 1 recipe Aioli (optional; page 200)

1. Sift the flour and baking powder into a medium-sized bowl.

2. In another bowl, whisk the egg and milk together with a wire whisk. Add this mixture gradually to the flour mixture, whisking all the time.

3. Add the seafood, parsley, jalapeño, garlic, salt, pepper, cayenne, lemon juice, Worcestershire sauce and Tabasco sauce to the egg-flour mixture, and combine well with a large spoon. Let stand for 5 minutes.

4. In the meantime, heat at least 2 inches of oil in an electric deep-fryer, deep saucepan or wok to 375 degrees F. Preheat the oven to 200 degrees F.

5. Using a teaspoon, drop about 9 or 10 teaspoonfuls of the mixture into the hot oil, and fry for 1 to 2 minutes on each side, or until golden brown.

6. Drain each batch of fritters on paper towels, and put them in a baking pan in the oven while you fry the rest. *Note*: Always wait until the oil has reached 375 degrees F before adding another batch.

7. Serve the fritters with lemon or lime wedges and one of the salsas or Aioli, if desired.

Poaching

To POACH SEAFOOD is to cook it in water, which is flavored with vegetables, herbs, seasonings and wine. Poached seafood can be ordinary daily fare or a special dish for a special occasion. You can serve it hot or at room temperature, garnished or not; if it is to be served at room temperature, you can, of course, prepare it beforehand. Poaching and boiling are similar in that the food is cooked in hot liquid; for poaching, the liquid must simmer.

Poaching is a time-honored practice, but I have the feeling that it causes some of the flavor of the seafood to disappear into the poaching liquid. However, it has its uses, as you will see from the recipes in this section, especially if the liquid is flavorful. When tackling a large whole fish, I prefer bake-poaching (see page 71), for it prevents much of the flavors and juices from escaping.

If you are poaching a large fish, prepare the liquid in a fish poacher. This is a long pan 4 to 8 inches high with a lift-out tray; it may be so large, it will stretch over two burners on your stove. For small whole fish, fillets or shellfish, you can use a large pot or baking pan with 4-inch sides. Fill the utensil you are using with enough liquid to cover the seafood. Add cut aromatic vegetables, such as onions, carrots and celery, and fresh herbs, such as thyme, oregano, marjoram, basil, coriander, tarragon and bay leaves. Fennel and lemon or orange peel can also be added. The liquid should be barely simmering when you lower the seafood into it. You can wrap the fish in cheesecloth, tying at both ends before immersing it in the poaching liquid, so that it can be easily lifted out of the liquid. Otherwise, be prepared to lift it out with wide spatulas.

You can poach many kinds of whole fish, although it is best to choose fish with firm flesh. Poached salmon is a classic, of course, but a whole poached trout, blackfish or cod can also look very attractive. Poach a whole fish for 10 to 45 minutes, depending on its size and thickness. You can skin a poached whole fish for better presentation, leaving the head and tail intact. Cover it with tiny thin slices of cucumber, and decorate it with dill or tarragon for a pleasing look.

With the exception of salmon, it is not a good idea to poach fish with dark or oily flesh, such as mackerel, sablefish, herring, sardines and bluefish. Poaching does nothing for their flavor.

Poaching is a plain way of cooking, so it is a good idea to serve seafood prepared this way with vegetables, perhaps those that were cooked in the poaching liquid. A whole poached fish with skin on can be garnished with these vegetables.

A coating of aspic will enhance a cold poached fish.

When you want to make a seafood salad by poaching shrimp, scallops and squid for a few minutes, immerse them in a strainer or colander so that they can be quickly removed and not overcooked. You can also use a slotted spoon to retrieve them.

To poach individual portions from fillets, lay them in a large baking pan and heat the oven to 350 degrees F. Pour boiling hot poaching liquid over the fish, cover the top of the pan with aluminum foil, and put it in the oven for 10 to 20 minutes, depending on the thickness of the fillets. This is a good way to poach salmon slices (see page 140). Fish fillets can be poached with skin on or off, but there will be less shrinkage if you leave the skin on.

You may also choose to liven up poached seafood with a flavorful sauce or mayonnaise. If so, there are plenty of sauce recipes to choose from (see page 195). When serving warm or cold poached individual portions, such as slices, serve the sauce on the plate under the fish or present it on the side.

Times and Temperatures

AFTER THE POACHING LIQUID has simmered for 25 minutes or so, the seafood can be added to it, or it can be added to the seafood. Depending on the thickness, the seafood will be cooked after 10 to 30 minutes. When poaching in the oven, portions of fish will be cooked between 10 and 15 minutes at 350 degrees F.

Health

NO FAT IS USED in this method, so unless you prepare a rich sauce to accompany the seafood—which, of course, your guests can choose to eat or pass up—the dish will be fat-free and therefore very healthful.

Poaching Liquid

Yields enough liquid to poach 2 to 10 pounds of seafood

Special equipment

Fish poacher or saucepan
or baking pan with
4-inch-high sides
Cheesecloth (optional)

Preparation time

10 minutes

Cooking time

20 to 25 minutes

THIS POACHING LIQUID takes only ½ hour to prepare—but be sure to make it flavorful. Extra poaching liquid can be strained and frozen for future use. The amounts of ingredients listed below are approximate; different amounts will be needed for different quantities of seafood. Let your judgment be your guide.

On those occasions when you are going to serve the vegetables with the seafood, cut them in a uniform and decorative fashion.

	Water to cover the seafood
¼-½	bottle dry white wine
2-4	carrots, peeled and thinly sliced
2-4	celery stalks, sliced into 1-inch lengths
1-2	medium onions, coarsely chopped
1-2	leeks, trimmed, halved lengthwise, rinsed and chopped into 2-inch lengths (optional)
1-2	lemon halves
2-6	garlic cloves, crushed with the flat of a chef's knife
5-10	sprigs of thyme or marjoram or basil or coriander or tarragon
6	parsley stems
2-6	bay leaves
2	or more tablespoons salt to taste (I mean it—taste the water!)
1-3	teaspoons black peppercorns

1. Fill the poacher, pot or pan with enough water to cover the seafood. (To ensure that the liquid will cover the seafood you are poaching, place the seafood in your poacher or pot. Pour in enough cold water to cover the seafood, then remove the seafood.)

2. Add the wine.

3. Lower the vegetables, lemon and herbs into the water. *Note*: You can first tie all the vegetables and herbs in cheesecloth. This is an especially good idea when cooking sliced fillets so that the

vegetables and herbs do not get mixed up with the seafood and they can be easily removed.

4. Add the salt and peppercorns.

5. Bring the liquid to a boil over high heat.

6. Turn the heat down to medium-low, and simmer for 20 to 25 minutes, until the liquid is full of flavor.

Poached Whole Fish

Serves 4 to 8

POACHED WHOLE FISH can be presented much like bake-poached whole fish, that is, decorated so that it makes a showy piece for a buffet and served either hot or cold. See step 17 on page 78 for these directions.

NUMBER SERVED	AMOUNT OF FISH NEEDED	APPROXIMATE POACHING TIME
4	1 fish weighing 3 pounds	20 minutes
5	1 fish weighing 4 pounds	30 minutes
6	1 fish weighing 5 pounds	35 minutes
8	1 fish weighing 6 pounds	45 minutes

1 recipe Poaching Liquid (previous page)
1 recipe appropriate sauce or mayonnaise (pages 196-208)
1 whole fish weighing 3-6 pounds, gutted and scaled, gills removed, head and tail left on

1. Prepare the poaching liquid.

2. While the poaching liquid is cooking, make the appropriate sauce or mayonnaise.

3. When the poaching liquid is barely simmering, lower the fish (wrapped and tied in cheesecloth if you want) into it. Check for doneness (see page 66) 5 minutes before the end of the recommended poaching time.

Fish choices
Choose whole fish such as
blackfish
grouper
red snapper
rockfish
salmon
tilefish

Special equipment
Fish poacher or saucepan or baking pan with 4-inch-high sides
Cheesecloth (optional)

Preparation time, including time to cook poaching liquid
30 to 35 minutes

Poaching time
20 to 45 minutes

4. Use either the fish-poacher tray or wide spatulas to lift the fish out of the liquid onto a platter.

5. Skin the fish or not, depending on the look you want (see page 77).

6. Use a slotted spoon to retrieve the vegetables from the stock, and surround the fish with them if you like. Serve with sauce or mayonnaise.

Poached Small Whole Fish or Fish Fillets

Serves 4

I T IS A GOOD IDEA to poach individual portions cut from fillets or small whole fish in a small baking pan instead of a large poacher.

In this recipe, when you are making the poaching liquid, I recommend tying the vegetables, herbs and seasonings in cheesecloth so they can be removed easily. Alternatively, if you wish, you can strain the liquid over the fish. Small whole fish can also be wrapped in cheesecloth or plastic wrap so that they will stay in perfect shape and can be retrieved easily. Tie the wrap at both ends.

Fish choices
Choose fish fillets such as
lingcod
salmon
or choose small fish such as
baby coho salmon
bass, various
brook trout
rainbow trout

Special equipment
Cheesecloth (optional)
Plastic wrap (optional)
Small baking pan

Preparation time, including time to make the poaching liquid
35 to 40 minutes

Poaching time
10 to 15 minutes

1 recipe Poaching Liquid (page 138)
1 recipe appropriate sauce or mayonnaise (pages 196-208)
  Oil or unsalted butter for coating
4 7-to-8-ounce fish fillets, pin bones removed, cut on the diagonal (see page 57)
  or
4 whole fish, weighing 8-12 ounces each, gutted and scaled, gills removed, head and tail left on
1 bunch chives, cut into 2-inch pieces
1 tomato, peel only
1 bunch parsley
1 lemon, cut into curls (see page 99)

1. Prepare the poaching liquid. (Tie the vegetables, herbs and seasonings in cheesecloth, or be prepared to strain the liquid over the fish.)

2. Make the sauce or mayonnaise to be served with the fish.

3. Preheat the oven to 350 degrees F.

4. Lightly oil or butter a baking pan that will fit the fish, so the fish doesn't stick to the bottom of the pan.

5. Place the fish, wrapped in cheesecloth or plastic wrap if you like, in the pan, and pour the poaching liquid over it. Discard the vegetables.

6. Cover the pan tightly with sheets of aluminum foil, and put it in the oven.

7. Cook for 10 to 15 minutes, checking for doneness after 7 minutes (see page 66).

8. Lift out the fish with a wide spatula onto serving plates or a platter.

9. Decorate the fish fillets with a crisscross of chives and thin strips of tomato peel, shaped into rounds. Skin the small whole fish if you like, and decorate with the chives and tomato peel (cut into thin strips) laid on the side of each fish body. Arrange the parsley sprigs and lemon curls around the fish. Serve the fish hot or at room temperature, with sauce or mayonnaise.

Shellfish Salad with Lime and Dill Vinaigrette

Serves 6 as a main course or 12 as an appetizer

Special equipment
Cheesecloth

Preparation time, including time to make the poaching liquid
30 to 45 minutes

Cooking time
15 minutes

Time needed for cooling in the liquid
10 minutes

Variation
Also use this method to poach shrimp, when serving them hot or cold with a spicy sauce or Aioli.

THIS SIMPLE SALAD requires seafood that has been previously poached (mussels can be poached or steamed). You may, of course, include more of one kind of seafood and less of another.

You need 6 to 8 ounces for each person if you are serving it as a main course and 3 to 4 ounces if you are serving it as an appetizer.

1	recipe Poaching Liquid (page 138)
1	recipe Lime and Dill Vinaigrette (page 202)
¾	pound medium (36-50) shrimp, shelled and deveined
	Ice water for cooling the seafood
¾	pound bay scallops, small tough muscles removed
¾	pound squid, cleaned and cut into ¼-inch slices
1½	pounds mussels, steamed (page 148) or poached and picked from their shells
3	tablespoons chopped fresh dill or tarragon or basil or parsley or coriander
	Boston lettuce, radicchio or endive leaves

1. Prepare the poaching liquid in a pot. (Tie the vegetables, herbs and seasonings in cheesecloth.)

2. In the meantime, make the vinaigrette.

3. If possible, find a strainer or colander that fits inside the poaching pot. Place the shrimp in it. When the liquid is barely simmering, place the shrimp in the colander and immerse it. Poach until opaque all the way through.

4. Remove the shrimp with a slotted spoon (if you didn't use a strainer or colander), and place them in the ice water.

5. Repeat with the scallops and squid, but check them after 30 seconds.

6. If the mussels are raw, add them to the liquid and cook until the shells open. Shuck them when cool.

7. Drain all the seafood well in a colander.

8. Put the seafood in a bowl, and add the vinaigrette and chopped herb. Refrigerate until ready to serve.

9. Place the salad leaves around a platter, and put the seafood salad in the middle.

Boiled Crawfish

Serves 1 to 6

IT IS ALWAYS BEST to make a zesty poaching liquid to cook crawfish in. This one suits their character.

1-2 garlic heads, cut in half crosswise
1-2 lemons, cut in half
2-4 tablespoons Old Bay Seasoning (optional)
1 or more tablespoons salt to taste (I mean it—taste the water!)
⅛-1 teaspoon cayenne
20-40 basil leaves, cut into thin strips
1-5 pounds crawfish, cleaned (see page 264)

1. Fill a pot with enough water to cover the crawfish.

2. Add the garlic and lemon halves, squeezing their juice into the water.

3. Add the Old Bay Seasoning, if desired, and the salt and cayenne.

4. Bring the mixture to a boil, and after 10 minutes, add the basil and crawfish. Cover, but check to see when the liquid comes to a boil again.

5. When the liquid boils, cook the crawfish for 1 minute, then turn off the heat and let them cool in the liquid for 10 minutes.

6. Drain and serve immediately.

Preparation time, including time to make the poaching liquid
30 to 45 minutes

Cooking time
15 minutes

Time needed for cooling in the liquid
10 minutes

Steaming

STEAMING IS ANOTHER HEALTHFUL WAY to cook seafood. It is a plain method, though the seafood can be enlivened with vegetables, herbs and seasonings. Small whole fish, such as bass and porgy, and fillets of fish can be steamed, as well as shrimp, lobster and scallops.

Steaming is done over water and/or wine in a utensil such as a basket steamer that fits closely on top of a saucepan or wok, or a metal steamer that fits inside a saucepan. The utensil must be covered with a lid so that the seafood cooks in the steam. If you use a metal steamer or fold-out steam basket, put a plate in the steamer and lay the seafood on it. (Of course, if you use a fold-out steam basket, you must remove the center post, if it has one.) Keep the liquid under the seafood at a medium boil over medium heat, and add more liquid only if necessary; this is hardly ever necessary, because seafood takes such a short time to steam.

When steaming seafood, place a bed of vegetables, such as onions or fennel, or a julienne of leeks and carrots on the plate in the steamer tray under the fish. Alternatively, you can lay the mixture on top of the fish. Sprinkle fillets with fresh herbs such as thyme, dill, parsley or mint. Suitable seasonings are a little butter, a squeeze of lemon juice and paprika, cumin, pepper or grated ginger. Rub small whole fish with a little oil and one of the aforementioned seasonings. Whole fish will better retain their shape and skin if they are wrapped lightly in cheesecloth. They can be pulled out of the steamer more easily this way too.

Steaming (on a fold-out vegetable steamer over 1 inch of water in a large pot) is a better way to cook lobster than boiling. One advantage is that you can count the cooking time from the moment you put the lobster on the steamer over the boiling water, instead of waiting for the water to begin boiling again after you place the lobster in the pot. Also, a steamed lobster does not get quite as waterlogged as one that is boiled.

To steam clams and mussels, put some wine and/or water and some fresh herbs in a large shallow skillet or saucepan with a fitted lid. Cook over high heat, shaking the pan occasionally until the mollusks are all open, about 5 minutes maximum. The juices are retained when you steam this way.

It is not advisable to steam oily fish, such as mackerel, herring, sardines, sablefish or bluefish, because steaming does nothing for their taste.

Times and Temperatures

IT TAKES NO LONGER to steam a fish or a fish fillet than it does to poach one: 3 to 30 minutes, depending on the thickness of the fish. Times for lobster steaming are given in the recipe on page 149. Other shellfish take from 3 to 10 minutes.

The steaming liquid must be kept at a medium boil over medium heat.

Health

LIKE POACHING, this method gives you a fat-free dish, unless you serve a rich sauce.

Steamed Seafood

Serves 2

Fish choices

Choose fillets of fish, preferably with skin on, such as

black sea bass
blackfish
catfish
cod
dolphinfish *(mahi-mahi)*
grouper
lemon sole
lingcod
monkfish
ocean perch
orange roughy
petrale sole
red snapper
salmon
sea robin *(skinned)*
sheepshead
skate
tilapia
tilefish
trout
whitefish
wolffish

or choose shellfish such as

bay or sea scallops
gooseneck barnacles
shrimp
squid

STEAMED FISH IS NEARLY FAT-FREE and therefore very healthful. To jazz up the taste, a few vegetables and a piquant sauce are served with it.

2   teaspoons olive or vegetable oil
2   6-to-8-ounce fish fillets, skin on, pin bones removed
    or
¾   pound scallops, small tough muscles removed, *or* shrimp, peeled and deveined, *or* squid, cleaned
2   small celery stalks, very thinly sliced or julienned
2   bok choy leaves, thinly sliced, *or* ¼ fennel bulb, thinly sliced, *or* ⅛ savoy cabbage, hard core removed and discarded, very thinly sliced, like a chiffonade
1   carrot, peeled and very thinly sliced or cut into julienne (like matchsticks)
2   scallions, sliced on the diagonal into 3-inch pieces
1   tablespoon finely chopped fresh dill or tarragon or parsley or thyme
    Salt to taste
    Freshly ground white pepper to taste
1   recipe Spicy Basic Topping or Lemon, Parsley and Garlic Topping (page 205) or an appropriate-flavored butter or sauce, such as Sweet Red Pepper Sauce (page 203), Honeycup Mustard Sauce (page 206) or Anchovy Butter (page 211), or a sauce of melted butter with lemon and parsley

1. Fill a saucepan halfway with water. (If using a flat fold-out vegetable steamer, use only 1 inch of water.) Bring the water to a boil over high heat.

2. Put the oil on a plate (one that will fit on or in the steaming utensil), and coat both sides of the seafood with the oil. Remove the seafood from the plate, and set aside.

3. Put the vegetables, three-quarters of the chopped herb, salt and white pepper on the plate. Lay a piece of cheesecloth on the

steamer, with some of it hanging over the edge, and place the plate on top of it. (Later, you will lift the hot plate out of the steamer using the cheesecloth.)

4. If you are cooking fillets that are less than 1 inch thick, put on the lid and steam the vegetables for 5 minutes before laying the fish on top of them. Otherwise, lay the fish, skin side down, or shellfish on top of the vegetables, turn the heat to medium, and cover the saucepan with the lid.

5. Steam for 3 to 10 minutes, until the fish or shellfish is opaque all the way through. Check after 3 minutes to see if it is cooked (see page 66).

6. When the seafood is cooked, turn off the heat. Lift the plate out with the cheesecloth, or use pot holders to remove it.

7. Serve from the plate, sprinkling the seafood with a little salt and white pepper, the remaining chopped herb and the topping, sauce or flavored butter of your choice.

Variation

Simple Steaming for Gooseneck Barnacles and Fish for Salads

Steam as above, but there is no need to use a plate or to steam vegetables with the seafood. Oil the surface of the steamer before placing the seafood on it. Two pounds gooseneck barnacles serves 2 and takes 3 to 5 minutes to steam. Serve gooseneck barnacles with Aioli (page 200) or melted butter. For 2 to 4 pounds of fish fillet, skin on or off, allow 5 to 15 minutes to steam.

Variation

Steamed Small Whole Fish

Choose whole dressed fish small enough to fit in the steamer, such as bass, blackfish, porgy or trout.

Steam as above, without vegetables, but add Spicy Basic Topping or Lemon, Parsley and Garlic Topping (page 205) halfway through steaming.

Special equipment
Chinese basket-weave steamer with a lid that fits on top of a wok or saucepan, or a metal steamer that fits on top of a saucepan with a lid, or a fold-out vegetable steamer that fits flat in a saucepan with a lid Cheesecloth

Preparation time
15 minutes

Steaming time
3 to 10 minutes

Steamed Mussels
or Soft-Shell Clams Marinière

Serves 2 as a main course or 4 as an appetizer

Special equipment

12-inch frying pan with a
* fitted lid*
Finger bowls

Preparation time

15 minutes

Standing time

½ hour

Steaming time

3 to 5 minutes

THIS SIMPLEST OF DISHES relies on some garlic, thyme, white wine and parsley.

¾ cup dry white wine
¼ cup finely chopped shallots (about 3 shallots) or
       scallions or onion
1 tablespoon finely chopped garlic cloves
2 pounds mussels, cleaned, beards removed, left to stand
       ½ hour (see page 300)
   or
2 pounds soft-shell (steamer) clams, cleaned and left to
       stand ½ hour (see page 246)
1 tablespoon fresh thyme or ½ teaspoon dried
2 tablespoons finely chopped fresh parsley
1 tablespoon unsalted butter or margarine or heavy cream
   (optional)

1. Put the wine, shallots or scallions or onion and garlic in the frying pan. Cover and cook over high heat for 2 minutes.

2. Add the mussels or soft-shell clams. They should lie in a single layer in the pan.

3. Cover the pan and cook, shaking the pan every ½ minute or so, until the mussel shells open (3 to 5 minutes). Discard any that do not open. *Note*: Soft-shell clam shells are already slightly open; when they cook, their shells gape further.

4. Pick the mussels or soft-shell clams out of the pan with tongs or a slotted spoon, and put them in soup bowls.

5. If you are serving mussels, add the thyme and parsley (and the butter, margarine or cream, if desired) to the wine mixture in the skillet. Swirl the mixture around over high heat, and when it is foamy, pour it over the mussels. At the table, use a pair of empty mussel shells as a pincer to pick the mussels from their shells.

If you are serving soft-shell clams, add the thyme and parsley and butter or margarine, if desired, but not the cream to the wine mixture in the skillet. When the butter has melted, strain the sauce through a fine mesh into little pots or ramekins.

At the table, dip the soft-shell clams (removed from their shells) in this sauce before eating. Have a bowl ready for the empty shells and finger bowls to rinse your fingers.

Steamed Lobster

LOBSTER IS BEST cooked plain by steaming or boiling and accompanied by lemon and melted butter. Beer adds some flavor to the lobster as it steams.

Special equipment
Large (16-quart) lobster pot with a lid
Flat fold-out vegetable steamer (remove the center post, if it has one)
Nutcrackers or a hammer (for large lobsters)
Lobster picks or forks

Preparation time
5 minutes

Steaming time
10 to 55 minutes

NUMBER SERVED	SIZE OF LOBSTER	STEAMING TIME
1	1 pound	10 minutes
1	1¼ pounds	12 minutes
1	1½ pounds	15 minutes
1	1¾ pounds	18 minutes
2	2 pounds	20 minutes
2	2½ pounds	25 minutes
2	3 pounds	30 minutes
4	5 pounds	55 minutes

1-2	cans lager-style beer
	Lobster or lobsters as needed
2-4	tablespoons unsalted butter or margarine per person
	Salt to taste
	Lemon juice to taste
	Lemon wedges

1. Pour the beer and enough water to measure 1 inch in your pot, and bring to a boil.

2. Lay the vegetable steamer in the pot, and place the lobster(s) on top. Hold the lobster by its body, near the head, and get its claws and head in first. Cover the pot. Count the cooking time from this point. *You have to be precise, because there is no way to tell if a lobster is cooked without breaking the shell open.*

3. In the meantime, gently heat the butter or margarine in a small pan until it is melted.

4. When cooked, place each lobster, right side up, in the kitchen sink.

5. Run a little cold water over each lobster to stop the cooking and let the lobster(s) stand for 5 minutes.

6. Using a dishcloth to protect you from the heat, turn each lobster on its back and cut it down the middle with a chef's knife. Use scissors to cut down the middle of the underside of the tail, if you want the tail meat in one piece.

7. Find and remove the little sac behind the eyes. It is advisable to remove the tomalley, because it may be contaminated.

8. Detach the claws, and crack them in several places with nutcrackers or with a hammer if they are large.

9. Arrange all the pieces on a platter in a decorative way.

10. Mix salt and lemon juice with the melted butter or margarine, and place the mixture in little pots or ramekins.

11. Serve the lobster(s) with lemon wedges and the melted butter.

Steamed Crabs

Serves 2

CRABS, ESPECIALLY BLUE CRABS, benefit from being steamed with a little added flavoring like crab boil. It is fun to eat them on a table laid with newspaper or butcher paper, with wooden mallets, nutcrackers and a small pail or container for empty shells.

The crabs must be bought alive—you've just got to keep out of the way of their claws. The best way to do this is to grab the crabs from behind or by the rear swimming legs or to use long-handled tongs after the crabs have been tranquilized by a half-hour stay in the freezer.

Steaming time does depend somewhat on the shape of the utensil you use. If you can fit the crabs in a large, wide pot in one or two layers, the steaming time will be as listed below. If you have to make more than two layers of crabs, of course the steaming will take longer. And don't forget that the crabs at the bottom will cook faster than those at the top.

NUMBER SERVED	CRABS NEEDED	APPROXIMATE STEAMING TIME
2	6 to 8 large blue crabs	20 minutes
4 or 5	12 large blue crabs	25 minutes
2	2 large Dungeness crabs	20 minutes
4	4 large Dungeness crabs	30 minutes

6-8 large blue crabs

   or

2 1-to-1½-pound Dungeness crabs

1 cup distilled white or white wine vinegar

3 tablespoons crab boil, available in bottled form from fish stores (optional)

4 tablespoons crab seasoning (store-bought or made from ½ teaspoon each freshly ground white pepper and black pepper, 1 tablespoon paprika, ½ teaspoon cayenne, ¾ teaspoon salt and 1 teaspoon dried oregano or thyme)

1. Put the crabs (in the bag they came in) in the freezer for 30 minutes to calm them down somewhat.

2. Bring an inch of water to a boil in a large pot, and add the vinegar and, if desired, the crab boil.

Special equipment
Large (16-quart) lobster pot with a lid
Flat fold-out vegetable steamer or rack
Wooden board (optional)
Wooden mallet (optional)
Nutcrackers

Preparation time
30 minutes in the freezer

Steaming time
20 to 30 minutes

3. Lay a flat fold-out vegetable steamer or rack in the pot, and place the crabs in one layer on top.

4. Sprinkle the crabs with crab seasoning, then add a second layer of crabs, and sprinkle again.

5. Cover the pot. Cook for 20 minutes; *you have to be precise, because there is no way to tell if a crab is cooked without breaking the shell open.*

6. Remove the crabs from the pot, place them on a platter, then take your time to enjoy this treat. It's best to crack the crabs on a wooden board with a wooden mallet and a nutcracker.

Braising

BRAISING IS A COMBINATION of cooking methods. First, you sear or sauté the seafood in a pan on top of the stove, then you add additional ingredients, such as a mixture of vegetables, flavorings like onion, garlic and herbs, and broth or wine. Next, depending on the size of the seafood, you can either transfer it to a baking dish and put it in the oven or leave it in its original pan and finish cooking it on top of the stove.

This is a particularly good method for seafood that tends to be bland, for the taste of the added ingredients is somewhat absorbed by the seafood. Large, fairly firm-fleshed fillets can be braised, as can slices or cubes of fish. Monkfish, sand shark, shrimp, squid, raw lobster in its shell (cut into sections), scallops and cooked octopus braise well. You can also use this method for smaller pieces of fish, such as thickly sliced fillets, medallions or steaks.

Times and Temperatures

WHEN YOU BRAISE FISH or shellfish, sear it just long enough to give it some color—a few minutes on each side. The oil or fat should be hot, so the pan must be set over medium to high heat. If you are going to finish cooking it in the oven, preheat the oven to 425 degrees F. Depending on the size of the seafood, it will be cooked in 10 to 50 minutes.

Health

USE JUST ENOUGH FAT or oil to sear the fish and brown it. After that is accomplished, you can leave the fat behind and transfer the fish to another pan before you add the additional ingredients and liquid to finish cooking. The braised fish ends up with little fat or oil.

Braised Monkfish Tail, Dolphinfish (Mahi-mahi) Fillets or Sand Shark

Serves 4

Special equipment

*Earthenware casserole dish
or Pyrex or other
ovenproof china dish
Frying pan*

Preparation time

20 minutes

Cooking time

40 to 50 minutes

THE FISH, WHICH IS SEARED IN BACON FAT, absorbs some of the hearty flavorings of white wine, chopped fresh tomatoes, thyme, basil or savory and seasonings. My thanks to the Minchelli brothers, chef-owners of restaurants in Paris, Geneva and the Seychelles, who gave me the idea for this recipe.

2 tablespoons olive oil

6 slices thick bacon, cut into 1-inch pieces

12 whole garlic cloves, peeled

3 pounds monkfish tail(s), on the bone, skinned (see page 54)

or

3 pounds sand shark (dogfish) in a piece, skinned, cut into 3-inch-thick steaks

or

2 pounds dolphinfish (mahi-mahi) fillets

1 cup dry white wine

3 medium tomatoes, skinned, seeded and coarsely chopped (2 cups)

1 teaspoon fresh thyme or basil or savory or ½ teaspoon dried

Salt to taste

Freshly ground black pepper to taste

1. In a frying pan large enough to hold the fish, heat the oil over medium heat.

2. Add the bacon pieces and garlic cloves. Separate the bacon pieces so they cook evenly.

3. Preheat the oven to 425 degrees F.

4. When the garlic is nearly brown and the bacon crisp, move them to the side of the pan. Add the fish, and brown it on one side and then the other. This will take from 3 to 5 minutes for each side.

5. Place the fish in an earthenware casserole dish or a Pyrex or other ovenproof china dish.

6. Remove the bacon and garlic cloves from the pan with a slotted spoon, and set aside.

7. Pour off the fat from the pan, put the pan back on the heat, and deglaze it with the wine.

8. Add the tomatoes, herb, salt and pepper, and cook for 1 minute.

9. Place the tomato mixture on and around the fish, and scatter the bacon and garlic cloves on the top.

10. Braise in the oven for 20 to 30 minutes, until the fish is just cooked through (see page 66).

11. Remove the fish from the oven, baste it with the juices, and serve.

Braised Fish Fillets, Steaks or Lobster with Provençal Sauce

Serves 4

Fish choices

Choose seafood such as

blowfish *(tails)*

carp *(1-inch-thick steaks)*

cod *(1-inch-thick steaks)*

eel *(1 inch-thick steaks)*

lingcod *(1-inch-thick steaks)*

lobster *(sections in shell)*

monkfish *(fillets, sliced into 2-inch-thick medallions)*

salt cod *(fillets, rehydrated; see page 250)*

sand shark (dogfish) *(1½-inch-thick steaks)*

sturgeon *(1-inch-thick steaks)*

tilefish *(1-inch-thick steaks)*

tuna *(2-inch-thick steaks)*

Preparation time

20 minutes

Cooking time

20 to 25 minutes

A 2-INCH-THICK TUNA STEAK is particularly good with Provençal Sauce. The sauce in this recipe can be made separately and used with any fish of your choice. Adding optional chopped jalapeño pepper (not typically Provençal) gives this sauce a different dimension—it will have heat in it.

- 4 tablespoons olive oil
- 1 medium onion, finely chopped (1 cup)
- 1-2 jalapeño peppers, seeded and finely chopped (optional)
- 3 garlic cloves, minced
- 1½-2 pounds fish steaks or monkfish fillets or blowfish tails

  or
- 2 2-to-2½-pound lobsters in their shells (cut into pieces)
- 4 medium tomatoes, skinned, seeded and chopped (2 cups)
- 3 tablespoons tomato paste

  Salt to taste

  Freshly ground black pepper to taste
- 1 cup dry white wine
- 3 tablespoons balsamic or red wine vinegar
- 20 fresh basil leaves, cut into strips at the last moment
- 12 black olives (Niçoise, Kalamata or California), pitted if desired
- 4 anchovies, cut into 1-inch pieces (optional)

1. Heat 3 tablespoons of the oil in a shallow casserole dish or skillet over medium heat.

2. Add the onion, and sweat it until the pieces are transparent.

3. Add the jalapeño, if desired, and garlic, and cook, stirring, for 2 minutes.

4. Put the vegetables aside, add the remaining 1 tablespoon oil, and brown the seafood briefly on all sides. There is no need to cook it through.

5. Add the tomatoes, tomato paste, salt, pepper and wine. Stir and cover.

6. Lower the heat, and cook for 7 to 10 minutes, depending on the thickness of the seafood. Check for doneness (see page 66).

7. When the seafood is cooked, stir in the vinegar and basil.

8. Scatter the black olives and anchovy pieces, if desired, over the seafood and sauce. Serve from the casserole dish or skillet, or spoon into a serving dish.

Soups and Stews

To MAKE A FISH SOUP in which the seafood is visible, first prepare a flavorful broth, then add seafood at the last moment. The broth is made with sautéed vegetables, wine and a stock made from fish bones or even lobster or shrimp shells (which of course are strained out). Or you can make a smooth soup by liquefying the ingredients in a blender or pushing them through a food mill.

To make a fish stew, sauté seafood and then add flavorings such as vegetables, herbs, wine and stock. A stew can be extended (with liquid) to make a sauce for pasta. You can cook a stew on top of the stove in a sauté pan, frying pan or saucepan.

You can use fish, shellfish or a mixture of both in a stew. Keep in mind that fish and shellfish will not take long to cook—unlike meat—so the basic liquid and flavorings should be simmered in advance for a little while before you add the seafood.

Thick fish fillets are suitable for soups and stews, although very oily fish, such as mackerel and herring, should be avoided unless you like strong tastes. Skin the fish fillets if you want, debone them, and cut across the grain into 1½-inch-thick slices.

Firm-fleshed fish, such as monkfish, blackfish, snapper, sea robin and the basses, are more suitable than flaky fish, which tend to break up in a soup or stew. With careful timing and handling, however, lean white fish that flakes easily, such as cod, can be used.

All shellfish are suitable for soups and stews, including mussels, clams, lobster pieces and thinly sliced squid. Clean any mollusks before using them.

Times and Temperatures

WHETHER YOU ADD SEAFOOD to a flavored broth or add flavors and broth to seafood, the fish and shellfish cook for only a few minutes. (The broth will take, at most, half an hour to prepare and must be simmering when the seafood is added or when added to the seafood.)

Health

FISH SOUPS AND STEWS are usually made with little oil or fat. Any fat used to sauté the fish or vegetables can be skimmed off before serving. Creamy Seafood Chowder (page 162) is the exception.

Fish Soup (Bourride)

Serves 4

THIS SOUP, a mixture of fish, shellfish and vegetables cooked in a fish stock, is a marvelous meal for a special occasion. Once you have prepared the stock, the dish is easily made and costs little, and most of the preparation can be done in advance.

You serve the soup with slices of French bread that have been rubbed with garlic and smeared with a garlic mayonnaise called Aioli. Some of the Aioli is stirred into the soup to flavor and thicken it. You can serve a salad before or after eating the soup.

Specific seafood is listed in the recipe; however, you may substitute as you like, as long as you use some fish, some crustaceans and some mollusks.

½ cup olive oil

2 celery stalks, finely chopped (¾ cup)

1 medium onion, finely chopped (¾ cup)

1 small fennel bulb, trimmed and chopped (¾ cup)

1 medium leek, trimmed, halved lengthwise, rinsed and finely chopped

1 small carrot, peeled and coarsely grated (½ cup)

3 garlic cloves—2 minced, 1 cut in half crosswise

4 medium to large tomatoes, peeled, seeded and chopped

1 teaspoon fresh thyme leaves or ½ teaspoon dried

Salt to taste

Freshly ground black pepper to taste

Pinch cayenne

4½ cups Fish Stock (page 164)

4 small red-skin potatoes (½ pound), scrubbed

Wide strip of orange zest, about 4 inches long

Wide strip of lemon zest, about 4 inches long

1 long loaf French bread

¼ cup dry vermouth

8 littleneck clams, scrubbed

½ pound monkfish or red snapper fillet, skinned, cut into 1½-inch chunks

1 pound mussels, cleaned

½ pound fillet of cod or scrod, skinned, cut into 1½-inch chunks

Fish choices

Choose lean fish fillets such as

black sea bass

blackfish

cod, scrod

grouper

lingcod

mako shark

monkfish

red snapper

sea robin *(skinned steaks)*

swordfish

tilefish

wolffish

and shellfish such as

clams

hard- or soft-shell blue crabs *or* **crabmeat**

mussels

oysters

scallops

shrimp

squid

Preparation time

45 minutes

Cooking time

40 to 45 minutes (Steps 1 to 4 can be done beforehand. Then the soup needs to be cooked for only 15 minutes.)

½ pound medium (36-50) or large (16-35) shrimp, with
   shells on or off
½ pound squid, cleaned, cut into ¼-inch-thick rings
1½ cups Aioli (page 200)
1 scallion, thinly sliced
2 tablespoons finely chopped fresh parsley

1. Heat the oil in a large casserole dish or pot over medium heat.

2. When the oil is hot, add the celery, onion, fennel, leek, carrot
   and minced garlic. Sauté, stirring occasionally, until the onion is
   transparent.

3. Add the tomatoes, thyme, salt, pepper and cayenne, and stir.

4. If you will be serving the soup immediately, preheat the oven to
   400 degrees F. Add the fish stock, potatoes and zests, and cook
   until the potatoes are very nearly cooked through, about 15
   minutes. (If you are preparing the soup in advance, refrigerate it
   now, and reheat it before proceeding.)

5. Slice the French bread into ½-inch-thick slices, and toast them
   lightly in the oven. Rub the toasted slices with the halved garlic.
   Set aside.

6. Add the vermouth to the hot soup.

7. Put the clams in, and watch to see when they open—they
   usually take 5 minutes or more.

8. Add the rest of the seafood. If using monkfish, put it in first,
   because it takes longer to cook than the other seafood. Take the
   pot off the heat as soon as the mussels open.

9. Remove the orange and lemon zests.

10. Stir in half of the Aioli, and sprinkle with a mixture of scallions
    and parsley.

11. Encourage your guests to spread the bread with the remaining
    Aioli and dip it into the soup as they eat.

Creamy Seafood Chowder

Serves 6

Fish choices

Choose skinned fillets of
lean flaky fish such as

blackfish

cod, scrod

haddock

halibut

lingcod

mako shark

pollock

rockfish

salt cod, pollock or cusk
  (rehydrated; see page
  250)

swordfish

or see the list of lean fish
on page 16, or choose
shellfish such as

cherrystone or razor
  clams

conch *(see page 255)*

crabmeat

geoduck clams *(see page*
  247)

medium shrimp

sea or bay scallops

or choose smoked seafood
such as

chub

haddock (finnan haddie)

mussels

sablefish

sea scallops

sturgeon

trout

whitefish

FOR A REALLY SPECIAL CHOWDER, try to use fish stock made from the bones and heads of the same species of fish you are going to use in the chowder—for instance, cod bones if you choose cod. If you make the chowder with shellfish, you can use two 8-ounce bottles of clam juice instead of the fish stock.

2   cups Fish Stock (page 164) or clam juice
6   tablespoons (¾ stick) unsalted butter or margarine
2   cups milk
1   cup half-and-half
1   medium onion, finely chopped (1 cup)
1   pound potatoes, peeled, coarsely grated and covered with cold water until ready to use
¼   pound bacon (5 slices), cooked until crisp and coarsely chopped (optional)
1   garlic clove, minced
3   tablespoons cornstarch
½   cup cold water
1   pound lean fish fillet, salt cod or smoked fish, skinned, pin bones removed
    or
12 ounces sea scallops, small tough muscles removed, cut into thin wafers
    or
12 ounces medium shrimp, shelled and deveined
    or
12 ounces crabmeat, picked over for cartilage
    or
2   cups shucked cherrystone or razor clams, minced in a grinder or food processor
    or
2   cups geoduck or conch strips, chopped
    Salt to taste
    Freshly ground white pepper to taste
2   tablespoons chopped fresh parsley or thyme

1. If you are using fish stock, make it as you are gathering the rest of the ingredients together.

2. Heat 3 tablespoons of the butter or margarine, the milk and the half-and-half in a double boiler over medium heat until hot.

3. Heat the remaining 3 tablespoons butter or margarine in a large saucepan over medium heat. When it is hot but not brown, add the onion.

4. Cook the onion until tender, about 5 minutes.

5. Add the potatoes, bacon, if desired, garlic and fish stock or clam juice. Cover and bring to a boil, then reduce the heat to low, and simmer until the potatoes are just tender, about 5 minutes.

6. In the meantime, whisk the cornstarch into the cold water in a small bowl.

7. When the milk mixture is hot, whisk in the cornstarch mixture to thicken it.

8. Add the fish or shellfish to the stock or clam-juice mixture. If you are using fish, cook until it is opaque all the way through, and stir the chowder so that the fish flakes. If you are using shellfish, pick a piece out of the soup and cut into it to see if it is opaque all the way through.

9. Pour the milk mixture into the soup, and stir. Remove from the heat as soon as it comes to a boil.

10. Add salt and white pepper, and sprinkle with the parsley or thyme.

Preparation time
15 minutes

Cooking time
20 to 25 minutes

Fish Stock

Makes 4½ to 5 cups

Fish choices

*Choose the bones, heads
and skin of lean fish
such as*

black sea bass

cod

flounder

haddock

hake

halibut

monkfish

Pacific cod

red snapper

rockfish

sea robin

sole

whiting

*or see the list of lean fish
on page 16, or buy whole*

whiting

or

sea robin *(cut into steaks)*

Special equipment

Cheesecloth

Preparation time

15 minutes

Cooking time

*25 minutes to 1 hour and
5 minutes*

This is a great recipe for a quick, light fish stock. Remember, all the fish must be scaled (if you are using the skin) and the gills removed—the scales can cloud the stock, and the gills can impart a bitter taste. Rinse off the bones if they are at all bloody. Also remember that this stock can be frozen for later use.

In a pinch, you can substitute bottled clam juice for the fish stock.

2 pounds fish bones, heads and skin
2 celery stalks, coarsely chopped
1 leek, trimmed, halved lengthwise, rinsed and chopped
½ fennel bulb, chopped (optional)
1 small onion, quartered
4 cups water
2 cups dry white wine

1. Put all the ingredients in a saucepan, and bring slowly to a boil. Skim with a tea strainer if you want a clear stock.

2. Turn down the heat so the stock just simmers, and cook it for 25 minutes.

3. Sniff the stock. If it smells good and of fish, it is ready to come off the fire.

4. Strain the stock through cheesecloth.

5. If you want a stronger stock, simmer and reduce it for another 40 minutes.

Seafood Stew or Pasta Sauce

Serves 4

MADE EITHER AS A STEW or as sauce for pasta, this delightful mixture of seafood and vegetables is economical, tasty and easily put together.

Specific seafood is listed in the recipe; however, you may substitute as you like. I suggest that you select a fish and a few shellfish.

¼	cup olive or vegetable oil
3	celery stalks *or* ½ fennel bulb, trimmed and chopped into ¼-inch dice
1	carrot, peeled and coarsely grated
3	garlic cloves, minced
2	soft-shell crabs, cleaned and cut in half
½	pound monkfish fillet, skinned and cut into 1¼-inch diagonal slices
½	pound mussels, cleaned
½	pound bay scallops, small tough muscles removed
½	pound squid, cleaned and cut into ¼-inch-thick rings
⅔	cup dry white wine
1	teaspoon fresh thyme or ½ teaspoon dried
	Salt to taste
	Freshly ground black pepper to taste
3	tablespoons finely chopped scallions
¼	cup finely chopped fresh parsley

1. Heat the oil in a large frying pan or shallow casserole dish (with a fitted lid) over medium heat.

2. When the oil is hot, add the celery or fennel, carrot and garlic, and cook for 5 minutes, turning occasionally, until tender.

3. Add the soft-shell crabs and monkfish, and cook for 1 to 2 minutes before adding the mussels. Lower the heat, cover the pan, and cook until the mussels open.

4. Add the bay scallops and squid, and stir them around in the pan.

Fish choices

Choose lean fillets of fish such as

black sea bass
blackfish
cod, scrod
grouper
lingcod
monkfish
porgy
red snapper
sand shark (dogfish)
tilefish
wolffish
or 1-inch-thick steaks of fish such as
mako shark
sea robin
and shellfish such as
clams
conch *(sliced cooked)*
crabmeat
mussels
octopus *(sliced cooked)*
scallops
shrimp
soft-shell crabs
squid

Preparation time
20 minutes

Cooking time
10 to 15 minutes

5. Add the wine, thyme, salt and pepper, and increase the heat to high for 1 minute. The seafood should all be cooked by this time. Check for doneness (see page 66).

6. Sprinkle the stew with the scallions and parsley. The dish may be served hot or at room temperature.

7. If serving as a pasta sauce, add a little of the pasta water to thin the stew to a sauce.

Smoking

SMOKING CAN ENLIVEN THE FLAVOR of many a dull piece of seafood and, some think, improve delicious ones, as with cold-smoked salmon.

Seafood is either cold-smoked (the usual commercial method) or hot-smoked, which is easily done at home. The finished product is flavored by brine and smoke—the different methods have different shelf lives. Hot-smoking generally must be eaten within a shorter period.

Cold-smoked seafood is first marinated in a brine and then smoked for a long time at low temperatures, 65 to 115 degrees F. It can be kept, refrigerated, for weeks or months, as long as it is vacuum-packed and stored at a temperature below 38 degrees F or frozen at minus 20 degrees F. When you buy smoked seafood, eat it within a couple of days unless it is kept under the above conditions.

Hot-smoking or smoke-cooking is a useful method of preservation when you have a glut of seafood. Many different utensils are available with which you can hot-smoke seafood—L.L. Bean and Sears stock several smoke-cookers—and, in addition, there are books available that teach you how to make your own. Smokers that you can make include primitive setups that use an old-fashioned icebox, an old refrigerator or a large drum barrel; commercially available smokers are covered barbecues fueled by electricity, charcoal, wood or gas. There are also small portable smokers that you can put on top of a burner on your stove or on an outdoor grill, using sawdust made from hardwoods as the smoke source, or electric smokers, some of which also use hardwood sawdust. I recommend that you carefully follow the directions given with your smoker until you can use it with confidence.

Hot-smoked seafood is usually marinated in brine for anywhere from an hour to 24 hours, depending on how strong a flavor is desired and how thick the seafood is. (Of course, if you want to smoke-cook the seafood and eat it right away, there is no need to marinate it in brine.) The brine or marinade for hot-smoked seafood consists mainly of water and salt. Salt is important, for it slows down or stops the growth of bacteria. Sugar can be added if you want, as well as a little paprika or ground chili powder (for color and flavor) and Cajun or Creole seasonings. You can also add flavor by mixing herbs such as rosemary and thyme into the marinade. Mixtures of paprika, ground chili powder, coriander seeds, cumin, cloves, salt, black and white pepper, cayenne and garlic are delicious.

After brining, rinse and dry the seafood and then smoke it for 10 minutes to 8 hours at temperatures ranging from 100 to 250 degrees F. Seafood smoked at lower temperatures demands longer smoking time, and of course, the size and thickness of the seafood or portion will determine the time necessary, just as in cooking. You can choose to have smoked seafood that is moist and soft or dry and firm, and adjust the smoking time accordingly.

Depending on your smoker, you may want to dry-smoke your seafood, which will help preserve it for a longer time, or water-smoke it with a pan of water in the smoker, which will produce a beautifully moist and flavorful piece of seafood that must be eaten within a day or so. With or without water, a pan in the smoker can catch any fat that may drip.

To obtain different flavors, use chips of hardwoods such as hickory, apple, oak, alder, peach, cherry, mesquite, maple or pecan. Or use dried corncobs, grapevines or fennel sticks. These should be soaked in water for half an hour to a few hours before being drained off and added to the main fuel. This damp fuel will smoke rather than burn and impart a delicious flavor to the seafood. You will need a fair amount to produce a nice, strong, smoky flavor, and you need to close down any openings in the smoker almost completely to concentrate the flavor and slow the cooking process. In some smokers, hardwood sawdust and chips are put in a pan above the main source of heat, and in others, the chips are put directly on the heat source; the fuel must be replenished as the seafood smokes. You can also scatter herbs such as rosemary and thyme directly on the heat source. Have fun and experiment.

Hot-smoked seafood can be eaten right away, either warm from the smoker or cold. Once cooled, you can store it in the refrigerator for a day or so, well wrapped in plastic wrap. Do not keep it any longer than this, for it must be treated like any conventionally cooked food. Hot-smoking does not usually cure food; it is just a fine way to cook and flavor seafood with heat and smoke. *If you want to store smoked seafood for up to 4 weeks, either freeze it or smoke it to an internal temperature of 180 degrees F for 30 minutes to make sure all the bacteria have been killed.*

Hot-smoked shellfish is done when the flesh has a good glaze on the outside and is firm but still fairly moist inside. Insert an instant-read thermometer into the thickest part of the flesh—140 degrees F is fine if you are not concerned with preserving the seafood for longer than a day or so, but the thermometer must read 180 degrees F for 30 minutes if you want bacteria-free seafood that can be preserved in the refrigerator for 4 weeks. Or you can freeze it.

When smoking, use good fresh seafood. Generally, oilier fish, such as bluefish, eel, mackerel, sablefish (black cod), salmon, sturgeon, whitefish and trout, smoke best. Other fish suitable for smoking are shad and its roe, swordfish, mako shark, marlin, tuna, monkfish, carp, catfish, mullet, porgy and croaker. Actually, any firm-fleshed fish can be smoked carefully. You can smoke whole dressed, butterflied or split fish, as well as fillets or steaks. Leave the skin on, and cut the fillets into portions as you like. It is advisable to make similar-sized whole fish or fish portions.

Most shellfish—clams, mussels, shrimp, scallops and oysters—smoke well.

Times and Temperatures

IT'S IMPOSSIBLE to give precise times and temperatures for smoking, because so many factors are involved: the strength of the fire, the size of the seafood and how much you are going to smoke, the strength of flavor you want, the differences in the smokers and how they function, the outside temperature and the wind. Generally, marinate seafood in brine for anywhere from 1 to 24 hours, depending on how strongly you want it to be flavored. Hot-smoke for 10 minutes (for small, thin fillets) to 8 hours at temperatures ranging from 100 to 250 degrees F.

Health

IF YOU ARE SALT-SENSITIVE, it's best to avoid smoked seafood, since it is often high in sodium. Still, who can resist smoked salmon, eel, trout, sturgeon, sablefish, chub and whitefish?

Hot-Smoking (Smoke-Cooking)

Serves 10 to 12

Fish choices

Choose whole fish,
butterflied or split fish,
or fillets or steaks such as
bluefish *(fillets)*
butterfish *(whole)*
carp *(fillets)*
catfish *(fillets)*
eel *(whole)*
haddock *(split or fillets)*
mackerel *(split or fillets)*
mako shark *(steaks)*
mullet *(whole)*
porgy *(whole)*
sablefish *(fillets)*
salmon *(fillets)*
sturgeon *(fillets)*
swordfish *(steaks)*
tilefish *(fillets)*
trout *(whole)*
tuna *(steaks)*
whitefish *(whole)*
or shellfish such as
mussels
oysters
scallops
shrimp

Special equipment

Smoker

CUT UP SMOKED SEAFOOD IN BITE-SIZED PIECES for cocktail snacks or serve with Honeycup Mustard Sauce (page 206) as canapés. Smoked fish can be sliced and arranged on small beds of salad greens for an appetizer or made into sandwiches. If extended with a plain cheese, such as farmer's cheese, with a little added horseradish, it becomes a spread.

Brining times, drying times and smoking times are dependent on many variants; refer to the explanation on page 167 or follow instructions for your particular smoker-cooker. I offer very general guidelines below.

Note: Small fish can be split or butterflied and spread open for smoking. Other fish can be filleted or cut into steaks. Smoke oysters on the half shell, and leave shrimp unshelled.

BRINE

    1   cup light brown sugar
    ⅔   cup salt
    ½   tablespoon freshly ground black pepper
    ½   teaspoon cayenne
    4   tablespoons packaged pickling spices or bottled shrimp
        and crab boil *or* a mixture of 1 teaspoon coriander
        seeds, 1 teaspoon mustard seeds, 1 teaspoon allspice,
        1 teaspoon fennel seeds, 2 dried chili peppers (seeds
        removed) and 3 bay leaves roughly crushed in a
        mortar with a pestle or processed for a few seconds in
        a coffee grinder
    1   garlic head, halved horizontally and crushed with the
        flat of a knife
        Juice of 1 lemon
    2   quarts (8 cups) water

4-5 pounds seafood

1. Mix all ingredients except for the seafood together in a nonaluminum pot or dish large enough to hold the seafood. Add the seafood.

2. To preserve the seafood, leave it in the brine for between 1 hour and 24 hours. If you are eating it right away, don't bother to brine at all, unless you want to give it extra flavor. I recommend brining ½-inch-thick fillets for 4 hours.

3. Rinse the seafood in cold water for 5 minutes. Pat it dry with paper towels or a dishcloth.

4. Put the seafood on a rack, and dry it in the wind (or use an electric fan) for 10 to 30 minutes, until you see a shiny skin form.

5. Smoke the seafood for at least 10 minutes and for up to 8 hours. I recommend smoking it for 1 hour at 300 degrees F.

6. Check for doneness (see page 66).

7. If you lightly smoked the seafood, eat it right away or within 2 days (refrigerated). If you smoked it to an internal temperature of 180 degrees F for 30 minutes, you can keep it for up to 4 weeks in the refrigerator. When the seafood is cool, wrap it in several layers of plastic wrap before refrigerating or freezing.

Fish preparation time
5 to 30 minutes

Brining time
1 to 24 hours

Rinsing time
5 minutes

Drying time
10 to 30 minutes

Total preparation time
Approximately 1 hour 20 minutes to 25½ hours

Smoking time
10 minutes to 8 hours

Microwave Seafood Cookery

GOOD, HEALTHFUL SEAFOOD DISHES can be cooked in the microwave oven, and of course all steaming, bake-poaching and stewing recipes work particularly well when prepared this way. For dishes in which the seafood is meant to have crisp or brittle skin or a colorful glaze, conventional methods such as broiling, grilling, barbecuing, roasting, baking, frying, sautéing or deep-frying are still preferable.

Seafood doesn't take long to cook by conventional methods, but then speed is not the main purpose of using the microwave oven in fish and shellfish cookery. The precision timing that the microwave offers can help cook seafood just right—tender and moist. The microwave can be set to cook for a few seconds to a few minutes, so we can't forget about a dish for a few moments as we can with conventional methods. Overcooking is a disaster for seafood—it becomes unappetizing, loses moisture, falls apart or, in the case

of shellfish, becomes rubbery—so when using a microwave, undercook the seafood at first and turn it halfway through cooking. If it is undercooked, set the oven to cook further at 30-second intervals until the seafood is cooked through.

Many of the recipes in this book for steaming and bake-poaching can be adapted for the microwave, although the amounts of liquid ingredients must be drastically reduced. Use microwavable dishes and plastic wrap to cover the seafood, leaving an open vent at one edge. Any juice that accumulates in the dish can be poured off to make a sauce. Or cover the dish with a paper towel if you want the moisture to be absorbed.

If you want a glaze, you can finish off the dish under the broiler for a minute or two. Also, you can begin cooking a whole fish or a larger fish in the microwave and finish it by broiling or grilling.

If the fish is in danger of being burned

before it is cooked through or if an open fire dies on you, you can finish cooking it in the microwave oven. (Of course, you can also do this in a conventional oven, though it will probably take longer.)

It's good to have a round or oval shallow casserole dish for microwave cookery. Place the seafood around the inside edge of the dish, with the thicker parts facing outward. If the seafood is of a uniform thickness, it will have to be moved around or turned over halfway through for even cooking. You can prepare dazzlingly handsome creations on platters or plates (depending on the size of the oven), with seafood, vegetables and sauce all cooked at the same time. The only draw-back is that if the microwave oven is small, you can cook only one plate at a time.

You can use the microwave to defrost seafood, but Marcia Cone and Thelma Snyder, in *Mastering Microwave Cookery* (Simon and Schuster, 1986), advise that you take it out before it is completely defrosted. Leave it at room temperature to finish defrosting; otherwise, you may cook the outside before the inside is defrosted.

Microwave ovens range in power from 500 to 700 watts. In the following recipes, the longer cooking time listed is for the less powerful microwave ovens. All times are approximate; use the shorter time to avoid overcooking. Most fish and shellfish should be cooked on High; only small whole fish, such as trout, will cook on Medium.

Microwaved Sole
with Endives and Béchamel

Serves 2

Special equipment

Small (6-by-8-inch) oval microwavable casserole dish
Plastic wrap

Preparation time

10 minutes

Cooking time

29 to 37 minutes

YOU WILL NEED TO COOK the endives and a béchamel sauce, then wrap the sole around the endive, cover it with béchamel and cook it for a few minutes before finishing it under the broiler.

2 large, fat endives or 4 medium leeks, trimmed and cleaned
¼ cup water
Salt to taste
1 cup milk
1 bay leaf
6 black peppercorns
¼ teaspoon salt
⅛ teaspoon freshly ground white pepper
Pinch ground nutmeg
2 tablespoons unsalted butter or margarine
3 tablespoons all-purpose flour
2 6-to-8-ounce fillets of sole (various) or flounder, skinned, pin bones removed
Juice of ½ lemon
1 tablespoon finely chopped fresh parsley

1. Trim any brown leaves from the endives or leeks, and make a crisscross cut at the root end of each. This should prevent the root ends from bulging during cooking.

2. Put the endives or leeks in a small oval microwavable casserole dish, and add the water and salt.

3. Cover the casserole with plastic wrap, leaving an open vent at one edge.

4. Cook on High for 12 to 15 minutes. Remove, and set aside.

5. To make the béchamel sauce, put the milk, bay leaf, peppercorns, salt, white pepper and nutmeg in a 4-cup microwavable measuring cup.

6. Cook on High for 2 to 4 minutes; do not boil.

7. Take the cup out of the microwave oven, stir, and let stand for 5 minutes.

8. Strain the mixture into a small saucepan or bowl.

9. Put the butter or margarine in the 4-cup measuring cup, and cook it on High for 50 to 60 seconds to melt it.

10. Add the flour to the melted butter or margarine, and whisk until smooth.

11. Gradually stir in the warm milk mixture, and whisk thoroughly.

12. Put this mixture in the microwave oven, and cook on High for 3 to 5 minutes, until it has thickened, stirring well every 2 minutes.

13. Wrap the endives or leeks with the sole or flounder fillets, and set them in the same oval dish. Sprinkle the fillets with the lemon juice, and cover them with the béchamel sauce.

14. Preheat the broiler.

15. Put the oval dish in the microwave oven, and cook on High for 4 to 5 minutes, until the sauce is bubbling.

16. For a nice brown glaze, put the dish under the broiler for less than 1 minute.

17. Sprinkle with the parsley, and serve.

Seafood Stew with Tomato and Green Pepper

Serves 6

Fish choices

Choose firm fish that you can cut into 1-inch cubes such as

blackfish

catfish

dolphinfish (mahi-mahi)

grouper

mako shark

monkfish

red snapper

sand shark (dogfish)

or choose shellfish such as

clams

crabmeat

mussels

sea scallops

shrimp

squid

Special equipment

Medium (8-inch) round microwavable casserole dish

Plastic wrap

Preparation time

20 to 30 minutes

Cooking time

15 to 20 minutes

THIS HEARTY STEW OF FISH and shellfish makes a great supper dish. Serve with rice or pasta if you like.

I have listed specific kinds of seafood in this recipe, but all you need is 2 pounds of seafood for 6 people, all cut about the same size (the fish should be cut into cubes), so substitute as you like, according to your taste and what is appealing in the market that day.

3 tablespoons olive oil

1 green bell pepper, cored and chopped into ¼-inch dice

1 medium onion, finely chopped (1 cup)

2 garlic cloves, minced

3 medium tomatoes, peeled and chopped (1½-2 cups)

½ cup red wine

2 tablespoons tomato paste

1 teaspoon fresh thyme or ½ teaspoon dried

⅛ teaspoon cayenne

Salt to taste

Freshly ground black pepper to taste

12 mussels (approximately 1 pound), cleaned

½ pound dolphinfish (mahi-mahi), skinned, cut into 1-inch cubes

½ pound squid, cleaned, cut into ¼-inch rings

2 tablespoons chopped fresh parsley

1. Put the oil, bell pepper, onion and garlic in a casserole dish. Cover with plastic wrap, leaving an open vent on one edge, and cook on High for 4 to 6 minutes, stirring after 3 minutes.

2. Add the tomatoes, wine, tomato paste, thyme, cayenne, salt and pepper. Cover again with wrap, leaving a vent, and cook on High for 1½ to 2 minutes, then uncover, stir, and cook for 1½ to 2 minutes more.

3. Add the mussels, and cook for a total of 6 to 8 minutes, until they open. They need to be moved around in the dish every 2 minutes. After 2 to 3 minutes, add the dolphinfish (total cooking time 4 to 5 minutes). After about 2 minutes, add the squid (total cooking time 1½ to 3 minutes). Stir and test for doneness

(see page 66). If the seafood is just on the verge of being cooked, remove it from the oven and let it stand for 2 minutes.

4. Sprinkle with the parsley, and serve.

Breaded Shellfish with Sweet Red Pepper Sauce

Serves 2

THIS DISH RESEMBLES TEMPURA but is not deep-fried. The seafood is spread with mayonnaise, which gives color and some crispness, before being coated with bread crumbs. I like to use the Japanese bread crumbs called *panko*, which are available at Japanese stores. (They look like shredded coconut.) I got the tip for using mayonnaise in this recipe from *Mastering Microwave Cookery* by Marcia Cone and Thelma Snyder.

½   recipe Sweet Red Pepper Sauce (page 203)
⅛   teaspoon cayenne
½   cup Japanese bread crumbs or dry bread crumbs
1   tablespoon salt
    Freshly ground white pepper to taste
½-¾   pound large shrimp (16-35 per pound), shelled and deveined (see page 340)

or

½-¾   pound sea scallops (¾ inch thick), small tough muscles removed
½   recipe Basic Mayonnaise (page 198) or store-bought
1   kirby cucumber

1. First make the Sweet Red Pepper Sauce in the microwave oven, adding the cayenne to taste to the recipe.

2. Mix the bread crumbs in a bowl with the salt and white pepper.

3. Insert brochette sticks or toothpicks through the middle of the shrimp so they lie flat. Some of the brochette stick or toothpick will protrude from the head end of each shrimp. There is no need to use brochette sticks or toothpicks for the scallops.

Fish choices
Choose shellfish such as
sea scallops
shrimp

Special equipment
6-inch thin wooden brochette sticks or long toothpicks (if using shrimp)

Preparation time
20 minutes

Cooking time for sauce
12 to 14 minutes

Cooking time for seafood
2 to 3 minutes, depending on the size of the seafood and the power of the microwave oven

4. Cover the shrimp or scallops all over with the mayonnaise, and spoon the bread-crumb mixture all over them. Place a paper towel on a plate with the shrimp or scallops on top. Cover them loosely with another paper towel.

5. Microwave on High for 2 to 3 minutes. Check for doneness (see page 66).

6. Pour the Sweet Red Pepper Sauce onto the center of each of two serving plates.

7. Thinly slice the cucumber on a diagonal, and fan the slices out on one side of the plate. Place the shrimp or scallops on top of the sauce, and serve.

Fish Fillets with Spinach and Ginger

Serves 2

Fish choices
Choose flatfish fillets or fillets of other fish not more than ½ inch thick such as
baby coho salmon
black sea bass
blackfish
cod, scrod
flounder
gray sole
lingcod
mackerel
orange roughy
rainbow trout
red snapper
various sole
weakfish (sea trout)

THE COMBINATION OF SPINACH AND GINGER enhances the flavor of many fish.

¾	pound fresh spinach
¾-1	pound fish fillets, skinned, pin bones removed
2	tablespoons olive oil
1	tablespoon unsalted butter
1	tablespoon finely chopped peeled ginger
1	garlic clove, minced
	Salt to taste
2	scallions, finely sliced on the diagonal
2	slices lemon

1. Wash the spinach, remove stalks, and dry in a salad spinner.

2. If using flounder or sole, cut the fillets in half lengthwise and fold them into thirds. Use appropriate-sized spinach leaves to cover each fillet partially. Set aside.

3. Put the oil, butter, ginger and garlic in a shallow microwavable casserole dish or on a microwavable plate. Cover with plastic wrap, leaving a vent open at the side, and cook on High for 1 to 2 minutes.

4. Place the rest of the spinach in the oil mixture, and turn the leaves over with your hands to coat them. Sprinkle with salt. Re-cover with plastic wrap, leaving a vent open at the side, and cook on High for 1 to 2 minutes.

5. Lay the fillets with the spinach on them around the outside edge of the dish on top of the wilted spinach, with the thickest part of each fillet facing the outside. Re-cover with plastic wrap, leaving a vent open at the side. After 2 to 3 minutes of cooking, sprinkle with the scallions. Cook on High for 5 to 7 minutes total. Check for doneness (see page 66).

6. Cook for 30 seconds longer if necessary.

7. Garnish with the lemon slices.

Special equipment
Shallow microwavable casserole dish
Plastic wrap

Preparation time
20 minutes

Cooking time
7 to 12 minutes

Seviche, Escabèche and Other Ways to Marinate Seafood

WE MARINATE FISH AND SHELLFISH for three different reasons. One purpose is to "cook" raw seafood with the acid of lime and lemon juices. Seafood prepared this way is called, variously, *seviche*, *cebiche* or *ceviche* in Central and South America and in the Caribbean.

The second purpose is to preserve and flavor cooked seafood—that is, fried or poached seafood—with vinegar, possibly mixed with wine or water. Seafood prepared this way is called *escabèche* or *caveach*. You can also use cider instead of vinegar or use ale to dilute the vinegar when "sousing" seafood (see page 186).

The third purpose is to flavor seafood before it is cooked or to give it a nice glaze as it cooks.

Seviche

SEVICHE IS RAW SEAFOOD marinated in lime juice or a mixture of lime and lemon juices. Essentially Latin American and Caribbean in origin, this preparation has the effect of firming the seafood so that it seems cooked. Then the seafood is served chilled or at room temperature. However, because the seafood remains raw, it poses the same health risks as raw fish. Be especially sure seafood for seviche is fresh. Also see "Tips for Careful Seafood Cookery," page 20. Raw lean fish, such as flounder and sole, and shellfish, such as conch and scallops, are marinated in the juice. You can add other flavorings as you wish, such as chopped scallions, garlic, jalapeño or serrano peppers, fresh coriander, fresh parsley, a little ginger, a little chopped tomato and salt and pepper to taste.

The time it takes to "cook" the seafood will depend on the acidity of the juices and the temperature of the kitchen. The more acidic the fruit and the warmer the kitchen, the speedier the process. Just to be sure, leave the seafood in the marinade in a nonmetal bowl for at least 4 hours at room temperature and then overnight in the refrigerator.

You can tell that the seafood is ready when it is opaque all the way through, just as with cooked fish.

Note: The seafood will exude moisture into the marinade if you leave it in too long—it will shrink and become "overcooked." Before serving seviche, and also when storing it, stop the process by draining off most of the juice and adding a little olive oil. You can usually keep it another 24 hours in the refrigerator.

All white lean-fleshed fish do well by this method. Choose fish that are not prone to have parasites (see page 21). Parasites can be killed by either freezing the fish for two days or cooking it to 140 degrees F. The acidity of the lime or lemon juice will not kill them. Fillet fish, and cut it into strips ½ to 1 inch wide or into ½-to-1-inch cubes. Sea scallops (cut into quarters or thin wafers) and whole bay scallops do fine, as does freshly garnered conch, but the flesh of squid and shrimp is too dense and cannot be prepared by this method. I like to add squid and shrimp to the seviche, so I blanch them in a poaching liquid (see page 138) until they are opaque all the way through. I throw them into ice water to stop further cooking, then drain them and toss them in a little oil before adding them to the marinade. This is a tip from Chef Felipe Rojas-Lombardi—tossing them in the oil prevents their color from being bleached out by the acid of the lemon or lime juice.

Escabèche

ESCABÈCHE, or *caveach*, introduced to Europe by the Moors in the fourteenth century, is cooked fish preserved and flavored with vinegar. More recently, in Central and South America and the Caribbean, cooks have greatly developed this preservation method, bringing more flavor to any number of escabèche dishes. Vinegar has great affinities with the basic sweetness of seafood. The Celts, Irish, Scots and Welsh all have their versions of escabèche too—for example, "soused" herring cooked in vinegar. Even the Japanese have their versions, using rice vinegar and mirin (sweet cooking wine made from rice).

First, seafood is lightly cooked, then vinegar that has been diluted with water or wine and cooked with additional flavorings is poured over the seafood to flavor and preserve it. You can eat the dish right away or leave it to stand an hour or so at room temperature. You can also chill it.

This is an especially good way to preserve fish when you are given a great deal of fish or shellfish or when you catch a lot at one time. In any case, it is a good idea to make a large batch. Store it in the refrigerator where it will last a few days (and up to a week). It's great being able to delve into the refrigerator over the next few days and treat yourself to a piece of cold seafood. You can also reheat it (gently) if you like.

Marinating for Flavor or Glaze

MARINADES FOR RAW SEAFOOD that will be cooked are various. Some people claim that milk sweetens, whitens and tenderizes fish such as shad, whiting and herring, as well as white-fleshed fish such as cod, but I find them tender enough already not to need such treatment. Others, like Frank Davis, author of *The Frank Davis Seafood Notebook* (Pelican Press, 1983), like to marinate soft-shell crabs in milk to make them even richer in taste—a good idea.

Olive oil and lemon juice make an appropriate marinade for cubes of fish like tuna, swordfish and mako shark that you might want to put on brochette sticks. A good marinade for meaty tuna is a light mixture of dry white wine, molasses and soy sauce, which gives the cooked flesh a nice glaze when broiled or barbecued.

Note: When marinating with acids such as lime juice, lemon juice, wine or vinegar, be sure to do so for only a short time—20 minutes will suffice. Otherwise, you might find that the fish is halfway "cooked" before you are ready to cook it with heat.

Health

SEVICHE IS A HEALTHY WAY to eat seafood, for there is little oil in the marinade. As a health precaution, freeze seafood before making it into seviche (see page 21).

Escabèche can have a light or heavy coating, or none at all, before the fish is fried, sautéed or deep-fried. The heavier the coating, the less healthy it is.

Some marinades, such as oil and wine, produce a healthy glaze; much of the oil will remain in the utensil or disappear when grilling or barbecuing.

Seviche

Serves 6 as an appetizer or 4 as a main course

RAW SEAFOOD is "cooked" in lime and lemon juices with a variety of other flavors and spices.

- 1 pound fish fillet, cut into strips ½-¾ inch wide by 2½ inches long or into ¾-inch cubes

  or

- 1 pound one or more kinds of shellfish, such as conch, very thinly sliced

  or

  mussels, steamed open and shucked (see page 148)

  or

  raw shucked littleneck clams

  or

  sea or bay scallops, small tough muscles removed, cut horizontally into thin slices if large

  or

  shrimp, shelled and deveined, or squid, previously poached (see page 142) and tossed in a little corn or olive oil

- ½ cup lime juice
- ¼ cup lemon juice
- 1 small tomato, diced
- ¼ cup chopped fresh coriander
- 1 scallion, thinly sliced
- 1 jalapeño pepper, seeded and finely chopped
- 1 inch piece of ginger, peeled and finely grated
- 1 garlic clove, minced
- 2 tablespoons olive oil

  Salt to taste

  Freshly ground white pepper to taste

- 4-6 Boston or Bibb lettuce leaves

1. Put the fish or shellfish in a nonmetallic bowl, and cover with the lime and lemon juices.

2. Let stand at room temperature for 4 to 6 hours, until the seafood becomes opaque. Chill in the refrigerator for 1 hour or so.

Fish choices

Choose skinned fillets of fish such as

baby coho salmon
black sea bass
blackfish
flounder
grouper
monkfish
orange roughy
red snapper
rockfish
salt cod *(rehydrated and cooked; see page 250)*
sole
swordfish
tilapia
tilefish
trout
tuna
wolffish
or shellfish such as
conch
littleneck clams
mussels
sea or bay scallops
shrimp
squid

Special equipment

4 to 6 wooden brochette sticks (optional)

Preparation time

15 minutes or 1 hour if using shrimp or squid

Marinating time

5 hours

Variation

*For an hors d'oeuvre,
string bay scallops on
brochette sticks.*

3. Add all the other ingredients, except the lettuce, and stir.

4. Set a lettuce leaf on each plate, and arrange the seafood on top.

Escabèche

Serves 4

FISH THAT HAS BEEN BRIEFLY FRIED, then marinated in a mixture of wine and vinegar, combined with saffron, carrots and onions, is a delight to eat hot or cold. This dish will keep for 3 days refrigerated.

Fish choices

*Choose whole small fish
such as*
baby coho salmon
black sea bass
herring
mackerel
perch
pompano
porgy
red snapper
rockfish
sardine
smelt
trout
*or fillets or steaks of fish
such as any of the above or*
blackfish *(fillets)*
bluefish *(fillets)*
cod *(fillets or steaks)*
dolphinfish (mahi-mahi)
  (fillets)
grouper *(fillets or steaks)*
halibut *(fillets or steaks)*
lingcod *(fillets or steaks)*
ocean perch *(fillets)*
orange roughy *(fillets)*
salmon *(fillets or steaks)*
salt cod *(rehydrated and
  cooked fillets; see page
  250)*
shad *(fillets)*
(continued)

3   cups white wine vinegar or distilled white vinegar
1½   cups dry white wine
½   teaspoon saffron threads and/or 1 small carrot, peeled
       and coarsely grated or sliced
4   bay leaves
1   medium onion, thinly sliced
4   garlic cloves, thinly sliced
     Olive oil or vegetable oil as needed
1½   teaspoons sugar
½   cup all-purpose flour
1   tablespoon paprika
1   teaspoon salt, plus more to taste
½   teaspoon freshly ground black pepper
4   small fish weighing 1-1½ pounds each, heads on or off,
       gutted and scaled, gills removed, left whole, boned or
       not, or butterflied or split
     or
4   fish fillets, skinned, pin bones removed, or steaks
       weighing 6-8 ounces each
     or
1½   pounds large shrimp (16-35 per pound), shelled and
       deveined, or sea scallops, small tough muscles removed
2   scallions, sliced lengthwise and cut into 2-inch lengths,
       or 1 red, yellow or green bell pepper, thinly sliced
⅛   teaspoon cayenne
     Freshly ground white pepper to taste
4   thin slices lemon

1. Bring the vinegar, wine, saffron and/or carrot and bay leaves to a boil in a saucepan over high heat.

2. Reduce the heat to medium, and cook for about ½ hour, until the mixture is reduced to 2 cups.

3. In the meantime, sauté the onion and garlic in 3 tablespoons of the oil in a skillet over medium heat. Add the sugar, and cook until the onion is well browned.

4. Add the onion and garlic to the vinegar-wine mixture as it is reducing.

5. While the marinade reduces, mix the flour, paprika, salt and pepper together and put on a plate.

6. Coat the fish or shellfish with the seasoned flour.

7. Heat ¼ cup oil oil in the skillet over medium-high heat.

8. When the oil is hot, fry the fish or shellfish on both sides until golden brown.

9. When the seafood has taken on good color, place it in a non-metallic dish or casserole dish with 2-inch sides. *Note*: The seafood need not be cooked all the way through, because it will continue to cook when the hot vinegar is poured on.

10. Add the scallions, more salt to taste, cayenne and white pepper to the boiling vinegar-wine mixture. Cook for another 2 minutes, or until the scallions are limp.

11. Pour the hot vinegar-wine mixture over the seafood, and decorate the seafood with the lemon slices.

12. Let stand for at least 10 minutes before eating. Eat warm or at room temperature. To store, cool and refrigerate, covered. Reheat gently in a 300-degree-F oven if you want to eat the escabèche hot.

southern kingfish (fillets or steaks)
sturgeon (fillets or steaks)
swordfish (steaks)
tilefish (fillets or steaks)
wolffish (fillets)
or shellfish such as
sea scallops
shrimp

Make-ahead tip
Steps 1 to 4 of this recipe can be done beforehand, and the marinade can be reheated.

Special equipment
Earthenware, Pyrex or ovenproof china casserole dish with 2-to-3-inch-high edges

Preparation time
15 minutes

Cooking time
45 minutes

Soused or Marinated Fish

Serves 2

Choose whole small fish such as

baby coho salmon

brook or rainbow trout

croaker

herring

ling (red hake)

mackerel

perch

porgy

sardine

smallmouth or largemouth bass

whiting

Special equipment

Earthenware, Pyrex or ovenproof china casserole dish with 2-to-3-inch-high edges

Preparation time

5 minutes

Cooking time

20 to 45 minutes

Cooling time

12 hours

Variations

You can use apple cider instead of vinegar and water; if so, use 1 table-spoon of fresh tarragon (or 1 teaspoon dried) instead of bay leaves and thyme. Or use dark brown ale instead of water; if so, use 8 cloves instead of thyme.

THE WORD "soused" is used in Great Britain to describe a fish marinated in a simple white-vinegar-and-onion mixture and served cold. It makes a good light meal with a salad.

> 4 small fish, weighing 4-6 ounces each (2 per person), heads on or off, gutted and scaled, gills removed, left whole, boned or not, or butterflied or split
>
> *or*
>
> 2 whole fish, weighing 8-12 ounces each (1 per person), prepared as above
>
> 2½ cups white wine vinegar or distilled white vinegar
>
> 2½ cups water
>
> 1 small onion, thinly sliced
>
> Freshly ground black pepper to taste
>
> 2 bay leaves
>
> 2 sprigs thyme or ¼ teaspoon dried
>
> 1 tablespoon salt

1. Preheat the oven to 400 degrees F.

2. Lay the fish in an earthenware, Pyrex or ovenproof china casserole dish.

3. Add the rest of the ingredients, draping the sliced onion over the fish and making sure that the vinegar just covers the fish.

4. Cover the dish with foil, and put it in the oven.

5. Cook small fish for 20 to 25 minutes, larger fish for 45 minutes. Or insert an instant-read thermometer—when it reads 120 degrees F, the fish is ready. The fish need not be cooked completely, because it will continue to cook in the liquid after it has been taken out of the oven.

6. Let the fish cool in the casserole dish to room temperature, then refrigerate overnight.

Marinade for Broiled, Grilled or Barbecued Seafood

Makes 1 cup marinade, enough for 2 pounds of seafood

THIS MARINADE is good for firm fish. Soy sauce, balsamic vinegar, lime juice and ginger are added for flavor. Marinate for only 20 minutes, or the acid in the marinade may "cook" the fish.

½ cup vegetable oil, such as peanut oil
¼ cup lime juice
3 tablespoons soy sauce
3 tablespoons balsamic or malt vinegar
1 ounce (1½ inches) fresh ginger, peeled and cut into julienne strips
Freshly ground black pepper to taste

1. Mix all the ingredients together in a bowl with a wire whisk.

2. Place the seafood in one layer in a nonmetallic casserole dish. Pour the marinade over the seafood.

3. Marinate the seafood for 20 minutes, turning occasionally.

4. Drain the seafood before cooking, but heat the marinade to a low boil before basting with it or serving it as a sauce for the seafood.

This marinade is suitable for fish such as
albacore *(fillets or cubes)*
bluefish *(whole or fillets)*
dolphinfish (mahi-mahi) *(fillets or cubes)*
lingcod *(cubes)*
mackerel *(fillets)*
mako shark *(cubes)*
marlin *(fillets or cubes)*
porgy *(whole)*
sablefish *(cubes)*
tuna *(cubes)*
or shellfish such as
shrimp *(shelled and deveined)*

Preparation time
3 minutes

Marinating time
20 minutes

Variation
You can add ¼ teaspoon hot and spicy (Sichuan-style) oil to the marinade.

Glaze for Broiled, Grilled or Barbecued Seafood

Makes ½ cup marinade, enough for 1 pound of seafood

This recipe is suitable for any cubed or filleted fish or shellfish that you are going to broil, grill or barbecue.

Preparation time
1 minute

Marinating time
5 minutes

THE GLAZE HELPS THE FISH TO BROWN QUICKLY, so it does not overcook.

¼ cup dry white wine
2 tablespoons molasses
2 tablespoons soy sauce
Freshly ground black pepper to taste

1. Mix all the ingredients together in a bowl with a wire whisk.

2. Marinate the seafood in the mixture for 5 minutes only.

3. Drain the seafood before cooking, and use the glaze to baste it.

Raw Seafood

THE JAPANESE HAVE, in recent years, made us aware of the delights of raw seafood, not only for its exquisite taste but for its beautiful appearance.

Several restaurants serving French and Italian dishes, such as steak tartare and carpaccio, are now making them with fish—salmon or tuna tartare and tuna carpaccio are some of the most recent variations.

To be eaten raw, seafood must be extremely fresh. Avoid eating raw freshwater fish because of the parasites they may carry; this also applies to salmon, which spend part of their life in fresh water. However, the vast amount of salmon farmed nowadays in ocean pens are free of parasites. Parasites carried by seafood are mostly harmless, and very few people have been affected by them in the United States. Parasites are killed when seafood is heated to 140 degrees F or when it has been frozen for at least 2 days. They are not killed when seafood is "cooked" with lime

and lemon juices, as in seviche, nor are they necessarily killed when seafood is brined, smoked, cured or pickled. Parasites look distasteful, and some fish are more apt to carry parasites than others. Cod is such a fish. When cod, haddock and other members of the cod family are processed in big plants, they are "candled," which means that the fillets are passed over translucent plastic shelves lit from below. Any imperfections or parasites that show are removed (see "Tips for Careful Seafood Cookery," page 20).

Sushi and Sashimi

SUSHI, which translates as "vinegared rice," is one kind of raw seafood served by the Japanese. In one sushi preparation, rice, seafood and vegetables are rolled up in dried seaweed (called *nori* in Japanese and "dried laver" in English). In another, rice is shaped into mounds that are about 2½ inches long and 1 inch wide, and raw seafood is then laid on top. I particularly like the sushi preparation in which the roll is made inside out: The seafood is enclosed in seaweed, the seaweed is surrounded by rice, the rice is rolled in sesame seeds, and the roll is then cut into logs.

Sashimi is raw seafood served without rice.

Sushi and sashimi are served with pickled ginger, wasabi paste, a soy dipping sauce and a number of artfully cut or decorated vegetables. All are delicious accompaniments.

Some of the kinds of seafood that can be used for sushi and sashimi are tuna, fluke, red snapper, bass, tilefish, bonito, salmon (it should be previously frozen to kill parasites), mackerel, yellowtail, geoduck, squid, octopus (cooked), abalone, scallops, shrimp (cooked or raw), sea urchin roe, flying fish roe, salmon roe and crabs or crab sticks.

Some of the cuts that can be used include:

♦ ¼-inch-thick slices of fish fillets, cut against the grain

♦ strips made from such slices, tangled up in a ball

♦ very thin slices of fish fillets, cut on a diagonal

♦ ½-inch cubes of fish fillets

♦ ¼-inch-thick slices of squid or cuttlefish, scored in a crisscross fashion with a knife

♦ slices of geoduck, octopus or abalone cut ⅛ inch thick or thinner, then cut into slices 3 inches long and 1 inch wide and finally tenderized gently with a mallet or scored in a crisscross fashion with a knife

♦ shrimp cut from the underside to make butterflies

As the handling of the raw seafood is critical in these Japanese dishes, I prefer to put myself in the hands of one of the many expert sushi chefs presiding in reputable Japanese restaurants. If the restaurants are well attended, you can be sure that the seafood is as fresh as it can be and is uncontaminated. Besides, it is fascinating to watch and learn from these experts. Sometimes I have fun and make my own sushi and sashimi when I know I can get very fresh seafood, especially if I or others have just caught the fish or shellfish. I'll take the precaution of freezing it for 2 days if it is fish from fresh water or other seafood that might be affected by parasites.

Seafood Salads

MADE WITH COOKED (LEFTOVER) FISH and shellfish, these salads are fast to assemble and delicious on hot days. Another recipe for shellfish salad is in the poaching section (see page 142).

Salsa-Flavored Fish Salad

Serves 6

Fish choices

Choose lean, white-fleshed, leftover cooked fish such as

bass

blackfish

catfish

cod

grouper

ocean pout

red snapper

salted cod (rehydrated and cooked; see page 250)

sea robin

sheepshead

skate

tilefish

whitefish

wolffish

Preparation time

25 minutes

Cooking time

None, unless leftover boneless fish is not available; 15 to 30 minutes if you must steam, bake or bake-poach raw fish

THIS FISH SALAD flavored with salsa is very quickly made, especially if you have leftover cooked fish and buy your favorite salsa.

1 recipe Tomato Salsa (page 196) or Tomatillo Salsa (page 197)

4 cups coarsely flaked cooked fish, skin and bones removed, if any

or

2 pounds steamed or baked fish fillets, skin and pin bones removed, if any

or

4 pounds steamed or bake-poached whole fish, skin and bones removed

Salt to taste

Freshly ground black or white pepper to taste

Boston lettuce, radicchio or endive leaves for decoration

1. Combine all the ingredients except the salad leaves in a bowl, being careful not to let the fish flake too much.

2. Line a platter with the salad leaves, and place the fish salad in the middle.

Summer Fish Salad

Serves 4

LEFTOVER FISH, POTATOES, CARROT, CELERY and dill create a fine summer dish.

¾ pound small red-skin potatoes, scrubbed

3 cups coarsely flaked cooked or smoked fish, skin and
 bones removed, if any

 or

1½ pounds steamed or baked fish fillets, skin and pin bones
 removed, if any

 or

3 pounds steamed or bake-poached whole fish, skin and
 bones removed

1 small carrot, peeled and coarsely grated

1 celery stalk, chopped into ¼-inch dice

3 tablespoons chopped fresh dill or parsley

¼ cup olive oil

¼ cup lemon juice

Salt to taste

Freshly ground black pepper to taste

Boston lettuce or radicchio leaves for decoration

1. Boil the potatoes in their skins for 20 minutes, until just tender and not falling apart. Run cold water over them, then drain and cut into quarters.

2. Combine all the remaining ingredients except the salad leaves in a bowl, being careful not to flake the fish too much.

3. Line a platter with the salad leaves, and place the fish salad in the middle.

Fish choices

Choose leftover boneless cooked or smoked fish such as

blackfish

bluefish

bonito

haddock

mackerel

mullet

ocean pout

porgy

sheepshead

trout

tuna

whitefish

Preparation time

30 minutes

Cooking time

20 minutes, plus 15 to 30 minutes if you must steam, bake or bake-poach raw fish

Scallop, Crab, Crawfish, Lobster or Shrimp Salad

Serves 2

Fish choices

Choose cooked shellfish, out of the shell, such as

bay or sea scallops *(small tough muscles removed)*

crabmeat *(picked over for cartilage)*

crawfish tail meat *(available frozen, peeled and deveined)*

lobster meat *(cut into ½-inch chunks)*

medium shrimp *(peeled, deveined and cut into ½-inch chunks)*

Preparation time

10 minutes

Cooking time

None

THIS CLASSIC SALAD is great served on lettuce leaves or in a roll.

8-12 ounces cooked shellfish meat, such as sea or bay scallops, crab, crawfish, lobster or shrimp
1-2 celery stalks, trimmed and chopped into ¼-inch dice
2 tablespoons finely chopped red bell pepper
¼ cup Basic Mayonnaise (page 198) or low-fat yogurt
2 teaspoons Dijon-type mustard (only for crabmeat salad)
2 tablespoons lemon juice
1 tablespoon chopped fresh dill or basil or coriander
Pinch cayenne or 6 drops Tabasco sauce
Salt to taste
Freshly ground white pepper to taste
Boston lettuce, radicchio or endive leaves for decoration

1. Combine all the ingredients except the salad leaves in a bowl.

2. Serve the shellfish salad on salad leaves arranged on individual plates.

Sauces and Condiments

Tomato Salsa

Makes 2 cups

Preparation time
15 minutes

Cooking time
None, except you must boil water to peel the tomatoes

TOMATO SALSA can accompany many fish dishes, particularly those using lean, white-fleshed fish and all fried or deep-fried fish dishes—it is far superior to ketchup and quite different.

3	medium to large ripe tomatoes, peeled, seeded and chopped into ¼-inch dice (see page 216)
¼	medium red onion, finely chopped (½ cup)
3	tablespoons chopped fresh coriander or parsley or basil
1	small jalapeño pepper, stems and seeds removed, finely chopped (1 tablespoon)
2	small garlic cloves, minced
3	tablespoons olive oil
3	tablespoons lemon juice
8	drops Tabasco sauce
	Salt to taste
	Freshly ground black pepper to taste

1. Drain the tomatoes for 15 minutes; you should have 2 cups drained.

2. Mix all the ingredients together.

3. Refrigerate, covered with plastic wrap, until chilled, about 20 minutes, before using.

Tomatillo Salsa

Makes 2 cups

YOU WILL FIND TOMATILLOS—green tomatolike vegetables from Mexico or California—in specialty produce stores and some Spanish supermarkets. They give a slightly more acidic—and distinctive—tomato taste to salsa than do tomatoes. Tomatillos are covered by papery husks, which are easily removed. They are really too acidic to eat raw and are best quartered and cooked until just tender.

Use the same ingredients as for Tomato Salsa (previous page), except use 1½ pounds tomatillos instead of tomatoes
1½ cups water
1 teaspoon sugar
Salt to taste

1. Remove the husks, and rinse the tomatillos.

2. Cut them into quarters, and put them in a saucepan with the water, sugar and salt.

3. Bring them to a boil over medium heat, and cook them for 2 to 3 minutes, just until they lose a little of their green color and are tender.

4. Drain them immediately, and run cold water over them.

5. Put them on a board, and chop them coarsely before proceeding with the Tomato Salsa recipe.

Preparation time
15 minutes

Cooking time
2 to 3 minutes

Basic Mayonnaise

Makes 1 cup

Preparation time
10 minutes

Cooking time
None

NOTHING BEATS HOMEMADE MAYONNAISE—it is simply a matter of practice to get it right. *Note*: This recipe contains a raw egg yolk. If you are worried about the possibility of contamination by salmonella, use commercial mayonnaise instead.

- 1 large egg yolk
- 1 tablespoon Dijon-style mustard
- ⅔ cup vegetable oil, such as canola, peanut, sunflower, safflower or corn oil
- ⅓ cup olive oil
- 1 tablespoon lemon juice, plus more to taste
  Salt to taste
- 1-2 tablespoons warm water if necessary

1. Using a wire whisk or an electric beater, beat the egg yolk and mustard together for about 3 minutes, until the mixture starts to turn a pale yellow.

2. Place the oils in a measuring cup or pitcher.

3. Add the oils, very gradually at first, in a thin stream as you continue beating the mixture. Then, as the mixture emulsifies and thickens, pour faster. *Note*: If the mixture separates and curdles, place another yolk in a clean bowl. Gradually introduce the curdled mixture, and it will emulsify again.)

4. Add the lemon juice and salt, and beat. Add the warm water if the mayonnaise needs thinning.

5. Taste for seasoning, adding more lemon juice and salt if necessary.

6. Place the mayonnaise in a clean bowl or container, and cover before refrigerating. It will keep for up to 5 days.

Mayonnaise for Lobster

Makes 1¼ cups

MAYONNAISE WITH ADDED LOBSTER ROE is a perfect accompaniment to hot or cold lobster meat. When cooking a female lobster, remove the roe or coral and break it up a little to separate, then mix it into Basic Mayonnaise.

Preparation time
15 minutes

Cooking time
None

Spicy Green Mayonnaise

Makes 1¼ cups

THIS MAYONNAISE CAN ACCOMPANY any cold seafood or cooked vegetables, such as broccoli or cauliflower, or coat a potato salad.

- 6 tablespoons finely chopped fresh parsley or coriander
- 1 small garlic clove, minced, then mixed and mashed with ¼ teaspoon salt
- 1 small jalapeño pepper, seeded and minced
- 1 teaspoon finely grated peeled ginger
- 1 recipe Basic Mayonnaise (previous page) or 1 cup commercial mayonnaise

Stir together the above ingredients until mixed well.

Preparation time
30 minutes

Cooking time
None

Harlequin Mayonnaise

Makes 3 cups

Preparation time
30 minutes

Cooking time
None

Tomato, yellow bell pepper, green olives and herbs make this a colorful and flavorful mayonnaise to accompany fish.

1 medium tomato, peeled, seeded and chopped into ¼-inch dice (see page 216)
1 medium yellow bell pepper cut into ¼-inch dice (1 cup)
10 Spanish olives (stuffed with pimientos), diced (¼ cup)
2 tablespoons finely chopped fresh parsley or tarragon
1 recipe Basic Mayonnaise (page 198) or
1 cup commercial mayonnaise

1. Drain the tomatoes for 15 minutes; you should have ¾ cup.

2. Combine all the ingredients, and mix well.

Aioli

Makes 2¼ cups

Preparation time
35 minutes

Cooking time
None

Aioli is a garlic mayonnaise that is an integral part of the fish soup called Bourride (page 160). It is also particularly tasty with steamed, grilled, broiled and deep-fried fish. For a delicious variation, you can spread it on fish fillets and broil, bake or steam them. *Note*: This recipe uses raw egg yolks. If you are worried about the possibility of contamination by salmonella, follow steps 1 and 2 and stir the ingredients into 2 cups commercial mayonnaise instead.

½ teaspoon saffron threads
2 tablespoons dry white wine
4 garlic cloves, peeled and crushed with the flat side of a heavy chef's knife
½ teaspoon coarse kosher salt
2 large egg yolks
1¼ cups vegetable oil, such as peanut, sunflower, safflower or corn oil
¾ cup olive oil
3 tablespoons lemon juice
1 or more tablespoons warm water if necessary

Salt to taste

Freshly ground white pepper to taste

1. Dissolve the saffron in the wine for 15 minutes, until the threads have softened.

2. Put the crushed garlic and coarse salt in a mortar or a medium-sized bowl, and work them together with a pestle or the back of a spoon until you have a coarse paste.

3. Transfer the garlic paste to a bowl if you used a mortar, and add the egg yolks.

4. Using a wire whisk or an electric beater, beat the garlic paste and egg yolks together.

5. Place the oils in a measuring cup or pitcher.

6. Add the oils, very gradually at first, then in a thin stream as you continue beating the mixture. As the mixture emulsifies and thickens, pour faster. *Note*: If the mixture separates and curdles, place another yolk in a clean bowl. Gradually introduce the curdled mixture, and it will emulsify again.

7. Add the lemon juice and the saffron mixture, and beat. Add the warm water if the aioli gets too thick.

8. Add salt and white pepper to taste.

9. Place the aioli in a clean bowl or container, and cover before refrigerating. It will keep for up to 5 days.

Lime and Dill Vinaigrette

Makes ⅔ cup
(Enough for seafood salad for 6 as a main course)

USE THIS VINAIGRETTE to make a seafood salad (page 142). *Note*: This recipe uses a raw egg yolk. If you are worried about the possibility of contamination by salmonella, use commercial mayonnaise instead.

Preparation time
15 minutes

Cooking time
None

- 2 tablespoons lime or lemon juice
- ½ large egg yolk or 2 teaspoons commercial mayonnaise
- 1 small garlic clove, minced
- ½ teaspoon salt
- ⅛ teaspoon freshly ground white pepper
- ½ cup olive oil
- 2 tablespoons finely chopped fresh dill or tarragon

1. Place the lime or lemon juice, egg yolk, garlic, salt and white pepper in a small bowl. Using a wire whisk or electric beater, beat together until light and frothy.

2. Add the oil in a thin stream until an emulsion is formed, then add it faster until the vinaigrette has thickened.

3. Stir in the dill or tarragon.

Sweet Red Pepper Sauce

Makes 1½ cups

THIS SAUCE GOES PERFECTLY with all kinds of seafood, for it is piquant—not hot and spicy, but sweet-sour. It has a wonderful color, and it can be made in exactly the same way with yellow bell peppers. This sauce can be made in advance and will keep covered in the refrigerator for 3 days.

- 3 red bell peppers (1-1½ pounds), stems, ribs and seeds removed, cut into 1½-inch squares
- 3 shallots, peeled and cut in half, or 1 small onion, coarsely chopped
- 3 garlic cloves
- ¼ cup olive oil
- 1 tablespoon water or dry white wine (optional)
- 1 tablespoon cider or raspberry vinegar
- 1 tablespoon lemon juice
- ¼ teaspoon salt
  Freshly ground white pepper to taste

1. *To cook on a stovetop*: Put the bell peppers, shallots or onion, garlic and oil in a medium-sized saucepan, and cover. Cook over low heat for 40 minutes, stirring occasionally, until all the vegetables are soft. Add the water or wine if the vegetables get dry.

2. *To microwave*: Put the bell peppers, shallots or onion, garlic, oil and water or wine in a small microwavable bowl or casserole dish, and cover with plastic wrap, leaving a vent at the edge. Cook on High for 12 to 14 minutes.

3. Process the bell-pepper mixture in a food processor or blender until very smooth, about 1 minute.

4. Add the vinegar, lemon juice, salt and white pepper; blend for another 5 seconds.

5. Store covered in the refrigerator for up to 3 days.

Special equipment
Small microwavable bowl or casserole dish (if using a microwave oven)
Plastic wrap (if using a microwave oven)

Preparation time
15 minutes

Cooking time
40 to 45 minutes (12 to 14 minutes in a microwave oven)

New Orleans-Style Barbecue Sauce

Makes 2 cups

Preparation time

5 minutes

Cooking time

15 minutes

THIS SAUCE IS HOT AND SPICY and suits a variety of seafood dishes. Serve this sauce as a dip with grilled, broiled or poached shrimp.

6 tablespoons (¾ stick) unsalted butter or ¼ cup olive oil (use butter if serving hot and oil if serving at room temperature)

3 garlic cloves, minced

¾ cup (6-ounce can) tomato paste

¼ cup Dijon-style mustard

1¼ cups cold water

1 teaspoon dried oregano

1 teaspoon freshly ground black pepper

½ teaspoon dried thyme

½ teaspoon cayenne

2 tablespoons Worcestershire sauce

2 tablespoons lemon juice

10 basil leaves, rinsed and dried, if necessary, finely shredded at the last moment

1. Heat the butter or oil in a medium frying pan over medium heat. When the butter or oil is hot, add the garlic and cook for 10 seconds, or until very lightly browned.

2. Lower the heat and add the tomato paste, mustard and water, stirring with a wire whisk. It will take a little time for these particular ingredients to mix together, but persevere.

3. Add all the remaining ingredients except the basil.

4. Cook for 10 to 12 minutes over low heat, stirring occasionally.

5. Just before serving, sprinkle on the shredded basil.

6. Store covered in the refrigerator for up to 3 days.

Spicy Basic Topping
FOR STEAMING, BROILING AND BAKING
OR FOR USE AS STUFFING

Makes ½ cup, enough for 2 pounds of seafood

GARLIC, GINGER, JALAPEÑO PEPPER and coriander or basil leaves can be sprinkled on fish as it is cooking or right afterward.

- 2 tablespoons minced garlic
- 2 tablespoons peeled and finely grated ginger
- 2 tablespoons chopped jalapeño pepper (seeded)
- 2 tablespoons finely chopped fresh coriander or basil

Mix all the ingredients together, and spread on seafood before cooking, or use as a stuffing for fish.

Preparation time
15 minutes

Cooking time
None

Lemon, Parsley and Garlic Topping
FOR STEAMING, BROILING AND BAKING
OR FOR USE AS STUFFING

Makes ¼ cup, enough for 1 pound of seafood

GRATED LEMON RIND, chopped parsley and minced garlic make a delicious topping for fish.

- 2 tablespoons finely grated lemon rind
- 2 tablespoons finely chopped fresh parsley
- 1 teaspoon minced garlic

Mix all the ingredients together, and spread on seafood before cooking, or use as a stuffing for fish.

Preparation time
2 minutes

Cooking time
None

Honeycup Mustard Sauce

Makes 1 cup

Preparation time

10 minutes

Cooking time

None

HONEYCUP MUSTARD IS SPICY and only somewhat sweet. Mixed with a little balsamic vinegar, olive oil and dill, it is a wonderful spread with gravlax, smoked salmon or other smoked fish. The ingredients for this sauce are a little unusual, but it is worth finding them, for the taste is highly addictive.

¼   cup honeycup mustard
1½ teaspoons balsamic vinegar
½   cup olive oil
1   tablespoon water
    Freshly ground white pepper to taste
1   packed tablespoon finely chopped fresh dill

1. Place the mustard and vinegar in a medium bowl.

2. Pour the oil into a measuring cup or pitcher, and add it slowly to the mustard mixture, whisking as if you were making mayonnaise.

3. Add the water and white pepper.

4. Fold in the chopped dill.

5. Store covered in the refrigerator for up to 1 week.

Lime, Ginger and Coriander Sauce

Makes 1 cup

SERVE THIS SPICY SAUCE with grilled, broiled or fried fish or shellfish.

Preparation time
10 minutes

Cooking time
None

Special equipment
Cheesecloth

1 tablespoon Dijon-style mustard
Grated zest of 1 lime
1 tablespoon lime juice
1 tablespoon finely grated ginger
¾ cup olive oil
Salt to taste
Freshly ground white pepper to taste
1 packed tablespoon finely chopped fresh coriander

1. Place the mustard, lime zest and juice in a medium bowl. Put the grated ginger in cheesecloth, and squeeze the juice into the bowl.

2. Using a wire whisk or electric beater, beat the mixture until opaque.

3. Place the oil in a measuring cup or pitcher, and add it to the mixture in a fine stream, as if you were making mayonnaise.

4. Add salt, white pepper and the coriander.

5. Store covered in the refrigerator for up to 2 days.

Coriander Pesto

Makes ⅔ cup

Preparation time
15 minutes

Cooking time
None

UNLIKE PESTO MADE WITH BASIL LEAVES, this coriander pesto does not need pine nuts and cheese to enrich it.

2 bunches coriander, leaves picked from stalks and rinsed and dried
1 garlic clove, minced
1 tablespoon lemon juice
¼ teaspoon salt
¼ cup olive oil

1. Place the coriander leaves, garlic, lemon juice and salt in a blender or food processor.

2. Blend or process for a minute or so until a fairly smooth puree is formed.

3. Finally, add the olive oil in a fine stream, and blend or process.

4. Store covered in the refrigerator for 1 day.

Flavored Butters

FLAVORED BUTTERS consist of different flavors folded or beaten into soft butter or margarine. The butters complement baked, broiled, grilled, steamed and poached seafood.

It is very easy to make these butters in a food processor; an electric beater or wire whisk can also be used. You can make some recipes up yourself—be as creative as you like, but be generous with the added flavorings, because the butter absorbs more than you would think.

To serve a flavored butter, you can pipe or spoon it onto cooked fish fillets or shellfish right away or shape the soft mixture into a log 1½ inches in diameter and roll it up in plastic wrap to be refrigerated and used later. (Flavored butters will generally keep for a week in the refrigerator. They can also be frozen.) When the log is fully chilled, you can cut it into wafers and place them on top of the cooked seafood, where they will melt and add zest to the dish. You can also place the butter on the side of the seafood, where it will melt as long as the plate is hot.

Basic Flavored Butter

Makes 1 cup

Preparation time
20 minutes

Cooking time
None

Butter seasoned with lemon juice, salt and pepper is a basic butter to which you can add other flavorings. When chilled in a log shape, it can be sliced and placed on freshly grilled, broiled or baked fish.

  1 cup (2 sticks) unsalted butter or margarine, each stick
       cut into 5 pieces
  2 tablespoons lemon juice
  ½ teaspoon salt or more to taste
       Freshly ground black or white pepper to taste

1. Take the butter or margarine out of the refrigerator to soften it. It can be softened in the microwave oven.

2. Put the butter or margarine in a food processor, and process until it gets airy and lightens in color.

3. Add the lemon juice, salt and pepper. *Note*: Do not add the salt if you are going to add salty ingredients, such as anchovies or soy sauce.

4. Add flavorful ingredients of your choice, and process until well blended, or scrape the butter into a bowl and fold in the other ingredients with a plastic spatula or spoon.

5. Use right away, or place on plastic wrap and shape into a log before storing in the refrigerator.

Anchovy Butter

Makes 1¼ cups

Anchovies, butter, lemon juice and mint leaves make up this tasty butter. Spread on bread, or serve with fresh broiled or grilled sardines.

1 cup (2 sticks) unsalted butter or margarine, each stick
    cut into 5 pieces
2 tablespoons lemon juice
    Freshly ground black or white pepper to taste
1 2-ounce can of anchovies or 15 anchovies drained of
    most of their oil
25 mint leaves, finely chopped
    Salt only to taste—the anchovies will salt the butter

Using a food processor, follow Basic Flavored Butter (previous page) instructions through step 3, using the ingredients above. Then add the rest of the ingredients.

Preparation time
20 minutes

Cooking time
None

Snail Butter
(Garlic and Parsley Butter)

Makes ¾ cup

This famous butter is used with snails, but it's also delicious with fish or steamed mussels or clams.

8 tablespoons (1 stick) unsalted butter or margarine,
    cut into 5 pieces
1 tablespoon lemon juice
½ teaspoon salt
    Freshly ground white pepper to taste
3 garlic cloves, minced
3 tablespoons finely chopped fresh parsley

1. Using a food processor, follow Basic Flavored Butter (previous page) instructions through step 3, then add the garlic.

2. Fold in the parsley with a plastic or rubber spatula.

Preparation time
20 minutes

Cooking time
None

Variation
For a milder, sweeter garlic taste, boil unpeeled garlic cloves for 10 minutes in water. Drain and peel the cloves, then mash with the flat side of a knife.

Garlic, Basil and Tomato Butter

Makes ¾ cup

Preparation time
25 minutes

Cooking time
None

USE THIS WONDERFUL BUTTER to brush on mussels on the half shell, then broil them. Or serve with broiled, grilled or sautéed fish.

- 8 tablespoons (1 stick) unsalted butter or margarine, cut into 5 pieces
- 1 tablespoon lemon juice
- 1 teaspoon salt
  Freshly ground black pepper to taste
- 3 garlic cloves, minced
- ¼ cup finely chopped fresh basil
- 3 tablespoons Tomato Concassée (page 216)

1. Using a food processor, follow Basic Flavored Butter (page 210) instructions through step 3, then add the garlic.

2. Fold in the basil and Tomato Concassée with a plastic or rubber spatula.

Chive and Toasted Sesame Seed Butter

Makes 1 cup

Preparation time
15 minutes

Cooking time
None

MAKE USE OF THIS ASIAN-FLAVORED BUTTER with fish such as black sea bass, red snapper or rockfish.

- 8 tablespoons (1 stick) unsalted butter or margarine, cut into 5 pieces
- 1 tablespoon lemon juice
- 1 tablespoon soy sauce
- 2 teaspoons sesame oil (Oriental-style)
- 2 tablespoons finely chopped fresh chives
- 2 tablespoons toasted sesame seeds

1. Using a food processor, follow Basic Flavored Butter (page 210) instructions through step 3, then add the soy sauce and sesame oil.

2. Fold in the chives and sesame seeds with a plastic or rubber spatula.

Shrimp, Lobster or Crawfish Butter

Makes 1¼ cups

THIS BUTTER IS DELICIOUS when spread on freshly cooked fish or added to a shrimp, lobster or crawfish bisque.

Preparation time
15 minutes

Cooking time
13 minutes

- 1 cup (2 sticks) unsalted butter or margarine, each stick cut into 5 pieces
- 4 cups uncooked shrimp shells from peeled raw shrimp

  or
- 4 cups broken lobster shells from cooked lobster, ground up in a food processor; do not use claw shells—they are too hard

  or
- 4 cups crawfish shells, collected from cooked crawfish, ground up in a food processor
- ½ cup dry white wine
- 1 teaspoon salt
- ½ teaspoon paprika
- ⅛ teaspoon cayenne

  Freshly ground white pepper to taste

1. Heat 1 stick of the butter or margarine in a frying pan over medium heat. Add the shellfish shells, and cook slowly, stirring occasionally for 7 to 10 minutes.

2. Put the shells and butter or margarine in the bowl of a food processor.

3. Stir the white wine and the salt, paprika, cayenne and white pepper. Add this to the food processor.

4. Process for 1 minute, then add the second stick of butter or margarine, and blend, scraping the sides of the bowl now and again.

5. Push the mixture through the fine mesh of a food mill or strainer (with a spatula).

6. Place it on plastic wrap, and shape it into a log before storing it in the refrigerator.

Related Cooking Techniques

How to Julienne Carrots, Leeks and Celery

A JULIENNE OF VEGETABLES is a pretty and appetizing accompaniment to many dishes. You need to achieve very thin matchstick or strawlike lengths of vegetable, about 2 to 3 inches long. Although it is a little tedious to do, the end result is most attractive. The thinner the julienne, the better.

Carrots

1. Peel a carrot.

2. Cut off the ends of the carrot, and cut it into 2-to-3-inch lengths.

3. Cut the carrot into very thin lengthwise slices, then cut these slices, stacked a few at a time, into thin julienne.

Leeks

1. Trim a leek at the bottom root end, and cut off the tough part of the green leaves.

2. Cut the leek in half lengthwise, and rinse it thoroughly.

3. Now cut the leek into 2-to-3-inch lengths.

4. Take a piece of the leek and put it on the board, inside down, and press it flat.

5. Cut it into very thin julienne.

Celery

This is the most difficult of the three to cut into a fine julienne.

1. Trim both ends of a celery stalk, and cut it into 2-to-3-inch lengths.

2. Holding the celery stalk in your left hand, with the inside of the stalk facing up, cut the stalk lengthwise into very thin slices or slivers, then cut these into very thin julienne.

How to Peel, Seed and
Chop Tomatoes (Tomato Concassée)

Preparation time

*Approximately 4 minutes
for each tomato*

Cooking time

30 seconds

CHOPPED TOMATO WITHOUT SKIN, seeds or juice is a must for some of the recipes in this book. Use ripe tomatoes, preferably sun-ripened. In the winter, I resort to plum tomatoes if they are the ones with the most color and flavor.

1. Bring a saucepan of water to a boil.

2. Immerse the tomatoes in the water for 30 seconds.

3. Take the tomatoes out of the water with a slotted spoon, and place them under cold running water.

4. Peel off the skins, and cut out the blossom ends.

5. Cut the tomatoes in half crosswise, and squeeze out the seeds and juice. Cut the flesh into ¼-inch-wide slices, ¼-inch-wide lengths and then into ¼-inch dice.

Clarified Butter

Makes ¾ cup

CLARIFIED BUTTER is useful for frying and sautéing fish. Because the milk solids and water are removed, it can stand high heat without burning. It is a good idea always to have some on hand; once made, clarified butter will keep for a week or so in the refrigerator.

Remember, clarified butter does not have the same flavor as whole butter.

Preparation time
1 minute

Cooking time
15 minutes

1   cup (2 sticks) unsalted butter

1. Cut each stick of butter into 5 pieces, and put the pieces in a saucepan over low heat.

2. When the butter is melted, take the pan off the heat and let it stand for 5 minutes.

3. Using a large spoon, spoon off the milk solids from the top and discard.

4. Pour the clarified butter into a bowl until you see the watery liquid at the bottom of the saucepan. Carefully spoon off the rest of the clarified butter, and discard the rest.

5. Let the clarified butter cool before refrigerating.

Herbs and Spices

These lists are only suggestions. Herbs and seasonings are a question of personal taste.

Herbs for lean fish

basil
bay leaf
chervil
coriander
dill
parsley
tarragon
thyme

Seasonings for lean fish

allspice
cumin
grated lemon rind
lemon juice
lime juice
mustard
nutmeg
paprika
saffron
salt
white pepper

Herbs for fatty fish

basil
dill
marjoram
mint
oregano
rosemary
savory
thyme

(Some of these herbs are mild, such as dill, but if used in quantity, they more than make up for their mildness.)

Seasonings for fatty fish

allspice
black pepper
chili peppers
cumin
dark or light Worcestershire sauce
fennel seed
garlic

ginger
ground coriander
lemon juice
lemon rind
lime juice
mustard
onion
paprika
salt
soy sauce
teriyaki marinade

When using fresh herbs such as parsley, basil, coriander, mint and dill, rinse the leaves, shake them free of water, pat them dry and take the leaves off the stems before chopping. Sprigs are very decorative and can be used on the finished plate.

It is impossible to gauge how hot fresh chili peppers will taste by looking at them.

Different chili peppers taste different—some are definitely hotter than others. Cross-pollination with a milder pepper may inadvertently cause some to lack heat altogether. The only reliable thing to do is to taste a very small piece of a chili pepper before using it. Use rubber gloves if you like when seeding and chopping hot peppers. Bottled and canned jalapeño peppers are perfectly all right to use if you cannot get them fresh.

I like the flat-leaf Italian parsley for flavor and looks. Curly parsley has its own character and is useful too. Do not chop these parsleys into a green dust—there is nothing worse. Chop finely. Separate parsley leaves picked off sprigs are a lovely decoration also.

I prefer using kosher salt when I cook, for it is pure and unadulterated. I have two pepper grinders: one for black peppercorns, the other for white peppercorns.

Wines

We usually drink white wines with seafood dishes because they complement each other particularly well. Dry, light white wines go very well with delicately flavored seafood, but heavier whites, such as the big rich Chardonnays, go beautifully with the stronger-flavored seafood, especially shellfish. Oysters deserve crisp, dry whites, and the spicy white wine Gewürztraminer stands up to smoked salmon, trout and mackerel.

A cold dry sherry such as a Fino or Manzanilla marries well with shrimp dishes. I also find that a light Chianti (red wine) is a wonderful complement to, for instance, a smoked haddock soufflé. A Merlot or Beaujolais, also red wines, are just fine as well. These red wines can be treated as white wines and chilled if you want.

There are innumerable fine white wines from all over the world at varying prices and quality. No doubt your local liquor store will have a large variety to choose from.

The following gives some idea of the types of wines that go with the different tastes of fish and shellfish and their cooking methods. Some wines are listed by the name of the grape, and others are named by type but rarely by the particular name of the producer.

It is best to avoid general brand names, for they usually denote large production of an inferior wine.

SIMPLE, DELICATELY FLAVORED PREPARATIONS

Vinho Verde (Portugal)
Galestro (Italy)
Vernaccia (Italy)
Bourgogne Aligoté (France)
Bordeaux Sauvignons (France)
Muscadet (Loire Valley, France)
Pouilly-Fumé (Loire Valley, France)
Very dry, ultra brut and brut sauvage
    champagnes (France)

Edelzwicker (Alsace)
New Zealand Sauvignons
Oregon Sauvignons and Chardonnays

CREAM AND BUTTER PREPARATIONS

Washington Sauvignons
White Burgundies (France)
White Riojas (Spain)
Torres Viña Sol (Spain)
Long Island Chardonnays
California Chardonnays

PREPARATIONS FOR RICH FATTY FISH

Sonoma Chardonnays (U.S.A.)
Pinot Grigio (Italy)
Sancerre (Loire Valley, France)
New Zealand Chardonnays
Chianti (Italy)
Beaujolais (France)
Merlot (France, Italy, U.S.A.)

SMOKED FISH AND GRILLED FISH

Gewürztraminer (Alsace)
Tokay (Alsace)
Riesling (Alsace)
Riesling (Germany)
Sylvaner (Germany)
Australian dry Sémillon

HOT AND SPICY PREPARATIONS

Chianti (Italy)
Beaujolais (France)
Australian Chardonnays
Riesling Spätlese (Germany)

In addition, here is a list of some wines I have enjoyed, particularly with fish and seafood dishes, in recent years.

FRANCE

Burgundy: Chardonnays, such as the delectable, crisp, elegant Chablis (not to be confused with the generic types), and fuller wines, such as Pouilly-Fuissé, Meursault, Puligny-Montrachet, Chassagne-Montrachet, Corton-Charlemagne from Burgundy and, on the lighter side, Mâcon-Villages, Bourgogne Aligoté, Montagny and Moreau Blanc.

Bordeaux: Dry Graves, Entre-Deux-Mers and Sauvignon Blancs.

Loire Valley: Pouilly-Fumé, dry Vouvray, Saumur, Sancerre, Saint Pourçain-sur-Sioule and Muscadet de Sèvre et Maine. These wines have been developed so that they are perfect with the freshwater fish of the Loire Valley and the shellfish from the nearby Atlantic Coast.

Provence: White and rosé Bandol, white Cassis and Côtes de Provence.

Midi: Listel Vin des Sables from the Camargue and Blanquette de Limoux, a sparkling dry white wine.

Alsace: Dry Gewürztraminers, Rieslings, Muscats, Tokays and the reasonably priced Edelzwickers.

FROM THE UNITED STATES

California: The most appropriate wines from California are from Sonoma County and the lower Napa Valley, where the lighter wines are produced. Sauvignon Blancs, Pinot Blancs and Chardonnays from Chateau St. Jean, Grgich-Hills, Stag's Leap, Trefethen, Wente, Robert Mondavi, Firestone, Sterling, Simi, Fetzer, Heitz, Stony Hill, Kalin, Domaine Michel, Silverado and Souverain.

Oregon: Chardonnays, Pinot Gris, dry Muscats and Pinot Noir Blancs from Knudsen Erath, Eyrie and Tualatin.

Idaho: Chardonnay and Chenin Blanc from Ste. Chapelle.

Washington: Riesling, Sauvignon Blanc and Sémillon from Château Ste. Michelle.

New York: Chardonnays, Rieslings and Seyval-Villards from Dr. Frank Konstantin, Heron Hill, Bully Hill and Wagner (Finger Lakes).

Sauvignons and Chardonnays from Hargrave, Lenz and Palmer (North Fork, Long Island) and Bridgehampton (South Fork, Long Island).

Pennsylvania: Chardonnay, Riesling and Seyval Blanc from Chaddsford Winery (Chadds Ford).

OTHER COUNTRIES

Italy: From northern Italy in the Alto Adige area (by the Alps) come the light, crisp Pinot Grigios and Pinot Blancs. Other northern wines from the Veneto region are Proseccos and the better Soaves. From Tuscany come other light wines such as the Vernaccia di San Gimignano and the lovely Orvietos such as Orvieto Bigi and Chiantis, both red and white. Look for the white Chianti called Galestro.

Far south there are fuller white wines, such as the Frascati from near Rome and the Verdicchios from the Adriatic coast. See the Verdicchio Castelli Gesi.

Portugal: Vinho Verde, particularly good when young, when it has a little spritz in it.

Spain: White Riojas: Marqués de Cáceres, Marqués de Riscal and Marqués de Murrieta (best to drink when young); Penedés, Torres Viña Sol; Sherries: Fino and Manzanilla.

Germany: Kabinett, quality Riesling and Silvaner. Look for *trochen* (dry) on the label (particularly in the Baden area).

Australia: Chardonnays, Rieslings and Muscats from Brown Brothers, Rosemount and Lindemans and a dry Sémillon from Hunter Valley.

New Zealand: Chardonnay and Sauvignon Blanc from Corbans. There are many exciting new wines being imported now from New Zealand. The temperate climate makes them fresh and fragrant—in particular, those made with the Sauvignon Blanc grape—and excellent with simply cooked seafood.

PART III

Profiles

A Guide to Common Fish and Shellfish

THE FOLLOWING PROFILES of the fish and shellfish that you are most likely to see at the fish store are meant to help you distinguish between them easily and learn the best ways to prepare and cook them. All but a few of these varieties are caught or garnered in fresh and sea waters in and around the United States; the rest are European species that are marketed here.

Some of the profiles group together related species of fish or shellfish. One profile, for example, discusses the various members of the cod group; another discusses drums, croakers and other members of the same family; still another, for purposes of convenience, groups together all the flatfish. If you have difficulty finding a particular variety of fish and shellfish, the index will direct you.

Each entry begins with the most common name of a fish, shellfish or group of related varieties, followed by the scientific name; this is the surest means of identifica-

tion, since it is the most consistent. Other names are also given, whether they are scientifically accurate or not, if they are commonly used by fishmongers.

Wherever possible, the profiles list statistical information relating to health—amounts of cholesterol in milligrams and omega-3 fatty acids and fat in grams per 100 grams (3.5 ounces) raw seafood. Omega-3 fatty acids include EPA (eicosapentaenoic acid) and DHA (docosahexaenoic acid) only. N/A indicates information is not available.

In addition, each profile designates the variety of seafood as low, moderate or high in fat—low fat means less than 5 percent, moderate fat is between 5 and 10 percent, high fat is more than 10 percent.

Each profile notes the forms (other than whole) in which the fish or shellfish is usually found in the fish store or the forms you can ask the fishmonger to prepare for you— fillets, steaks, split, pan-dressed, chunks. (See

"Useful Terms You Will Need to Know," page 23.)

Each profile also provides a description of the taste and texture of the fish or shellfish when cooked. Keep in mind that these descriptions are relative—I have described only some kinds of seafood as "mild," but in fact, all seafood is mild-tasting when raw or cooked, although some varieties have more flavor than others. (If seafood tastes really strong, it is probably old and should be thrown away, although strong tastes can also come from curing with salt or salty brines.) I have also described some kinds of fish as "firm," not because they never flake but because they do not flake as easily as other varieties. (All fish will eventually flake if overcooked.)

A description is given of each variety of fish or shellfish, including its usual marketed size, its colors, its availability and where it can be found or caught. Seafood is available year-round from one body of water or another. Generally speaking, a number of kinds of fish become more available from south to north up the east coast (to take an example) as the waters warm during spring and summer.

Most of the profiles include a table listing available forms or cuts, cooking methods for these cuts and suggestions for how much to buy for a given number of people. Each profile ends with a choice of recommended recipes from Part II.

Abalone

Genus *Haliotis*

Cholesterol: 85 Omega-3: N/A Fat: 0.8

Fat content
low

**Form usually
prepared**
slices

Taste
sweet and buttery

Texture
firm but melting

THE ABALONE IS A UNIVALVE. We eat the flesh that lies inside its single beautiful shell. The shell is iridescent mother-of-pearl inside, and the outside ranges in color from pink to red, green or black. The flesh is much treasured because it is so delicious; it is unfortunately also hard to come by nowadays, which probably adds to its attraction.

Abalone are found in the Pacific Ocean off Alaska, California, Chile and Southeast Asia. In the Pacific, not only have they been overfished, but the otters that populate the west coast of the United States relish them. The supply of abalone is also suffering because supplies of the seaweeds upon which they live are dwindling.

A European abalone called the ormer is found off Jersey in the Channel Islands.

Baby abalone are farmed in Hawaii and California. These flavorful little morsels make a delightful appetizer. Save the shells—they are very decorative. Most recently, Alaskan waters have begun producing some varieties of abalone that are small but slightly larger than those farmed farther south. These have red shells, and the flesh inside weighs about 4 ounces, enough for a main course.

Abalone are usually available at Japanese fish stores and at other specialty fish stores. They are usually sold in the shell at a set price per piece. They should be alive when you buy them. If there is some reaction when you touch the dark fringe and flesh in the shell of an abalone, then it is alive. The flesh of a commercially available abalone weighs from 1 to 8 ounces.

How to Shuck Abalone

♦ Push a wide spatula or a knife under the abalone flesh to detach it from the shell. Once the flesh is out of the shell, use a sharp knife to cut off the dark fringe that surrounds the flesh and scrape off any dark skin. Cut away the dark intestinal vein. Now you should have a nice piece of slightly off-white flesh.

♦ You can eat abalone raw or cook it very briefly. To eat it raw, cut the flesh (downward if the abalone is large and horizontally if it is small) into very thin slices. To cook it, cut the flesh into slices ¼ inch thick and pound gently with a smooth-headed mallet—be careful not to pound too hard, or you will tear the flesh. Or cut slices ⅛ inch thick and do not pound them. Fry them only for a few seconds. The flesh becomes unusually sweet and flavorful when cooked.

COOKING METHODS

Cut	Cooking Methods	Serves	How Much to Buy
Thin slices	Frying	1	4 ounces
Thin slices	Sushi, sashimi	1	4 ounces

CHOICE OF RECIPES

Fried Abalone à la Meunière, page 122
Sushi and Sashimi, page 189

Anchovy

Canned or salted
Cholesterol: N/A   Omega-3: 2.0   Fat: 9.7

Fresh
Cholesterol: N/A   Omega-3: 1.4   Fat: 4.1

A NCHOVIES ARE HARVESTED worldwide. Those native to the United States are found in both the Atlantic (*Anchoa hepsetus*) and the Pacific (*Engraulis mordax*). There are many species, and most are caught too small to do anything with, other than deep-fry whole, ungutted, as you would with whitebait. However, larger anchovies—like those from the Mediterranean (*Engraulis encrasicholus*) and, on rare occasions, from U.S. waters—can be gutted (pull out the gills; see page 42 for instructions) and then grilled. They are delicious little silvery streamlined creatures. Those anchovies which are not sold fresh or canned are used for bait or made into fish meal.

Of course, we usually buy canned anchovies, either in oil or salted. By the way, anchovies are not naturally salty; the salt is part of the cure. Either people like these flavorsome fish or they don't, but anchovies can be intriguing in many dishes, and they are practically unrecognizable when cooked into a meat or game stew to deepen flavor. Be sure to tell people that the anchovies are there, for some dislike them intensely and others are allergic to them. They do well as a garnish for salade niçoise, with roasted red bell peppers, on top of a pizza or in a cheese pie. Rinse canned salted anchovies before using.

Fat content
high (canned or salted anchovies); low (fresh anchovies)

Forms usually prepared
fillets (canned or salted); whole (fresh)

Taste
strong, salty (canned or salted); mild (fresh)

Texture
firm (canned or salted); flaky (fresh)

Anchovies are also made into a paste, which is a handy way of using them in some dishes. Anchovy butter, a mixture of butter and ground-up canned or salted anchovies, is a great accompaniment to many fish—for example, sardines or even milder lean white-fleshed fish such as red snapper. (See the recipe on page 211.)

COOKING METHODS

Cut	Cooking Methods	Serves	How Much to Buy
Whole	Grilling	1	¾ to 1 pound
Whole	Broiling	1	¾ to 1 pound
Whole	Deep-frying	1	6 to 8 ounces

CHOICE OF RECIPES

Broiled Whole Roundfish, page 98
Grilled Whole Fish or Shellfish, page 107
Deep-Fried Seafood with Seasoned Flour, page 131

Bass, Black Sea

Centropristis striata
Cholesterol: 41   Omega-3: 0.6   Fat: 2.0

Fat content
low

Forms usually prepared
fillets, butterflied or split fish

Taste
mild

Texture
flaky

THE BLACK SEA BASS, which is often just called the sea bass, is a magnificent fish. Its flesh is very similar in excellence to that of red snapper and striped bass. It is wonderful-looking, black with light coloring under each scale and beautiful articulated spiny fins, also black, striated with white markings. It's one of my favorite fish. Black sea bass tastes sweet, and its flesh is firm, lean and white.

The black sea bass is fished from the Atlantic, from Maine down to Florida. It usually weighs between 1 and 3 pounds when caught, but it does grow to 5 pounds. By the way, don't confuse the black sea bass with the blackfish, also called the tautog or tog, which is another species altogether (see page 232).

At the fish store, black sea bass are usually sold whole. Of course, you can ask the fishmonger to fillet one for you or split it—that is, butterfly it—as described on page 47. The beauty of this fish's skin is retained not only when it is cooked whole but also when it is cooked in filleted form with the skin showing.

Black sea bass can be prepared by many cooking methods.

COOKING METHODS

CUT	COOKING METHODS	SERVES	HOW MUCH TO BUY
Whole	Roasting	4	3 pounds
Whole	Broiling, grilling	1 to 4	1 to 3 pounds
Whole pan-dressed	Frying	1	¾ to 1 pound
Whole	Deep-frying	1	¾ to 1 pound
Whole	Poaching	1	1 pound
Fillets	As listed below	1	6 to 8 ounces
Butterflied or split	As listed below	1	8 to 10 ounces

CHOICE OF RECIPES

Baked Lean Fish Fillets, page 75

Bake-Poached Fish Fillets, page 79

Oven-Steamed Seafood en Papillote, page 80

Roast Whole Fish, page 89

Broiled Whole Roundfish, page 98

Broiled Fillets, Butterflied or Split Fish, Steaks, Escalopes or Medallions, page 100

Grilled Whole Fish, page 107

Grilled Fish Fillets, Butterflied or Split Fish, Steaks or Medallions, page 109

Fried Whole Fish or Pan-Dressed Fish, page 124

Fish Croquettes, page 125

Deep-Fried Seafood with Cornmeal Coating, page 132

Poached Small Whole Fish or Fish Fillets, page 140

Steamed Seafood, page 146

Fish Soup (Bourride), page 160

Seafood Stew or Pasta Sauce, page 165

Fish Fillets with Spinach and Ginger, page 178

Seviche, page 183

Escabèche, page 184

Salsa-Flavored Fish Salad, page 192

Bass, Striped
Morone saxatilis
Cholesterol: 80   Omega-3: 0.8   Fat: 2.3

Fat content
low

Forms usually prepared
fillets, steaks

Taste
sweet

Texture
firm

ALAS, the fish from the Atlantic Coast, also called the striper and the rockfish down Chesapeake Bay way, is not always available. There are restrictions on its catch because of overfishing and pollution in the rivers where it is hatched before it migrates to the ocean. Sportsmen, however, are allowed to catch fish that measure 36 inches and up. Striped bass have been successfully transplanted to the Pacific off California, where they are important for recreational fishing.

Some smart farmers are breeding a hybrid freshwater striped bass, which is some consolation. White bass or white perch (freshwater fish) have been interbred with striped bass to produce this hybrid (*M. chrysops* x *M. saxatilis* and *M. americanus* x *M. saxatilis*), which has excellent flesh—firm and sweet but a little bland in overall taste. It is incorrectly called white bass in the Chesapeake Bay area. In my opinion, this breed is just not the same and can't compare with the lovely striped bass from the Atlantic Ocean, which has such a fine yet firm texture and an exquisite taste. Treat the freshwater striped bass much like other bass, red snappers or rockfish.

Whole striped bass, when available, grow up to 125 pounds, though they are usually caught at less than 50 pounds. Freshwater hybrid striped bass are available only at weights ranging from 1½ to 3 pounds, usually ungutted.

COOKING METHODS

Cut	Cooking Methods	Serves	How Much to Buy
Whole	Roasting	2 to 14	1½ to 9 pounds
Whole	Broiling, grilling	1 to 8	1 to 6 pounds
Whole	Frying	1	1 pound
(freshwater striped bass only)			
Chunks	Roasting	2 to 8	1½ to 4 pounds
(wild striped bass only)			
Fillets	As listed below	1	6 to 8 ounces
Steaks	As listed below	1	6 to 8 ounces
(wild striped bass only)			

CHOICE OF RECIPES

Baked Lean Fish Fillets, page 75

Bake-Poached Fish Fillets, page 79

Roast Whole Fish, page 89

Roast Stuffed Fish Chunk, page 92

Broiled Whole Roundfish, page 98

Broiled Fillets, Butterflied or Split Fish, Steaks, Escalopes or Medallions, page 100

Grilled Whole Fish, page 107

Grilled Fish Fillets, Butterflied or Split Fish, Steaks or Medallions, page 109

Fried Fish Fillets or Fish Steaks à la Meunière, page 122

Fried Whole Fish or Pan-Dressed Fish, page 124

Fish Croquettes, page 125

Bass, White

Morone chrysops

Cholesterol: 68   Omega-3: 0.6   Fat: 3.7

THIS FRESHWATER FISH comes from the lakes, reservoirs, rivers and estuaries of the United States and Canada from the East Coast across to the Mississippi. It's a small fish but a good fighter and a favorite with sports fishermen. The flesh is white and firm and can be treated like black sea bass, striped bass, snapper or rockfish. The fish is silvery and is marketed at weights from ½ to 2 pounds; it is essentially a pan fish.

There are numerous other freshwater fish called bass, such as the smallmouth, largemouth, redeye, rock and spotted varieties. These are actually members of the sunfish family (see page 353). White sea bass from the Pacific, also called white bass and *corbina* (the Spanish name for the croaker), and channel bass from the Gulf of Mexico are members of the drum and croaker family (see page 267). Also see the discussion of sea bass of the grouper family (page 283).

Fat content
low

Form usually prepared
pan-dressed fish

Taste
mild

Texture
flaky

COOKING METHODS

Cut	Cooking Methods	Serves	How Much to Buy
Whole pan-dressed	Broiling, grilling, frying	1	¾ to 1 pound
Fillets	Broiling, grilling	1	6 to 8 ounces
Butterflied or split	Broiling, grilling	1	8 to 10 ounces

Blackfish

Tautoga onitis

Cholesterol: *N/A* **Omega-3:** *N/A* **Fat: 0.2**

THE BLACKFISH is a member of the wrasse family (Labridae). It is also called by the American Indian name *tautog* or just plain *tog*. This creature with mottled coloring has thick lips (the male has thicker lips than the female), a set of four long, very humanlike teeth in the front of its mouth and more molars behind. With these teeth, it eats its diet of crustaceans and mollusks.

Blackfish are caught in the Atlantic from Cape Cod down to the Carolinas and are available most of the year, although they are most plentiful during the summer. It is fun to catch them with hook and line around rocks.

The usual size of a blackfish is 2 to 5 pounds. Blackfish are sold whole and in filleted form. The flesh is white and firm but fairly bland, and it needs a flavorful sauce or accompaniment such as Sweet Red Pepper Sauce (page 203) or one of the other sprightly mixtures to brighten its taste. The skin can be lifted off easily when serving. I like to poach blackfish whole, with head and tail, to show off their blotchy skin and strange teeth.

Fat content
low

**Form usually
prepared**
fillets

Taste
mild

Texture
slightly firm

COOKING METHODS

CUT	COOKING METHODS	SERVES	HOW MUCH TO BUY
Whole	Poaching	6	5 pounds
Fillets	Blackening	1	8 to 10 ounces
Fillets	As listed below	1	6 to 8 ounces

CHOICE OF RECIPES

Blowfish

Sphaeroides maculatus

Cholesterol: N/A   Omega-3: N/A   Fat: (Cooked flesh) 0.7

Fat content
low

Form usually prepared
skinned tail pieces

Taste
sweet

Texture
flaky

BLOWFISH, also known as northern puffers, pufferfish, sea squabs, swellfish, swell toads, blow toads and chicken of the sea, live in the waters along the eastern Atlantic Coast. They are easy to catch in inshore waters, but they are not always available, for their appearance in these waters comes and goes. They are usually caught when they are 3 to 8 inches long.

Blowfish have white bellies and are brown on top (this color changes to yellow), and they have powerful teeth. They puff up their prickly skin when in danger. If you catch a blowfish yourself, handle it with rubber gloves. Cut off the head, and turn the skin inside out to expose the flesh. Pull off the flesh. Dispose of the guts, and it is ready to cook; you do not need to fillet it. Under no circumstances should the skin, roe or digestive system of a blowfish be eaten, because they contain toxins. Blowfish are available in fish stores already skinned and ready to cook (see page 54).

The blowfish is a delicious fish to eat once skinned. Its central backbone is covered with sweet, moist flesh, and as there are no other bones to contend with, it can be eaten with the fingers like a chicken drumstick. Blowfish are delicious quickly sautéed, broiled, grilled or braised. Depending on the size of the blowfish, one person can eat up to five pieces.

COOKING METHODS

Cut	Cooking Methods	Serves	How Much to Buy
Whole, skinned, tail pieces	As listed below	1	6 to 8 ounces

CHOICE OF RECIPES

Broiled Fillets, Escalopes or Medallions, page 100
Grilled Whole Fish, page 107
Sautéed Blowfish, page 126
Braised Fish Fillets with Provençal Sauce, page 156

Bluefish

Pomatomus saltatrix

Cholesterol: 59   Omega-3: 0.8   Fat: 4.2

THESE FINE FISH are favorites of mine, especially in the summer. They are attractive-looking, with their silvery blue skin and streamlined bodies, and they have rich and flavorful flesh. What a delight they are to cook and eat!

Bluefish are caught year-round along different parts of the western Atlantic Coast, from Cape Cod down to Florida, most notably between North Carolina and Massachusetts, where large and small ones appear in the late spring and summer as the waters grow warmer. Bluefish are also found in the eastern Atlantic, especially in the Mediterranean and off the coast of South Africa, as well as off the east coast of Australia.

Many of these fierce and lively fighting fish are caught by sports fishermen, who sell them to commercial markets or give them away to friends if they have caught more than they need—many friends have given me freshly caught bluefish during the summers on Long Island. Bluefish travel in large schools and can sometimes be seen near the surface of the ocean when they are pursuing other fish—which may, incidentally, be close to their own size. Anglers of all ages have fun catching bluefish from the ocean surface as well as in deep ocean waters, in fast-running inlets and even off docks, when they are "running." John Hersey has written a wonderful book called *Blues*—a beautiful, lyrical discourse on fishing for bluefish in New England waters.

Bluefish are voracious eaters, and consequently, they grow fast. They are caught at weights up to 20 pounds, although they are usually sold weighing 1 to 10 pounds. Young bluefish weighing a pound or two are called snappers; when larger, they may be called choppers or harbor blues. Snappers have lighter, sweeter flesh, probably because they are young.

Bluefish are sold whole or as skin-on fillets. They are very reasonable in price. Even more than most fish, they are at their most delicious when they are fresh. The flesh of bluefish is somewhat soft and perishable, so I eat only extremely fresh blues. Their flesh should look firm and translucent and be a light blue-gray with a brownish tinge. They should be gutted as soon as possible to help forestall deterioration. I cannot stress this enough—amateur fishermen

Fat content
moderate

Forms usually prepared
fillets, chunks

Taste
mild

Texture
soft and flaky

should be aware that this is the first consideration. A properly, promptly gutted bluefish is a wonderful gift—a carelessly treated one, a damn shame.

The bone structure of a bluefish is simple, so the fish is easy to eat when cooked whole or filleted. It is easy to pull the pin bones out of a raw fillet of a small bluefish using pin-nose pliers; these bones can be cut out of a large bluefish.

Although the flesh of a large bluefish is quite dark and oily, it lightens up when it is cooked. It can take strong herbs, such as rosemary, in small quantities, and lemon or lime juice will counteract the oiliness of the flesh. Bluefish is excellent broiled, roasted or baked. It can also be cooked over charcoal on an open grill.

Small bluefish are wonderful cooked over charcoal in an oiled two-sided hinged grill or pan-dressed and fried.

A fish salad made with bluefish is a breeze. The cooked flesh flakes easily, and adding grated carrot, chopped cooked small red potatoes, lemon juice, dill and other seasonings is all that is needed.

A note on health: Many people worry about eating bluefish because of reports that these fish may be contaminated with dangerous amounts of polychlorinated biphenyls (PCBs). Bluefish spawn at sea, where they are not likely to be affected by PCBs, but they are at the top of the food chain, and they eat other fish that may be affected by PCBs. Larger bluefish may absorb significant quantities of PCBs, but it is certainly fine to eat bluefish that weigh less than 6 pounds, and in fact, there is no government health advisory against doing so. When toxic material is present in a bluefish, most of it collects in the dark red, fatty band that stretches along the lateral line on the side of the fish (this is also where the omega-3 fatty acids lie), and you can cut this muscle out if you want. Because the benefits of eating fish far outweigh the dangers—heart disease kills more Americans than cancer, and omega-3s do so much good—I don't believe there is any harm in eating bluefish a few times a year.

COOKING METHODS

Cut	Cooking Methods	Serves	How Much to Buy
Whole	Roasting	Part of a buffet for 25	Two 6-pound fish
Whole	Roasting	Dinner for 8	6 pounds
Whole	Grilling on an open fire	Dinner for 8	6 pounds
Whole	Bake-poaching	Dinner for 8	6 pounds
Chunks	Roasting	4	3 pounds
Whole snappers (small bluefish)	Grilling on an open fire	1	¾ to 1 pound
Fillets	Blackening	1	8 to 10 ounces
Fillets	As listed below	1	6 to 8 ounces

CHOICE OF RECIPES

Baked Fatty Fish Fillets, page 73

Bake-Poached Whole Fish, page 76

Bake-Poached Fish Fillets, page 79

Oven-Steamed Seafood en Papillote, page 80

Baked Fish Fillet Casserole with Light Tomato Sauce, page 83

Baked Cajun Fish Casserole, page 85

Roast Whole Fish, page 89

Roast Stuffed Fish Chunk, page 92

Broiled Whole Roundfish, page 98

Broiled Fillets, Butterflied or Split Fish, Steaks, Escalopes or Medallions, page 100

Grilled Whole Fish, page 107

Grilled Fish Fillets, Butterflied or Split Fish Steaks or Medallions, page 109

Whole Fish Steamed in Foil on the Grill, page 116

Blackened Fish Fillets, page 128

Hot-Smoking (Smoke-Cooking), page 170

Escabèche, page 184

Marinade, page 187

Summer Fish Salad, page 193

Buffalofish

Smallmouth Buffalofish *Ictiobus bubalus*
Bigmouth Buffalofish *I. cyprinellus*

Cholesterol: *N/A* ***Omega-3:*** *N/A* ***Fat:*** *16.6*

Fat content
high

Form usually prepared
fillets

Taste
mild

Texture
firm

SMALLMOUTH AND BIGMOUTH buffalofish, which belong to the sucker family, live in fresh water. They are found in large lakes and rivers of North America. They have a slight hump where their shoulders are, which undoubtedly prompted someone to find a resemblance to a buffalo. The smallmouth has the more pronounced hump and is the preferred species of buffalofish.

Both buffalofish and, incidentally, carp look like large goldfish, although the buffalofish is colored a dull gray to olive brown. Its internal structure is not quite as bony as the carp's, but it does have tiny, free-floating bones shaped like the letter Y in its upper part—its back—which are a nuisance. Learn to cut them out of the flesh if they are a bother to you. The scales are large, like those of the carp, and can be removed with the skin in one piece. To do this, insert a knife under the skin at the tail end of the fish and gradually loosen the skin from the flesh. The scales are embedded in the skin, and you can peel them off as a single armored sheet. This is a neat trick that I learned from my local fishmonger, Paul Diminio.

Buffalofish weigh 2 to 10 pounds when caught, although the bigmouth variety can grow to 50 pounds. Buffalofish are sold fresh or frozen whole. The fish are cheap; supply exceeds demand. The flesh is firm, sweet and pink and turns white when cooked. It's very filling and has high fat content, so it lends itself well to being smoked.

COOKING METHODS

Cut	Cooking Methods	Serves	How Much to Buy
Fillets	As listed below	4	1½ to 2 pounds

CHOICE OF RECIPES

Baked Fatty Fish Fillets, page 73
Baked Fish Fillet Casserole with Light Tomato Sauce, page 83
Broiled Fillets, Escalopes or Medallions, page 100
Grilled Fish Fillets or Medallions, page 109

Butterfish

Peprilus triacanthus
Cholesterol: 65   Omega-3: N/A   Fat: 8.0

Harvestfish

P. alepidotus
Cholesterol: N/A   Omega-3: N/A   Fat: N/A

BUTTERFISH ARE SMALL, round fish with compressed bodies. They are silvery blue in color. They are also known as dollarfish, as they are round, silver and flat.

Butterfish are found in the Atlantic Ocean, from New York down to Florida. Most butterfish are between 4 and 9 inches long when caught and weigh a few ounces to half a pound.

Butterfish are ideal for smoking, as their flesh is oily. They are delicious pan-dressed (gutted, scaled and trimmed) and then fried. Butterfish can also be broiled or grilled. Their gray flesh turns white when cooked.

In the summer in Montauk, Long Island, I have heard the fishermen say that a shortage of butterfish accounts for a shortage of tuna—butterfish are among the tuna's favorite foods, along with squid.

Harvestfish are sold as star butterfish or starfish at New York's Fulton Fish Market. Although similar, they are another species altogether.

Fat content
high

Forms usually prepared
pan-dressed, butterflied or split fish

Taste
sweet

Texture
flaky

COOKING METHODS

Cut	Cooking Methods	Serves	How Much to Buy
Whole pan-dressed	As listed below	1	4 to 10 ounces

CHOICE OF RECIPES

Broiled Whole Roundfish, page 98

Grilled Whole Fish, page 107

Fried Whole Fish or Pan-Dressed Fish, page 124

Hot-Smoking (Smoke-Cooking), page 170

Carp

Cyprinus carpio

Cholesterol: 66   Omega-3: 0.4   Fat: 5.6

CARP RESEMBLE LARGE GOLDFISH. They are golden to brown in color and have large scales. Carp are cultivated in ponds and reservoirs, and they also live in rivers, streams, lakes and swamps all over the United States. They have been known to survive 40 years or more, although most live 20 years if not caught before then.

The carp that are commercially available weigh up to 10 pounds. Their scales and skin, like those of buffalofish, can be peeled off in one piece (see page 238).

Carp can be cooked whole or filleted. As the carp is fatty, I remove the dark, oily streak of flesh next to the skin along its lateral band before cooking it in filleted form. Since the flesh is very meaty, tough and bony, a little goes a long way.

Carp are traditionally used (along with pike and whitefish) to make gefilte fish, which is eaten at the Seder at Passover time. The flesh is ground, which makes it less bony; long cooking softens the bones.

Fat content
moderate

Form usually prepared
fillets

Taste
mild

Texture
firm

COOKING METHODS

Cut	Cooking Methods	Serves	How Much to Buy
Fillets and steaks	As listed below	1	6 to 7 ounces

CHOICE OF RECIPES

Broiled Fillets, Butterflied or Split Fish, Steaks, Escalopes or Medallions, page 100

Grilled Fish Fillets, Butterflied or Split Fish or Medallions, page 109

Braised Fish Fillets with Provençal Sauce, page 156

Hot-Smoking (Smoke-Cooking), page 170

Catfish

Freshwater

Cholesterol: 58   Omega-3: 0.4   Fat: 4.3

Ocean

Cholesterol: 50   Omega-3: N/A   Fat: 2.9

THOUGH SOME HOLD that catfish is an unbecoming name, the name does suit, for these fish have streamlined bodies and "whiskers" (barbels) around their mouths. I don't think they are ugly, and I like the fine, firm texture of their flesh.

There are 2,500 species of catfish in the world, including:

Brown Bullhead
Ictalurus nebulosus
White Catfish
I. catus
Channel Catfish
I. punctatus
Flathead Catfish
Pylodictis olivaris
Gafftopsail Catfish
Bagne marinus
Hardhead Catfish
Ariopsis felis

Fat content
low to moderate

Forms usually prepared
fillets, steaks, nuggets

Taste
sweet

Texture
firm

All very confusing, but there you are. Most are from fresh water, with the exception of the gafftopsail and hardhead catfish, which are from the sea.

Catfish taken from rivers in the southern states have been regional favorites for many a year, but now that catfish are raised on farms, they have gained popularity in the rest of the United States as well. The industry began in 1965 and has grown enormously since 1974. Mississippi produces the most farm-raised catfish; other farms are in Arkansas, Alabama, Louisiana, Georgia, Idaho, California, North Carolina and South Carolina. Up to 5,000 pounds of fish can be produced from a one-acre pond, and the fish are now available year-round. Farm-raised catfish are excellent—no more can we complain of a muddy taste, for they are raised in fresh water in large ponds on flat land that holds groundwater well. The flesh of farm-raised catfish is pure white, and the taste is sweet. They are high in protein and low in calories, fat and cholesterol.

Catfish weigh 1½ pounds and up. Most commonly, they are skinned and their heads are removed. Much catfish flesh is filleted and sold fresh or frozen. Fillets usually weigh between 5 and 20 ounces. Catfish fillets can be smoked. Catfish can also be bought as steaks or as diagonally cut strips of flesh called nuggets. Farm-raised catfish are processed right after they are taken from the pond, so we generally do not have the bother of skinning or filleting them ourselves.

Catfish are often deep-fried with a coating of cornmeal and served with a piquant or spicy sauce, but they can be cooked by various other methods—in fact, I can't think of one that does not suit them, except roasting whole. The firm, sweet flesh is conducive to strong flavorings as well as mild ones. I like to bake the fillets in a casserole dish, where they retain their shape beautifully. The firmness of the flesh is a great feature of this fish.

COOKING METHODS

Cut	Cooking Methods	Serves	How Much to Buy
Whole, head off, skinned	Deep-frying	1	12 ounces
Fillets	Blackening	1	8 to 10 ounces
Fillets	As listed below	1	6 to 8 ounces

CHOICE OF RECIPES

Baked Lean Fish Fillets, page 75

Baked Fish Fillet Casserole, page 82

Baked Cajun Fish Casserole, page 85

Casserole of Fish Fillets with Potatoes and Coriander Pesto, page 86

Broiled Fillets, Butterflied or Split Fish, Steaks, Escalopes or Medallions, page 100

Grilled Fish Fillets, Butterflied or Split Fish, Steaks or Medallions, page 109

Fish Croquettes, page 125

Blackened Fish Fillets, page 128

Deep-Fried Seafood with Beer Batter, page 133

Steamed Seafood, page 146

Hot-Smoking (Smoke-Cooking), page 170

Seafood Stew with Tomato and Green Pepper, page 176

Salsa-Flavored Fish Salad, page 192

Char, Arctic

Salvelinus alpinus
Cholesterol: *27*
Omega-3: *N/A* **Fat:** *7.9*

ARCTIC CHAR is becoming a popular "new" fish. Some are
farmed, some are wild. Farmed char come from Iceland, the wild
come from cold Alaskan waters, Canada, Greenland, Iceland and
Norway. It looks like a salmon with slightly larger spots on it, and in
the wild it behaves like salmon. The flesh is an attractive strong pink
to orange color. The smaller fish weigh 2 to 6 pounds, the wild up to
and over 10 pounds. Many of the latter are smoked. Cook Arctic
char as salmon or trout, depending on its size.

COOKING METHODS

Cut	Cooking Methods	Serves	How Much to Buy
Whole	Roasting	Dinner for 10	8 pounds
Fillets	As listed below	2	12 ounces

CHOICE OF RECIPES

Cook small fish as you would baby coho salmon (10 to 12 ounces
each), page 323.
Cook larger fish as you would salmon, page 323.

Fat content
moderate to high

**Form usually
prepared**
fillets, boned, head on

Taste
sweet, rich

Texture
flaky

Clams

Cholesterol: *34* **Omega-3:** *0.1* **Fat:** *1.0*

THERE ARE MANY delicious species of clams. These bivalve
(double-shelled) mollusks are found in both the shallow and the
deep cool waters of the Atlantic and the Pacific. They live a pretty
stationary life in the sand or mud on the floor of the ocean. Quahogs
(hard-shell clams), some razor clams and soft-shell clams are from
the Atlantic, while butter, Manila, common Pacific littleneck, geoduck and other razor clams are found in the Pacific.

Many clams are found in shallow sandy bays or freshwater inlets,
and it is fun to collect them (but watch out for razor clams—they can
cut your toes). Large Atlantic surf or bar clams are dredged up commercially from deeper waters.

Hard-shell clams are sold by the dozen. Other clams are sold by
the pound. All clams must be alive when you buy them. Make sure

Fat content
low

**Form usually
prepared**
in shell

Taste
sweet and slightly salty

Texture
soft

that the shells are tightly closed, except for soft-shell, razor and geoduck clams, which gape naturally. If hard-shell clams do gape a little, give them a good knock, and if they close, all is well: they are alive. As with all bivalves, you must be sure they are fished from clean waters. Here you have to trust your fishmonger. If you collect your own, check for local laws that set limits on your take, and make sure that the water is considered clean by the local office of the Environmental Protection Agency or by local health authorities.

Quahogs (Hard-Shell Clams)
Mercenaria mercenaria
Cholesterol: 40 Omega-3: 0.2 Fat: 1.0

The smallest of the hard-shell quahog clams are the littleneck clams. They have hard off-white shells with striations (fine ridges) encircling them. You must scrub and rinse these and other clams to rid them of sand. These clams are delicious eaten raw, but they can be briefly sautéed until their shells open or put, at the last moment, into a fish soup or even a paella. They will toughen if they are cooked too long. It's best to eat them as soon as their shells open.

Cherrystones are the next largest hard-shell clams. They are also delicious eaten raw or chopped for chowders.

As quahog clams grow larger, they are called chowder clams. Their flesh gets tougher and needs to be ground or chopped and then cooked.

Ocean quahogs (*Arctica islandica*), also called mahogany or black clams, are large clams, up to 4 inches wide. These are used to make chowder and may also be called chowder clams. They are also minced and canned.

Atlantic surf clams (*Spisula solidissima*), also called bar or sea clams, are even larger—4 to 7 inches wide. They are usually cut into strips and fried—Howard Johnson restaurants couldn't exist without them.

Soft-Shell Clams
Mya arenaria
Cholesterol: 25 Omega-3: 0.2 Fat: 1.2

Soft-shell clams—also called steamers, softs, gapers, squirts or even "pissers"—have soft shells, that is, shells which are brittle and break easily. A soft-shell clam's shell never closes completely, because the neck, or siphon, sticks out. Steam soft-shell clams open, and serve them with broth and melted butter, or dip them in a batter and deep-fry them.

These clams are nirvana for me, and I hunt up and down the highways for the stand or small restaurant serving the best fried clam rolls whenever I visit Long Island or Cape Cod, where these rolls are popular. They have to be coated with a light batter and must be supercrisp. I specify that I want bellies, not just fried strips—the bellies burst with sweet flavor in my mouth.

Razor Clams
Cholesterol: 107
Omega-3: 0.3 Fat: 1.5

The Atlantic and Pacific razor clams are shaped like lozenges, up to 6 inches long. Other species, such as the common razor (from the Atlantic, *Ensis directus*) and the jackknife clam (from the Pacific, *Tagelus californianus*), look like the old-fashioned strap razors and grow as long as 10 inches. They have sweet flesh and can be prepared in the same way as soft-shell clams. In some markets, they may be sold by the pound already shucked.

Manila Clams
Tapes semidecussata
Cholesterol: N/A Omega-3: N/A Fat: 0.8

Manila clams, which are native to the western Pacific but are now also found in the Pacific off British Columbia, are wonderful little mollusks that are best cooked, in my opinion. They need only be sautéed with a little oil, garlic, fresh herbs and wine for a few minutes until they open. You can make a great pasta sauce with them or add them to fish soups such as Bourride (page 160). The Manila clam is thin-shelled but not as brittle as a soft-shell clam and is light to dark brown with striations that extend from its hinged part to the edges of its shells. Manila clams are small and round, about 1¼ to 1½ inches in diameter.

Geoduck Clams
Panopea abrupta
Cholesterol: N/A Omega-3: N/A Fat: N/A

Geoduck (pronounced "gooeyduck") clams, large relatives of soft-shell clams, weigh 1 pound or more. They are harvested from the Pacific Northwest. The geoduck clam has a very long siphon, or neck, that protrudes at great length from the shell, and it is lewd-looking, to say the least. It has the most delicious, sweet, rich flesh. We eat the peeled neck and the strip of flesh that runs around the belly. Japanese fish stores sell the geoduck already prepared. Eat it raw or cooked, but cook it ever so briefly; otherwise, it will toughen.

New Zealand Cockles

Chione stutchburyi

Cholesterol: *N/A* **Omega-3:** *N/A* **Fat:** *N/A*

Cockles, from New Zealand, can be cooked as Manila clams: sautéed or added to stews, soups or rice or pasta dishes. They are thin-shelled, about 1¼ inches in diameter. Cockles are sometimes available cooked and shucked.

How to Shuck Clams

♦ Before eating clams, whether raw or cooked, scrub them under cold running water with a brush and put them in a bowl of cold water for 20 to 30 minutes so that they can rid themselves of any sand they may have in their bodies. Don't soak them any longer than that, for fresh water will eventually kill them.

♦ As you shuck clams, work over a clean empty bowl that has a fine sieve or cheesecloth in it, so you can catch the juice and free it of sand or pieces of shell. Pick up each clam, and put it in your left hand (or your right if you are left-handed), with the hinged thick part of the clam in your palm near your thumb. Insert a clam knife that has a blunt tip or a thin paring knife where you can easily see the division between the shells. If it is difficult or even impossible to insert the knife, you can resort to putting the clam in the freezer for ½ hour until it gives up and opens its shells a little, or try twirling the clam on a board—to make it dizzy and give up resistance! When your knife is between the shells, don't let it go in too far, because you might cut the clam in half inadvertently. Using just the tip of the knife, slide it up close to the inside of the shells so that you cut the two muscles holding the shell together. Open the clam and release the flesh on both shells by sliding your knife under it—you will end up with all the flesh on the bottom shell. This is called a clam on the half shell.

♦ If you are serving clams raw, pull off the top shell of each clam and display the flesh on the lower shell. Pour some of the strained juice you have collected on the flesh. Serve with lemon wedges.

♦ Always save the clam juice—it helps to flavor soups and chowders. You can freeze it if you like. When you are going to cook clams for a chowder or a sauce, you can put them in a hot oven for a few minutes until they open or steam them open using very little water.

How to Prepare Geoduck Clams

♦ Loosen the flesh from the shell with a thin knife, and put the whole creature in a bowl of hot water for 5 minutes. Then rinse it in cold water. Peel off the skin from the siphon and the strip surrounding the belly. Discard the belly. You are left with the siphon and the strip that was around the belly.

♦ Cut the siphon away from the strip, and trim off the tip. Cut the siphon lengthwise but not all the way through. You will see that the siphon is hollow like a pipe. Spread it open, and cut it into very thin slices on the horizontal. Cut across the slices every 1¼ inches, and you will have little butterfly shapes.

♦ You can tenderize geoduck clams by pounding them very gently with a smooth mallet or, as the Japanese do, by making very fine incisions in the flesh.

COOKING METHODS

FORM	COOKING METHODS	SERVES	HOW MUCH TO BUY
Littleneck and cherrystone	On the half shell	1	6 to 9
Same	Soup	1	2
Same and razor	Chowder	6	2 cups shucked (20 to 30)
Soft-shell	Deep-frying, steaming	1	¾ to 1 pound
Geoduck sliced	Frying	1	4 ounces
Geoduck chopped	Chowder	6	2 cups (2 pounds)
Geoduck sliced	Raw	1	4 ounces
Manila	Frying	1	6 to 8 ounces

CHOICE OF RECIPES

Clams Steamed in Foil on the Grill or in the Oven, page 118
Fried Geoduck Clam Slices à la Meunière, page 122
Deep-Fried Seafood with Beer Batter, page 133
Steamed Soft-Shell Clams Marinière, page 148
Fish Soup (Bourride), page 160
Creamy Seafood Chowder, page 162
Seafood Stew or Pasta Sauce, page 165
Seafood Stew with Tomato and Green Pepper, page 176
Seviche, page 183

Sushi and Sashimi, page 189
Littlenecks or cherrystones on the half shell (serve 6 to 9 per person)

Cod Group

THE COD GROUP includes Atlantic and Pacific cod, haddock, white hake, red hake (ling), European whiting, Atlantic pollock, Alaskan pollock and cusk.

Cod and its group are lean, white-fleshed creatures that are marvelous for our health; the flesh is low in fat and calories and high in protein.

Cod can be deep-fried, broiled, baked in a casserole or in a baking pan, bake-poached, steamed, braised and stewed, used in a salad or made into croquettes (fish cakes), just to name a few methods of preparation.

Fillets from larger fish have firmer flesh with large flakes. The smaller fish produce softer, flakier flesh. For this reason, cod cannot be grilled with much success.

Fat content
low

Forms usually prepared
fillets, steaks

Taste
mild

Texture
flaky

Atlantic Cod
Gadus morhua
Cholesterol: 43   Omega-3: 0.2   Fat: 0.7

Cod has made men rich on both sides of the North Atlantic, and indeed there is nothing to compare with its pearly white flesh, which is lean, sweet, flaky and delicious. Hardy fishermen battle the North Atlantic in all weathers to catch these cold-water fish.

William Warner, in his book *Distant Water*, describes the start of a week of cod fishing on the trawler Tremont out of Boston:

> After supper the breeze stiffens and a quarter moon, waxing, hangs halfway up the night sky. Cables sway and the net gear shifts and clanks, tugging at stop lines, on the spray-swept steel of the main deck. To the south the distant flashes of Cape Cod lighthouses are easily seen on the horizon. Race Point, Highland, Nauset Beach—each conjures up its full share of summer memories. But the Tremont is hurrying

along at twelve knots, pushed by quartering seas, and the lights fall off fast to starboard. Soon they are no more than smudged and irregular twinkles, frequently obscured by heaving seas. A pyramidal wave rises up in the dark, showing a large white crest, and slams hard against the Tremont's side. Water explodes through the crack of a hinged scupper and hisses across the deck. It is reminder enough. We are going somewhere else. And summer is over.

Huge amounts of Atlantic cod are caught off Georges Bank (United States and Canadian fishing territory) and the Grand Banks (Canadian territory), sand formations on the continental shelf teeming with fish. Most of this cod is gutted at sea, then iced down and landed fresh. Much of it is then frozen in the Northeast before being sent off to the rest of the country. Unfortunately, the Georges Bank area has been overfished, and the catch has been restricted temporarily.

The Atlantic cod lives close to the bottom of the ocean. It has olive-green to gray skin that changes to white at the belly. It has a whitish lateral line from its head to its tail and a hooked barbel (a fleshy, whiskerlike protuberance) under its jaw. Its belly is large; when emptied of the guts, the belly leaves a huge hollow. There is little flesh covering the rib bones, except on a heavy fish.

Codfish up to 200 pounds have been caught, but the average cod taken weighs 10 pounds or less. The names scrod and schrod used to refer to codfish and other members of the same family weighing less than 3½ pounds. Nowadays, the terms are used rather loosely for any sized cod or any member of the same family.

In the fish trade, "market cod" refers to a fish with head and tail on, and "steak cod" is the name used when the head is cut off. You seldom see a whole codfish in the store, because so much is processed and filleted before it reaches us. Boneless filleted cod is, after all, the way most cod lovers like their fish.

Cod fillets and steaks are sold fresh or frozen. I don't care for the frozen fillets or steaks, because they exude an unnecessary amount of moisture as they defrost and they tend to dry out when cooked. Let's hope we get to see more whole fish and fresh, not frozen, fillets.

Salt cod, popular in regions around the world as diverse as the warm Caribbean, the Mediterranean countries and the cold countries of Scandinavia, is now mostly produced by Canada, Iceland,

Spain and Norway and exported across the world. It is called, variously, *bacalhau* in Portugal, *bacalà* in Italy, *morue* (*seche*) in France and *bacalao* in Spain and the West Indies.

Many other fish of the cod family are salted and dried and may also be called salt cod. The actual name of the fish that has been salted, such as pollock, cusk or haddock, should be on the package.

Salt cod can be prepared in different ways: Some are dried on the bone, and some are prepared boneless and skinless. Some are salted down and partially dried, so they come to us in a somewhat moist condition. Another preparation entails salting the fish and then drying it out until it becomes hard as wood and sometimes has to be cut with a saw. The Norwegians use this method.

Stockfish (*stoccafisso* in Italy) is a similar product, but it is not salt cod. Stockfish is preserved by drying—no salt is used.

How to Prepare Salt Cod for Cooking

♦ All salt cod must be soaked for a number of hours, or overnight, in running water or several changes of water so that it loses its salt and its flesh is reconstituted. The length of time will depend on the method by which the cod was salted and dried. When buying salt cod, you can judge for yourself if it will need a long soaking time: Very dry fish will require longer soaking than moist fish.

♦ When the flesh is soft, put it in a saucepan of cold water. Bring to a boil, lower the heat, and simmer it for 10 minutes, or until tender. Strain. Cut it into slices or flake it according to the recipe you are using. The saltiness of the cod is usually washed away during the rinsing period, and you may find that you have to add salt to your dish—but be sure to taste it first.

Salt cod can be used to make a delicious variety of dishes, such as those listed on page 254.

Cod is often smoked instead of haddock to make finnan haddie. The dish is good with either.

Cod roe is edible—it can be delicious fried—but it is more popular in Europe than in North America. It is sold both canned and fresh. Cod roe is also smoked, and it can be used successfully to make the lovely Greek spread or dip called *taramasalata*.

If you can find cod cheeks, buy them, for they are wonderful small morsels of tender flesh, which can be quickly sautéed and served with brown butter.

Pacific Cod
Gadus macrocephalus
Cholesterol: 37   Omega-3: 0.2   Fat: 0.6

This cod is also known as the gray cod because of its coloration, although it is colored brown to gray. It is also called the true cod to distinguish it from the lingcod, rock cod and black cod, which are also from the Pacific and are not of the cod family at all.

It is caught in the Pacific from Oregon to Alaska and can weigh up to 10 pounds.

It is sold whole and in filleted form, and its flesh is similar to that of Atlantic cod. Cook as you would Atlantic cod.

Haddock
Melanogrammus aeglefinus
Cholesterol: 57   Omega-3: 0.2   Fat: 0.7

Haddock is found in much the same waters as Atlantic cod. Its skin is gray to purplish gray. It has a thin, black lateral stripe along its body, with a dark smudge behind the pectoral fin. Its body is more streamlined than the cod's; its flesh is so similar to the cod's that all the cod recipes listed on page 253 and 254 can be prepared with haddock. It appears in the fish store in cuts like those used for cod, but it commands a higher price.

Haddock smokes well. Smoked haddock is called finnan haddie, after a town called Findon in Scotland, where a very good product is made. The flavor of smoked haddock on the bone is definitely superior to that of smoked haddock fillets, but the former is not always available.

White Hake
Urophycis tenuis
Cholesterol: 39   Omega-3: 0.22   Fat: 0.5

White hake, also called hake, is caught at weights up to 50 pounds from Newfoundland down to North Carolina. Its flesh is white, and it is usually sold filleted. Often, there is a line of beige muscle running along the center and sides of the fillet. This fish has a large stomach cavity and therefore a fairly low yield of flesh. Nearly all white hake is landed dressed, so the consumer doesn't have to worry about yield. It is sometimes sold as cod or scrod. Don't confuse it with the European hake, page 284.

Red Hake (Ling)

Uroplycis chuss

Cholesterol: 35   Omega-3: N/A   Fat: 0.6

The red hake is also called the squirrel hake and the ling. It is smaller than the white hake, growing to only about 3 pounds. It is caught off the coasts of New England, Canada and the mid-Atlantic region. In the mid-Atlantic states, it is sold whole and dressed. It is also salted or canned. Not to be confused with the European hake, page 284, or lingcod, page 288.

European Whiting

Merlangius merlangus

Cholesterol: N/A   Omega-3: N/A   Fat: N/A

Fished in great quantities from northern European waters and the Mediterranean, this is a popular fish in Europe. The whiting found in American waters is profiled on page 285.

Atlantic Pollock

Pollachius virens

Cholesterol: 71   Omega-3: 0.4   Fat: 1.0

The Atlantic pollock, also known incorrectly as the Boston bluefish and the blue cod in the United States and as the saithe and the coley in England, is a fine fish that resembles cod (its skin is darker, without the light spots) but is sold at half the price, probably because the flesh is gray-pink before it is cooked. The flesh does turn white when cooked, and it has a mild flavor. The average Atlantic pollock sold is between 4 and 8 pounds. These fish are taken from the North Atlantic in great quantities.

Atlantic pollock is sold whole, in chunks, in fillets and, occasionally, in steak form. It is often frozen. I used to feed my gorgeous Persian cat this fish in England, but now the fish is better appreciated, and the price is up. It can be baked, fried, broiled, grilled and stuffed and roasted. It is often salted down like salt cod, and it is good smoked.

Alaskan Pollock

Theragra chalcogramma

Cholesterol: N/A   Omega-3: N/A   Fat: N/A

The Atlantic pollock should not be confused with the Alaskan walleye pollock, which is caught in huge quantities in the Bering Sea and the Gulf of Alaska. The walleye pollock is smaller and has white flesh. Much is frozen at sea and then reprocessed to make surimi, which, with the addition of flavorings, is made to resemble crab, scallops, shrimp and even lobster. I can't say I like the taste of surimi, for processors add sugar and monosodium glutamate to it.

Cusk

Brosme brosme

Cholesterol: 41   Omega-3: N/A   Fat: 0.7

Cusk, important to the Maine fishing industry, is sold primarily in New England. It is available year-round and has white flesh, reminiscent of cod. The fish has one dorsal fin and one anal fin; they stretch all the way down to its tail in a continuous line.

Cusk is sold in filleted form and can be cooked like cod.

COOKING METHODS

Cut	Cooking Methods	Serves	How Much to Buy
Cod			
Whole	Roasting	6 to 8	6 pounds
Chunks	Roasting	4 to 5	2 pounds
Fillets and steaks	As listed below	1	2 to 8 ounces
Red Hake and Whiting			
Whole	Roasting	1	¾ to 1 pound
Whole	Grilling	1	¾ to 1 pound
Whole	Deep-frying	1	¾ to 1 pound
Whole	Sousing	1	¾ to 1 pound
Fillets and steaks	As listed below	1	2 to 8 ounces

CHOICE OF RECIPES

Cod

Baked Lean Fish Fillets, page 75

Bake-Poached Fish Fillets, page 79

Oven-Steamed Seafood en Papillote, page 80

Baked Fish Fillet Casserole, page 82

Baked Fish Fillet Casserole with Light Tomato Sauce, page 83

Casserole of Fish Fillets with Potatoes and Coriander Pesto, page 86

Roast Whole Fish, page 89

Roast Stuffed Fish Chunk, page 92

Broiled Fillets, Butterflied or Split Fish, Steaks, Escalopes or Medallions, page 100

Grilled Fish Fillets, Butterflied or Split Fish, Steaks or Medallions, page 109

Fish Fillets Steamed in Foil on the Grill, page 116

Fried Fish Fillets or Fish Steaks à la Meunière, page 122

Fish Croquettes, page 125

Deep-Fried Seafood with Seasoned Flour, page 131

Steamed Seafood, page 146

Braised Fish Fillets or Steaks with Provençal Sauce, page 156

Fish Stock, page 164

Fish Soup (Bourride), page 160

Creamy Seafood Chowder, page 162

Seafood Stew or Pasta Sauce, page 165

Hot-Smoking (Smoke-Cooking), page 170

Fish Fillets with Spinach and Ginger, page 178

Escabèche, page 184

Marinade for Broiled, Grilled or Barbecued Seafood, page 187

Salsa-Flavored Fish Salad, page 192

All of the above recipes can also be prepared using other members of the cod family, including European hake, except smaller members such as the red hake (ling) and European whiting (the recipes suitable for these fish are listed below).

Salt Cod

Fish Croquettes, page 125

Fritters, page 134

Braised Fish Fillets or Steaks with Provençal Sauce, page 156

Creamy Seafood Chowder, page 162

Seviche, page 183

Escabèche, page 184

Salsa-Flavored Fish Salad, page 192

Red Hake (Ling), European Whiting and American Whiting

Bake-Poached Fish Fillets, page 79

Roast Whole Fish, page 89

Grilled Whole Fish, page 107

Grilled Fish Fillets, Butterflied or Split Fish, Steaks or Medallions, page 109

Deep-Fried Seafood with Cornmeal Coating, page 132
Fish Stock, page 164
Soused or Marinated Fish, page 186

Conch

Strombus spp
Cholesterol: N/A Omega-3: N/A Fat: N/A

Whelks

Busycon carica, B. canaliculatum
Cholesterol: 65 Omega-3: 0.1 Fat: 0.4

T HE CONCH (pronounced "conk" or "conch") is found in the warm waters off the Florida Keys and in the Caribbean. Queen conch (*Strombus gigas*) is the best known in the United States. The pretty single shell of this mollusk is shaped a bit like that of a snail, with a pointed, striated turret or crown at one end. The shell is thick, and the flesh spirals up into the turret. Once extracted from the shell, the flesh is a delight to eat raw with lime juice. Getting the flesh out without giving in to an urge to break the whole shell to pieces on the nearest rock is tricky.

Knobbed and channeled whelks, often called conch or scungilli (from the Italian word for "conch"), are similar in shape and are found down the east coast from Rhode Island to the Gulf of Mexico. Whelks consume other shellfish and fish. The whelk manages to break open the shells of oysters, clams and mussels with its knobbed turret and extract the flesh with its "tongue." Conch are herbivorous.

Conch and whelks have fascinating sweet flesh with a slightly smoky taste; the flesh is smooth and chewy when cut. You can slice the flesh and pound it to tenderize it or cook it whole. Be sure a conch or whelk is alive if you want to eat it raw: Tap the operculum (a thin hard covering at the opening), and if there is some movement or response, the creature is alive. Before you eat a conch or whelk raw, the flesh must be shaved into very thin

Fat content
low

Form usually prepared
shucked

Taste
sweet yet smoky

Texture
firm

slices. You can tenderize these thin slices by making very fine incisions in the flesh or by pounding it lightly. The queen conch is better than the whelk for eating raw.

Conch and whelks are sold by the piece when alive in their shells. Conch meat is often sold frozen. Whelk meat is usually partially or fully cooked and then frozen. This meat is not like the fresh article, but it is perfectly fine for making fritters or stews. Conch and whelk meat—cooked or raw, fresh or frozen—is sold by the pound.

Scungilli marinara, a fine southern Italian dish much appreciated in the United States as well, is made with conch or whelk.

How to Extract the Flesh from a Conch or Whelk Shell

METHOD 1

♦ It is easier to extract the meat from a conch or whelk shell after dunking it into boiling water for a minute or two. When its muscles relax, pull on the flesh from the opening and extract it.

METHOD 2

♦ The flesh of a conch or whelk is attached to a spiral column inside the pointed, conical spire at the top or turret, and it is necessary to detach this muscle to extract the flesh. Make a hole in the turret about one inch from the top. Insert a sharp, pointed knife in the hole, and scrape the muscle free. Put the tip of the knife under the operculum (the thin hard covering) at the opening of the shell, and pull out the flesh. Cut off the operculum and the long, tough pointed appendage (its tongue). Clean off the intestines, and peel off any tough skin, especially if you will be eating the conch or whelk raw.

♦ If you are going to cook the conch or whelks whole, put the extracted flesh in boiling water without cleaning off the intestines, and cook it in lightly salted boiling water until tender. Remove the intestines, and skin the flesh before using it.

COOKING METHODS

FORM	COOKING METHODS	SERVES	HOW MUCH TO BUY
Out of shell	As listed below	1	6 to 8 ounces

CHOICE OF RECIPES

Grilled Shellfish, page 107
Fritters, page 134
Creamy Seafood Chowder, page 162
Seafood Stew or Pasta Sauce, page 165
Seviche, page 183

Crab

As ANYONE who frequents the shores of this country knows, many species of crab are available in shallow waters, bays and estuaries. These feisty creatures, which may tickle your toes or even nip you with their meaty claws, are most delicious to eat. Other notable crabs are found in very deep waters.

West Coast people think the Dungeness crab is the best, East Coast and Gulf people love their blue crabs and stone crab claws, and I like them all for their different qualities. Dungeness and blue crabmeat are mild, sweet and tender. Stone crab claw meat tastes like lobster and crabmeat all at once. Picked crabmeat can be made into all sorts of delicious hot or cold preparations, such as crab cakes, deviled crab and crab salads.

On the East Coast, you can buy live hard- and soft-shell blue crabs. Some fish stores in the East have live Dungeness crabs from the Pacific in tanks; these crabs are also sold cooked and frozen in the East. On the West Coast, you can buy live Dungeness crabs and, sometimes, live snow crabs kept in tanks. Some live hard- and soft-shell blue crabs can survive the journey from the East Coast and may be for sale in the West. Packaged, picked cooked blue crabmeat travels well also, either pasteurized or frozen.

Snow and king crab legs are available on the West Coast cooked and frozen; their sweet meat is a treat. On the East Coast, cooked legs and shoulders of Atlantic and Pacific snow crabs are available, as well as legs and claws of northern Pacific king crabs. Also available in the East are cooked blue crab claws and cooked claws from stone crabs, which are taken from Florida waters and the Gulf of Mexico.

On both coasts, fresh or frozen crabmeat picked from cooked crabs is sold in different grades. (See pages 25 and 26 for details.) Cooked crabmeat is picked over for cartilage before it is sold, but it is worth picking over it again when you get it home, because it is not pleasant to find bits of shell in your mouth.

When alive, crabs have various colorings, including green, brown, red and blue, but they turn orange-red when cooked.

Fat content
low

Forms usually prepared
various

Taste
sweet

Texture
flaky

Blue Crab
Callinectes sapidus
Cholesterol: 78   Omega-3: 0.3   Fat: 1.1

Blue crabs are found along the Atlantic Coast, from Cape Cod down the Eastern Seaboard into the Gulf of Mexico, with a large concentration in the Chesapeake and Delaware Bay areas off Maryland and Virginia. A wonderful book called *Beautiful Swimmers* by William Warner, to whom I am beholden for a lot of information, tells in a delightful way much more about these crabs than I can here.

The blue crab has a green-brown body with blue claws and a shell measuring 5 to 9 inches across. The female can be distinguished by her orange-red-tipped claws. When cooked, the crabs turn orange-red all over. The immature female, called a she-crab, has a V-shaped tail (apron) on the underside of her body. After her last molt, when she is ready for mating, her apron becomes round with a tiny V shape on the top, and then she is a mature sook. The male crab, called a jimmy, has a very small apron. Live blue crabs are steamed or boiled. Chesapeake people choose to eat jimmys, for they contain a slightly higher yield of flesh than the females. They usually cost more. New Yorkers choose to buy the females, with their pretty orange-red-tipped claws.

In the summer, blue crabs are fairly easy to catch. Even young children can have the fun of baiting up some string with a piece of chicken or fish, for instance, and pulling in a blue crab. As soon as you know you have a crab on the bait, use a net to get it into a tall container—crabs can pinch and come out fighting, seemingly all claws. As a rule, blue crabs are trapped by using either pots baited with bits of fish, such as menhaden, or trotlines (lines stretched 2,000 feet or so between buoys) from shallow saline estuarine water during the summer months in the Chesapeake Bay area. In the winter, they are dredged from this area; in the Gulf of Mexico, they can be trapped year-round.

An acquaintance of mine who lives in Washington, D.C., and goes crabbing on weekends tells me that he usually uses eel as bait on his trotline. However, when eel gets too expensive, he alternates it with pieces of cow or ox lips—he says he is tempting the crabs with "surf and turf."

Live blue crabs are sold by the dozen or by the piece. They stay alive in bushel baskets for up to 5 days.

The soft-shell blue crab season, happily, is nice and long; from about May 15 to September 15. Soft-shell crabs are best sautéed, broiled or grilled. A soft-shell blue crab is a hard-shell blue crab that is caught within 6 hours after it has shed its hard outer shell. All crabs do this periodically so that they can grow larger. During the season, "peelers" ready to shed their shells are sold to soft-shell crab producers who keep them in pens, pick them out as they molt and sell them at fish markets. (Crawfish and lobsters also shed their hard shells.)

Soft-shell blue crabs are graded and priced according to size. (See page 26 for details.) They are packed with seaweed or straw in flat boxes, where they stay alive for 3 to 4 days. Many are frozen, but I like to see signs of life in the soft-shell crab before I prepare it for cooking.

Rock Crab
Cancer irroratus
Jonah Crab
Cancer borealis
Red Crab
Geryon quinquedens
Cholesterol: 74   Omega-3: 0.3   Fat: 1.3

Other crabs from the North Atlantic are the rock and Jonah crabs. Most of their meat is contained in their claws, which resemble those of the stone crab but have black tips. Most body meat of the Jonah crab is picked and canned in Maine. Some rock crabs are sold live in the fall and spring from tanks. The cooked claws of both rock and Jonah crabs are also available. A company in Virginia sells a small number of soft-shell rock crabs during the winter months when blue "softies" are out of season. Until more become available, they will continue to be expensive.

The deep-sea red crab, also from the Atlantic, is processed on board and is marketed as picked meat, legs and claws.

Stone Crab
Menippi mercenaria
Cholesterol: N/A Omega-3: N/A Fat: N/A

There are three species of stone crab, two from the Gulf of Mexico and one from Chile. The stone crab's claws are very popular, for the flesh tastes like a marvelous cross between crab and lobster. One large, smooth, rounded claw is picked off each crab, then the animal is returned to the water to grow another. The missing claw gradually grows back, and then the other claw may be picked off. The claws are cooked right away and are sold fresh, frozen or defrosted. Stone crab claws are priced according to their size—the largest ones are the most expensive. When cooked, they are bright orange-red with black tips. Stone crabs are in season year-round in the Gulf of Mexico and from November to May in Florida waters.

Cooked stone crab claws must be cracked with a mallet or nutcracker and can be served with lemon or lime wedges, mayonnaise or Lime and Dill Vinaigrette (page 202).

Dungeness Crab
Cancer magister
Cholesterol: 59 Omega-3: 0.3 Fat: 1.0

Dungeness crabs come from the North Pacific. They are large, weighing 1 to 3 pounds, with a high yield of the most delicious meat. Buy them live, and steam them yourself, then eat them hot or cold in a salad. You should beware of their strong claws when they are alive, although they are usually held together with rubber bands.

King Crab
Cholesterol: 42 Omega-3: N/A Fat: 0.6

King crabs also come from the North Pacific. There are three king crabs, two of the genus *Paralithodes*, the red king crab (*P. camtschaticus*) and the blue king crab (*P. platypus*), and one of the genus *Lithodes*, the golden or brown king crab (*L. aequispina*). King crabs have spiny shells and long legs, and it is in the legs that we find the meat. The legs and claws are cooked and then sold whole or split, fresh or frozen. Picked king crabmeat is also sold canned or frozen. King crabmeat is excellent in salads, or reheated under the broiler or on the grill.

Snow Crab
Chionoecetes bairdi, C. oplio
Cholesterol: 55   Omega-3: 0.4   Fat: 1.2

Snow crabs, also called tanner and queen crabs, come from the North Atlantic and the Pacific. They have long legs. The claws, legs and shoulders are cooked and then sold in clusters, fresh or frozen, or as picked meat. Snow crabs have smoother shells than king crabs. Prepare snow crab like king crab.

How to Eat Whole Steamed Blue, Dungeness, Rock or Jonah Crabs

♦ You will need plenty of napkins, a wooden or plastic board, a nutcracker or a small wooden mallet, a nutpick or lobster pick (optional) and a container for the empty shells.

♦ First remove the tail (apron) under the main body, then break off the claws and legs so you can eat them later. Pull the top shell that covers the body off from the rear end. (You can stuff the shell with cooked crabmeat and serve it hot or cold.) Brush off the feathery gills, and break the body in two. Break the two halves again so you have quarters. You can use your fingers or a pick to take out the meat. Use a small wooden mallet or a nutcracker to crack the claws and legs. Of course, you can use your teeth to crack the softer legs and suck the meat out.

♦ A few beers and a side plate of coleslaw will complete the feast.

How to Prepare Hard-Shell Crabs for Deep-Frying or Grilling

Follow the steaming instructions on page 151, but steam the crabs for only a minute or two, or until they stop moving. Rinse them in cold water. take off the top shell of each crab, clean the insides, and cut each crab in half.

How to Prepare Soft-Shell Crabs for Cooking

♦ Fresh soft-shell crabs should be alive shortly before being cooked. A "softy" cannot really hurt you, but you may want to use rubber gloves when preparing one. First remove the tail (apron) from under the main body. Then lift up each pointed side of the body, and remove the feathery gills with scissors or your fingers. Cut off the face, which includes the eyes and mouth. Behind this opening, you will find a little sac that is like a bubble—pull it out and discard it.

♦ Or you can ask your fishmonger to clean soft-shell crabs for you. Frozen soft-shell crabs are already cleaned. Be sure to defrost them in a colander or sieve so they shed some of the moisture accumulated during the freezing process.

COOKING METHODS

TYPE OF CRAB	COOKING METHODS	SERVES	HOW MUCH TO BUY
Blue crab	Steaming, soup	1	2 to 6 in shell, depending on size
Soft-shell blue crab	Grilling	1	2 to 4 in shell, depending on size
	Deep-frying		
	Sautéing		
	Soup		
	Stew		
Dungeness crab	Steaming	1	1 pound in shell
King or snow crabs	As suggested on page 261	1	½ to 1 pound in shell
Stone crab claw	As suggested on page 260	1	¾ to 1 pound
Picked crabmeat	Croquettes (crab cakes)	1	4 to 8 ounces
	Fritters		
	Chowder		
	Stew		
	Salad		

Crawfish

Louisiana Red Swamp Crawfish
Procambarus clarkii
Louisiana White River Crawfish
Procambarus acutus
Pacific Northwest Crawfish
Pacifasticus leniusculus

Mixed Species
Cholesterol: 139   Omega-3: 0.2   Fat: 1.1

Fat content
low

Form usually prepared
tail meat

Taste
sweet

Texture
tender

CALLED CRAYFISH up North, crawfish or crawdads in the South, these small freshwater creatures look like miniature lobsters. In Louisiana, where most of them come from, they live in streams, bayous and rice fields and are harvested in the wild and farmed. Crawfish are also harvested in the wild and from farms in Oregon, California and Washington State. They grow in streams and rivers all over the country and can be caught by hand.

Crawfish 3 to 5 inches long are shipped to market very tightly packed in string bags or boxes where, out of water but in a cool environment, they survive nicely for several days.

If you want crawfish, you'll need to order them in

advance, unless, of course, your fish store is close to the source. Be sure to buy them live. (It's easy to tell—they will splay their claws as you pick them up and even try to nip you.) Do not cook dead crawfish, for their flesh deteriorates quickly. Some stores sell crawfish already cooked, with a spicy coating.

Crawfish are highly decorative on a plate. As with lobster, the meat is mostly in the tail, which contains a sweet wonderful tidbit, but there is also a small amount in the claws.

You can boil whole crawfish, and they can be served hot or cold. You can enjoy the tail and claw meat and suck out the juices and fat from their heads. You'll need a finger bowl, napkins and a bowl for the discarded shells. Unless the crawfish are large, you won't need a nutcracker or mallet—you can crack the shells with your teeth and extract the meat easily.

You can pick the meat from crawfish and make a salad or pie from it. You can also use the meat to make crawfish bisque, a sumptuous soup; you'll also need the shells for flavor.

Crawfish tail meat is available, usually frozen in packages. Coated and deep-fried, it is a popular snack or appetizer known as Cajun popcorn.

Soft-shell crawfish are now available to restaurants and specialty fish stores. They are simply delicious deep-fried.

How to Clean Crawfish

Put the crawfish in a bowl of running water, and stir them around for a few minutes with a long wooden spoon. When they are clear of mud, drain them through a colander and run more water over them for a minute. Discard any dead crawfish.

How to Shell and Devein Boiled Crawfish

♦ Boil and drain crawfish as directed on page 143. When they are cool enough to handle, break the tail end of each crawfish away from the head; with it will come the orange-yellow "fat" (tomalley). Peel the tail, leaving on the fins at the end of the tail. Straighten the tail with one hand, take hold of the middle fin with the finger and thumb, give it a twist, and pull. The vein should come out all in one piece. If it doesn't, cut a very shallow groove down the top of the tail meat and extract it.

♦ The twisting and pulling technique to rid the crawfish of the vein is somewhat fancy, but it keeps the tail meat intact. Once you get used to the procedure, it can be done quickly.

COOKING METHODS

FORM	COOKING METHODS	SERVES	HOW MUCH TO BUY
Whole	Boiling	1	6 to 12 (½ to 1 pound)
Tail meat	Deep-frying	1	6 to 8 ounces
	Salad		

CHOICE OF RECIPES

Deep-Fried Seafood with Seasoned Flour, page 131
Boiled Crawfish, page 143
Crawfish Salad, page 194

Croakers

see Drum and Croaker, page 269

Cusk

see Cod Group, page 253

Dab

see Flatfish, page 273

Dolphinfish (Mahi-mahi)

Coryphaena hippurus
Cholesterol: 73   Omega-3: 0.1   Fat: 0.7

DOLPHINFISH, now more commonly known by the Hawaiian name *mahi-mahi*, are not the mammals we call dolphins. They are brilliantly colored fish with blue to turquoise backs, iridescent emerald-green bodies and yellowish bellies. Most of their color fades, however, as they die: Their skin turns a silvery gray the longer they are out of water. Lord Byron wrote:

> Parting day
> Dies like the dolphin, whom each pang imbues
> With a new colour as it gasps away,
> The last still loveliest, till—'tis gone—and all is grey

The bodies of dolphinfish are very compressed, and the males have high foreheads.

Fat content
low

Form usually prepared
fillets

Taste
sweet

Texture
firm

Dolphinfish come from all over the world, inhabiting the tropical waters of the Pacific from one side to the other, the Atlantic Ocean from Long Island down to the Caribbean and the Gulf of Mexico and the Central and South American waters off Costa Rica, Ecuador, Peru and Brazil. (In Latin America, dolphinfish are also known by the Spanish name *dorado*.)

Dolphinfish are caught at weights up to 88 pounds. They are marketed at 15 pounds and under. They are sold whole and in filleted form, fresh and frozen. Fillets are of even thicknesses. The texture of dolphinfish flesh is firm; it is dark along the lateral line and off-white elsewhere, but it lightens up as it cooks.

Dolphinfish are best broiled, grilled or baked. The flesh is firm enough to be braised with strong flavors. The thick skin should be removed before cooking.

COOKING METHODS

Cut	Cooking Methods	Serves	How Much to Buy
Fillets	Blackening	1	8 to 10 ounces
Fillets	As listed below	1	6 to 8 ounces

CHOICE OF RECIPES

Baked Lean Fish Fillets, page 75

Baked Fish Fillet Casserole, page 82

Baked Cajun Fish Casserole, page 85

Casserole of Fish Fillets with Potatoes and Coriander Pesto, page 86

Broiled Fillets, Butterflied or Split Fish, Steaks, Escalopes or Medallions, page 100

Grilled Fish Fillets, Butterflied or Split Fish, Steaks or Medallions, page 109

Blackened Fish Fillets, page 128

Steamed Seafood, page 146

Braised Dolphinfish (mahi-mahi) Fillets, page 154

Seafood Stew with Tomato and Green Pepper, page 176

Escabèche, page 184

Marinade for Broiled, Grilled, or Barbecued Seafood, page 187

Drum and Croaker

D RUMS AND CROAKERS are so named because they are capable of making grunting or drumming sounds in the water.

Redfish

Sciaenops ocellatus

Cholesterol: 64   Omega-3: 0.1   Fat: 0.8

The redfish, a member of the drum family, is also called the channel bass, red drum, puppy drum, spottail bass and red bass. It is found along the southeastern coast of the United States and in the Gulf of Mexico. It has been overfished, and its catch is now prohibited in most waters, at least partly as a result of the popularity of blackened redfish, the dish made famous by Chef Paul Prudhomme of New Orleans. The redfish has reddish bronze skin with one or two spots on its tail and pinky white flesh that turns white when it is cooked.

White Sea Bass

Atractoscion nobilis

Cholesterol: N/A   Omega-3: N/A   Fat: N/A

The white sea bass, or Chilean sea bass, is a member of the croaker family found in the Pacific from California down to Chile. White sea bass weighing up to 10 pounds are caught.

In Central and South American countries, white sea bass are called *corbinas* (Spanish for "croakers"). White sea bass flesh is similar to that of striped bass or grouper and can be treated as such.

Black Drum

Pogonias cromis

Cholesterol: N/A   Omega-3: 0.2   Fat: 1.5

Northern Kingfish

Menticirrhus saxatilis

Cholesterol: N/A   Omega-3: N/A   Fat: N/A

Fat content
low

Forms usually prepared
fillets, butterflied or split fish

Taste
sweet and mild

Texture
soft and flaky

Southern Kingfish
Menticirrhus americanus
Cholesterol: *N/A* **Omega-3:** *0.4* **Fat:** *5.1*

Other members of the drum family include the black drum, the northern kingfish (Maine to Florida), sometimes sold as whiting in Virginia, and the southern kingfish from the Gulf of Mexico, also known as the Gulf kingfish. All have white, lean flesh. Northern and southern kingfish are not related to the king mackerel, which is sometimes called the kingfish.

Weakfish (Sea Trout)
Cynoscion regalis
Mixed Species
Cholesterol: *83* **Omega-3:** *0.4* **Fat:** *3.6*

The weakfish, also called the squeateague or gray sea trout, is a silvery fish with small speckles on its skin. Its flesh is gray before it is cooked, but it then turns white. The name weakfish does not refer to the texture of the flesh but, rather, to the fish's weak mouth, which is easily torn by fishhooks. Weakfish are caught all along the Atlantic Coast, from Massachusetts to Florida; they are in season much of the year. Weakfish weighing up to 40 pounds are caught, but those sold usually weigh 2 to 10 pounds. They can be cooked whole or in filleted form, and they are very good to eat. Interestingly enough, they have no pin bones.

Spotted Sea Trout
Cynoscion nebulosus
Cholesterol: *83* **Omega-3:** *0.4* **Fat:** *3.6*

The spotted sea trout, also called the speckled trout or southern spotted weakfish, is prized in the South, where it is fished from the waters of the southeastern coast and the Gulf of Mexico. It has firmer flesh than the weakfish. Its skin is silvery in color, and it is spotted.

Freshwater Sheepshead

Aplodinotus grunniens

Cholesterol: 64   Omega-3: 0.5   Fat: 4.9

The freshwater sheepshead—also known as the freshwater drum, gasperou, gaspergou and graybass—is not to be confused with the sheepshead from the Sparidae family, a saltwater fish that lives along the Atlantic Coast (see page 338). Freshwater sheepsheads are caught in the lakes and rivers of the United States and Canada and are very popular in the Midwest and the southern states around the Gulf of Mexico. The flesh is white and flaky when cooked. Freshwater sheepsheads weighing up to 20 pounds are caught, but those marketed usually weigh 1 to 5 pounds.

Spot

Leiostomus xanthurus

Cholesterol: N/A   Omega-3: 0.6   Fat: 4.9

The spot, also called the Lafayette, goody and Norfolk spot, is a croaker. Spots are caught mainly along the southeastern coast. Most are small—they usually weigh ¼ pound each—but they can grow to as much as a pound. They have lean, flaky flesh and are best pan-fried.

Atlantic Croaker

Micropogonias undulatus

Cholesterol: 61   Omega-3: 0.2   Fat: 3.2

The Atlantic croaker, sometimes called the hardhead (a name also applied to catfish), is a pretty little fish with silvery bronze skin, a dark back and reddish brown spots that form lines going down to a white belly. Atlantic croakers are fished along the mid-Atlantic Coast. They weigh as much as a pound in the summer but are caught at 2 to 3 pounds in the fall. They are sold whole and can be pan-dressed or filleted and fried. They have a lot of taste; their flesh is firm and has small flakes when cooked.

COOKING METHODS

Cut	Cooking Methods	Serves	How Much to Buy
Redfish			
Fillets	Blackening	1	8 to 10 ounces
Fillets	As listed below	1	6 to 8 ounces
White Sea Bass			
Cook like grouper or striped bass (see pages 283 and 230).			
Black Drum			
Seldom marketed; cook small individuals like Atlantic croaker.			
Northern Kingfish			
Cook like European or American whiting (see page 254).			
Southern Kingfish			
Fillets	As listed below	1	6 to 8 ounces
Steaks	As listed below	1	6 to 8 ounces
Weakfish (Sea Trout)			
Whole	As listed below	1	¾ to 1 pound
Fillets	As listed below	1	6 to 8 ounces
Spotted Sea Trout			
Fillets	As listed below	1	6 to 8 ounces
Freshwater Sheepshead			
Fillets	As listed below	1	6 to 8 ounces
Spot			
Whole pan-dressed	As listed below	1	¾ pound
Atlantic Croaker			
Whole pan-dressed	As listed below	1	¾ pound

CHOICE OF RECIPES

Redfish

Baked Cajun Fish Casserole, page 85

Broiled Fillets, Butterflied or Split Fish, Steaks, Escalopes or Medallions, page 100

Grilled Fish Fillets, Butterflied or Split Fish, Steaks or Medallions, page 109

Blackened Fish Fillets, page 128

Southern Kingfish

Broiled Fillets, Butterflied or Split Fish, Steaks, Escalopes or Medallions, page 100

Grilled Fish Fillets, Butterflied or Split Fish, Steaks or Medallions, page 109

Escabèche, page 184

Weakfish (Sea Trout)

Baked Lean Fish Fillets, page 75
Bake-Poached Fish Fillets, page 79
Oven-Steamed Seafood en Papillote, page 80
Baked Fish Fillet Casserole, page 82
Baked Fish Fillet Casserole with Light Tomato Sauce, page 83
Casserole of Fish Fillets with Potatoes and Coriander Pesto, page 86
Roast Whole Fish, page 89
Broiled Whole Roundfish, page 98
Broiled Fillets, Butterflied or Split Fish, Steaks, Escalopes or
    Medallions, page 100
Grilled Whole Fish, page 107
Grilled Fish Fillets, Butterflied or Split Fish, Steaks or Medallions,
    page 109
Whole Fish Steamed in Foil on the Grill, page 116
Fried Fish Fillets or Fish Steaks à la Meunière, page 122
Fish Croquettes, page 125
Fish Fillets with Spinach and Ginger, page 178

Spotted Sea Trout

Baked Lean Fish Fillets, page 75
Baked Cajun Fish Casserole, page 85
Broiled Fillets, Butterflied or Split Fish, Steaks, Escalopes or
    Medallions, page 100
Grilled Fish Fillets, Butterflied or Split Fish, Steaks or Medallions,
    page 109

Freshwater Sheepshead

Fried Whole Fish or Pan-Dressed Fish, page 124

Spot

Broiled Whole Roundfish, page 98
Grilled Whole Fish, page 107
Fried Whole Fish or Pan-Dressed Fish, page 124

Atlantic Croaker

Roast Whole Fish, page 89
Broiled Whole Roundfish, page 98
Grilled Whole Fish, page 107
Fried Whole Fish or Pan-Dressed Fish, page 124
Soused or Marinated Fish, page 186

Eel
Mixed Species Other Than Conger Eels

Fat content
high
low (conger)

Forms usually prepared
fillets, steaks

Taste
sweet and mild

Texture
firm

EELS ARE LONG AND SNAKELIKE, with continuous dorsal and anal fins stretching the length of their brownish cylindrical bodies. A cross section of the eel's bone structure resembles the symbol of a Mercedes-Benz.

American Eel
Anguilla rostrata
Cholesterol: 126   Omega-3: 0.1   Fat: 11.66

American eels, also known as freshwater eels, are catadromous—that is, they grow up in fresh water and spawn in the ocean. They are found in waters from Newfoundland down to the West Indies, and also inland in rivers, streams, reservoirs, lakes and brackish water.

The American eel spawns in the Atlantic Ocean, and the young are helped to the east coast of the United States by ocean currents. It is an astonishing story, for it seems that both the European and American eels spawn in the same area, the Sargasso Sea, but each finds its way back to its own homeland. The trip for the young European eels takes more than a year. The small eels that take a year to reach our shores in the springtime are called elvers. Mature eels contain high levels of fat and are extremely fine food when smoked. They are good fried and used in soups or stews.

Baby European eels are called *angulas* in Spain, where they are a great delicacy. The baby eels are rinsed, dried and quickly fried in oil with garlic. Some Spanish restaurants in New York serve them when they are in season. A typical English dish is jellied eel, which I find delicious.

Other species of eel are found in Japan and New Zealand, but not along the west coast of the United States.

American Conger Eel
Conger oceanicus
Cholesterol: 49   Omega-3: N/A   Fat: N/A

This silvery gray eel, which grows much larger than the American eel, is found in the Atlantic along the east coast of the United States. It is not catadromous. It does not reach many fish markets, for it is not commonly caught and there is little demand for it. It is closely related to the European conger eel (*Conger conger*), which is a fine fish. When the American conger eel is available, buy it, for its flesh is most suitable for cooking in stews, braising or frying. It is firm, white and not as fatty as the smaller eel.

COOKING METHODS

CUT	COOKING METHODS	SERVES	HOW MUCH TO BUY
Whole	Smoking	6	1 pound (appetizer)
Skinned steaks	As listed below	1	7 ounces
Skinned fillets	As listed below	1	7 ounces

CHOICE OF RECIPES

Broiled Fillets, Steaks, Escalopes or Medallions, page 100
Grilled Fish Fillets, Steaks or Medallions, page 109
Braised Fish Fillets or Steaks with Provençal Sauce, page 156
Hot-Smoking (Smoke-Cooking), page 170

Flatfish

Mixed Flounder and Sole Species
Cholesterol: 48   Omega-3: 0.2   Fat: 1.2

FLATFISH ARE SO CALLED because their bodies are compressed laterally into flat oval shapes. A flatfish starts life swimming in a vertical position, as other fish do. Gradually, it begins to swim in a "flat" (horizontal) position, and it is during this time that the eye on its bottom side joins the eye on its top side. The eyes of a flatfish may be on the left or right side of its head. Most flatfish caught in U.S. waters are right-eyed. Knowing the difference between left-eyed and right-eyed flatfish is important in identifying species.

The upper part of a flatfish is colored variously from sandy brown to reddish brown, brown, green, gray and black. With the exception of the gray sole (witch flounder) and Greenland turbot, flatfish are white or nearly white underneath. The dark top skin is a flatfish's camouflage. Because of it, flatfish can hide or bury themselves on the ocean floor in the sandy, rocky or muddy soil where they live.

Every flatfish has continuous dorsal and anal fins, starting at its head and running along its body down to its tail. The tail is rounded on a small flatfish and convex on larger flatfish such as the halibut.

Fat content
low
high (turbot)

Forms usually prepared
fillets, steaks

Taste
bland to mild and sweet

Texture
flaky to soft

European flatfish include the Dover sole (the true sole), plaice, turbot and brill. Flatfish from the United States and Canada include the flounder, fluke, plaice, dab and halibut from both the cold and warm parts of the Atlantic and Pacific oceans. Many flatfish are called "sole" in the United States, even though there are no commercially important true soles in North American waters. In the North Atlantic, flatfish are part of a group of fish called groundfish, which includes cod, haddock, pollock, hake and ocean perch—all of which are caught from one of the world's richest sources for fine fish, the relatively shallow cold water above the continental shelf on Georges Bank (U.S. and Canadian fishing territory) and Grand Banks (Canadian fishing territory). Catches on Georges Bank have been temporarily restricted because of overfishing.

Flatfish are very desirable, lean fish. They cook beautifully on the bone (when you see a small, gutted whole flatfish in your store, buy it and try cooking it under the broiler) as well as in filleted form, although we see more filleted than whole flatfish in fish stores. The sparkling double fillets, which weigh a few ounces to a pound each and are usually skinned, are cut by suppliers or fishmongers from whole flatfish such as flounder, fluke, plaice and "sole." The fillets are boneless, because the skeletal construction of a flatfish is very simple (see page 50). As flatfish are not round-bodied, their flesh is more evenly distributed than the flesh of roundfish, which is an advantage if you are cooking fillets. Fillets from different species have slightly different textures, although most are smooth, with firm flesh. Flatfish flesh is translucent white to light gray when raw. However, note that the fillet from the top of a flatfish (the dark-skinned side of the fish) is thicker than the bottom fillet and is usually slightly off-white in color. Flatfish fillets turn white and opaque when cooked, and the flesh flakes easily.

On the East Coast, flatfish fillets are not usually identified by the actual names of the fish from which they are cut. Various flounders are called fillets of flounder, sole, lemon sole or gray sole.

Fillets of black-back (winter) flounder are called variously fillet of flounder and fillet of sole. When it weighs more than 3 pounds, it is called lemon sole. Gray sole fillets come from the witch flounder.

Atlantic Sole

There are a few species of true sole along the east coast that have some amusing names. They are naked, fringed, lined and crawled sole. There is also one called the hogchoker (which has been known to make its way into fresh water). All these fish are small and commercially insignificant.

The true sole from the northeast Atlantic is the Dover sole, available from the North Sea, Channel Islands and the Bay of Biscay. This fish is much prized for its firm texture, sweet taste and lean flesh. It's a pity it does not inhabit the western part of the Atlantic, because it is a particularly fine eating fish. This sole is flown over to the United States from Europe. You can find it in a few fish markets, but you are more likely to see it served up in restaurants.

Atlantic Flounder, Fluke, "Sole" and Plaice

Flounders and fluke from the west Atlantic are often called "sole," but they are technically flounder. There are many species of flounder available from the western Atlantic, up and down the east coast of the United States. They have white, mild-tasting, fine flesh and are very popular, for their fillets are boneless. They are easy to cook and can be prepared in countless ways, both simple and elaborate.

Blackback Flounder
Pseudopleuronectes americanus

This right-eyed fish is also called the winter flounder; when it weighs over 3 pounds, it is called the lemon sole. It is available nearly all year from the northwest Atlantic, mostly from Canadian and New England waters. Fillets of blackback flounder are variously called fillets of flounder, sole or lemon sole at the fish store.

Witch Flounder
Glyptocephalus cynoglossus

This fish, known as the gray sole, has dark gray skin. It is found in cold water from Labrador down to North Carolina. Fillets of witch flounder are usually more substantial than other flounder fillets but not as wide. The fillets lie very much in the middle of the fish on top of the backbone, and they do not stretch across the fish to the dorsal and anal fins as on other flatfish.

Sea Dab
Hippoglossoides platessoides

The sea dab (also known as American plaice) is reddish brown and is caught in waters from the Grand Banks down to Rhode Island. Sea dabs weigh up to 14 pounds. The fillets are sold as flounder in fish stores.

Yellowtail Flounder
Limanda ferruginea

This fish, caught in Canadian and New England waters, is yet another flounder, not to be confused with the yellowtail, a member of the jack family (see page 370).

Turbot
Reinhardtius hippoglossoides
Cholesterol: 46   Omega-3: 0.9   Fat: 13.8

This fish is also called the Greenland halibut, although, since it is not a halibut, use of that name is illegal. Not all turbot are caught near Greenland—they are caught in both the North Atlantic and the Pacific. Turbot have a relatively high fat content compared with flounders. Most are filleted and then frozen.

Summer Flounder
Paralichthys dentatus

This fish, also known as the fluke, is left-eyed. It can weigh up to 25 pounds, but those sold usually weigh up to 5 pounds. The summer flounder is available in the winter from Virginia and North Carolina waters and in the summer from waters as far north as Massachusetts. The Japanese like to use this heavy flatfish for sushi and sashimi.

Southern Flounder
Paralichthys lethostigma

This left-eyed flounder is fished from the southeastern Atlantic, from North Carolina to Florida and into the Gulf of Mexico.

Gulf flounder are found in the same waters, although the landings are small.

Pacific Sole, Flounder and Dab

Some flatfish species from the Pacific are described below. Most of these fish are sold in filleted form and are equally good broiled, fried, deep-fried, bake-poached, baked or steamed.

West Coast Dover Sole
Microstomus pacificus

The West Coast Dover sole is usually sold at weights ranging from 2 to 6 pounds, but it can grow larger.

English Sole
Parophrys vetulus

The English sole, also called the lemon sole, is a small fish that ordinarily weighs ¾ pound but can grow larger.

Butter Sole
Isopsetta isolepis

Sometimes available in the fish store, this fish weighs less than 1¼ pounds.

Petrale Sole

Eopsetta jordani

The petrale sole, also called the sand sole, is the best of the Pacific flatfish, a 1-to-8-pound fish with thick, flavorsome fillets.

Rex Sole

Glyptocephalus zachirus

Pacific Sand Dab

Citharichthys sordidus

The rex sole, also known as the brill sole, and the Pacific sand dab are small fish that cook well whole and as fillets. The Pacific sand dab is left-eyed.

Rock Sole

Lepidopsetta bilineata

The rock sole is considered to have excellent flesh and is usually filleted.

Yellowfin Sole

Limanda aspera

Curlfin Sole

Pleuronichthys decurrens

Starry Flounder

Platichthys stellatus

These flounders are also sold as flounder or sole.

Arrowtooth Flounder

Atherethes stomias

The arrowtooth flounder, sometimes marketed as the Pacific turbot, does not have consistently good flesh—it tends to be very soft when cooked, so it falls apart. It is mostly used for mink food.

Halibut

Atlantic Halibut
Hippoglossus hippoglossus
Pacific Halibut
Hippoglossus stenolepis
California Halibut
Paralichthys californicus

Mixed Species (Atlantic and Pacific)
Cholesterol: 32   Omega-3: 0.4   Fat: 2.3

Halibut are large flounder, harvested in both the Atlantic, from New York up to Greenland, and the Pacific, from Oregon to the Bering Sea. Atlantic halibut weighing 10 to 400 pounds are sold, although females can grow to 750 pounds. Pacific halibut grow to 500 pounds but are usually caught at weights of up to 10 pounds. The smaller California halibut, not a true halibut, is closely related to the East Coast fluke. They are caught in California and northern Mexico and grow up to 50 pounds, although most are sold at weights under 10 pounds.

Halibut are usually cut into steaks in the store. A halibut can be filleted easily, and a "roast" can be made with the tail end of the fish. Halibut has lean, firm, sparkling-white flesh that can be broiled, grilled, bake-poached or steamed. It has ideal flesh for skewering on brochettes because of its firmness. Be sure to have steaks cut at least 1 inch thick, preferably 1¼ inches thick; these steaks can then be cut into 1¼-inch cubes for brochettes.

COOKING METHODS
Flounder, Sole, Dab, Fluke, Turbot and Halibut

CUT	COOKING METHODS	SERVES	HOW MUCH TO BUY
Whole (all except gray sole, petrale sole and turbot)	Broiling	1	1 to 1¼ pounds
Tail ends (halibut)	Roasting	4	3 pounds
Steaks (halibut)	As listed below	1	6 to 8 ounces
Fillets	As listed below	1	6 to 8 ounces

CHOICE OF RECIPES

A recipe that includes a flatfish as one of its ingredients can generally be made with any other flatfish. (An exception is halibut, which is much larger than other flatfish and therefore has a distinct recipe list.) Note, however, that gray sole and petrale sole have thicker and firmer fillets than other flatfish.

Flounder, Lemon Sole, Sole, Sand Dab and Turbot

Oven-Steamed Seafood en Papillote, page 80

Broiled Whole Flatfish, page 96

Broiled Fillets, Butterflied or Split Fish, Steaks, Escalopes or
    Medallions, page 100

Grilled Fish Fillets, Butterflied or Split Fish, Steaks or Medallions,
    page 109

Fish Fillets Steamed in Foil on the Grill, page 116

Fried Fish Fillets or Fish Steaks à la Meunière, page 122

Deep-Fried Seafood with Seasoned Flour, page 131

Steamed Seafood, page 146

Fish Stock, page 164

Microwaved Sole with Endives and Béchamel, page 174

Fish Fillets with Spinach and Ginger, page 178

Seviche, page 183

Gray and Petrale Sole

Baked Lean Fish Fillets, page 75

Oven-Steamed Seafood en Papillote, page 80

Baked Cajun Fish Casserole, page 85

Casserole of Fish Fillets with Potatoes and Coriander Pesto, page 86

Broiled Fillets, Butterflied or Split Fish, Steaks, Escalopes or
    Medallions, page 100

Grilled Fish Fillets, Butterflied or Split Fish, Steaks or Medallions,
    page 109

Fish Fillets Steamed in Foil on the Grill, page 116

Fried Fish Fillets or Fish Steaks à la Meunière, page 122

Deep-Fried Seafood with Seasoned Flour, page 131

Steamed Seafood, page 146

Microwaved Sole with Endives and Béchamel, page 174

Fish Fillets with Spinach and Ginger, page 178

Fluke

All of the above recipes for Gray and Petrale Sole

Sushi and Sashimi, page 189

Halibut

Baked Fish Fillet Casserole, page 82

Baked Cajun Fish Casserole, page 85

Roast Stuffed Fish Chunk, page 92

Broiled Fillets, Butterflied or Split Fish, Steaks, Escalopes or Medallions, page 100

Grilled Fish Fillets, Butterflied or Split Fish, Steaks or Medallions, page 109

Grilled or Broiled Seafood Brochettes, page 110

Grilled or Broiled Seafood and Vegetable Brochettes, page 112

Fried Fish Fillets or Fish Steaks à la Meunière, page 122

Fish Croquettes, page 125

Fish Stock, page 164

Creamy Seafood Chowder, page 162

Escabèche, page 184

Flounder

see Flatfish, page 273

Fluke

see Flatfish, page 273

Gooseneck Barnacle

Polliicipes polymerus (North and South America),
Mitella polliicipes, also known as *Polliicipes cornucopia*
(Spain, Portugal and North Africa)
Cholesterol: *N/A* ***Omega-3:*** *N/A* ***Fat:*** *N/A*

Fat content
low

Form usually prepared
in shell

Taste
sweet

Texture
firm to soft

ALTHOUGH MANY EDIBLE BARNACLES are found in the Atlantic and Pacific, the most appealing and best-tasting is the gooseneck barnacle, also known as the leaf barnacle. Gooseneck barnacles grow in dense clusters on boats, rocks, buoys and pilings that are washed by the tides. They also grow on whales and floating logs.

The gooseneck barnacle is a remarkable-looking creature. Its neck can be up to 6 inches long (the reason for its name), on top of which it has a configuration of pointed, naillike plates that fit closely together and look a lot like a collection of pointed hooves or big-toe nails. Feathery appendages extend between the plates when the barnacle is gathering food.

Gooseneck barnacles are popular in Spain and Portugal, and as they are now scarce there, people in British Columbia are exporting them to these markets. Some are also supplied to restaurants in the Pacific Northwest, and some others are dropped off in New York restaurants, where I first had the opportunity to cook and eat them.

Barnacles should show signs of life before being rinsed in cold water. They should be steamed above boiling water for 3 to 5 minutes—no longer than that. The peeled little pink necks are what we eat—when they are cool enough to handle, peel the skin off each neck to expose a pink-orange stem. You can dip barnacle necks into a container of melted butter and lemon or a garlic sauce, though they are quite wonderful on their own. I think they taste like mussels, though others say they taste like crab, shrimp or lobster.

Gooseneck barnacles are not generally available in retail fish stores yet, but if you live in the Northwest, you can garner them yourself from coastal rocks with a little effort. Check with the local health and fish and game authorities before harvesting them.

My friend Bruce Stutz has written a short, amusing piece of history about the gooseneck barnacles called "Goosefeathers" in *Natural History* magazine. He recounts that "Irish priests were caught eating geese during Lent. Because they had never seen the Arctic nests of these migrating birds, the priests believed they arose from the goose-necked shells with the feathery tendrils. So they considered them seafood, not fowl." In 1215, the pope had forbidden the eating of geese during Lent; but likewise, a rabbi in France decided that if the geese did indeed grow from the gooseneck barnacles, Jews should be forbidden to eat them, as they were considered shellfish.

COOKING METHOD

FORM	COOKING METHOD	SERVES	HOW MUCH TO BUY
In shell	Steaming	1	½ to ¾ pound

CHOICE OF RECIPE

Steamed Seafood, page 146

Grouper and Sea Bass

Genus *Epinephelus, Mycteroperca* and *Paranthias*
Mixed Species
Cholesterol: 37   Omega-3: 0.2   Fat: 1.0

THIS LARGE FAMILY OF FISH includes groupers and sea bass. (Also see the profile of the black sea bass on page 228.)

Most groupers and sea bass are fished in temperate and tropical waters. There are 385 species of grouper worldwide. To name but a few, Atlantic Ocean groupers include the yellowfin grouper, Nassau grouper, black grouper, red grouper, rock hind, red hind, speckled hind, gag, scamp, Warsaw grouper and giant jewfish, while Pacific Ocean groupers include the California sea bass and the cabrilla.

The jewfish can grow to 800 pounds, and other groupers have been known to grow to 1,200 pounds—in Queensland, Australia, for instance. I expect you have seen those huge monsters of the deep in aquariums; they are so large, they take a few minutes to swim by you. In the fish stores, we see groupers weighing from 2 to 20 pounds, and they are just fine for eating.

Some groupers are as colorful as their names—the red grouper, popular on the East Coast, has a reddish hue—but most have brown-gray skin. They have large heads and spiny dorsal fins. Their excellent flesh is similar to that of red snapper—firm, sweet, white and lean. Whole groupers, both large and small, are very good roasted; filleted groupers are good baked, broiled or grilled. Cook them as you would red snapper or black sea bass.

Fat content
low

Form usually prepared
fillets

Taste
mild to sweet

Texture
quite firm

COOKING METHODS

Cut	Cooking Methods	Serves	How Much to Buy
Whole	Roasting	4	3 pounds
Whole	Roasting	Part of a buffet for 15	9 pounds
Fillets	Blackening	1	8 to 10 ounces
Fillets	As listed below	1	6 to 8 ounces

CHOICE OF RECIPES

Baked Lean Fish Fillets, page 75
Bake-Poached Whole Fish, page 76
Baked Fish Fillet Casserole, page 82
Baked Fish Fillet Casserole with Light Tomato Sauce, page 83
Baked Cajun Fish Casserole, page 85

Haddock
see Cod Group, page 251

Hake, Red (Ling)
see Cod Group, page 252

Hake, White
see Cod Group, page 251

European Hake and American Whitings

European Hake
Merluccius merluccius
Cholesterol: *N/A* **Omega-3:** *N/A* **Fat:** *N/A*

The European hake and the U.S. whiting used to be considered
members of the cod family, but it is now established that they belong
to a separate family called Merlucciidae.

Hake is called *merluza* in Spain, *pescada* in Portugal and *merlu* or *colin* in France. Hakes are caught off the Bay of Biscay and the Irish coast. Prized in Spain and Portugal, they are used often in soups and stews. They can also be baked, fried or deep-fried. The Spanish smoke hake. The flesh, when cooked, resembles that of cod, so hake can be used in recipes that call for cod (see page 253).

American Whiting
Merluccius bilinearis
Cholesterol: 67   Omega-3: 0.2   Fat: 1.3

Also called the silver hake, New England hake and frostfish, this fish abounds in the northwestern Atlantic. It is silvery brown with a dark lateral line.

The flesh of American whiting is made up of small flakes, because it is usually quite a small fish. It is off-white before it is cooked but turns clear white when cooked. The taste is quite bland. Because whiting is small, it makes good individual helpings, either whole or filleted. It can be fried, deep-fried or used in stews (in steak form). One wonderful method of cooking it is to place its tail in its mouth, fix the tail there with its very sharp teeth, then souse it (see page 186) or deep-fry it.

It is easy to remove the fillets from a cooked whiting. When you have taken the first fillet off, just pull the skeleton free from the rest of the flesh.

Whiting is usually very cheap, and I often use it to make a light fish stock when other, richer fish bones are not available.

Cook whiting like red hake (ling) and European whiting (see page 254).

Pacific Whiting
Merluccius productus
Cholesterol: N/A   Omega-3: 0.5   Fat: 1.6

Caught abundantly in the northeastern Pacific, this fish does not often reach the fish stores, because it is used primarily for fish meal.

Halibut, Atlantic, Pacific and Californian
see Flatfish, page 273

Fat content
low

Forms usually prepared
fillets, steaks

Taste
mild

Texture
flaky

Fat content
high

Forms usually prepared
fillets, butterflied or split fish

Taste
mild to strong

Texture
soft

Herring

Atlantic Herring
Clupea harengus harengus
Cholesterol: 60   Omega-3: 1.6   Fat: 18.0

Pacific Herring
Clupea harengus pallasi
Cholesterol: 77   Omega-3: 1.7   Fat: 16.4

HERRING ARE CAUGHT both in the North Atlantic and in the Pacific, from California to Alaska. These silvery blue elongated creatures have moderately fat flesh that is delicious, especially when broiled or grilled.

Herring are sold at weights up to about 8 ounces. When fresh and young, small Atlantic herring are sold as sardines, and most of them are canned as such. Many herring are frozen or cured in some form or other: When smoked, they are called kippers; when pickled in brine or flavored vinegars, they are called rollmops, matjes herring, Bismarck herring and soused herring.

The flesh of herring is soft and tends to spoil quickly, so it is fairly rare that one finds a fresh herring in this country.

When herring are available fresh (or defrosted), whole and ungutted, they can be split or butterflied from the back. The fishmonger is used to doing this with herring and should be willing to do it for you. Another good way to serve them is gutted through the head (see page 42). They can also be filleted like other roundfish.

Herring roe is important to the Japanese. It is exported from Alaska, where roe-bearing herring are caught. A very limited season is imposed so the herring can maintain their population.

COOKING METHODS

Cut	Cooking Methods	Serves	How Much to Buy
Whole	Roasting	1	½ to ¾ pound
Butterflied or split	As listed below	1	½ to ¾ pound
Fillets	As listed below	1	6 to 8 ounces

Jack

Pacific Crevalle Jack
Caranx caninus
Cholesterol: *N/A* ***Omega-3:*** *0.7* ***Fat:*** *3.9*

Amberjack
Seriola rivoliana
Cholesterol: *43* ***Omega-3:*** *N/A* ***Fat:*** *1.8*

Jackmackerel
Trachurus symmetricus
Cholesterol: *N/A* ***Omega-3:*** *N/A* ***Fat:*** *N/A*

Fat content
moderate

Form usually prepared
fillets

Taste
sweet

Texture
firm flake

THERE ARE MANY SPECIES OF JACKS roaming the tropical and warm temperate waters of the world. They are bright silvery creatures with compressed bodies. Some sport yellow or orange tinges on their sides. All of them have forked tails, and many have a row of bony scutes (hard bony scales) on each side.

The best-known jacks from the Atlantic are the Florida pompano (see page 314), the permit and the palometa. Other important jacks are the Pacific crevalle jack, the amberjack, the yellowtail (which is farmed in Japan for sushi and sashimi and is also caught off the California coast; see page 370) and the Pacific jackmackerel. Large species may contain ciguatera toxin, which can cause food poisoning (see page 21).

Apart from the Florida pompano, jacks are not as yet available in many fish markets. As more jacks appear in markets, take advantage of the firm, sweet flesh. Remove the dark, oily flesh along the lateral line of the fillets before cooking.

Cook crevalle jack like pompano (see page 315).

Ling

see Red Hake, Cod Group, page 252

Lingcod

Ophiodon elongatus
Cholesterol: 52   Omega-3: 0.2   Fat: 1.1

Fat content
low

Forms usually prepared
fillets, steaks

Taste
mild

Texture
firm

LINGCOD, also incorrectly called cultus cod, green cod, leopard cod and buffalo cod, is not related to the Atlantic cod but is part of the greenling family. It inhabits the waters of the Pacific from Alaska down to California; most lingcod is caught off Alaska and British Columbia.

This brownish green mottled and spotty creature looks similar to a cod, but it has a more elongated body. It can weigh up to 70 pounds, although 10 to 40 pounds is more usual. When cooked, its flesh is white, firm-textured and mild-tasting. Its scales are negligible because they are so small and smooth.

Lingcod is sold whole and as fillets and steaks. It is available fresh, frozen and smoked.

Cook lingcod like cod (see page 253).

Lobsters

Northern Lobster
Homarus americanus
Cholesterol: 95   Omega-3: N/A   Fat: 0.9

THE NORTHERN, or American, lobster is a fascinating-looking crustacean with large claws, an armored head and tail and antennae as long as its body. It is black with dark brown, red or green hues; when cooked, it turns a lovely bright orange-red. Its flesh is white with red tinges.

These lobsters thrive in the cold waters of the North Atlantic. They are caught in wooden traps from Labrador down to Virginia. The largest supplies come from waters off the coasts of Canada, Massachusetts and Maine; most of the rest come from waters off Rhode Island, New Jersey, New York and Connecticut.

Although they can live to a grand old age and can weigh as much as 45 pounds, lobsters are generally sold at weights ranging from 1 pound to about 5 pounds. Those weighing 1 to 1½ pounds are suitable for individual helpings. Larger lobsters—those weighing 3 pounds and up—have meat which is just as flavorful as that of smaller ones, and a steamed or broiled lobster this size can be shared by two people, since it can easily be cut in half. Lobsters command high prices, which are affected by supply and demand.

Lobsters must be kept alive in tanks of aerated salt water until shortly before they are cooked. In some fish stores, they are kept on ice, but it's not a very efficient way. Be sure a lobster shows real signs of life before you buy it: The claws and tail should splay out when it is picked up. The tail may also curl tightly under when it is picked up. If your lobster dies on the way home, cook it immediately and eat it as soon as possible. If it is a lively lobster, you can keep it for a few hours or even overnight in an open paper or plastic bag in the refrigerator. Make sure it is covered with a damp dishcloth or paper towels, or nestle it in seaweed.

Lobsters have firm, high-quality meat. You don't want to let the meat dry out—it becomes firm naturally as it cooks, and it must not lose any moisture, or it will toughen. Lobsters are best simply steamed or boiled, then served with melted butter and lemon juice (or lemon juice alone). Your fishmonger may sell cooked lobsters or

Fat content
low

Forms usually prepared
Northern lobsters: alive and cooked
Cooked lobster meat: pasteurized, canned and frozen lobster meat
Spiny lobsters: alive and cooked, frozen tails

Taste
sweet

Texture
firm

be willing to steam a lobster for you—be sure to choose a lively one. Broiling or grilling a lobster is tricky but not impossible, and the cooked shell does impart a very special flavor to the meat when prepared by these methods. Follow the accompanying instructions if you want to prepare a lobster for broiling or grilling, if you want to make a dish such as *lobster à l'americaine*, which calls for lobster in sections, or if you need raw lobster meat for a terrine or ravioli stuffing. These instructions are not for the squeamish. You can also ask your fishmonger to prepare lobsters for you in these ways.

Apart from the shell, the only parts of a lobster that are not edible are the little sac found behind the eyes and the feathery gills found at the base of the legs inside the body. The vein (which, incidentally, is edible but unsightly) running down the back of the tail meat, usually shrinks up when cooked and nearly disappears. If, when you cut the tail lengthwise, you see the vein, pull it out before serving. It is advisable to discard the tomalley, because it may be contaminated. The coral (roe) is edible; it is a dark green substance that turns bright red when cooked and is found only in the female. (You can tell the sex of a lobster by looking under the tail at the tiny claws nearest the body—if they are very thin and feathery, the lobster is a female, whereas if the lobster is a male, the claws will be thick and bony.) I think coral is delicious eaten along with the lobster meat or sieved, when raw, into a sauce to thicken it. Cooked coral added to a mayonnaise served with the lobster gives added dimension.

In addition to whole lobsters, your fishmonger may also sell cooked lobster meat, which you can use to make a nice salad, and lobster meat that is pasteurized, canned or frozen.

How to Kill a Lobster for Broiling, Grilling or Sectioning

Always pick up the lobster by its body. Put the lobster on a board in the sink, and pierce it with the point of a heavy chef's knife where there is a little crease halfway down the back of the body. This will kill the lobster instantly, but the nervous system will continue to cause movement for a few minutes, so leave the lobster alone until it is still.

How to Prepare a Lobster for Broiling or Grilling After Killing It

♦ Put the lobster on its back, and cut through the middle of its body lengthwise. Do not cut all the way through the back shell. Use kitchen scissors to cut through the middle of the shell on the underside of the tail. Spread the two halves apart with your hands, leaving the lobster partly joined at the back.

♦ Remove the little sac from behind the eyes. Leave the pale green tomalley and the dark green coral (if there is any) inside the body.

♦ It is not absolutely necessary to remove the intestinal vein that runs along the back of the tail, but it can be unsightly if it is exposed when cooked. Here are two methods for removing it from a raw lobster (if you don't succeed, leave it in—you can easily discard it as you are eating):

I have to say that this method does not always work, because the vein is fragile. Straighten out the uncooked tail with one hand, twist the middle tail fin and pull gently: The vein should come out in one piece.

Take hold of the vein from inside the body, and pull it out gently. Now you are ready to boil or grill the lobster.

How to Section a Lobster After Killing It

To obtain lobster sections, first sever the tail from the body. (It's easy to remove the vein now.) Twist off the claws, cut the body in two lengthwise, remove the little sac behind the eyes, pull off the leg sections, and remove the feathery gills near the base of the legs. Discard the tomalley. You now have two halves of tail, two leg sections, two claws and some coral (if any).

How to Kill a Lobster to Obtain Raw Meat

♦ Kill the lobster by putting it in boiling water for 1 or 2 minutes, making sure the lobster shell turns red all over. The preliminary heating of the shell helps separate the flesh from the shell so that extraction of the raw meat will be easier.

♦ To extract the raw meat, first twist off the claws. Cut the body (not the tail) in two lengthwise. Using scissors, cut the underside of the tail shell down its length. Do not cut the tail meat. Pry open the tail shell and pull out the flesh in one piece. Remove the vein running down the back of the tail meat. Collect the coral (if there is any), and put it in a bowl; discard the tomalley. Crack the claws with a mallet or nutcracker, and extract the flesh. Pick the meat out of the body where the legs are attached.

Spiny Lobsters

West Indies Lobster
Palinurus argus

California Spiny Lobster and Other Species
Panulirus interruptus

Mixed Species
Cholesterol: 70   Omega-3: 0.4   Fat: 1.5

West Indies spiny, or rock, lobsters are fished in warm waters from the Florida Keys down to Brazil. On the west coast of North America, California spiny lobsters are caught from Los Angeles and San Diego down to Baja California. Other spiny lobsters are caught in Hawaiian waters and in the cold waters of Australia and New Zealand. Live spiny lobsters have a reddish brown color mottled with yellow, orange, green and blue. They may be called crawfish, but they should not be confused with those little freshwater crustaceans.

Spiny lobsters are clawless. They are known for their tail meat, which is often sold frozen. Spiny lobster tails are graded by size, and prices differ accordingly—cold-water tails are more expensive than warm-water tails.

Dublin Bay Prawn
Nephrops norvegicus
Cholesterol: N/A   Omega-3: N/A   Fat: N/A

Dublin Bay prawns are neither shrimp nor prawns but miniature lobsters. They have claws about 4 to 6 inches long and are colored pink to white. They are fished from the east Atlantic, the North Sea and the Mediterranean. They are called *langoustines* by the French and *scampi* by the Italians. In the United States, these lobsters are sometimes available at restaurants and are rarely found in retail fish stores.

COOKING METHODS

Form	Cooking Methods	Serves	How Much to Buy
Northern Lobster			
Whole, live	Broiling	2	Two 1¼-pound (see table, page 101)
	Grilling	2	Two 1¼-pound (see table, page 114)
	Steaming		(see table, page 149)
Sectioned, raw	Braising	4	Two 2-2½-pound
Cooked lobster meat	Salad	2	8 to 12 ounces
Spiny Lobster			
Whole	Steaming	2	2½ pounds
Tails	Broiling	1	6 to 8 ounces
	Grilling	1	6 to 8 ounces

CHOICE OF RECIPES

Broiled Lobster, page 101

Grilled Lobster, page 114

Steamed Lobster, page 149

Braised Lobster with Provençal Sauce, page 156

Lobster Salad, page 194

Mackerel

THE MACKEREL FAMILY consists of 49 species, including all the tunas. Some mackerels we are familiar with are the Atlantic, Spanish, king, chub and Pacific varieties. All have beautifully shaped and colored bodies and are excellent to eat when fresh. Their flesh is gray (sometimes pink), soft and oily before it is cooked and is best broiled, grilled or baked. Once cooked, the flesh firms up and turns off-white.

Fat content
high to low

Forms usually prepared
fillets, butterflied or split fish

Atlantic Mackerel

Scomber scombrus

Cholesterol: 70   Omega-3: 2.3   Fat: 13.9

Taste
mild

Texture
flaky

These beautiful fish, also known as Boston mackerel, have silvery blue streamlined bodies and greenish backs that are striated with dark, uneven, wavy little stripes. The "mackerel" sky, with its thin, unevenly waved clouds, undoubtedly takes its name from the skin of

Atlantic mackerel. These fish seem to be scaleless—their scales are so minute and smooth as to be negligible. They range in size from ½ pound to 7 pounds.

Atlantic mackerel are available from both sides of the North Atlantic. On this side of the ocean, they are primarily available in the spring, when they migrate from south to north between Cape Hatteras and Labrador, and in the autumn, when they return south. During the summer, they are found in the Gulf of Maine and the Gulf of Saint Lawrence.

The Atlantic mackerel is a soft-fleshed fish and must be eaten when very fresh. It is sold whole, usually ungutted. You have to ask the fishmonger to gut it and split, butterfly or fillet it for you or do these things yourself. One of the best ways to gut a small Atlantic mackerel (called a *tinker* in England and a *lizette* in France) is through the head (see page 42).

Smoked Atlantic mackerel is available, imported from Europe. Fillets of Atlantic mackerel, sometimes both smoked and peppered, can be used for a cold lunch or brunch or can be made into a smoked pâté.

Pacific and Chub Mackerel
Scomber japonicus
Cholesterol: 47 Omega-3: 1.4 Fat: 7.9

These fish are identical. They look like the Atlantic mackerel but are smaller. They are very plentiful in the Pacific and are found in the Atlantic, where they are called chub mackerel. They can be cooked like Atlantic mackerel.

Spanish Mackerel
Scomberomorus maculatus
Cholesterol: 76 Omega-3: 1.3 Fat: 6.3

This colorful mackerel has a silvery body and yellow to deep orange spots on its sides. It is available in waters from the Chesapeake Bay area down to southern Florida and the Gulf of Mexico. It can be treated like Atlantic mackerel, although it has paler flesh and is not as strong-tasting.

King Mackerel

Scomberomorus cavalla

Cholesterol: 53   Omega-3: 0.3   Fat: 2.0

King mackerel, also called kingfish (but not to be confused with the kingfish of the drum family), come from the warm waters off Florida and the Gulf Coast. They grow large, up to 100 pounds. Cook them as you would Atlantic mackerel. They are usually sold as steaks at the fish store.

COOKING METHODS

CUT	COOKING METHODS	SERVES	HOW MUCH TO BUY
Whole	Roasting	1	¾ to 1 pound
Whole	Broiling	1	¾ to 1 pound
Whole	Grilling	1	¾ to 1 pound
Whole	Sousing	1	8 to 12 ounces
Split	As listed below	1	6 to 8 ounces
Fillets	As listed below	1	6 to 8 ounces

CHOICE OF RECIPES

Baked Fatty Fish Fillets, page 73

Bake-Poached Fish Fillets, page 79

Oven-Steamed Seafood en Papillote, page 80

Baked Fish Fillet Casserole with Light Tomato Sauce, page 83

Roast Whole Fish, page 89

Broiled Fillets, Butterflied or Split Fish, Steaks, Escalopes or Medallions, page 100

Grilled Whole Fish, page 107

Grilled Fish Fillets, Butterflied or Split Fish, Steaks or Medallions, page 109

Hot-Smoking (Smoke-Cooking), page 170

Fish Fillets with Spinach and Ginger, page 178

Escabèche, page 184

Soused or Marinated Fish, page 186

Marinade for Broiled, Grilled or Barbecued Seafood, page 187

Summer Fish Salad, page 193

Monkfish

Cholesterol: 25 Omega-3: N/A Fat: 1.5

Fat content
low

Form usually prepared
fillets

Taste
mild

Texture
firm

THE MONKFISH, also known as goosefish and by at least 14 other names, is an excellent fish to eat but hardly easy to look at in its natural state. Most of the names given to it refer to its looks and its habits. Anglerfish and fishing frog allude to the fact that the monkfish entices fish into its extraordinarily large mouth with the aid of a dorsal spine that sports a fleshy tab on its tip and resembles a bit of food. This little "fishing rod" protrudes above the head, and when lowered over the mouth, the tissue acts as bait or lure. The monkfish will eat nearly anything, including fish, shellfish and water birds, and it has an insatiable appetite, hence the name bellyfish. Its mouth is very wide and the fish is ugly, hence the names bullmouth, allmouth, frogfish, bellowsfish and devilfish. As for the names monkfish, abbotfish and lawyerfish, these are beyond my comprehension, unless they refer to the silken, mottled, dark brown skin and side appendages that "enrobe" the monkfish. My friend Richard Lord, formerly head of the Fulton Fish Market Information Services, suggests that monkfish might have attained their name because they were taken by monks who used to go through the catch discarded by fishermen.

One species of monkfish (*Lophius americanus*) is fished in the Atlantic from North Carolina up the entire east coast to Newfoundland. A European monkfish (*L. piscatorius*) is caught in the eastern Atlantic and the Mediterranean. Other monkfish species are caught near Japan.

Monkfish is popular in France, where it is called *lotte* and *baudroie*, in Spain, where it is called *rape*, and in Italy, where it is called *coda di rospo* and *rana pescatrice*. In Japan, it is much appreciated for its delicious liver (sometimes served here in Japanese restaurants) as well as its flesh. In America, monkfish has only recently found a market. Enterprising people have discovered its culinary merits, and it is now relatively well known and still reasonably priced.

The monkfish can weigh up to 50 pounds. We seldom see the entire fish, for the head is nearly always cut off and discarded before the fish reaches the market, although in Europe, the head is used to make stock. As a rule, we eat only the tail section of the fish, which consists of firm white flesh surrounding a central backbone that has no rib bones protruding from it. I have handled monkfish tails that weighed as much as 10 pounds and others that weighed less than a pound.

The fish should be skinned, and the pinkish-purplish dark outer flesh should be removed; what remains is flesh that is pearly white. Thereafter, it should be extremely easy to cut fillets from each side of the backbone (see page 54); and the tough fiber on the side of the fillet that was nearest to the backbone should also be cut away.

If you like, you can then cut the fillets into individual portions, depending on the size of the tail. Cubes can be cut and cooked in stews or skewered for grilled or broiled brochettes. Using the whole tail end for a braised dish is one of my favorite ways of preparing monkfish. Even though they are easy to cut, monkfish steaks are not practical, for the flesh contracts and shrinks around the central backbone while cooking, and the backbone protrudes, making it impossible to cook the steak evenly on both sides.

The flesh is firm, white and lean. It will not flake unless cooked for a long time, so it is perfect for soups, stews and brochettes. It can be braised, fried, steamed, broiled or grilled. It tastes sweet, and its texture is like that of lobster meat, so it is sometimes called "the poor man's lobster." The flesh loses quite a bit of moisture as it cooks and shrinks, so you must buy a little more of this fish than you usually would of other fish, and when cutting fillets, you should cut the portions larger than usual.

The flesh absorbs flavors readily, so you can use many delicious ingredients, such as garlic, tomatoes, fresh herbs, wine and stocks, to flavor it.

When monkfish cheeks are available, buy them, for they are wonderfully easy to prepare and are skinned before being sold. They are beautiful little round nuggets of firm white flesh. You need three or four per portion.

COOKING METHODS

CUT	COOKING METHODS	SERVES	HOW MUCH TO BUY
Whole tail ends	Braising	Part of a buffet for 20 to 30	10 pounds
Whole tail ends	Braising	Dinner for 2	1½ pounds
Fillets	As listed below	1	8 ounces
Slices, medallions	As listed below	1	8 ounces
Cubes (brochettes)	Grilling, broiling	1	6 to 8 ounces

CHOICE OF RECIPES

Broiled Fillets, Butterflied or Split Fish, Escalopes or Medallions, page 100

Grilled Fish Fillets, Butterflied or Split Fish or Medallions, page 109

Grilled or Broiled Seafood Brochettes, page 110

Grilled or Broiled Seafood and Vegetable Brochettes, page 112

Fried Fish Fillets à la Meunière, page 122

Steamed Seafood, page 146

Braised Monkfish Tail, page 154

Braised Fish Fillets with Provençal Sauce, page 156

Fish Soup (Bourride), page 160

Fish Stock, page 164

Seafood Stew or Pasta Sauce, page 165

Seafood Stew with Tomato and Green Pepper, page 176

Seviche, page 183

Mullet, Striped
Mugil cephalus
Cholesterol: 49   Omega-3: 0.3   Fat: 3.8

Mullet, White
Mugil curema
Cholesterol: N/A   Omega-3: N/A
Fat: N/A

Fat content
low

Forms usually prepared
fillets, butterflied or split fish

Taste
mild

Texture
flaky

THERE ARE SEVERAL SPECIES of mullet, two of which are the striped mullet, also called the jumping mullet, and the white mullet, also called the silver mullet. Long but stout-bodied, with silvery blue skin and large, loose scales, they are herbivorous and often inhabit brackish waters. They form large schools and may be seen jumping from the water.

Striped mullet are found worldwide in warm waters. They are important as food fish. White mullet are caught in the Atlantic from Cape Cod down to Florida, in the Gulf of Mexico and on down to South America. Some are farmed in ponds.

Mullet are marketed weighing up to 5 pounds. They are sold whole and in filleted form.

Mullet flesh is firm, mild and nutty-tasting. Both the flesh and roe smoke well.

You can all but eliminate the muddy taste a mullet may have by skinning it and removing the dark lateral strip of fatty flesh.

COOKING METHODS

Cut	Cooking Methods	Serves	How Much to Buy
Whole	Roasting	1	¾ to 1 pound
Fillets	As listed below	1	6 to 8 ounces

CHOICE OF RECIPES

Baked Lean Fish Fillets, page 75

Bake-Poached Fish Fillets, page 79

Roast Whole Fish, page 89

Broiled Fillets, Butterflied or Split Fish, Steaks, Escalopes or Medallions, page 100

Grilled Fish Fillets, Butterflied or Split Fish, Steaks or Medallions, page 109

Fried Fish Fillets or Fish Steaks à la Meunière, page 122

Fish Croquettes, page 125

Hot-Smoking (Smoke-Cooking), page 170

Summer Fish Salad, page 193

Mussels

Blue Mussel

Mytilus edulis

Cholesterol: 28   Omega-3: 0.4   Fat: 2.2

THIS ATTRACTIVE BIVALVE has become widely popular in the United States relatively recently, but why it took so long I don't know. Europeans have enjoyed mussels for centuries for their distinctive taste and versatility. The near-black shells are attractive in many dishes, and their flesh, though briny, is rich and sweet.

A wild mussel affixes itself to a rock, pier or pole by means of its byssus (also known as its "beard"), a tuft of dark threads that it makes itself. Mussels are also farmed: Farmers dangle ropes from large rafts above the ocean floor, and the mussels attach themselves. Great quantities of mussels are gathered commercially in the North Atlantic from North Carolina up to Canada and in the Pacific from

Fat content
low

Forms usually prepared
live in shell and sometimes frozen; cooked and shucked, fresh, bottled or canned

Taste
sweet

Texture
soft to firm

Alaska to California; in addition, the aquaculture of mussels is a large, expanding business.

You can also collect your own mussels, but be sure they are from clean, uncontaminated water—check with the local department of health or the fish and game department. Red tides that occasionally invade some Atlantic and Pacific coastal waters are dangerous to humans who eat bivalves, and these shellfish should not be picked when such tides are present.

Mussels that are sold commercially range up to 3 inches in length, although they may grow larger. Mussels in their shells are sold by the pound, fresh or sometimes frozen; mussels are also cooked, shucked and then canned or bottled.

Mussels must be alive shortly before they are prepared. If the shells are tightly closed, you can be sure they are living. Throw out any that are broken or gaping open or any that are extra heavy—they may be filled with only sand or mud. (If you suspect that a mussel is filled with mud or sand, try sliding the shells apart with your finger and thumb. If there is flesh inside, there will be resistance. Wild mussels are often washed before going to the consumer, but some may have barnacles on them or may be sandy inside. This is a nuisance, but they can be cleaned easily—see the instructions that follow. Cultivated mussels are usually far cleaner than wild mussels; their shells are thin and light, and they are less prone to grow "pearls" or be sandy.

How to Clean Mussels

♦ Put the mussels in a large bowl, bucket or sink under cold running water. Discard any broken, gaping shells or shells filled with mud or sand (see above). Rub the mussels together vigorously for 2 to 3 minutes until you rid them of barnacles and sand (you might want to wear rubber gloves for this). It is the rubbing together that cleans them. If some stubborn barnacles do not rub off, use a paring knife or wire brush to scrape them off.

♦ Put the cleaned mussels in a container of cold, lightly salted water, and sprinkle them with a teaspoon of flour so they plump up and disgorge any sand. (This is not absolutely necessary for farmed mussels, which are usually free of sand.) Leave them to stand for up to 1 hour (no longer, for the fresh water will kill them), then pull off the beards just before cooking them or serving them raw. The mussels will die within hours without their beards. You can tell they are dead when their shells gape open.

You can use mussels cold in salads or hot in soups; you can bake them on the half shell or add them to a risotto. One simple way to cook mussels is to put them in a shallow covered skillet with a little dry white wine, fresh herbs, shallots and fresh parsley and steam them just until their shells open. This takes only 4 to 5 minutes, and then they are ready to eat. (You can never tell what color their flesh is going to be once it's cooked—it can vary from a bright orange to a dull gray. I'm told that this may have to do with their sex or what they are feeding on.) If you are going to use the mussels cooked and shucked, shuck them as soon as they are cool enough to handle and put them in their own juice, so they won't dry out and shrivel.

Incidentally, it is best to eat mussels during the fall, winter and spring, before they spawn. After they spawn, their flesh is depleted, and you will not find the plump morsels for a while.

Green-Lipped Mussel
Perna canaliculus
Cholesterol: N/A *Omega-3:* N/A *Fat:* N/A

The green-lipped mussel, imported from New Zealand, is another wonderful shellfish. Not only do green-lipped mussels look beautiful, but their orange and white flesh is exquisite to eat. Their shells are usually larger than those of blue mussels; they range in color from light brown at one end to bright green at the tip, and they are striated with thin dark brown stripes. Their inside shells are iridescent mother-of-pearl.

Green-lipped mussels are farmed and arrive in this country perfectly clean. You are likely to find them on restaurant menus. They are not generally available in fish stores, but some supermarkets carry them already cooked and frozen.

The best way to cook these beautiful mussels is to steam them open like blue mussels and savor their unique flavor, either hot or cold.

COOKING METHODS

FORM	COOKING METHODS	SERVES	HOW MUCH TO BUY
In shell	As listed below	1	¼ to 1 pound

Ocean Perch

Sebastes marinus

Deepwater Redfish

Sebastes mentella

Mixed Species

Cholesterol: 42   Omega-3: 0.3   Fat: 1.6

Fat content
low

Form usually prepared
fillets

Taste
mild

Texture
flaky

OCEAN PERCH—also known as golden redfish, Atlantic redfish, redfish, rosefish, deep-sea perch and red perch—are found in the cold northwestern waters of the Atlantic off the coasts of the United States and Canada. They are members of the rockfish family, Scorpaenidae.

Ocean perch are commercially important fish for Canada, the United States and other countries. Most weigh up to 3 pounds when caught, although they grow larger. They have fine, attractive red to orange skin and small scales.

Ocean perch are sold whole and filleted; the fresh skin-on fillets are pink in tone. The flesh has a fine, flaky texture and is mild-tasting.

Deepwater redfish, marketed as ocean perch, have large eyes, which are often distended because the fish are taken from very deep water.

COOKING METHODS

Cut	Cooking Methods	Serves	How Much to Buy
Fillets	As listed below	1	6 to 8 ounces

CHOICE OF RECIPES

Oven-Steamed Seafood en Papillote, page 80

Baked Fish Fillet Casserole with Light Tomato Sauce, page 83

Broiled Fillets, Butterflied or Split Fish, Steaks, Escalopes or Medallions, page 100

Fried Fish Fillets or Fish Steaks à la Meunière, page 122

Steamed Seafood, page 146

Escabèche, page 184

Ocean Pout

Macrozoarces americanus

Cholesterol: 52   Omega-3: *N/A*   Fat: 0.9

OCEAN POUT is a member of the eelpout family. It is found in the northwestern Atlantic. It resembles an eel, with its streamlined body and continuous fins running down the top and bottom of its body. Mottled in appearance, it is colored from brown to yellow to green. Ocean pout are caught weighing up to 12 pounds, December through April.

Fat content
low

Form usually prepared
fillets

Taste
mild, sweet

Texture
flaky

COOKING METHODS

Cut	Cooking Methods	Serves	How Much to Buy
Fillets	As listed below	1	6 to 8 ounces

CHOICE OF RECIPES

Oven-Steamed Seafood en Papillote, page 80

Baked Fish Fillet Casserole, page 82

Fried Fish Fillets or Fish Steaks à la Meunière, page 122

Steamed Seafood, page 146

Fish Soup (Bourride), page 160

Salsa-Flavored Fish Salad, page 192

Octopus

THE OCTOPUS has a scary reputation as an eight-armed creature that can enfold its victims in its tentacles and puff out black ink to avoid being seen. It is terrifying to some but delicious eating. Indeed, octopus do grow large, but those available to us weigh 1 pound up to 3 or 4 pounds. They are found worldwide. Octopus, like squid, are cephalopods, that is, "head-footed," meaning that their tentacles or legs are attached to their heads.

In this country, most octopuses are sold partially cooked and then frozen or frozen raw. Many are imported from Portugal. However, fresh whole octopuses are available in November and December on the East Coast. Most of these are sold cleaned. The octopus has a delicate ink sac embedded in its head that is obtainable only if it has not been cleaned, so if you are buying a cleaned whole octopus and you want to use the ink (it is a marvelous flavoring for sauces and can also be used for a risotto), arrange in advance for your fishmonger to remove the sac and save it for you.

Octopus skin may look gray when raw, but when cooked, it turns a purplish color that contrasts with the solid white inner flesh. Octopus flesh is firm and flavorful. It can be cooked ever so briefly, or because it toughens quickly, boil it for an hour or so until tender. Then finish it with a sauce, put it in a stew, marinate it, grill it or broil it. The flesh is unlikely to fall apart; however, take care not to cook it so long that it loses its firm texture.

The Japanese have a wonderful way of preparing octopus: They rub it with salt and then pickle it in rice vinegar. The skin turns a bright, deep, nearly unreal purple.

The people of the Mediterranean use this creature in many dishes, and I have seen the Greeks tenderize the octopus by repeatedly throwing it on a rock.

Common Atlantic Octopus
Octopus vulgaris
Cholesterol: 48   Omega-3: 0.2   Fat: 1.0

The Atlantic octopus is found in U.S. waters from Connecticut all the way to Mexico.

Fat content
low

Forms usually prepared
fresh or frozen, raw or partially cooked

Taste
mild

Texture
firm

How to Prepare Octopus for Cooking

Turn the head inside out, and clean it under running water. You will find the delicate ink sac inside—carefully free it from the attached membrane and save it. Turn the head right side out, and cut off the part where the eyes are.

How to Cook Octopus

1 garlic head, cut in half horizontally
3 inches fresh ginger, sliced
4 dried chili peppers
1 tablespoon whole allspice
6 bay leaves
  Salt to taste
1 1-to-4-pound octopus

1. Bring a pot of water (enough to cover the octopus) to a boil with all of the ingredients except the octopus.

2. Add the octopus, and cook slowly for 40 minutes. Then turn off the heat, and let stand for 40 minutes before draining.

3. After the octopus is cooked, scrape and pull off the outside layer of purplish skin from the head and tentacles with your fingers, and cut it into suitable-sized pieces.

COOKING METHODS

Cut	Cooking Methods	Serves	How Much to Buy
Previously cooked and cut into pieces	As listed below	1	6 to 8 ounces

CHOICE OF RECIPES

Broiled Fillets, Butterflied or Split Fish, Steaks, Escalopes or Medallions, page 100

Grilled Fish Fillets, Butterflied or Split Fish, Steaks or Medallions, page 109

Seafood Stew or Pasta Sauce, page 165

Sushi and Sashimi, page 189

Orange Roughy

Hoplostetheus atlanticus

Cholesterol: 23   Omega-3: N/A   Fat: 0.7

THE ORANGE ROUGHY (pronounced "ruffy") is a relative new-comer to the commercial fish scene, even the name had to be invented. Discovered in marketable quantities in 1975 and marketed only since 1979, it is fished from the Tasman Sea in the South Pacific and off the coasts of New Zealand and Australia. It has bright red-orange skin and firm white flesh. It is usually frozen at sea, thawed on shore and then filleted and refrozen.

The market for this fish has grown enormously, as has the price, in recent years. It is exported all over the world in large quantities. This excellent if somewhat bland fish can be cooked in many ways.

Fat content
low

Form usually prepared
fillets

Taste
mild

Texture
flaky

COOKING METHODS

Cut	Cooking Methods	Serves	How Much to Buy
Fillets	As listed below	1	6 to 8 ounces

CHOICE OF RECIPES

Broiled Fillets, Butterflied or Split Fish, Steaks, Escalopes or Medallions, page 100

Grilled Fish Fillets, Butterflied or Split Fish, Steaks or Medallions, page 109

Fish Croquettes, page 125

Steamed Seafood, page 146

Fish Fillets with Spinach and Ginger, page 178

Seviche, page 183

Escabèche, page 184

Also see the suggested recipes for cod (fillets) on page 253 and for red snapper (fillets) on page 348.

Oysters

Eastern Oyster
Crassostrea virginica
Cholesterol: 55   Omega-3: 0.4   Fat: 2.5

Pacific Oyster
Crassostrea gigas
Cholesterol: N/A   Omega-3: 0.7   Fat: 2.3

Olympia Oyster
Ostrea lurida
Cholesterol: N/A   Omega-3: 0.45   Fat: 2.5

Belon Oyster

Ostrea edulis

Cholesterol: N/A   Omega-3: 0.24   Fat: 1.7

Fat content
low

Form usually prepared
shucked

Taste
salty, sweet to flinty

Texture
soft

THESE OYSTERS are also called "flat oysters"—they are not true belons, which belong to France. The craggy bivalves, each of which contains a plump, meaty morsel, are much appreciated the world over. Supplies may come and go, but many oysters are commercially grown nowadays, and production seems to be keeping up with demand.

The above listed oysters are those which are harvested in U.S. and Canadian waters. Common eastern oysters are found in the Atlantic, from the Gulf of Saint Lawrence down the east coast to the Gulf of Mexico, in brackish waters close to shore. They vary greatly in shape, size, taste and name, according to the region they come from. Everyone has favorites. The best-known eastern oysters are the Apalachicola (Florida), Blue Point (Long Island), Bristol (Maine), Caraquet (New Brunswick), Chatham (Massachusetts), Kent Island (Chesapeake Bay), Chincoteague (Maryland and Virginia), Cotuit and Wellfleet (Cape Cod), Malpeque (Prince Edward Island), and Louisiana and Texas Gulf oysters.

Pacific oysters, introduced from Japan, are found from northern California up to British Columbia. Their shapes, sizes, flavors and names differ according to the region. Some of the best-known Pacific oysters are the Golden Mantle (British Columbia), Hog Island Sweetwater and Tomales Bay (north of San Francisco, California), Kumamoto (Washington and California), Penn Cove (Washington), Quilcene (Washington), Rock Point (Dahob Bay, Seattle, Washington), Westcott Bay (Washington), Willapa Bay (Washington) and Yaquina Bay (Oregon).

Belon flat oysters, indigenous to France, are now farmed off the coasts of Maine, New Hampshire, California and Washington.

Olympia oysters are harvested off the coast of Washington State.

Some oysters are marketed fresh and sold by the pound (in Cape Cod), by the piece or by the dozen. Others are shucked and sold by volume (pint, quart or gallon). Still others are cooked, smoked and canned.

Be sure you obtain your oysters from reliable fish stores or eat them in good restaurants, for they can become contaminated by tainted water. Be sure that oysters are alive and have tightly closed shells if you are going to eat them raw, and store them in an open container in the refrigerator with a damp towel, a paper towel or seaweed.

Oysters spawn as the waters warm, so it is best to avoid eating them during the summer months—they get milky and tasteless, and they tend to perish more quickly out of water at this time. However, the time to eat the Malpeques from Prince Edward Island, the Caraquets from New Brunswick and the Bristols from Maine is from May to November—they are harvested when the ice melts, and the cold water they come from keeps them in good condition for eating in the summer. The triploid oysters from the West Coast never spawn and are therefore plump and good to eat year-round.

The saltiness of oysters can vary a lot, from mild to strong. They usually have a full sweet flavor with a delicious flinty overtone. Surely the best way to eat them is on the half shell with a squeeze of lemon juice. Warmed oysters are also a delight, but warm them only until they plump up, or if you cook them, cook them only until their edges curl. If you deep-fry them, use good oil at the right temperature (375 degrees F) and cook them for a minute only.

Incidentally, oysters have far less cholesterol than previously thought, which is encouraging. It turns out that in their calculations, scientists mistakenly included the plant sterols contained in oysters—in fact, these sterols work against cholesterol accumulation.

How to Shuck Oysters

♦ You will need an oyster knife to shuck oysters—no other knife will do. This is a strong pointed knife available in fish stores or kitchen-supply stores; it usually has a guard, a curved piece of metal placed between the blade and the handle. I like simple, sturdy, narrow-pointed oyster knives with or without a guard.

♦ Scrub the oysters with a wire or plastic brush under running water just before shucking. Wrap a dishcloth around your hand so that you can hold the oyster down firmly and protect yourself in case the knife slips. With the rounded shell down, find the hinged, pointed end of the oyster and push the tip of the knife into it, between the shells. When you get inside, twist the knife a little to loosen the shell—you'll hear a click. Insert the knife, and scrape close to the top shell to cut the muscle that keeps the shells together. Discard the top shell. Slide your knife under the oyster so it sits freely on the bottom shell. Retain as much juice as you can, and strain out any pieces of broken shell before serving.

♦ If you need shucked oysters without shells, break the thin end of each shell with a hammer, then slide your knife around the shell to release the oyster.

COOKING METHODS

FORM	COOKING METHODS	SERVES	HOW MUCH TO BUY
Shucked, half shell	Raw, hot-smoking	1	6 to 9
Shucked	Deep-frying	1	12 (½ to 1 pint)
Shucked	Soup	1	2 to 3

CHOICE OF RECIPES

Deep-Fried Seafood with Beer Batter, page 133
Fish Soup (Bourride), page 160
Hot-Smoking (Smoke-Cooking), page 170
Raw on the half shell

Perch Group
Mixed Species
Cholesterol: 90   Omega-3: 0.3   Fat: 0.9

Fat content
low

Form usually prepared
fillets

●

Taste
mild

Texture
flaky

All of the following fish are lean and can be treated like pike (see page 313):

Yellow Perch
Perca flavescens

Yellow perch are small freshwater fish caught in lakes, streams, rivers and low-saline estuaries from Canada down to South Carolina. These are colorful creatures with brown bands of color striping their backs. In the winter, they are caught through the ice.

Walleye
Stizostedion vitreum
Cholesterol: 86   Omega-3: 0.3   Fat: 1.2

Walleyes, also called pickerel, walleye pike or walleyed pike (although no relative of pike), are freshwater fish variously colored yellowish to greenish. They have large, glassy-looking eyes. They are much treasured as game fish, have excellent fine white flesh and grow up to 20 pounds.

Sauger

Stizostedion canadense

The sauger is a smaller version of the walleye but can grow to 8 pounds in, for instance, the Missouri River.

COOKING METHODS

CUT	COOKING METHODS	SERVES	HOW MUCH TO BUY
Whole perch	Frying	1	¾ pound to 1 pound
Whole perch	Sousing, marinating	1	8 to 12 ounces
Whole walleye	Roasting	4	3 pounds
Fillets	As listed below	1	6 to 8 ounces

CHOICE OF RECIPES

Oven-Steamed Seafood en Papillote, page 80

Baked Fish Fillet Casserole with Light Tomato Sauce, page 83

Roast Whole Fish, page 89

Broiled Fillets, Butterflied or Split Fish, Steaks, Escalopes or Medallions, page 100

Grilled Fish Fillets, Butterflied or Split Fish, Steaks or Medallions, page 109

Fried Fish Fillets or Fish Steaks à la Meunière, page 122

Fried Whole Fish or Pan-Dressed Fish, page 124

Fish Croquettes, page 125

Escabèche, page 184

Soused or Marinated Fish, page 186

Periwinkle, Common

Littorina littorea

Cholesterol: *N/A* ***Omega-3:*** *0.4* ***Fat:*** *3.0*

Fat content
low

Form usually prepared
in shell

Taste
smoky

Texture
firm

THE COMMON PERIWINKLE, called a winkle in England and *bigorneau* in France, is just one of many species of the periwinkle family. Common periwinkles look like little sea snails and live on pilings and rocks up and down the Atlantic Coast. They are brownish-grayish black, and they come about 40 to 60 a pound. Although they are not often sold in retail fish stores, you can collect your own from safe, clean waters.

Make sure periwinkles are alive when you buy them: Touch the lid or operculum, and if it moves slightly, the periwinkle is alive. They should also smell good, with just a slight aroma of the sea.

You can eat periwinkles hot or cold in a stew or a salad or just plain steamed; they can also be used as a pretty and highly edible garnish for other dishes. You must have patience when eating them. After you've prepared them, push off the tiny hard lid (operculum) of each, and then with a long tailor's pin, lobster pick or fork, pull out the little creature. You can dip periwinkles in lemon, garlic butter, malt vinegar or balsamic vinaigrette.

Periwinkles are delicious, but it's hard to describe their flavor—they are inevitably a little rubbery in texture, and their flesh is nutty and a bit smoky. They are particularly good when boiled in cayenne-flavored water.

How to Clean and Boil Periwinkles

1. Wash the periwinkles in cold water until the water runs clear. Rub them together with your hands.

2. Put the clean periwinkles in a pot, and cover them with cold water. Optional: Add ¼ teaspoon cayenne or 4 dried chili peppers to each pound of periwinkles.

3. Bring to the boil for 3 minutes, then drain and put under cold running water for a few seconds.

4. Remove the tiny thin foot (operculum) from each periwinkle with a tailor's pin, the point of a small, sharp knife or a small lobster pick or fork, and extract the meat.

COOKING METHOD

Form	Cooking Method	Serves	How Much to Buy
In shell	Steaming	1	4 to 8 ounces

CHOICE OF RECIPES

Hot and spicy periwinkles—as above
Steamed (as above) and served with balsamic vinaigrette

Pike

Northern Pike

Cholesterol: 39   Omega-3: 0.1   Fat: 0.7

PIKE LIVE IN THE LAKES, streams and rivers of the central and southern United States. Varieties of pike include the redfin pickerel (*Esox americanus*), chain pickerel (*E. niger*), northern pike (*E. lucius*) and muskellunge, or muskie, (*E. masquinongy*). Their large mouths, which are like the bills of spoonbills, are full of teeth that they use to satisfy their appetite for fish. Because pike are voracious eaters and can live for years, they can be the scourge of a stream or river. For this reason, and also because of their size (northern pike are caught at weights up to 20 pounds, while muskellunge are caught at weights up to 60 pounds), they are prize catches for the sports fisherman—particularly as their demise gives other fish a chance to live and be caught.

Pike are not widely distributed. When available, they are sold whole, usually with heads off, at weights of ½ pound and up, or in filleted form.

The northern pike has a silvery brown belly with a dark back and pale yellow spots along its sides. Its flesh is yellow; when cooked, white, with small flakes. The upper half of the fish has tiny floating bones that are a nuisance. Either be patient and bone out the fillets, or do as others do and use the meat in dishes that call for it to be ground.

Pike flesh is widely used to make the fine French dumplings known as *quenelles de brochet*. Pike is also used (along with whitefish and carp) to make gefilte fish.

The other members of the pike family are similar in looks, although their coloring differs slightly.

Fat content
low

Form usually prepared
fillets

Taste
sweet to bland

Texture
flaky

COOKING METHODS

CUT	COOKING METHODS	SERVES	HOW MUCH TO BUY
Whole	Roasting	4	3 pounds
Fillets	As listed below	2	6 to 8 ounces

CHOICE OF RECIPES

Baked Lean Fish Fillets, page 75
Roast Whole Fish, page 89

Broiled Fillets, Butterflied or Split Fish, Steaks, Escalopes or
  Medallions, page 100
Grilled Fish Fillets, Butterflied or Split Fish, Steaks or Medallions,
  page 109
Fried Fish Fillets à la Meunière, page 122

Plaice
see Flatfish, page 275.

Pollock, Alaskan
see Cod Group, page 253

Pollock, Atlantic
see Cod Group, page 252

Pompano, Florida
Trachinotus carolinus
Cholesterol: 50   Omega-3: 0.56   Fat: 9.5

THIS MARVELOUS-LOOKING FISH comes primarily from the
waters off Florida. Related species include the round pompano
(*T. ovatus*) and the gafftopsail pompano (*T. glaucus*),
which are mostly fished off the Carolinas and
Florida and from the Gulf of Mexico as far
west as the Texas coast. Other related
species are the permit (*T. falcatus*) and the
palometa (*T. goodei*), which are fished in
waters from Massachusetts to Argentina, and another
gafftopsail pompano (*T. rhodopus*), which is fished in Pacific waters
from southern California to Peru. The Florida pompano is a small-
ish fish weighing ¾ pound to 2 pounds. It has a blue back and a silvery belly when it has just been taken from the water; after it dies, it
turns silver all over, with tinges of yellow and blue. The Florida pompano is extremely flat-bodied for a roundfish, with a compact small
head, a tiny mouth and a forked tail. Its scales are negligible, and so
it does not need to be scaled.

The Florida pompano is particularly suited to being halved
before cooking (see page 49); it can also be cooked whole or in filleted form. Broiling, baking, grilling, bake-poaching and roasting are

Fat content
moderate

**Form usually
prepared**
fillets

Taste
sweet

Texture
firm-flake

good cooking methods for this firm-fleshed fish. Its anatomy is much like that of a flatfish such as flounder, so it is easy to eat when cooked on the bone. Always try, if you can, to show the skin, because it is very beautiful. The flesh of this fish is much appreciated, as it is sweet and firm.

COOKING METHODS

Cut	Cooking Methods	Serves	How Much to Buy
Whole	Roasting	2	1½ to 2 pounds
Fillets	As listed below	1	6 to 8 ounces
Halved	Broiling, grilling	1	6 to 8 ounces

CHOICE OF RECIPES

Bake-Poached Fish Fillets, page 79
Oven-Steamed Seafood en Papillote, page 80
Roast Whole Fish, page 89
Broiled Whole Roundfish, page 98
Broiled Fillets, Butterflied or Split Fish, Steaks, Escalopes or Medallions, page 100
Grilled Fish Fillets, Butterflied or Split Fish, Steaks or Medallions, page 109
Escabèche, page 184

Porgy, Northern
Stenotomus chrysops
Cholesterol: *N/A* **Omega-3:** *N/A*
Fat: *2.7*

Fat content
low

Forms usually prepared
butterflied or split fish, pan-dressed fish

Taste
sweet to mild

Texture
flaky

NORTHERN PORGIES, also known as scups, are members of the sea bream family. Related species include the whitebone porgy, also called the chocolate porgy; the knobbed porgy, also called the Key West porgy; and the red porgy, also called the pink porgy or silver snapper. Northern porgies are caught in waters from Cape Hatteras down to Florida and also in the Gulf of Mexico. They are easily caught, even by children, with a stout rod and a bent pin.

Porgies are flat-bodied. They are silver to gray, and they have spiny fins. Some porgies weighing more than 8 pounds have been caught, but most weigh ½ pound to 3 pounds.

Porgies are usually cheap. They are more than likely to be sold pan-dressed (scaled and gutted with heads and tails removed). You can ask for them to be split also. If you catch your own, you can do your own pan-dressing.

The flesh of porgies is lean, flaky and not quite white; when cooked, it becomes whiter. Because the flesh of porgies is lean and very flavorful, it can be accompanied by some strong seasonings.

COOKING METHODS

Cut	Cooking Methods	Serves	How Much to Buy
Whole	Roasting, broiling, sousing	2	1½ to 2 pounds
Pan-dressed or split	Grilling, frying, broiling, hot-smoking	2	1½ to 2 pounds
Fillets	As listed below	1	6 to 8 ounces

CHOICE OF RECIPES

Roast Whole Fish, page 89

Broiled Whole Roundfish, page 98

Broiled Fillets, Butterflied or Split Fish, Escalopes or Medallions, page 100

Grilled Whole Fish, page 107

Grilled Fish Fillets, Butterflied or Split Fish or Medallions, page 109

Fried Whole Fish or Pan-Dressed Fish, page 124

Fish Croquettes, page 125

Seafood Stew or Pasta Sauce, page 165

Hot-Smoking (Smoke-Cooking), page 170

Escabèche, page 184

Soused or Marinated Fish, page 186

Marinade for Broiled, Grilled or Barbecued Seafood, page 187

Summer Fish Salad, page 193

Rockfish

Sebastes spp
Mixed Species
Cholesterol: 35 Omega-3: 0.3 Fat: 1.6

SEE ALSO two other members of the Scorpaenidae family, the Atlantic ocean perch (*Sebastes marinus*) and the deepwater redfish (*S. mentella*). There are numerous species of rockfish worldwide—approximately 330.

Pacific rockfish must not be confused with "rockfish," the name given to striped bass in the Chesapeake Bay area. Fishing for rockfish is a major industry on the West Coast: In the Pacific, they are harvested from southern California up to Oregon, Washington, British Columbia and Alaska. There are 65 species found there, and I would need to write a separate volume to describe them all.

Rockfish are colorful, and different species are named for all the colors of the rainbow—species include black (*S. melanops*), copper (*S. caurinus*), brown (*S. auriculatus*), blue (*S. mystinus*), canary (*S. pinniger*), vermilion (*S. miniatus*) and yelloweye (*S. ruberrimus*). Indeed, these fish are accurately named. Other popular species of rockfish are the widow (*S. entomelas*), bocaccio (*S. paucispinis*), china (*S. nebulosus*), rosethorn (*S. helvomaculatus*), tiger (*S. nigrocinctus*), quillback (*S. maliger*) and chili pepper (*S. goodei*).

Rockfish have heavily armored gill covers, and they are somewhat similar in looks to fish from the snapper family, with their large heads, spiny fins and colorful skins. Some are spotted, some are striped; they are a very colorful bunch. Put them together, and we have numerous clowns for a fish circus.

Rockfish weigh up to 15 pounds but are usually sold at weights ranging from 1½ pounds to 5 pounds. They are sold whole and as fillets.

Rockfish flesh is lean, white and flaky—it is similar to the flesh of fish from the snapper family and some bass. These fish can all be cooked in like fashion. Some rockfish have firmer flesh than others and can be eaten in filleted form, while others with softer flesh will do better by being cooked whole; your fishmonger should be able to guide you on this. The Chinese steam or deep-fry whole rockfish with added flavorings such as ginger, soy sauce and scallions.

A word of warning: Red-skinned rockfish are shamelessly

Fat content
low

Form usually prepared
fillets

Taste
mild

Texture
flaky

labeled "red snapper" or "Pacific red snapper," which is actually legal in California but not elsewhere. Some people consider red snapper a finer-tasting fish.

COOKING METHODS

Cut	Cooking Methods	Serves	How Much to Buy
Whole	Roasting	4	3 pounds
Fillets	As listed below	1	6 to 8 ounces

Also see the tables for black sea bass and red snapper on pages 229 and 347.

CHOICE OF RECIPES

Baked Lean Fish Fillets, page 75
Bake-Poached Fish Fillets, page 79
Baked Fish Fillet Casserole, page 82
Baked Fish Fillet Casserole with Light Tomato Sauce, page 83
Baked Cajun Fish Casserole, page 85
Roast Whole Fish, page 89
Broiled Fillets, Butterflied or Split Fish, Steaks, Escalopes or Medallions, page 100
Grilled Whole Fish, page 107
Grilled Fish Fillets, Butterflied or Split Fish, Steaks or Medallions, page 109
Fried Fish Fillets or Fish Steaks à la Meunière, page 122
Fried Whole Fish or Pan-Dressed Fish, page 124
Fish Croquettes, page 125
Blackened Fish Fillets, page 128
Poached Whole Fish, page 139
Creamy Seafood Chowder, page 162
Fish Stock, page 164
Seviche, page 183
Escabèche, page 184

Also see the recipes for black sea bass and red snapper on pages 229 and 348.

Sablefish

Anoplopoma fimbria

Cholesterol: 49   Omega-3: 1.4   Fat: 15.3

THE SABLEFISH, also known as the black cod and (in local fish stores) as the butterfish when in filleted form, is not a member of the cod family but of the skilfish family. It is a sleek fish that ranges in color from blue-black to gray, and it is commercially available at weights ranging from 5 to 100 pounds. It is fished in the Pacific from California to the Bering Sea, off the coast of Alaska.

The flesh is white with large flakes. It is very oily and is eminently suitable for smoking—a great deal of it is marketed this way as smoked Alaskan black cod or sablefish. I can recommend smoked sablefish, and you can, if you want, have the pleasure of smoking your own (see page 167).

Sablefish fillets and steaks are fine grilled, broiled or baked. A large chunk or roast can be roasted.

Fat content
high

Forms usually prepared
fillets, steaks, chunks

Taste
sweet and rich

Texture
flaky

COOKING METHODS

Cut	Cooking Methods	Serves	How Much to Buy
Steaks	Grilling, broiling	1	6 ounces
Chunks	Roasting	5 to 6	3 pounds
Fillets, steaks	As listed below	1	6 ounces

CHOICE OF RECIPES

Roast Stuffed Fish Chunk, page 92

Broiled Fillets, Butterflied or Split Fish, Steaks, Escalopes or Medallions, page 100

Grilled Fish Fillets, Butterflied or Split Fish, Steaks or Medallions, page 109

Blackened Fish Fillets, page 128

Creamy Seafood Chowder, page 162

Hot-Smoking (Smoke-Cooking), page 170

Salmon

Fat content
low (pink) to high (chinook)

Forms usually prepared
fillets, steaks, chunks

Taste
rich and buttery

Texture
flaky

Atlantic Salmon
Salmo salar
Cholesterol: 55   Omega-3: 1.4   Fat: 6.3

Chinook Salmon (King Salmon)
Oncorhynchus tshawytscha
Cholesterol: 66   Omega-3: 1.4   Fat: 10.4

Chum Salmon (Dog or Keta Salmon)
Oncorhynchus keta
Cholesterol: 74   Omega-3: 0.6   Fat: 3.8

Coho Salmon (Silver Salmon)
Oncorhynchus kisutch
Cholesterol: 39   Omega-3: 0.8   Fat: 6.0

Pink Salmon (Humpback Salmon or Humpie)
Oncorhynchus gorbuscha
Cholesterol: 52   Omega-3: 1.0   Fat: 3.5

Sockeye Salmon (Red or Blueback Salmon)
Oncorhynchus nerka
Cholesterol: 62   Omega-3: 1.2   Fat: 8.6

THE SALMON is a beautiful fish, all silver, black and shiny. One can imagine the hidden strength it uses in making arduous sea and river journeys during its lifetime. Its body is perfectly proportioned to move swiftly through the water or fly into the air as it makes its way up waterfalls or fast streams to spawn or to grab at an angler's teasing fly hook. You are fortunate, indeed, if you can obtain the freshest of salmon, caught by rod and fly.

Wild salmon are anadromous, that is, they spend most of their lives in the sea but return to the streams and rivers of their birth to spawn. Most wild salmon are fished on their return to fresh or coastal waters.

Salmon flourish in both the North Atlantic and the North Pacific, not only in the wild state but also farmed. In this aquaculture, young salmon bred from large, fecund females are transferred to controlled areas, which may be inland lakes or protected sea pens. Farming of Atlantic salmon in Norway, Canada, Scotland and Ireland is extensive and accounts for some of the best salmon available. Atlantic and coho salmon are farmed in Chile; other salmon are farmed in Australia and New Zealand. In the United States, some chinook and coho salmon have been successfully introduced into the Great Lakes.

Most of the salmon fished in the United States come from Alaskan waters; the rest come from Washington State, Oregon and California. Chinook salmon from the Pacific (with flesh the color of a blood orange) have good texture and taste and command the highest price; coho salmon cost somewhat less. Some chinook salmon have white flesh; these fish are much treasured, especially by the Japanese. Chum salmon have pale pink flesh, sockeye salmon have bright orange-red flesh, and pink salmon have pale pink flesh. Most chum, sockeye and pink salmon are canned, but some chum and sockeye are available fresh and frozen.

Atlantic salmon have moist flesh and a beautiful, rich pink color. They are well handled by the farmers, so they usually reach the fish store in pristine condition. Wild Atlantic salmon are rarely available.

Salmon trout are sea-run rainbow, brown or brook trout. For a discussion of trout, which are related to salmon, see page 359.

Also available are farm-raised baby coho salmon with pink-orange flesh from the West Coast and silver coho from Chile. They are the size of trout, weighing 8 to 10 ounces. They are sold boned and butterflied, ready to cook, and are quite delicious.

When filleting salmon, notice that the pin bones are thin and feathery and can easily be pulled out with pin-nose pliers or tweezers.

The taste of cooked salmon appeals to almost everyone. The pink to red flesh is moist and tender when properly prepared. It is important just to cook the flesh through, and perhaps leave it a tiny bit underdone to ensure that it does not dry out. Take into account that the fish will continue to cook in its own heat once it is removed from the stove or grill.

You can cook salmon by many methods. Broiling, grilling and baking give the pink-orange flesh added color; poaching and roasting are favorite ways to cook it, and the flesh retains an inviting, unadulterated blush color.

It is not a good idea to eat wild salmon raw, either in the form of sushi or as salmon tartare, because no matter how fresh the fish is, a wild salmon has spent some of its life in fresh water and may contain parasites. (You can freeze salmon for a couple of days to kill any parasites; see page 21.) Farmed salmon spend their lives in ocean pens. I like the way the Japanese prepare salmon skin: broiled and then wrapped around rice, in the manner of the seaweed sheets called nori. These fatty skins have the benefit of being rich in omega-3 fatty acids.

Salmon is marvelously suitable for smoking—witness the popularity of smoked salmon. The Swedish preparation known as *gravlax*, which is salmon cured with salt, sugar and dill, is very popular. Lox is salmon cured in a salted brine for up to a year, rinsed and then only sometimes smoked.

Most everyone has his or her own particular taste when it comes to choosing smoked salmon—I can only say that the intensity of the brine and method of smoking make the difference. The flavor you prefer seems to depend on the salt content, the oiliness and the moisture. I prefer moist, sweet, slightly salty smoked salmon. In any case, before buying smoked salmon—whether Scottish, Norwegian, Irish, Canadian, Pacific or nova—decide for yourself by tasting a little piece.

When preparing a whole side of smoked salmon, you will usually need to shave off a thin layer of the flesh or skin that has formed from the brine and smoking and then pull out the pin bones before slicing it.

COOKING METHODS

Cut	Cooking Methods	Serves	How Much to Buy
Whole	Roasting	Part of a buffet for 20	8 pounds
Whole	Poaching	Dinner for 10 to 12	8 pounds
Whole	Bake-poaching	1	½ to ¾ pound
Chunks	Roasting	5 to 6	3 pounds
Fillets, steaks, escalopes and medallions	As listed below	1	6 to 8 ounces
Smoked		Appetizer for 1	2 to 4 ounces

CHOICE OF RECIPES

Baby Coho Salmon (8 to 10 ounces each)

Oven-Steamed Seafood en Papillote, page 80

Broiled Fillets, Butterflied or Split Fish, Steaks, Escalopes or Medallions, page 100

Grilled Whole Fish, page 107

Grilled Fish Fillets, Butterflied or Split Fish, Steaks or Medallions, page 109

Poached Small Whole Fish or Fish Fillets, page 140

Fish Fillets with Spinach and Ginger, page 178

Seviche, page 183

Escabèche, page 184

Soused or Marinated Fish, page 186

Salmon

Baked Fatty Fish Fillets, page 73

Bake-Poached Whole Fish, page 76

Bake-Poached Fish Fillets, page 79

Baked Fish Fillet Casserole with Light Tomato Sauce, page 83

Roast Whole Fish, page 89

Roast Stuffed Fish Chunk, page 92

Broiled Fillets, Butterflied or Split Fish, Steaks, Escalopes or Medallions, page 100

Grilled Fish Fillets, Butterflied or Split Fish, Steaks or Medallions, page 109

Grilled or Broiled Seafood Brochettes, page 110

Grilled or Broiled Seafood and Vegetable Brochettes, page 112

Fish Croquettes, page 125

Poached Whole Fish, page 139

Sardine

Atlantic Herring
Clupea harengus harengus
Pacific Herring
Clupea pallasi
Pacific Sardine
Sardinops sagax
European Sardine
Sardina pilchardus

Mixed Species
Cholesterol: 52   Omega-3: 1.5   Fat: 6.8

Canned in oil
Cholesterol: 52   Omega-3: 1.0   Fat: 11.5

Fat content
moderate
high (canned in oil)

Form usually prepared
butterflied fish

Taste
mild to strong

Texture
flaky

SARDINES THRIVE on both sides of the Atlantic and Pacific. The European pilchard is a member of the herring family, which when young is called a sardine. In the western Atlantic, there are no pilchards, but the Atlantic and Pacific herrings are called sardines when juvenile. On the East Coast in Maine, these sardines are mostly canned. In Europe, the sardines are also canned but can be found fresh, frozen or defrosted from the Mediterranean and the eastern Atlantic. If you can find them in specialty fish markets on the East Coast, by all means buy them, for they are delicious grilled or broiled. I don't find American sardines (Atlantic herring) as flavorful as European sardines (pilchards). I refer to those delicious fat sardines, grilled outdoors on charcoal, that one can eat in Spain, Portugal and France. (Pacific sardines are no longer a viable commercial catch because the stock is depleted, and those few which are caught are usually used for bait.)

The sardine is a silvery bullet-shaped fish that grows to only about 8 inches long. The fresh sardines that are commercially available weigh up to 5 ounces or so.

You can gut sardines through the head (see page 42), brush off the loose scales, oil them lightly, roll them in coarse salt and broil, grill or roast them. The flesh of sardines is fat and oily, so they need a good squeeze of lemon when cooked and a nice crusty bread to accompany them. They can also be boned (fiddly work), rolled up and baked; if you want to butterfly and bone sardines, follow the instructions on pages 47 and 48.

Brisling (sprats), pilchards and sils are very similar to sardines and, like sardines, are mostly available canned. All these fish are delightful in sandwiches and salads and are full of healthy minerals and calcium, if you eat the bones.

COOKING METHODS

Cut	Cooking Methods	Serves	How Much to Buy
Whole	Grilling, roasting, broiling, sousing, escabèche	1	¾ to 1 pound
Boned, butterflied or split	Broiling, grilling	1	6 to 8 ounces

CHOICE OF RECIPES

Roast Whole Fish, page 89

Broiled Whole Roundfish, page 98

Broiled Fillets, Butterflied or Split Fish, Steaks, Escalopes or Medallions, page 100

Grilled Fish Fillets, Butterflied or Split Fish, Steaks or Medallions, page 109

Escabèche, page 184

Soused or Marinated Fish, page 186

Scallops

Cholesterol: 33   Omega-3: 0.2   Fat: 0.8

Sea Scallop

Placopecten magellanicus
Cholesterol: 37   Omega-3: 0.19   Fat: 0.8

Bay Scallop

Argopecten irradians
Cholesterol: N/A   Omega-3: 0.13   Fat: 0.06

Calico Scallop

Argopecten gibbus
Cholesterol: N/A   Omega-3: 0.13   Fat: 0.06

Fat content
low

Form usually prepared
shucked

Taste
sweet

Texture
quite firm

THE SEA SCALLOP IS A BIVALVE MOLLUSK that thrives in deep Atlantic waters from Canada down to North Carolina. Other scallops are found worldwide—in Alaskan, Peruvian, Icelandic, Central American and Japanese waters, as well as in other waters off the coast of the United States.

Unlike other mollusks that stay sedentary, most scallop species swim by snapping their shells together, using the muscle in the center of their shells. This large, round, white muscle, called the adductor muscle, is the sweet, rich, scallop meat we eat.

We buy scallop meat by the pound. (Scallops are sold by the piece and by the pound in Europe.) Scallops can be sautéed, broiled, grilled, baked in the shell and made into salads and seviche. They are highly successful when placed on brochette sticks, because they keep their shape.

Use high heat when cooking scallops. When sautéing, do a few at a time so the temperature of the fat does not drop. Scallops are cooked when they are opaque all the way through.

Scallop shells are seldom seen nowadays because scallops are shucked at sea, but we all know the shape from the Shell gasoline logo or from Botticelli's *Birth of Venus*, in which Venus stands on a large scallop shell. Many designers and architects have made use of this shell in decorating doors and mantelpieces through the ages.

It is useful to have a few sea scallop shells around, for many a delightful dish can be baked in them. Even though the Atlantic sea scallops have smoothish shells, more attractive grooved shells are available from Europe and other parts of the world. The small pink scallops from the Pacific Northwest are nicknamed "singing scallops." They come with their roe and are cooked in their shells. After eating the sweet little morsels, we can keep the charming pink shells. Excellent farmed scallops come from Rhode Island.

Unfortunately, the scallop's roe, or coral, is usually discarded at sea by American fishermen, mostly because it can cause the meat to spoil during the long trip at sea. In Europe, the roe is prized for its color and flavor and is sold with the scallop on the half shell. Scallops with roe are imported from France, Holland, the Isle of Man and New Zealand. Some fishermen on the East Coast are now selling the roe with scallops. The roe ranges in color from a deep purple to a coral to a pale gray.

Sea scallops have shells up to 8 inches wide. The white meat inside is round like a drum, measuring up to 2½ inches in diameter and 2 inches high. The flesh is sweet and firm when cooked.

How to Prepare Sea Scallops for Cooking
Remove the tough little muscles from the side of each scallop before cooking. If the scallops are of very different sizes, wafer them (cut them crosswise) so they are the same thickness.

Bay scallops, the small cousins of the sea scallops, are even sweeter and more delicate. Try eating them raw when they are fresh—they taste as sweet as candy. They are wonderful sautéed quickly over high heat, steamed and added to salads or made into seviche.

Calico scallops are southern bay scallops harvested off Florida. Steam-shucked at processing plants, they are usually not as sweet as other scallops. Cook these scallops like bay scallops.

COOKING METHODS

FORM	COOKING METHODS	SERVES	HOW MUCH TO BUY
Shucked	As listed below	1	4 to 8 ounces

CHOICE OF RECIPES

Sea Scallops

Oven-Steamed Seafood en Papillote, page 80

Casserole of Large Sea Scallops with Potatoes and Coriander Pesto, page 86

Broiled Shellfish, page 100

Grilled Shellfish, page 107, page 109

Grilled or Broiled Seafood Brochettes, page 110

Grilled or Broiled Seafood and Vegetable Brochettes, page 112

Sautéed Scallops, page 126

Steamed Seafood, page 146

Fish Soup (Bourride), page 160

Creamy Seafood Chowder, page 162

Seafood Stew or Pasta Sauce, page 165

Hot-Smoking (Smoke-Cooking), page 170

Seafood Stew with Tomato and Green Pepper, page 176

Breaded Shellfish with Sweet Red Pepper Sauce, page 177

Seviche, page 183

Escabèche, page 184

Sushi and Sashimi, page 189

Scallop Salad, page 194

Bay and Calico Scallops

Sautéed Scallops, page 126

Shellfish Salad with Lime and Dill Vinaigrette, page 142

Fish Soup (Bourride), page 160

Creamy Seafood Chowder, page 162

Seafood Stew or Pasta Sauce, page 165

Seviche, page 183

Scallop Salad, page 194

Sea Robin

Prionotus carolinus

Cholesterol: 32   Omega-3: N/A   Fat: 1.9

THE SEA ROBIN, called the *grondin* in French and the *capone* in Italian, is popular in Europe for its delicate flavor. In the United States, where it is also known by the English name "gurnard" and is sometimes incorrectly referred to as the angelfish, the sea robin is not much favored. On the Eastern Seaboard, sea robins are caught along with flukes and flounder but are often thrown back or used as bait for larger fish; a few are marketed in the United States, however, and they can sometimes be found in ethnic fish stores. The two species most likely to be seen in the Northeast are the striped sea robin and the northern sea robin.

When these creatures are hooked, they flutter and fly and even squeal in indignation. They appear, to some, to be prehistoric or medieval-looking—and a little scary-looking—for they have rays that jut out and spiny winglike fins which they use to swim, find food or bury themselves in the sandy seabed. They have wide, flat, bony heads and bodies that taper off to very narrow tails. Different species can be colored orange, red, gray or brown; some are mottled and others are striped. They grow to weights of as much as 3 pounds.

Sea robin flesh is firm, lean, flavorful and sweet, but you do want to get rid of the skin, for it is rough and unpleasant. The fish is bony: The rib bones extend into the flesh, and you can see the ends of them sticking out when you fillet the fish. The best way to get rid of these bones is by pulling them out with pin-nose pliers. Alternatively, since the flesh is firm when cooked, you can cook it by poaching or baking, for instance, then flake the flesh and pick out the bones at the same time.

Sea robin cut into steaks can be added to fish soups, as it is in a French bouillabaisse. Poached sea robin can be made into a salad. Sea robin can be grilled or steamed.

How to Prepare Sea Robin for Cooking

♦ Gut the fish by making a cut from the anal vent toward the head, bypassing each side of the Y-shaped flat bone behind the mouth, at the base of the head.

♦ Turn the fish over, cut off the head, and discard it. The guts will come away with the head. Cut off the spiny fins. Rinse the fish.

Fat content
low

Forms usually prepared
fillets, steaks

Taste
mild

Texture
quite firm

How to Remove the Skin of a Sea Robin

♦ Loosen the skin at the head end with a sharp-pointed knife, and then pull it off with your fingers or pliers. (I find it easier with pliers.)

♦ Or blanch the fish in boiling water for 10 seconds, then rinse it in cold water and peel off the skin with a knife or your fingers.

How to Fillet Sea Robin

Cut down each side of the backbone. You will feel the knife cutting through the rib bones. When you have two fillets, feel for the rib bones with your fingertips. Pull these out with pliers or tweezers.

COOKING METHODS

CUT	COOKING METHODS	SERVES	HOW MUCH TO BUY
Whole, skinned	Grilling	1	½ to 1 pound
Fillets and steaks	As listed below	1	6 to 8 ounces

CHOICE OF RECIPES

Broiled Fillets, Butterflied or Split Fish, Steaks, Escalopes or
    Medallions, page 100
Grilled Whole Fish, page 107
Grilled Fish Fillets, Butterflied or Split Fish, Steaks or Medallions,
    page 109
Fish Croquettes, page 125
Steamed Seafood, page 146
Fish Soup (Bourride), page 160
Fish Stock, page 164
Seafood Stew or Pasta Sauce, page 165
Salsa-Flavored Fish Salad, page 192

Sea Urchin

Strongylocentrotus droebachiensis
Cholesterol: 498   Omega-3:   Fat: 3.21

VARIOUS SPECIES of sea urchin inhabit the Atlantic Ocean, from Canada down through the West Indies, and the Pacific, from Canada down to Baja California. Sea urchins have spherical shells, called tests, that measure up to 6 inches in diameter and are covered with spines like the bodies of porcupines. Those from U.S. waters can be red, green or purple. Sea urchins grow on rocky shores, eat kelp and can be a nuisance to swimmers because they're spiny.

In the United States, we eat the gonads of these creatures, also called roe, which are a delicious treat. There is nothing quite like them—they are bright orange-yellow and shaped like little tongues, and they taste sweet and are unctuous at the same time. Europeans are also keen on sea urchin gonads and cook them in a number of dishes—for example, they mix them with eggs, a preparation that is very high in cholesterol indeed.

Sea urchin gonads develop during spawning season, and urchins must be harvested prior to spawning. In the Pacific, and particularly on the British Columbian coast near Vancouver, mostly red sea urchins thrive; their season is from October to May. Harvested by humans, they are also favored by sea otters, which are quite capable of cracking large ones on rocks. The gonads of the British Columbian red sea urchins are mostly exported to Japan on shallow trays, in very fresh condition, as they are eaten raw as sushi. I particularly like the preparation *uni-maki* (*uni* is the Japanese word for "sea urchin"), sea urchin roe rolled up in nori (seaweed sheets).

The green urchins from the Atlantic are in season from November to March on the East Coast of the United States. I enjoy eating the gonads of green urchins straight out of the shell, especially at the Oyster Bar in New York City's Grand Central Station.

The little trays of sea urchin gonads prepared for Japanese consumption are fortunately available in Japanese food stores in large cities throughout the United States. They are very convenient to use and contain ½ pound of gonads.

If you buy whole sea urchins, choose those which show some signs of life before extracting the gonads. The spines should be erect, and if they move when you touch them, the sea urchin is alive.

Fat content
low

Form usually prepared
gonads

Taste
sweet

Texture
unctuous

How to Extract Sea Urchin Roe or Gonads

Wear heavy gardening or rubber gloves so the spines do not pierce the skin of your fingers. Hold the sea urchin so the "mouth" side of the shell (the bottom) is uppermost. Insert scissors into the shell about 1½ inches below the mouth, and cut around it so you have a lid. Discard the lid and with a small spoon, scoop out the orange-yellow gonads, avoiding the brown viscera. There are five little gonad sacs to each sea urchin, and you will need between 10 and 20 gonad sacs to obtain ½ pound of roe.

PREPARATION METHOD

FORM	COOKING METHODS	SERVES	HOW MUCH TO BUY
Raw gonads	Sushi, sashimi	1	Up to 4 ounces

CHOICE OF RECIPE

Sushi and Sashimi, page 189

Shad

American Shad

Alosa sapidissima

Cholesterol: N/A Omega-3: 1.4 Fat: 13.6

SHAD, which are members of the herring family (Clupeidae), are anadromous—that is, they are hatched in fresh water, go out to sea to grow and return later to spawn in the rivers in which they were born. Shad are marvelous to look at, sporting bright silver coloring, small heads and compressed bodies. They weigh as much as 4 to 5 pounds.

The American shad and the hickory shad (*Alosa mediocris*) are related species which inhabit the rivers that spill into the Atlantic, from the Gulf of Saint Lawrence down to Florida. American shad is the important food fish. The American shad season along the east coast is from February to May, when the fish return to the rivers of their birth to spawn. The season starts down south, gradually moving north as the waters warm. American shad are also caught along the west coast, from California to Alaska. One of their home rivers is the Columbia River, where they return to spawn from May through July.

Fishmongers rarely carry whole shad—these fish are nearly always sold in filleted form. It is the females that are filleted. Filleting them is an art known to only a few patient and skillful people, for the shad has an inordinate amount of bones in its bone structure. I'm told by a man who fillets shad at the Fulton Fish Market in New York that there are 365 bones in this fish. Whether there are or not, we do know that there are double rows of bones in each fillet. I do not fillet my own shad—I leave this task to others.

It is perfectly possible to cook a split shad or its fillets without boning it completely, for with long cooking, the bones will eventually soften. The softening process can be helped along by sprinkling the shad or fillets with lemon juice or another acid. Shad from the Delaware River in Pennsylvania are pickled without being boned.

The sweet-fleshed boned fillets are best broiled, baked or fried. The precious roe has to be cooked gently, only until firm all the way through, so that it does not dry out and the membrane which surrounds the eggs does not split.

Planking is an interesting way to cook shad: The shad is fastened to a board spread-eagled (butterflied), a few pieces of bacon are stretched across it, and then the fish is baked in the oven.

Fat content
high

Forms usually prepared
fillets, roe

Taste
sweet

Texture
quite flaky

COOKING METHODS

Cut	Cooking Methods	Serves	How Much to Buy
Fillets	As listed below	1	6 to 8 ounces
Roe	Frying	1	1 pair

CHOICE OF RECIPES

Shad
Baked Fatty Fish Fillets, page 73
Oven-Steamed Seafood en Papillote, page 80
Baked Fish Fillet Casserole, page 82
Broiled Fillets, Butterflied or Split Fish, Steaks, Escalopes or Medallions, page 100

Grilled Fish Fillets, Butterflied or Split Fish, Steaks or Medallions, page 109
Fried Fish Fillets à la Meunière, page 122
Hot-Smoking (Smoke-Cooking), page 170
Escabèche, page 184

Shad Roe
Fried à la Meunière, page 122

Shark
Mixed Species
Cholesterol: 51 Omega-3: 0.8 Fat: 4.5

Fat content
mostly low

Forms usually prepared
fillets, steaks

Taste
mild

Texture
firm

SHARKS INHABIT ALL THE OCEANS worldwide. Because of their voracious appetites, we have been somewhat reluctant to think of sharks as food. But, not too late, we have discovered that many species, including the larger mako, blacktip and thresher sharks and the smaller species of dogfish, are highly edible.

The sharks I want to see more of in the markets and on restaurant menus are the smooth dogfish (*Mustelus canis*), also called the sand shark, and the spiny dogfish (*Squalus acanthias*), also called sand shark and grayfish. Another common name for these sharks is cape shark. These two sharks are very similar in looks: Both have light gray to brown backs and white bellies. The spiny dogfish has short spines on its fins and is sometimes spotted. The flesh of this shark happens to be fattier than other sharks (12.2 milligrams per 100 grams of raw fish). These sharks weigh up to 10 pounds and are caught up and down the Atlantic Coast and in the Pacific. They are easily obtainable in Europe (lightly battered and deep-fried, they are among the fish used for England's famous fish and chips) and are good eating. Unfortunately, they are rarely available in fish stores here, for there currently is not a big enough demand for them. Many that are caught on the east coast, as an incidental catch along with other fish, are thrown away because they are a nuisance to the fishermen (who cannot get a good price for them) and because they tend to mess up fishing nets. We must change this situation, for the fish are delicious. I like sand shark fried (coated only with seasoned flour); it is also good baked or braised in a casserole with tomatoes.

From the Pacific and Atlantic oceans, we have angel sharks (*Squatina californica*), which have small "wings" like skates. They weigh up to 60 pounds and constitute a large part of the shark catch in California. They are sold in the form of fillets and steaks.

Blacktip sharks (*Carcharhinus limbatus*) and spinners (*C. brevipinna*) from the requiem family (Carcharhinidae) of sharks are found worldwide in temperate waters. They weigh up to 80 pounds. They are gray with black tips on each fin.

Mako sharks (*Isurus glaucus*) are caught in the Atlantic from Massachusetts down to the Gulf of Mexico and in the southern hemisphere too.

Threshers (*Alopias vulpinus*) are found worldwide. Soupfin (*Galeorhinus zyopterus*) and bonito (*Isurus oxyrinchus*) sharks are found in the Pacific off California.

The flesh of the larger shark that we eat—like angel, blacktip, soupfin, mako and thresher—is white to pink with red tinges when raw and turns nearly white when cooked. The flesh is similar to that of swordfish, but it is not quite as flaky or sweet. Sand shark flesh is quite different from that of other sharks: Because sand sharks are smaller, their flesh is softer and has small flakes. It is firm, sweet and white when cooked, although it is pink when raw.

All sharks have cartilaginous skeletons and no rib bones or other smaller bones to bother the cook. They must be bled within minutes after they are caught, for the urea in their blood, flesh and skin will produce an ammonia smell. If a shark has a strong ammonia smell, don't buy or use it, but if the smell is faint, soak it in acidulated water (for example, a mixture of vinegar and water or lemon juice and water) or milk for an hour or so.

When you catch a sand shark, it is best to cut the gills if you can or quickly cut off the tail, or at least cut to the backbone at the tail end to bleed it. Remove the head, gut the shark, then ice it down.

The larger sharks, such as mako and thresher sharks, are cut into loins or wheels and then into steaks or cubes for brochettes. Sand sharks are skinned and then cut into steaks, fillets or cubes for brochettes.

How to Skin a Sand Shark

♦ Cut off the fins, and make a slit in the skin along the back, from head to tail. Loosen the skin from the flesh at the head end of the fish, and use pliers to pull it off down to the tail end. Repeat with the other side of the fish. You can cut off and discard the belly flaps if you wish—they are very fatty, though they are often exported to Europe, where they are smoked.

♦ Now you can fillet the fish—this is easily done by cutting along both sides of the cartilaginous "backbone"—or you can simply cut the fish into 1-inch-thick steaks (cut across the grain of the fish) or 3-inch-long chunks.

COOKING METHODS

Cut	Cooking Methods	Serves	How Much to Buy
Sand shark fillets	Baking, broiling, grilling, frying, stewing	1	6 to 8 ounces
Sand shark steaks	Frying, broiling, grilling, stewing, braising	1	6 to 8 ounces
Mako and thresher steaks	Broiling, grilling, hot-smoking	1	8 to 10 ounces
Mako and thresher cubes	Broiling, grilling, soup, stew	1	4 to 6 ounces

CHOICE OF RECIPES

Sand Shark Fillets

Baked Fish Fillet Casserole, page 82

Baked Fish Fillet Casserole with Light Tomato Sauce, page 83

Baked Cajun Fish Casserole, page 85

Broiled Fillets, Butterflied or Split Fish, Steaks, Escalopes or Medallions, page 100

Grilled Fish Fillets, Butterflied or Split Fish, Steaks or Medallions, page 109

Fried Fish Fillets or Fish Steaks à la Meunière, page 122

Seafood Stew or Pasta Sauce, page 165

Seafood Stew with Tomato and Green Pepper, page 176

Sand Shark Steaks

Broiled Fillets, Butterflied or Split Fish, Steaks, Escalopes or Medallions, page 100

Grilled Fish Fillets, Butterflied or Split Fish, Steaks or Medallions, page 109

Grilled or Broiled Seafood Brochettes, page 110

Grilled or Broiled Seafood and Vegetable Brochettes, page 112

Fried Fish Fillets or Fish Steaks à la Meunière, page 122

Braised Sand Shark, page 154

Braised Fish Fillets or Steaks with Provençal Sauce, page 156

Seafood Stew or Pasta Sauce, page 165

Seafood Stew with Tomato and Green Pepper, page 176

Steaks and Cubes of Mako, Thresher and Other Large Sharks

Broiled Fillets, Butterflied or Split Fish, Steaks, Escalopes or Medallions, page 100

Grilled Fish Fillets, Butterflied or Split Fish, Steaks or Medallions, page 109

Grilled or Broiled Seafood Brochettes, page 110

Grilled or Broiled Seafood and Vegetable Brochettes, page 112

Fish Soup (Bourride), page 160

Creamy Seafood Chowder, page 162

Seafood Stew or Pasta Sauce, page 165

Hot-Smoking (Smoke-Cooking), page 170

Seafood Stew with Tomato and Green Pepper, page 176

Marinade for Broiled, Grilled or Barbecued Seafood, page 187

Sheepshead

Archosargus probatocephalus

Cholesterol: N/A Omega-3: 0.3 Fat: 2.4

THE SHEEPSHEAD is a round, flat-bodied saltwater porgy. The strong wide stripes that cross its body from back to belly inspired another name for it—the convict. Sheepshead have thick lips and extremely strong teeth, with which they eat all sorts of shellfish, including barnacles.

Sheepshead Bay in New York was named after these fish, but they are no longer found in those waters, which have turned too cool for them. Sheepshead are fished in the Atlantic, from New York down to the Florida Keys. They are also found in the Gulf of Mexico and off South America. They are caught at weights up to 15 pounds. They are sold whole or pan-dressed, and a small quantity are filleted. Their flesh is white and firm when cooked.

Sheepshead flesh is delicious. I took a tip from Susan Herrmann Loomis, author of *The Great American Seafood Cookbook,* and mixed some steamed sheepshead fillet with a little crab seasoning. Voilà! It tasted like crab.

Fat content
low

Forms usually prepared
fillets, split fish

Taste
sweet

Texture
firm flake

COOKING METHODS

Cut	Cooking Methods	Serves	How Much to Buy
Whole	Roasting	2	1½ pounds
Pan-dressed	Frying	2	1½ pounds
Fillets	As listed below	1	6 to 10 ounces

CHOICE OF RECIPES

Oven-Steamed Seafood en Papillote, page 80

Baked Cajun Fish Casserole, page 85

Roast Whole Fish, page 89

Broiled Fillets, Butterflied or Split Fish, Steaks, Escalopes or Medallions, page 100

Grilled Fish Fillets, Butterflied or Split Fish, Steaks or Medallions, page 109

Fried Whole Fish or Pan-Dressed Fish, page 124

Blackened Fish Fillets, page 128

Steamed Seafood, page 146

Salsa-Flavored Fish Salad, page 192

Summer Fish Salad, page 193

Shrimp
Mixed Species
Cholesterol: 152   Omega-3: 0.5   Fat: 1.7

SHRIMP DISHES ARE WIDELY POPULAR—and no wonder. There are myriad ways to prepare the delicately flavored shrimp, and all of these methods are delicious as long as the shrimp are cooked well, that is, not too long, for they will toughen and lose flavor.

Shrimp are found worldwide, and we import many from such diverse places as India, Bangladesh, Thailand and most of the Central and South American countries, where many shrimp are farmed. The largest exporters of shrimp to the United States are Ecuador, China and Mexico, in that order. Nearly all the shrimp from these countries are sold frozen with heads removed.

Several species of shrimp are found in our coastal waters. Northern shrimp (*Pandalus borealis*) are harvested from the waters off Maine from December through March. They are usually sold cooked, peeled and frozen, but some are available fresh in the spring. Look out for them—they are pink when raw, small and fragile, and should be steamed whole as quickly as possible. They are great eating—don't forget to suck the head of a northern shrimp after you break it away from the tail for the delicious piece of "fat" (liver, pancreas and roe) inside. *P. jordani*, another pink shrimp, is harvested from the waters of the Pacific near Oregon.

Brown (*Penaeus aztecus*) and white shrimp (*P. setiferus*) are harvested in waters from South Carolina to the Gulf of Mexico. Pink shrimp (*P. duorarum*) are harvested from the Gulf of Mexico off southwest Florida. Most are sold frozen, but in some markets, they are available fresh with heads on.

Another shrimp harvested from fresh water is called the blue prawn or sweet-water prawn (*Machrobrachium rosenbergii*). Similar in appearance to other shrimp, blue prawns have marvelous-looking armored heads; they are blue with red tinges on their long antennae and claws. These prawns are farmed primarily in Hawaii and also in Puerto Rico, Jamaica, Brazil and the southern states. Blue prawns are rushed to restaurants for immediate cooking. They are most delicious.

Spot shrimp or prawns (*Pandalus platyceros*) are an exceptionally well-flavored shrimp from the Pacific. It's best to buy and eat them when on the West Coast, for they are highly perishable.

Fat content
low

Form usually prepared
headless, in and out of shell

Taste
mild

Texture
firm

Head-off shrimp are available in fish stores frozen or defrosted, cooked or raw, with shell on or peeled. Some fish stores sell shrimp that are peeled, deveined and cooked. Frozen, cooked and peeled shrimp are also sold in cans. Many chefs will use only fresh, not frozen, shrimp when they are in season; you should buy fresh local whole shrimp when you can, but know that the other shrimp you see (about 95 percent of the available shrimp) have been defrosted and should be cooked quickly. Be sure they smell fresh; that is, be sure they have no odor of ammonia. The color of raw shell-on shrimp can vary from a transparent light brown to gray to pink and orange and even to black (the color of oriental tiger prawns), but when shrimp are cooked, the shells are nearly always pink to red and the flesh turns an attractive pearly white with pink and red shadings. Sometimes a pink-shelled shrimp may look cooked when it is actually raw. If you aren't sure, ask your fishmonger.

Shrimp are graded by size—the larger the shrimp, the higher the price. They range in weight from 400 to the pound (tiny shrimp that are peeled, cooked and frozen, called "titi" in the trade) to 8 to the pound (extra-colossal shrimp).

Incidentally, it is useful to know that in English-speaking countries the names "shrimp" and "prawn" refer to the same creature, though local usage may differ. In England, tiny shrimp in cans are called "shrimp," but all other larger shrimp are called "prawns." Dublin Bay prawns (*Nephrops norvegicus*), however, are neither shrimp nor prawns but miniature lobsters (see page 292). To add to the confusion, *scampi* is the Italian name for the Dublin Bay prawn, but in restaurants here in the United States, shrimp scampi refers to a dish of sautéed shrimp with a butter-and-garlic sauce.

How to Devein and Peel or Shell Shrimp

I have had to shell and devein thousands of shrimp in my life, and it's really not such a chore, as some would have it.

Every shrimp has a vein running down its back that is unsightly but edible—this is its digestive tract. All too often, however, just when I am trying to explain the deveining process during cooking demonstrations, I find empty-veined shrimp that look as if they are veinless. You can imagine my frustration, but I proceed to show the method anyway.

♦ Use a pair of scissors. Hold each headless shrimp with the head end toward you and insert the point of the scissors under the shell on the top (back) of the shrimp. Cut the shell down to the next to last section before the tail. Now peel the shell off, and discard it. You will see that the vein is exposed, so just pull it out and rinse the shrimp. Voilà! The shrimp is ready, and it looks attractive with the tail shell still attached.

♦ It is my firm opinion that tiny headless shrimp need not be shelled or even deveined, for the vein will be negligible and the shell, which is soft and edible, will impart a special flavor to the flesh when it is cooked. Large shrimp cooked in their shells are delicious, but you must be willing to peel them with your fingers, which I enjoy if I have plenty of napkins and a finger bowl.

♦ Cooking lightly marinated shell-on shrimp on an outdoor grill or even in a cast-iron frying or grill pan makes them taste fantastic. You can also poach peeled shrimp for salads, steam them with vegetables, broil them, braise them or cook them in a stew, soup, paella, gumbo or jambalaya.

How to Butterfly a Shrimp

To butterfly a shrimp, peel and devein it, then make a cut down the back nearly all the way through, and spread it open.

COOKING METHODS

Form	Cooking Methods	Serves	How Much to Buy
Head-off	As listed below	1	4 to 8 ounces
Fresh head-on	Steaming	1	6 to 8 ounces

CHOICE OF RECIPES

Oven-Steamed Seafood en Papillote, page 80

Broiled Shellfish, page 100

Grilled Shellfish, page 107, page 109

Grilled or Broiled Seafood Brochettes, page 110

Grilled or Broiled Seafood and Vegetable Brochettes, page 112

Sautéed Shrimp, page 126

Deep-Fried Seafood with Seasoned Flour, page 131

Shellfish Salad with Lime and Dill Vinaigrette, page 142

Steamed Seafood, page 146

Fish Soup (Bourride), page 160

Creamy Seafood Chowder, page 162

Seafood Stew or Pasta Sauce, page 165

Hot-Smoking (Smoke-Cooking), page 170

Seafood Stew with Tomato and Green Pepper, page 176

Breaded Shellfish with Sweet Red Pepper Sauce, page 177

Seviche, page 183

Escabèche, page 184
Shrimp Salad, page 194

Skate and Ray

Cholesterol: 56   Omega-3: 0.3   Fat: 0.7

THESE GRACEFUL CREATURES glide through the water like futuristic airplanes. In U.S. waters, they are found in the Atlantic (from Canada to Florida) and the Pacific; in addition, many species inhabit the oceans of the world. Some of the better known are the big (*Raja binoculata*), thorny (*R. radiata*), smooth (*R. senta*), clearnose (*R. eglanteria*) and barndoor (*R. laevis*) skates, the cownose rays (*Rhinoptera bonasus*) and many species of stingray. It is not easy to distinguish the different species when we see only their wings.

Although the names skate and ray are used interchangeably, we usually refer to the more common edible creatures as skates. The French, however, use the name *raie*. Skates and rays are very similar-looking. They have cartilaginous skeletons, and their young are hatched from little egg cases called mermaid's or sailor's purses, which we find along the seashore and beaches. Both skates and rays have long tails, and in some species, such as the stingray, a spine on the tail is poisonous. Skates have thick skin covered by a viscous coating. Their skin is brownish gray on top and light underneath, like a flatfish's.

Fat content
low

Form usually prepared
wings

Taste
sweet

Texture
tender, filamentous

Skates and rays have triangular "wings" protruding in a fan shape from the sides of their bodies; these undulating wings are what we eat. The wings are enlarged pectoral fins, and skates and rays use them to swim and to burrow in the sand for food or hiding places. A wing can measure up to 2 inches thick and be near zero thickness at its edge. In some species, tiny thornlike spines stick out of the tops of the wings, hence the name given to one species—the thorny skate.

The composition of the flesh and cartilage is as follows: filaments or strands of flesh in one layer, then a layer of cartilage and more strands of flesh underneath. The thin part of the cartilage is soft and edible. The flesh easily slides off the layer of cartilage "bone." It is this flesh which is so delicious: sweet and white. I refuse to believe the story which is bandied about that people used to cut "scallops" out of the flesh and sell them as such. It is just not likely that anyone could be fooled by this deception, because skate is made up of distinctly separate strands of flesh, tenuously held together, which tend to separate easily after the flesh is cooked.

Skate wings are eaten all over Europe—*raie au beurre noir* is a marvelous French dish, using browned butter and capers as a sauce—and skate cheeks and livers are also favored. Unfortunately, in this country, skates are caught as a by-product of the catch of other groundfish and are often thrown back in the water. Recently, more skate is being processed for the home market, and restaurants serve it in many dishes. When the wings do reach the market, they are very cheap, and you should snap them up.

You can buy whole wings or parts of the wings. Sometimes fishmongers fillet these wings, which I think is highly unnecessary, as the flesh falls so easily off the cartilaginous bones when cooked. Whole skate wings weigh 1 pound or more.

Unless skates are bled immediately, the urea in their flesh will produce an ammonia smell. The ammonia smell is a natural phenomenon in the shark and skate family, for these fish carry urea in their blood and tissue to keep a natural balance of salt in their bodies. Blanch skates in vinegar mixed with water, or soak them in salt water, milk or lemon juice and water. Bleeding skate properly when they are first caught will also help to keep their flesh white. Eat them when they are very fresh.

How to Skin Skate Wings

♦ Raw skate wings can be skinned by pulling the skin off (across the wing) with heavy pliers.

♦ Or you can remove the skin by cooking the skate:

  Water to cover the skate wings
  ½ **cup dry white wine**
  1 **carrot, peeled and sliced**
  ½ **teaspoon black peppercorns**
  2 **celery stalks, coarsely chopped**
  Skate wings

1. Bring the water to a boil with the other ingredients except the skate.

2. Turn the heat to low and simmer for 10 minutes

3. Immerse the skin-on skate wings in the liquid, one at a time, and cook over very low heat for 1 to 2 minutes, depending on how large they are. *Note*: If you want to poach the skate wings, cook them for another 4 to 5 minutes, until they are cooked all the way through. Insert a fork or knife, and pull the flesh apart to see the flesh.

4. Lift the skate wings out of the water with wide spatulas and let them drain on a plate or dishcloth for a minute or so.

5. Use a thin, pointed knife to remove the skin. It should come off easily. Also remove any part of the flesh which is dark so that only strands of completely white flesh remain. There is no need to pull the bottom (white) skin off.

You can broil, fry, grill or steam skate. You can make lovely salads with it. Little wings look nice on a plate, and the larger ones can be cut into portion-sized pieces or into little strips about 1½ inches wide that can be placed in a star pattern on the plate.

Skates need to be accompanied by a sauce or dressing with acid, such as the Lime and Dill Vinaigrette (page 202). Tomatillo Salsa (page 197) is also a good accompaniment.

COOKING METHODS

Cut	Cooking Methods	Serves	How Much to Buy
Whole wings	As listed below	1	8 to 12 ounces
Fillets	As listed below	1	6 to 8 ounces

CHOICE OF RECIPES

Broiled Fillets, Escalopes or Medallions, page 100
Grilled Fish Fillets or Medallions, page 109
Fried Skate Wings à la Meunière, page 122
Poached Small Whole Fish or Fish Fillets, page 140
Steamed Seafood, page 146
Salsa-Flavored Fish Salad, page 192

Smelt

Rainbow Smelt
Osmerus mordax
Cholesterol: 70   Omega-3: 0.7   Fat: 2.4

Eulachon
Thaleichthys pacificus
Cholesterol: N/A   Omega-3: N/A   Fat: N/A

MOST OF THESE BEAUTIFUL, iridescent little fish are anadromous (that is, they live in the sea but spawn in rivers) and are caught when returning to fresh water to spawn. Others have adapted to life in fresh water and now inhabit cold-water lakes and streams; this means they are available for much of the year, which is good news for those who love to eat them. Most smelts are caught from the Atlantic, primarily off the coast of Canada, especially at New Brunswick, as well as off the coast of Maine. They are also caught in the Pacific and the Great Lakes.

There are many species of smelt. Varieties include the eulachon, a West Coast fish that is also known as the icefish, frostfish and candlefish because of its oiliness; and the rainbow smelt, a pale olive-green fish with a yellow and silver belly and a bright silver lateral band running down its body. On the West Coast, many fish are called smelts when they are actually from the silversides family, Atherinidae—jack smelts, for example, are silversides.

Smelts weigh as much as ⅓ pound. They are sold whole and gutted and sometimes beheaded, fresh and frozen. They are so small that they can be easily gutted through the head: Pull out the gills, and the guts will follow (see page 42). If you feel roe inside the fish, either squeeze the fish gently like a toothpaste tube to get the roe out or leave it in. It is a delight to eat along with the fish.

The flesh of smelts is sweet with fine flakes when cooked. Deep-fry, fry or broil them whole, filleted or butterflied. I prefer whole smelt that has been gutted through the head. I eat it with my fingers, chewing up the bones and head if they are very small, and if they are large, I pull the flesh off either side of the backbone with my teeth to savor the delicious, sweet flesh.

Fat content
low

Form usually prepared
butterflied or split fish (sometimes headless)

Taste
sweet

Texture
flaky

Cut	Cooking Methods	Serves	How Much to Buy
Whole	Roasting, deep-frying, escabèche	1	8 to 12 ounces
Butterflied and fillets	Frying, broiling, grilling, escabèche	1	6 to 8 ounces

CHOICE OF RECIPES

Roast Whole Fish, page 89

Broiled Fillets, Butterflied or Split Fish, Escalopes or Medallions, page 100

Grilled Fish Fillets, Butterflied or Split Fish or Medallions, page 109

Fried Fish Fillets à la Meunière, page 122

Deep-Fried Seafood with Seasoned Flour, page 131

Escabèche, page 184

Snapper, Red

Lutjanus campechanus
Mixed Species
Cholesterol: 37   Omega-3: 0.3   Fat: 1.3

Fat content
low

Form usually prepared
fillets

Taste
mild

Texture
flaky

ALTHOUGH THERE ARE MANY MEMBERS of the snapper family (Lutjanidae) bearing many different names and 103 species of the *Lutjanus* genus, there is only one true red snapper, according to the Food and Drug Administration. Also called the American red or northern red snapper, this is truly a special fish that can command good prices. It is handsome with spiny fins, a large head with a strong gill cover, large scales, eyes with red irises and black pupils and beautiful pink-tinged skin. It is also magnificent in taste. The red snapper is caught in the Atlantic in warm waters off North Carolina, off the Florida "snapper banks," off the coasts of Texas and Louisiana and from the Campeche Bank off Mexico.

Around the world, there are many other snappers with similar looks to the red snapper. Some are the mutton snapper (*L. analis*), blackfin snapper (*L. buccanella*), gray or mangrove snapper (*L. griseus*), lane snapper (*L. synagris*) and mahogany snapper (*L. mahogoni*). Silk snappers (*L. vivanus*), incorrectly called queen snappers, whose eyes have yellow irises, are also called yelloweye snappers. Yellowtail snappers (*Ocyurus chrysurus*) and vermilion snappers

(*Rhomboplites aurorubens*) are from the same family but not the same genus; they are similar in looks, with yellow markings. The vermilion snapper is red-skinned, while the red snapper is pink-skinned. Vermilion snappers are more streamlined, and they do not grow so large.

Snappers generally have wonderful flesh, and none should be shunned. A large number of snappers are imported from Central and South American waters; they are similar-tasting fish. They usually come to us already gutted and with gills removed. But look carefully for the true American red snapper—other snappers may be called by this name to justify a high price. On the West Coast, a red-skinned rockfish may be called a red snapper and marked up accordingly. This is allowed in California but not in interstate trade.

Red snappers weighing up to 30 pounds and more are caught, although we usually see 1-to-3-pounders at the fish store. True red snapper is sold whole and in filleted form, nearly always with its skin left on, for that is one of the main attractions of this fish, and it also helps to identify the fish. (On the East Coast, be suspicious of "skinned red or white snapper fillets"—they're probably tilefish.) When buying whole red snappers, keep in mind that true red snappers have large, heavy heads (the South American species have smaller heads).

Snappers are easy to fillet once you know how to fillet roundfish (see page 43). However, I prefer to roast these creatures whole: Take a snapper weighing 1 to 1½ pounds, and roast it with a good variety of vegetables, or take one weighing 10 to 15 pounds that is stuffed very simply with fresh herbs and seasonings, and roast it on a bed of sliced onions. Red snapper flesh is especially white and sweet when cooked.

The frames (heads, bones and skin) of snappers make wonderful stock.

COOKING METHODS

Cut	Cooking Methods	Serves	How Much to Buy
Whole	Roasting, broiling, grilling, frying	2	1½ to 2 pounds
Whole	Roasting	Dinner for 10	10 pounds
Whole	Roasting	Part of a buffet for 20	10 pounds
Whole	Bake-poaching	Dinner for 8 to 10	7 pounds
Fillets	As listed below	1	6 to 10 ounces

CHOICE OF RECIPES

Baked Lean Fish Fillets, page 75

Bake-Poached Whole Fish, page 76

Bake-Poached Fish Fillets, page 79

Oven-Steamed Seafood en Papillote, page 80

Baked Fish Fillet Casserole, page 82

Baked Fish Fillet Casserole with Light Tomato Sauce, page 83

Roast Whole Fish, page 89

Broiled Whole Roundfish, page 98

Broiled Fillets, Butterflied or Split Fish, Steaks, Escalopes or Medallions, page 100

Grilled Whole Fish, page 107

Grilled Fish Fillets, Butterflied or Split Fish, Steaks or Medallions, page 109

Fried Fish Fillets or Fish Steaks à la Meunière, page 122

Fried Whole Fish or Pan-Dressed Fish, page 124

Blackened Fish Fillets, page 128

Poached Whole Fish, page 139

Steamed Seafood, page 146

Fish Soup (Bourride), page 160

Fish Stock, page 164

Seafood Stew or Pasta Sauce, page 165

Seafood Stew with Tomato and Green Pepper, page 176

Fish Fillets with Spinach and Ginger, page 178

Seviche, page 183

Escabèche, page 184

Sushi and Sashimi, page 189

Salsa-Flavored Fish Salad, page 192

Sole: Gray, Lemon, Dover, English, Butter, Petrale, Rex and Rock

see Flatfish, page 273

Spot

see Drum and Croaker, page 269

Squid

Squid, Long-Finned or Winter
Loligo pealeii
Squid, Short-Finned or Summer
Illex illecebrosus
Squid, Pacific
Loligo opalescens

Mixed species
Cholesterol: 233   Omega-3: 0.5   Fat: 1.4

SQUID ARE TENTACLED "head-footed" creatures—cephalopods—meaning that the eight arms and two tentacles are attached to the head. Squid are mollusks. A squid has a thin internal quill, or pen, that supports its soft body. It can swim at great speeds and therefore can migrate great distances.

Squid are caught in both the Atlantic and the Pacific in some abundance. The biggest fisheries are in Japanese waters, off Argentina in the Pacific and off Morocco in the Atlantic. Squid are also caught in the Mediterranean: There is nothing so good as the tiny squid of Greece, which, when I stayed there, we refused to eat if they were any larger than the first joints of our thumbs. On the East Coast of North America, the two main commercial species are the summer squid, also known as the short-finned squid, which is taken primarily from Canadian Atlantic waters, and the winter squid, also known as the long-finned squid, which is taken from the Atlantic waters of the United States. The biggest markets are the Orient, Spain, Italy and the United States.

In the fish store, we see squid tubes (bodies) that range in size from 3 to 12 inches long, although squid grow to some 30 feet long. They are sold cleaned and uncleaned, with head, arms and tentacles, fresh and frozen. Much squid is processed at sea and even frozen on board. Look for creamy white flesh under a brown, mottled membrane on the summer squid and the same pearly flesh on the winter squid, with a membrane that turns purplish the longer it is out of the water.

Also known as *calamari* (Italian) or *calmar* (French), squid are often sold in restaurants as fried rings, stuffed or in seafood salad. Because of their pocketlike shape, they are perfect for stuffing. Cut

Fat content
low

Forms usually prepared
cleaned, uncleaned

Taste
mild

Texture
firm

small, they make a flavorful addition to soups and stews. The arms and tentacles may be unsightly for some, but they can be chopped for stuffings or added to soups. Large giant squid are cut into round or oval "steaks" on the West Coast; they can be nearly an inch thick and are tenderized before being grilled or broiled.

Ink is usually found in a little sac in the body, although sometimes the sac is too small or nonexistent (perhaps the squid blew all its ink away in fright at being caught or hadn't developed any yet). Squid ink is also available in little sachets at a reasonable cost in specialty stores. It is worth collecting to flavor sauces or a black risotto. Some black pasta is made with squid ink.

How to Clean Fresh Whole Squid

♦ Gently pull the head, arms and tentacles from the body. Remove the creamy-colored viscera and plasticlike quill from the inside of the body. Rinse well to remove sand, and pull off the outer membrane. Find the ink sac near the head and inside the eyes; reserve it if needed. Cut the arms and tentacles from the head, and remove the small beak from it. (The beak is a little, hard, round ball with a beak like a bird's inside it.) Cut the large tentacles in two, and use them for a stock, stuffing, soup or stew.

♦ Squid ink is very thick and viscous. Have a 2-cup measuring cup ready with ½ cup water in it. Squeeze the ink from the sac into the water and also rinse your fingers in the water. This way you will catch all the ink.

♦ If the squid has been "cleaned" by the processor or the fish store, you will need to rinse it well for sand and pull off the outer membrane if it is still on.

♦ Squid flesh will toughen easily with overcooking, so cook a small squid very quickly at high temperatures. If it toughens, you must cook it until it gets tender again. This might take a long time. Large squid take slightly longer than small squid to cook.

COOKING METHODS

Cut	Cooking Methods	Serves	How Much to Buy
Cut into rings	As listed below	1	6 to 8 ounces (uncleaned squid)
Cut into rings	As listed below	1	4 to 6 ounces (cleaned squid)

CHOICE OF RECIPES

Sautéed Squid, page 126

Deep-Fried Seafood with Seasoned Flour, page 131

Shellfish Salad with Lime and Dill Vinaigrette, page 142

Steamed Seafood, page 146

Fish Soup (Bourride), page 160

Seafood Stew or Pasta Sauce, page 165

Seafood Stew with Tomato and Green Pepper, page 176

Seviche, page 183

Sushi and Sashimi, page 189

Sturgeon
Mixed Species
Cholesterol: N/A Omega-3: 0.3 Fat: 4.0

THE ANADROMOUS STURGEONS are the grand old prehistoric fish of river and sea. As the source of the best caviar (treated eggs or roe), they are precious to us. Their flesh is also in high demand, for it is delicious when cooked or smoked. Sturgeon flesh is better known as a smoked product, but that is changing as more people begin to appreciate it freshly cooked.

Sturgeons grow to a large size, a mature old age and a great weight (they are caught at weights up to 350 pounds, although weights of 40 to 50 pounds are more common). Sturgeons have five rows of bony scutes (strong bony plates or scales) running along their bodies. The mouth is a long snout with whiskers on the bottom that are used to search for food in dark, sometimes muddy waters. They are colored olive-gray, brown, green or gray. The sturgeon has a primitive cartilaginous "backbone" that surrounds its notochord (spinal cord); the notochord can be removed by twisting and pulling it out all in one piece. Isinglass, used to clarify

Fat content
*low (ocean species),
high (lake species)*

Forms usually prepared
steaks, fillets

Taste
mild

Texture
firm

liquids, used to be prepared from air bladders of sturgeon, as well as from other fish.

As a consequence of overfishing, sturgeons are scarce, and rigid fishing limitations have been set. The Atlantic sturgeon from Nova Scotia to North Carolina (*Acipenser oxyrhynchus*) and the shortnose sturgeon (*A. brevirostris*) from Cape Cod to Florida have been nearly fished out. The white sturgeon (*A. transmontanus*) and the green sturgeon (*A. medirostris*) are still found in rivers, bays, lakes and coastal waters from California to Alaska; the Columbia River is the largest source of these West Coast sturgeons. Lake sturgeon (*A. fulvescens*) once inhabited the Great Lakes but are scarce nowadays. Shovelnose (*Scaphirhynchus platorynchus*) and pallid sturgeons (*S. album*) inhabit the lakes and rivers of the Mississippi Valley. Some sturgeons are also farmed in California.

The flesh of sturgeon is cut into fillets as well as steaks. It is delightful if grilled or braised.

Salted American sturgeon eggs, or roe, can be sold as caviar as long as they are marketed as "American caviar" to distinguish them from the imported sturgeon caviars of Russia and Iran. Roe from other fish, such as whitefish and lumpfish, can also be treated and sold as caviar as long as the name of the fish is included in the name—for example, "golden whitefish caviar" or "black lumpfish caviar."

COOKING METHODS

Cut	Cooking Methods	Serves	How Much to Buy
Steaks and fillets	As listed below	1	6 to 8 ounces

CHOICE OF RECIPES

Baked Fatty Fish Fillets, page 73

Broiled Fillets, Butterflied or Split Fish, Steaks, Escalopes or Medallions, page 100

Grilled Fish Fillets, Butterflied or Split Fish, Steaks or Medallions, page 109

Fried Fish Fillets or Fish Steaks à la Meunière, page 122

Braised Fish Fillets or Steaks with Provençal Sauce, page 156

Creamy Seafood Chowder, page 162

Hot-Smoking (Smoke-Cooking), page 170

Escabèche, page 184

Sunfish

Mixed Species

Cholesterol: 67   Omega-3: 0.1   Fat: 0.7

SUNFISH ARE COLORFUL FISH that are caught in fresh water in lakes, rivers and streams all over the inland United States and southern Canada. There are many species—bluegill, green, warmouth, pumpkinseed, redbreast, spotted, longear and redear, to name just a few. Other very similar species are the black and white crappies. Largemouth and smallmouth bass are also members of the sunfish family.

Sunfish have lean and delicate flesh and are best pan-fried, grilled or roasted. Watch out for bones!

COOKING METHODS

Cut	Cooking Methods	Serves	How Much to Buy
Whole	Roasting, grilling	2	1½ to 2 pounds
Pan-dressed or split	Broiling, grilling, frying	2	1½ to 2 pounds

CHOICE OF RECIPES

Roast Whole Fish, page 89

Broiled Fillets, Butterflied or Split Fish, Steaks, Escalopes or Medallions, page 100

Grilled Whole Fish, page 107

Grilled Fish Fillets, Butterflied or Split Fish, Steaks or Medallions, page 109

Fried Whole Fish or Pan-Dressed Fish, page 124

Fat content
low

Form usually prepared
pan-dressed

Taste
mild

Texture
flaky

Swordfish

Xiphias gladius

Cholesterol: 39   Omega-3: 0.6   Fat: 4.0

R ANGING THE WARM WATERS of the world, the swordfish, which grows up to 1,000 pounds but is usually caught at about 250 pounds, is a favorite. This fish, a member of the billfish clan and also called the broadbill, is aptly named for the flat swordlike protrusion that extends from the upper part of its jaw. It uses this "sword" to swat and stun its diet of fish. The swordfish has a torpedo-shaped body that tapers off narrowly at the tail end and strong fins which help get it through the water with speed.

Swordfish are caught in the Atlantic from Newfoundland (when the waters get warm) down to Argentina. In the Pacific, they are found from Chile up to California. Swordfish are imported to America from places like Chile, Japan, Taiwan, Spain, Brazil, Ecuador, Portugal and Greece (Spain is the largest producer), but Americans favor the swordfish caught off the east coast of New England, because it is very well handled by the fishermen—that is, it is bled on board fishing boats and not stored for too long.

Swordfish are usually beheaded at sea (some fishermen save and exhibit the swords if they are very large). When the fish are brought to shore, distributors cut them into large "wheels," which are cuts across the body. In the fish store, you will most likely see swordfish already cut into steaks obtained from these wheels. Try to persuade your fishmonger that you like them 1¼ inches thick—this thickness will help to keep the steaks moist as you cook them. The same is true for cubes cut for brochettes—they should be 1¼ inches square. *Note*: Sometimes the large girth of the swordfish creates problems when cutting steaks weighing 7 to 10 ounces—the proper size for a portion. You may have to cut them less than 1¼ inches thick. If a swordfish steak is less than 1 inch thick, cook it very carefully.

Swordfish flesh is firm, lean and sweet. It can be gray, orange, white or pink when raw, but it turns white when cooked. The only bothersome bone in a swordfish steak is the central backbone, which is large and easily avoided. There is a dark red muscle running through the fish that some feel they must cut out before cooking, but it is, in fact, edible.

Fat content
low

Forms usually prepared
steaks, cubes

Taste
mild

Texture
firm

COOKING METHODS

Cut	Cooking Methods	Serves	How Much to Buy
Steaks	Broiling, grilling, hot-smoking, escabèche	1	7 to 10 ounces
Brochette cubes	As listed below	1	4 to 8 ounces

CHOICE OF RECIPES

Broiled Steaks, Escalopes or Medallions, page 100

Grilled Steaks or Medallions, page 109

Grilled or Broiled Seafood Brochettes, page 110

Grilled or Broiled Seafood and Vegetable Brochettes, page 112

Blackened Fish Fillets, page 128

Fish Soup (Bourride), page 160

Creamy Seafood Chowder, page 162

Hot-Smoking (Smoke-Cooking), page 170

Seviche, page 183

Escabèche, page 184

Tilapia

Tilapia rendalli

Cholesterol: 19   Omega-3: 0.1   Fat: 0.9

TILAPIA IS A GENERAL NAME given to several species of fish that have been bred for years all over the world in freshwater ponds, although they can also grow in seawater. Africa (from Egypt down to the Cape of Good Hope), India, Bangladesh, Indonesia, Jamaica, Hawaii and Taiwan are just a few of the places where these fish are bred. Israel has now started to farm and export tilapia, and many tilapia farms have been established all over the United States, primarily in southern states such as Florida, Texas and Arizona.

The beauty of tilapia is that they can reach the table in a day or so, because they can be processed so quickly and efficiently from the ponds and they stay fresh longer than saltwater fish. These fish grow in great profusion in small ponds; when the ponds are kept clean, the tilapia produced are excellent food fish. Tilapia grow fast in warm water—80 degrees F produces large fish, though they cannot survive in water less than 60 degrees or more than 85 degrees. In the southern states of the United States, where they are bred, it is easy

Fat content
low

Form usually prepared
fillets

Taste
mild

Texture
firm

to keep the water temperatures high; in other states, breeders either use water from naturally warm springs or warm the water artificially.

Tilapia have good-looking skin that, as a rule, is black and white, like salt and pepper—black with light shadings where the scales were. Breeders in Florida, Texas and Arizona have developed hybrids with an attractive pink-red skin.

Tilapia grow up to 3 pounds, but most of those marketed weigh less. They are available whole or filleted, fresh or frozen; the fillets weigh 3 ounces or more, and those bred in Israel are usually filleted with the skin on. The texture of the flesh is not unlike that of catfish—firm yet light and sweet when cooked.

Tilapia is most versatile for cooking. It will suit most cooking methods, but remember to feature its good-looking skin.

Note: Up to now, the Food and Drug Administration has insisted that these fish be called tilapia, but some (for instance, some of the tilapia bred in Israel) can slip by as Saint Peter's fish in supermarkets. Some tilapia from Florida, Texas and Arizona are given names such as sunshine snapper and cherry snapper, which are also not correct.

COOKING METHODS

Cut	Cooking Methods	Serves	How Much to Buy
Whole	Roasting	2	1½ pounds
Pan-dressed	Frying	1	¾ to 1 pound
Fillets	As listed below	1	6 to 8 ounces

CHOICE OF RECIPES

Bake-Poached Fish Fillets, page 79

Oven-Steamed Seafood en Papillote, page 80

Baked Fish Fillet Casserole with Light Tomato Sauce, page 83

Roast Whole Fish, page 89

Broiled Fillets, Butterflied or Split Fish, Steaks, Escalopes or Medallions, page 100

Grilled Fish Fillets, Butterflied or Split Fish, Steaks or Medallions, page 109

Fried Whole Fish or Pan-Dressed Fish, page 124

Steamed Seafood, page 146

Seviche, page 183

Tilefish

Lopholatilus chamaeleonticeps
Cholesterol: N/A Omega-3: 0.4 Fat: 2.3

Fat content
low

Forms usually prepared
fillets, steaks

Taste
mild

Texture
flaky

THE TILEFISH, also most aptly called the golden tilefish and the rainbow tilefish, bears all the colors of the rainbow. Its blue-green back extends to a blue head, which is tinged with rose and yellow. Its back and head are dotted with yellow and gold spots, and its sides, which are pink and yellow, shade to a white-silver belly. Sadly, once out of water, the fish tends to lose some of this fine coloring.

Although its colors might suggest that the tilefish belongs in tropical waters, it is fished from the Gulf of Mexico up the east coast to Cape Cod. Much tilefish is caught off the New Jersey coast year-round; Barnegat Light in New Jersey has been called the tilefish capital of the world. The usual weight is between 5 and 20 pounds, although tilefish weighing up to 60 pounds have been caught.

Tilefish are cut into steaks at the fish store or sold in filleted form. If you want a whole fish, know that the head is big and heavy (only the cheek is edible) and the relative percentage of flesh to bone is not large. Tilefish exudes a fair amount of moisture as it cooks, so there is some shrinkage. Compensate for this by buying slightly more than you would of other fish. At present, tilefish commands reasonable prices.

Pin bones run along the fillets to just short of the tail. Loosen them with pin-nose pliers or cut them away with a knife if they are hefty.

This splendid-looking fish is very good to eat. It has lean white flesh and a flaky texture (somewhat like that of grouper or even cod) when cooked. The flavor is quite sweet but bland, and you will need to use a cooking method and seasonings that will make it interesting. For this reason, I find deep-frying, sautéing, broiling and grilling good cooking methods for this fish, and I season it strongly with fresh herbs and seasonings and flavorful sauces.

COOKING METHODS

CUT	COOKING METHODS	SERVES	HOW MUCH TO BUY
Whole	Roasting	Part of a buffet for 15	10 pounds
Whole	Roasting, poaching	Dinner for 8	7 pounds
Chunks	Roasting	Dinner for 4 or more	10 to 12 ounces per person
Fillets and steaks	As listed below	1	6 to 8 ounces

CHOICE OF RECIPES

Trout

Genus *Oncorhynchus*, *Salmo* and *Salvelinus*

TROUT ARE VERSATILE FISH to cook. These attractive fish are marketed at just the right size for individual servings. Those in the wild are a joyous catch for the fly fisherman or angler when they are caught in lakes, streams and rivers.

Most trout and chars belong to the Salmonidae family (salmon). Some, such as lake trout, survive only in fresh water, while others are anadromous—that is, they spend some time in the sea before returning to their freshwater birthplace to spawn. Anadromous trout become silvery when they go to sea but regain their skin colors upon returning to fresh water. They also grow larger during their stay in the sea and become fat before entering the rivers to spawn.

Most of the trout we buy at fish stores have been farmed in spring-water-fed ponds. Rainbow trout is the predominant species that is farmed, but brook trout and brown trout are also farmed.

In the wild, we have rainbow trout all over the United States, brook and brown trout in the eastern United States and the Canadian Atlantic Provinces, lake trout from the northern United States and all over Canada and cutthroat trout and Dolly Varden char from rivers to the sea on the West Coast, to mention just a few.

Salmon trout is the name given by fish suppliers to the rainbow, brown or brook trout that go to sea. Rainbow trout gone to sea on the West Coast are called not only "salmon trout," but, more correctly, "steelhead." Some steelheads are bred to 8 to 12 ounces each. Steelhead is also the name given to some rainbow trout that live in the Great Lakes and never get to the sea.

Farmed trout are most often marketed at 8 to 10 ounces (though they do grow larger). They are boned (butterflied) or filleted and sold fresh or frozen.

Trout are delicate and mild and must not be overwhelmed with strong sauces. A simple way to enhance them is with a little butter, lemon and parsley. The color of trout flesh ranges from white to pink, orange and red. Take advantage of this lovely color when cooking this fish.

Fat content
low to moderate

Form usually prepared
butterflied or split fish

Taste
mild

Texture
flaky

Rainbow Trout

Oncorhynchus mykiss

Cholesterol: 57   Omega-3: 0.6   Fat: 3.4

The rainbow trout is a freshwater fish that sports a lot of color: It has a green or blue back, silvery sides with a red strip along each side, a white belly and little dark spots all over.

The West Coast steelhead trout, which is a rainbow trout that goes to sea, loses some of this color when in the sea and becomes silvery and very bright, with a green and pink lateral band. Steelhead trout grow larger than inland rainbow trout, but they are also marketed at the same size as rainbow trout (8 to 10 ounces).

Rainbow trout originated in the western part of the United States but are now farmed all over America—in fact, all over the world. Idaho has the largest number of trout farms in the United States. Most of them are located in the Magic Valley, which has a lot of natural spring water.

Brook Trout

Salvelinus fontinalis

Cholesterol: 68   Omega-3: 0.4   Fat: 3.2

Brook trout are an angler's treat. These fish, also called eastern brook trout, grow in the wild in cool lakes and streams in the eastern United States and Canada; some are anadromous and go to sea.

The brook trout has a green-brown back and green sides, and its skin is mottled with yellow spots and red spots surrounded with blue halos. Fins on its lower body are outlined in black with white edges.

Aquafarmed brook trout are available in fish stores in the same form as rainbow trout.

Brown Trout

Salmo trutta

Cholesterol: N/A   Omega-3: N/A   Fat: N/A

The brown trout originated in Europe and was brought over by settlers. It now inhabits inland waters throughout the United States and Canada; some brown trout go to sea (the Atlantic) and are known as sea or salmon trout. The fish is brownish with dark spots on its back and sides and a white belly.

Lake Trout

Salvelinus namaycush

Cholesterol: 36   Omega-3: 1.4   Fat: 9.4

These trout are not farmed but thrive in the cold-water lakes and rivers of the northern United States and all of Canada. They do not go to sea. They grow large and are colored brown and silver with yellow spots. They are very high in fat and do not have as much food appeal as other trout. I find them too oily.

COOKING METHODS

Cut	Cooking Methods	Serves	How Much to Buy
Whole and pan-dressed	As listed below	1	8 to 10 ounces
Butterflied or split	As listed below	1	6 to 10 ounces
Fillets	As listed below	1	Two 3-to-4-ounce fillets

CHOICE OF RECIPES

Baked Fatty Fish Fillets, page 73

Oven-Steamed Seafood en Papillote, page 80

Casserole of Fish Fillets with Potatoes and Coriander Pesto, page 86

Roast Whole Fish, page 89

Broiled Fillets, Butterflied or Split Fish, Steaks, Escalopes or Medallions, page 100

Grilled Whole Fish, page 107

Grilled Fish Fillets, Butterflied or Split Fish or Medallions, page 109

Fried Whole Fish or Pan-Dressed Fish, page 124

Poached Small Whole Fish or Fish Fillets, page 140

Steamed Seafood, page 146

Creamy Seafood Chowder, page 162

Hot-Smoking (Smoke-Cooking), page 170

Fish Fillets with Spinach and Ginger, page 178

Seviche, page 183

Escabèche, page 184

Soused or Marinated Fish, page 186

Summer Fish Salad, page 193

Tuna

Fat content
low to moderate

Forms usually prepared
steaks, cubes

Taste
mild to bland

Texture
firm flakes

TUNA ARE MEMBERS OF THE MACKEREL FAMILY, and a large number of species roam the temperate and subtropical waters of the world. Many people know tuna only as a canned product, but for the rest of us, fresh is best—there is no comparison. Fresh tuna has superb flesh, and it can be cooked or enjoyed raw in sushi or sashimi.

A typical tuna is silver with a bluish back, large round eyes lying flat against its head and little finlets stretching down to the tail behind the dorsal and anal fins. It is capable of achieving great speed in the water—most tuna have voracious appetites, so they need speed and endurance for their long migrations away from their spawning grounds in search of food. A tuna's body is torpedo-shaped—just about round at the center and tapering off toward the head and tail ends. Its fins can be retracted into its body so it can become more streamlined and therefore swim faster. The differences among tuna species lie in the sizes they attain (bluefin tuna grow to 1,000 pounds, while yellowfin and bigeye tuna grow to around 400 pounds, and blackfin, skipjack, albacore and bonito weigh less than 100 pounds), the markings on their skin and the sizes of their eyes.

The best varieties of tuna for eating raw or cooked are bluefin, bigeye, yellowfin, bonito and blackfin. The Japanese, who buy up the best tuna from New England, New York and other parts of the world and fly it fresh to their country for the sashimi trade, pay very high prices for bluefin; the catch has now been restricted because of overfishing, and consequently, these fish are becoming very scarce. Skipjack and yellowfin are mostly canned as light tuna, while albacore is mostly canned as white tuna.

Tuna flesh differs in quality from fish to fish, and it takes years of experience to recognize the quality differences. The Japanese assign three grades to tuna: Grade-1 and grade-2 tuna are considered sashimi quality—they are fresh, have a high fat content and are a glossy, translucent red (brownish tuna is oxidized)—while grade-3 tuna, which must be fresh but may have less color, is considered good enough for cooking. The quality of the flesh depends on the size of the fish, the time of year it was caught (the fat content varies with the season, and the fatter the flesh, the more delicious it is), the way it was caught and its subsequent handling—tuna have been known to "cook" themselves in their struggle to survive when caught, and when this happens, their flesh deteriorates quickly. Of course, the higher a tuna's grade, the more expensive it is.

As a rule, a tuna that is marketed is cut into four boneless loins.

In the fish store, we see these loins as well as steaks, chunks and sometimes cubes cut from the loins. The tuna at your fish store may be fresh or defrosted.

When buying tuna for sashimi, you should look for deep red, glistening flesh—ask for a thin little slice and rub it between your fingers to make sure it is oily. (Incidentally, the marbled flesh from the belly, or *toro*, as it is called in Japanese, is considered the most delicious part of the tuna.) If you are going to cook the tuna, you need not be as fussy, but be sure the tuna is fresh and colorful. Buy steaks that are cut 1¼ inches thick—you are less likely to overcook them.

The dark red fatty muscle found near the skin along the lateral line has a different texture and is rich and flavorful, but you may want to remove it. You can cook tuna like swordfish or mako shark; you can also marinate it in oil and herbs and then grill or broil it, or you can sauté or braise it. You can, for a change, grill a thick (2-inch) steak on an open fire or in a grill pan, then finish cooking it in the oven; this makes for a most impressive dish. Tuna flesh has large flakes when cooked and is flavorful and firm. It turns a light gray as it cooks. Be sure to undercook it slightly, as it dries out easily. After cooking tuna, just add some freshly ground black pepper and a squeeze of lemon juice for flavor.

Tuna freezes well. The Japanese are experts at freezing tuna and may keep it frozen for up to a year.

Bluefin

Thunnus thynnus
Cholesterol: 38   Omega-3: 1.2   Fat: 4.9

Bluefin tuna are found in the waters of the eastern Atlantic (from Norway to the Mediterranean), the western Atlantic (from Labrador to South America) and the Pacific. Atlantic bluefin grow to weights of 1,400 pounds; Pacific bluefin are smaller. Bluefins caught in the western Atlantic spawn in the Gulf of Mexico and the Mediterranean and swim north as the waters warm in the summer.

Bluefins have blue-black backs that shade to silver at the belly; their finlets are yellow outlined with black. Bluefin flesh is dark red. Although their catch is limited now that they have been overfished, bluefins command high prices for their high fat content, which occurs in the late summer and fall. They are very much sought after by the Japanese, who eat them raw. Bluefin tuna are sold fresh or defrosted.

Yellowfin

Thunnus albacares

Cholesterol: 45 Omega-3: 0.2 Fat: 1.0

Yellowfin tuna are found worldwide in warm waters. They grow to weights of as much as 500 pounds. They look similar to bluefin tuna but have yellow bellies, fins and finlets.

Bigeye

Thunnus obesus

Cholesterol: 66 Omega-3: N/A Fat: 1.6

The bigeye tuna is found from Cape Cod down to Brazil. It is colored blue and silver and has yellow finlets and large eyes. It grows to weights of 400 pounds and is excellent eating.

Blackfin

Thunnus atlanticus

Cholesterol: N/A Omega-3: N/A Fat: N/A

Blackfin is another highly edible tuna. It is found in the Atlantic from Cape Cod to Brazil. It grows to weights of only about 40 pounds. It has a brownish stripe on its back and a silvery belly.

Albacore

Thunnus alalunga

Cholesterol: 38 Omega-3: 2.1 Fat: 7.2

Also called the longfin tuna, the albacore looks like other varieties of tuna, with its blue and silver coloring, but it has long pectoral fins. Albacore tuna grow to weights of 90 pounds. Most are caught in the Pacific, though they are also found in the Atlantic. Some albacore tuna goes in the can—albacore is the white meat of canned tuna—but it is also delicious fresh. Take care to keep it moist.

Atlantic Bonito
Sarda sarda
Pacific Bonito
Sarda chiliensis

Mixed Species
Cholesterol: N/A   Omega-3: N/A   Fat: 5.5

Bonitos are fished on both sides of the temperate Atlantic as well as in the Pacific. In looks, they resemble small tuna with stripes on their backs, and they grow to weights under 20 pounds. Bonitos have dark red flesh; when they are bled, their flesh turns an apricot color. Japanese cooks sometimes broil bonitos very briefly and serve them uncooked at the center.

Skipjack
Euthynnus pelamis
Cholesterol: 47   Omega-3: 0.3   Fat: 1.0

Similar in looks to other tuna, the skipjack has stripes on its belly and grows to weights of as much as 70 pounds. It is caught predominantly in the Pacific, but it is also found in the warm waters of the Atlantic. Much skipjack is canned or frozen.

Little Tunny
Euthynnus alletteratus
Cholesterol: N/A   Omega-3: N/A   Fat: N/A

Also called the false albacore, the oceanic bonito and the spotted bonito, the little tunny has spots on its belly under the pectoral fin and has wavy stripes on its back. It is fished abundantly in the warm waters of the Atlantic, mostly by sports fishermen.

COOKING METHODS

Cut	Cooking Methods	Serves	How Much to Buy
Brochette cubes	Grilling	1	6 to 8 ounces
	Broiling	1	6 to 8 ounces
Chunks	Braising	4	2 pounds
Steaks	As listed below	1	6 to 10 ounces

CHOICE OF RECIPES

Broiled Fillets, Butterflied or Split Fish, Steaks, Escalopes or Medallions, page 100

Grilled Fish Fillets, Butterflied or Split Fish, Steaks or Medallions, page 109

Grilled or Broiled Seafood Brochettes, page 110

Grilled or Broiled Seafood and Vegetable Brochettes, page 112

Blackened Fish Fillets, page 128

Braised Fish Fillets or Steaks with Provençal Sauce, page 156

Hot-Smoking (Smoke-Cooking), page 170

Seviche, page 183

Sushi and Sashimi, page 189

Summer Fish Salad, page 193

Whitebait

Silversides
Atherinopsis affinis
Sand Lances
Ammodytes americanus, A. hexapterus

Cholesterol: N/A *Omega-3:* N/A *Fat:* N/A

Fat content
moderate

Form usually prepared
whole

Taste
mild

Texture
flaky

WHITEBAIT ARE ANY VERY SMALL FISH found in waters worldwide that are as tiny as minnows; these include silversides and sand lances. Whitebait are silvery in color and practically transparent. They are sold in some fish stores, although restaurants seem to get most of them.

We eat whole whitebait, bones, eyes and all. They are most delicious deep-fried after having been coated lightly with seasoned flour. (They should be rinsed in a colander with cold running water, then drained and patted dry before being coated.) Pile them up on the plate, sprinkle them with a little cayenne, and serve them with lemon wedges. This preparation is extremely popular in England.

COOKING METHOD

Cut	Cooking Method	Serves	How Much to Buy
Whole	Deep-frying	Appetizer for 1	6 to 8 ounces

CHOICE OF RECIPE
Deep-Fried Seafood with Seasoned Flour, page 131

Whitefish
Mixed Species
Cholesterol: 60   Omega-3: 1.3   Fat: 5.9

LAKE, MOUNTAIN (*Prosopium williamsoni*) and round (*P. cylindraceum*) whitefish inhabit the lakes and streams of the United States. Lake whitefish is the most important.

Fat content
moderate

Lake Whitefish
Coregonus clupeaformis
Cholesterol: 48   Omega-3: 1.3   Fat: 9.0

Forms usually prepared
fillets, steaks

Lake whitefish have certain similarities to their relatives, the salmon, being freshwater fish with silver-colored skin and scales and streamlined bodies. Lake whitefish have more compressed bodies than salmon and very small heads, so they yield a lot more flesh than other fish.

Caught in cold freshwater lakes and rivers, lake whitefish are imported from Canada in considerable numbers. They are caught at weights up to 7 pounds and are sold whole or filleted. They can be broiled, fried, grilled, roasted or baked. Their flesh is white, firm and sweet-tasting. As they are moderately fatty fish, many are smoked very successfully.

Chub, a small freshwater fish, is also another name for a small smoked whitefish.

Taste
mild to sweet

Texture
flaky

COOKING METHODS

Cut	Cooking Methods	Serves	How Much to Buy
Whole	Roasting	4	3 pounds
Fillets	As listed below	1	6 to 8 ounces

CHOICE OF RECIPES

Baked Fatty Fish Fillets, page 73

Oven-Steamed Seafood en Papillote, page 80

Baked Fish Fillet Casserole with Light Tomato Sauce, page 83

Roast Whole Fish, page 89

Broiled Whole Roundfish, page 98

Broiled Fillets, Butterflied or Split Fish, Steaks, Escalopes or Medallions, page 100

Grilled Fish Fillets, Butterflied or Split Fish, Steaks or Medallions, page 109

Fish Croquettes, page 125

Steamed Seafood, page 146

Creamy Seafood Chowder, page 162

Hot-Smoking (Smoke-Cooking), page 170

Salsa-Flavored Fish Salad, page 192

Summer Fish Salad, page 193

Wolffish
Anarhichas lupus
Cholesterol: 46   Omega-3: 0.6   Fat: 2.5

Wolf-Eel
Anarrhichthys ocellatus
Cholesterol: *N/A*   ***Omega-3:*** *N/A*   ***Fat:*** *N/A*

THE WOLFFISH is indeed an interesting if not somewhat astonishing creature to see and deal with, for in many ways it does not resemble a marine fish: The head is round like the head of a cat (it is sometimes called the ocean catfish). It has large eyes, long front teeth and powerful back teeth that allow it to eat shellfish, thereby creating delicious flesh. And then there is its body, which has continuous dorsal and anal fins down to the tail, like an eel.

Some wolffish are dark gray or nearly black, while others are gray and black with darker strips and spots. Wolffish are scaleless.

There are two other species of wolffish in the Atlantic—the northern wolffish (*Anarhichas denticulatus*) and the spotted wolffish (*A. minor*). The wolf-eel (*Anarrhichthys ocellatus*) is from the Pacific. The wolffish and the wolf-eel are extremely similar in looks, and both are known to bite viciously when caught.

Wolffish is not widely marketed, which is a real shame, because once you get past its strange looks, you will find it has marvelous flesh—white, sweet, lean and firm with small flakes. A whole wolf-fish may weigh up to 20 pounds. Fishmongers usually sell fillets that can be fried, baked, broiled or grilled.

Fat content
low

Form usually prepared
fillets

Taste
mild to sweet

Texture
flaky

COOKING METHOD

Cut	Cooking Method	Serves	How Much to Buy
Fillets	As listed below	1	6 to 8 ounces

CHOICE OF RECIPES

Baked Fish Fillet Casserole, page 82

Baked Cajun Fish Casserole, page 85

Broiled Fillets, Butterflied or Split Fish, Steaks, Escalopes or Medallions, page 100

Grilled Fish Fillets, Butterflied or Split Fish, Steaks or Medallions, page 109

Fried Fish Fillets or Fish Steaks à la Meunière, page 122

Steamed Seafood, page 146

Fish Soup (Bourride), page 160

Seafood Stew or Pasta Sauce, page 165

Seviche, page 183

Escabèche, page 184

Salsa-Flavored Fish Salad, page 192

Yellowtail

Seriola quinqueradiata

Cholesterol: *N/A*   **Omega-3:** *N/A*   **Fat:** *5.2*

Yellowtail, California

Seriola lalandei

Cholesterol: *N/A*   **Omega-3:** *N/A*   **Fat:** *N/A*

Fat content
high

Forms usually prepared
raw slices (yellowtail); fillets (California yellowtail)

Taste
sweet and mild

Texture
flaky

THE YELLOWTAILS are members of the jack family, closely related to the amberjack. Their name can cause some confusion, for there are other fish bearing the same name: the yellowtail flounder (from the North Atlantic), yellowtail rockfish (from the Pacific) and yellowtail snapper (from the South Atlantic).

The species *S. quinqueradiata* is aquafarmed in Japan. It is expertly frozen, defrosted slowly, then cut into diagonal slices for sushi and sashimi and is called *hamachi*. It has a delicious buttery flesh.

The California yellowtail, equivalent to the East Coast amberjack, is considered a game fish and is not often obtainable in fish stores. When marketed, it is sold whole and as fillets and steaks. Broil or grill it. (Remove the dark fatty flesh along the lateral line before you cook it.)

COOKING METHODS

Cut	Cooking Methods	Serves	How Much to Buy
Fillets	Broiling, grilling	1	6 to 8 ounces
Fillets	Raw	1	3 to 4 ounces

CHOICE OF RECIPES

Broiled Fillets, Butterflied or Split Fish, Steaks, Escalopes or Medallions, page 100

Grilled Fish Fillets, Butterflied or Split Fish, Steaks or Medallions, page 109

Sushi and Sashimi, page 189

Equivalency Tables

LIQUID AND DRY MEASURE EQUIVALENCIES

CUSTOMARY	METRIC
¼ teaspoon	1.25 milliliters
½ teaspoon	2.5 milliliters
1 teaspoon	5 milliliters
1 tablespoon	15 milliliters
1 fluid ounce	30 milliliters
¼ cup	60 milliliters
⅓ cup	80 milliliters
½ cup	120 milliliters
1 cup	240 milliliters
1 pint (2 cups)	480 milliliters
1 quart (4 cups, 32 ounces)	960 milliliters (0.96 liters)
1 gallon (4 quarts)	3.84 liters
1 ounce (by weight)	28 grams
¼ pound (4 ounces)	114 grams
1 pound (16 ounces)	454 grams
2.2 pounds	1 kilogram (1,000 grams)

OVEN TEMPERATURE EQUIVALENCIES

DESCRIPTION	°FAHRENHEIT	°CELSIUS
Cool	200	90
Very slow	250	120
Slow	300-325	150-160
Moderately slow	325-350	160-180
Moderate	350-375	180-190
Moderately hot	375-400	190-200
Hot	400-450	200-230
Very hot	450-500	230-260

Bibliography

Audubon Society Staff and Norman A. Meinkoth. *The Audubon Society Field Guide to North American Seashore Creatures.* New York: Alfred A. Knopf, 1981.

Audubon Society Staff et al. *The Audubon Society Field Guide to North American Fishes, Whales, and Dolphins.* New York: Alfred A. Knopf, 1983.

Commonwealth of Massachusetts. Division of Marine Fisheries. *The Northeast Seafood Book: A Manual of Seafood Products, Marketing and Utilization.* Boston: Division of Marine Fisheries, 1984.

Davidson, Alan. *North American Seafood.* New York: The Viking Press, 1980.

Eschmeyer, William N., and Earl S. Herald. *A Field Guide to Pacific Coast Fishes: North America from the Gulf of Alaska to Baja California.* Peterson's Field Guide Series. Boston: Houghton Mifflin, 1983.

Fletcher, Anne M. *Eat Fish, Live Better.* New York: Harper & Row, 1989.

Gosner, Kenneth L. *A Field Guide to the Atlantic Seashore.* Peterson's Field Guide Series. Boston: Houghton Mifflin, 1982.

Krzynowek, Judy, and Jenny Murphy. *Proximate Composition, Energy Fatty Acid, Sodium and Cholesterol Content of Finfish, Shellfish and Their Products.* Springfield, Va.: National Oceanic and Atmospheric Administration Technical Report National Marine Fisheries Services 55. National Technical Information Service, July 1987.

Lamb, Andy, and Phil Edgell. *Coastal Fishes of the Pacific Northwest.* Madeira Park, B.C., Canada: Harbour Publishing, 1986.

Loomis, Susan Herrmann. *The Great American Seafood Cookbook.* New York: Workman Publishing, 1988.

Manooch, Charles S., III. *Fisherman's Guide: Fishes of the Southeastern United States.* Raleigh, N.C.: North Carolina State Museum of Natural Sciences, 1984.

McClane, A.J. *McClane's Field Guide to Freshwater Fishes of North America.* New York: Henry Holt, 1978.

Morris, Percy A. *A Field Guide to Atlantic Coast Shells.* 3rd ed. Peterson's Field Guide Series. Boston: Houghton Mifflin, 1973.

Nettleton, Joyce. *Seafood and Health.* Huntington Station, N.Y.: Osprey Books, 1987.

Ray, G. Carleton, and C. Richard Robins. *A Field Guide to Atlantic Coast Fishes.* Peterson's Field Guide Series. Boston: Houghton Mifflin, 1986.

U.S. Department of Agriculture. Human Nutrition Information Service. *Composition of Foods: Finfish and Shellfish Products.* Agriculture Handbook No. 8-15. Washington: U.S. Government Printing Office, 1987.

U.S. Department of Health and Human Services. Food and Drug Administration. *Food and Drug Administration Guide to Acceptable Market Names for Food Fish Sold in Interstate Commerce 1993.* Washington: U.S. Government Printing Office, 1993.

Warner, William W. *Beautiful Swimmers.* Boston: An Atlantic Monthly Press Book; Little, Brown, 1976.

Index

About the Author

SHIRLEY KING is regarded as one of the foremost authorities on fish in the United States. She has spent the last 25 years in the food business, as a caterer, restaurant chef, consultant and writer. She teaches fish-cookery classes and appears frequently on the radio to talk about seafood. Also the author of *Saucing the Fish* and *Dining with Marcel Proust*, Shirley King lives in New York City.